The Principalship

A REFLECTIVE PRACTICE PERSPECTIVE

Sixth Edition

Thomas J. Sergiovanni

Trinity University
San Antonio, Texas

PEARSON

Boston   New York   San Francisco
Mexico City   Montreal   London   Madrid   Munich   Paris
Hong Kong   Singapore   Tokyo   Cape Town   Sydney

Editor-in-Chief: *Paul Smith*
Series Editorial Assistant: *Anne Whittaker*
Senior Marketing Manager: *Erica DeLuca*
Editorial Production Service: *Omegatype Typography, Inc.*
Composition Buyer: *Linda Cox*
Manufacturing Buyer: *Linda Morris*
Electronic Composition: *Omegatype Typography, Inc.*
Cover Administrator: *Linda Knowles*

For related titles and support materials, visit our online catalog at
www.pearsonhighered.com.

Between the time website information is gathered and then published, it is not unusual
for some sites to have closed. Also, the transcription of URLs can result in typographical
errors. The publisher would appreciate notification where these errors occur so that they
may be corrected in subsequent editions.

Library of Congress Cataloging-in-Publication Data

Sergiovanni, Thomas J.
    The principalship : a reflective practice perspective / Thomas J.
Sergiovanni.—6th ed.
      p.   cm.
    Includes bibliographical references and index.
    ISBN 13: 978-0-205-57858-0 (casebound)
    ISBN 10: 0-205-57858-6 (casebound)
    1. School principals—United States.   2. Educational leadership—
United States.   3. School management and organization—United States.
4. School supervision—United States.   5. School improvement programs—
United States.   I. Title

LB2831.92.S47   2009
371.2'012—dc22

                                                                    2007039935

Printed in the United States of America

10 9 8 7 6 5 4 3   RRD-VA   12   11   10

**Allyn and Bacon
is an imprint of**

www.pearsonhighered.com

ISBN-10:   0-205-57858-6
ISBN-13:   978-0-205-57858-0

ABOUT THE AUTHOR

Thomas J. Sergiovanni is Lillian Radford Professor of Education at Trinity University, San Antonio, Texas, where he teaches in the school leadership program and in the five-year teacher education program. Prior to joining the faculty at Trinity, he was on the faculty of education administration at the University of Illinois, Urbana-Champaign, for 19 years, and he chaired the department for 7 years. A former associate editor of *Educational Administration Quarterly,* he serves on the editorial boards of *Journal of Personnel Evaluation in Education* and *Catholic Education: A Journal of Inquiry and Practice.* Among his recent books are *Moral Leadership* (1992), *Building Community in Schools* (1994), *Leadership for the Schoolhouse* (1996), *The Lifeworld of Leadership: Creating Culture, Community, and Personal Meaning in Our Schools* (2000), *Strengthening the Heartbeat: Leading and Learning Together in Schools* (2005), *Supervision: A Redefinition* (2007), and *Rethinking Leadership* (2007).

Important Ideas

IN THIS NEW EDITION

- A basic idea is that the management of responsibility involves the internalization of values and purposes that obligate people to meet their commitments. Responsibility for following up can be shared but not delegated.

- Teacher leadership is key. Without teacher leadership we can change how things look but not how things work.

- A strong heartbeat is a school's best defense against the obstacles leaders face as they work to change schools for the better.

- Strengthening the heartbeat of a school requires that we rethink what leadership is, how leadership works, and what leadership and learning are like.

- As schools struggle to become communities, they need to address questions such as the following:

  What can be done to increase the sense of connections, neighborliness, and collegiality among the faculty of a school?

  How can the faculty become more of a professional community where everyone cares about each other and helps each other to grow, to learn together, and to lead together?

  What kinds of relationships need to be cultivated with parents that will enable them to be included in this emerging community?

  How can the web of relationships that exists among teachers and between teachers and students be defined so that they embody community?

  How can teaching and learning settings be arranged so that they are more like a family?

  How can the school, as a collection of families, be more like a neighborhood?

  What are the patterns of mutual obligations and duties that emerge in the school as community is achieved?

Contents

part two

Toward a New Theory

part four

Instructional Leadership

chapter *13*   **Clinical Supervision, Coaching, Peer Inquiry, and Other Supervisory Practices   291**

part five

Motivation, Commitment, and Change

chapter *14*   **Motivation, Commitment, and the Teacher's Workplace   317**

Preface

*E*verywhere you look there is someone with an easy solution for improving schools. "Research says" if you put these principles in place—if you teach, manage, or supervise using this list of behaviors—all will be well. Careers are built, journals are filled, and, for some with entrepreneurial bents, fortunes are amassed as the "solutions" are proposed.

The engine that drives this grand solutions machine is our search for simple answers. This searching, I fear, drives us to think in the rationalistic tradition about our work, to make unwarranted assumptions about the linearity and predictability that exist in the world, and to overestimate the tightness of links between research and practice. The result is the adoption of management theories and leadership practices that look great on paper, sound compelling when heard, and maybe even make us feel good, but that don't fit the actual world of schooling very well.

The term *rationalistic* is chosen over *rational* or *irrational* deliberately, for what is often thought to be irrational is actually rational, and vice versa. Winograd and Flores (1986) sort the differences as follows:

> In calling it [traditional theory] "rationalistic" we are not equating it with "rational." We are not interested in a defense of irrationality or a mystic appeal to nonrational intuition. The rationalistic tradition is distinguished by its narrow focus on certain aspects of rationality which often lead to attitudes and activities that are not rational when viewed in a broader perspective. Our commitment is to develop a new ground for rationality—one that is as rigorous as the rationalistic tradition in its aspirations but that does not share the presuppositions behind it. (8)

In a similar vein, Kozlov (1988) uses the categories "Neats" and "Scruffies" to sort researchers in the field of artificial intelligence as follows: "For a Neat, if an idea about thinking can't be represented in terms of mathematical logic, it isn't worth thinking about. For a Scruffy, on the other hand, ideas that can't be proved are the most interesting ones" (77–78).

It isn't easy for anyone to be a Scruffy. After all, it's very comfortable to be a Neat. You have all the answers, and you fit nicely into our bureaucratic, technical, and rational culture. Fitting nicely reaps many career rewards. But still, many of us feel uncomfortable with the position of the Neats. A frequent first response to this discomfort is to try to change the world to fit our theories and to damn those aspects of the world that will not cooperate. A better alternative, I propose, is for us to change our theories to fit the world. A scruffy world needs scruffy theories. Reflective practice, as I will argue in Chapter 3, is key to making scruffy theories work. John Stuart Mill wrote, "No great improvements in the lot of mankind are possible, until a great change takes place in the fundamental constitution of their modes of thought." His prophetic statement describes the situations we face today. If we want better schools, we are going to have to learn how to manage and lead differently. This book doesn't provide the answers, but it can help you find them.

The key to accepting the challenges of leadership in a scruffy world is for principals to understand leadership differently. When writing articles and books for principals, it is common to point out how important a principal is to the successful functioning of the school. Part of this ritual is to portray the principal as some sort of superhero who combines the best qualities of strong "instructional leadership" with a messianic ability to inspire people to great heights. It turns out that principals are indeed important, and their leadership is indeed indispensable, but in different ways than commonly thought.

From the perspective of the Neats, principals practice leadership directly by calculating what levers to pull to get the school structured differently and what buttons to push to get people motivated to do what is needed. Neat principals are highly visible players in the drama of leadership. Everything revolves around them. Should neat principals fail to provide the needed leadership, things go awry.

Scruffy principals view the problem of leadership differently. Their leadership is much more subtle and aimed at building substitutes for leadership into the school. Substitutes, they argue, are the keys needed to encourage teachers and students to become self-managing. The sources of authority for leadership, as scruffy principals see it, need to be idea based and anchored to moral commitments. Their job is to create new connections among people and to connect them to an idea structure. They do this by practicing leadership through binding and bonding. Their aim is to build a followership in the school. For the secret to leadership, they argue, is to have something worth following—something to which followers become morally committed.

A key theme in this book is that what we believe to be true about management and leadership depends on the metaphor we use to understand the school. Schools, for example, have traditionally been understood as formal *organizations* of one kind or another, and this metaphor encourages us to think in certain ways about school organizational structure, teacher motivation, power and authority, curriculum development, and supervision and evaluation. If the metaphor were changed to *community*, these ways of viewing the world of school management and leadership would no longer make sense. Instead, a new management and leadership would need to be invented to be more congruent with what communities are and how they function. Key would be the development of communities of practice throughout the school. Communities of practice are known as Professional Learning Communities in some places and as Critical Friends Groups in other places.

Members of communities of practice are committed to learning, sharing, and caring for each other. They come together voluntarily because they feel an obligation to do so. Without this voluntary commitment and practice, little of consequence happens in schools for very long. Trusting relationships are key. Why do we need communities of practice? Because today's learning requirements can only be met when collegiality leads to a shared practice of teaching. Communities of practice, we will soon see, are not cozy collections of people who are committed to group harmony and little else. They are committed to doing what is right for students.

Learning is often scary and is always hard work. As Wilson and Berne (1999) remind us, "You read, you think, you talk. You get something wrong, you don't understand something, you try it again. Sometimes you hit a wall in your thinking, sometimes it is just too frustrating. Yes, learning can be fun and inspiring, but along the way, it usually makes us miserable. And to move forward we often have to acknowledge that which we do not know" (200). Important learnings emerge when teachers' extant assumptions are challenged—when they experience disequilibrium. "Productive disequilibrium offers useful territory for teachers' learning" (Ball and Cohen, 2000, cited in Wilson and Berne, 1999:200).

But why learn together? Because the greatest asset a school has is its collective intelligence. Leaders have to figure out how to harness this intelligence, to grow it, and to use it to help the school achieve its purposes. This intelligence, however, is too often divided among individuals, and this division dilutes its effectiveness. Thus, as we shall see in this book, school leadership should not just be about making individuals smarter for their own sake. It should also be about making schools smarter. Schools get smarter when individual intelligences are aggregated. And smart schools lead to smart students.

The concept of *lifeworld* is introduced in Chapter 1. We might think of the lifeworld as a school's local values, traditions, meanings, and purposes as embodied in traditions, rituals, and norms that define a school's culture. The lifeworld is important because it is at the core of a school's organizational character. Character is what gives a school a special focus, an idea structure, and an orientation toward purpose that has consistently been linked to more effective schooling as measured by levels of civility and student achievement. Chapter 1 also examines how standards can either help or hinder the development of a school's character depending on whether they are driven by that school's lifeworld or imported from afar.

Throughout the book, readers will find a number of inventories and questionnaires. Their purpose is to help raise and clarify issues, stimulate thought, encourage reflection, and provide a basis for discussion of concepts and ideas. They are not presented as fine-tuned measurement devices suitable for "research purposes"; however, faculties and groups may benefit from collecting school data and using results as a basis for discussion and reflection.

*A*CKNOWLEDGMENTS

I would like to thank the following reviewers for their time and input: Philip V. Bender, Indiana State University; Gregory Moss, Newman University; and Diane Ricciardi, Clemson University.

*R*EFERENCES

Ball, D. L., and D. K. Cohen. 2000. "Developing Practice, Developing Practitioners: Toward a Practice-Based Theory of Education," in Linda Darling-Hammond and G. Sykes (Eds.), *Teaching as the Learning Profession: Handbook of Policy and Practice.* San Francisco: Jossey-Bass.

Kozlov, Alex. 1988. "Aristotle in the Fast Lane," *Discovery* 9(7), 77–78.

Wilson, Suzanne M., and Jennifer Berne. 1999. "Teacher Learning and the Acquisition of Professional Knowledge: An Examination of Research on Contemporary Professional Development," in Asghar Iran-Nejad and P. David Pearson (Eds.), *Review of Research in Education.* Washington, DC: American Educational Research Association, 173–209.

Winograd, Terry, and Fernando Flores. 1986. *Understanding Computers and Cognition.* Norwood, NJ: Ablex.

THE MORAL DIMENSION

1

SETTING THE STAGE
Administering as a Moral Craft

*W*e begin by setting the stage for leadership in the principalship and by providing a framework for bringing leadership together as a coherent strategy for change and as a moral spearhead for its practice. Leadership practice in the principalship is challenging for sure. But successful principals are everywhere. They know that for every challenge there is a reward for them, their school, and the children they serve. Few professions offer as much in return for the required dedication and commitment.

Michael Fullan (2003) points the way as follows:

> Leading schools—as in any great organization—requires principals with the courage and capacity to build new cultures based on trusting relationships and a culture of disciplined inquiry and action. That school leaders with these characteristics are in short supply is the point. Leading schools through complex reform agendas requires due leadership that goes far beyond improving test scores. Admittedly, developing trust and discipline in an organization that doesn't have it is a huge challenge. But . . . [t]here are cases where it has been done. We need to learn from these schools, focus on the right things, and create the conditions under which new leaders can develop and flourish. (45)

For Fullan, overcoming this challenge is the moral imperative of school leadership. But there are obstacles. Prime among them are the social relationships in schools

1

that too often keep us apart. Yet it is the quality of these relationships that helps schools develop the relational trust necessary for lasting change. Relational trust is a powerful concept that we discuss below. It is also a necessary ingredient in any attempt to bring about change for the better.

Roland Barth suggests that relationships within schools can be categorized in four ways: as parallel play, as adversarial, as congenial, and as collegial. For parallel play, he uses the metaphor of young children playing in a sandbox. "To illustrate, imagine two 3-year olds busily engaged in opposite corners of a sandbox. One has a shovel and a bucket; the other has a rake and a hoe. At no time do they share their tools, let alone cooperate to build a sandcastle" (Barth, 2006:10). When relationships become adversarial, notes Barth, "We educators have drawn our wagons into a circle and trained our guns—on each other" (Barth, 2006:10). Congenial relationships, by contrast, are interactive and positive, personal and friendly, reflecting consideration for others and being helpful when we can. Despite their value, congenial relationships represent promises unfulfilled. There seems to be a line that teachers and others dare not cross. Being involved in the teaching life of others, sharing one's practice with them by working together, and in other ways coming together on behalf of the teaching and learning success for all children may come about, but these characteristics are rarely realized on the congenial side of the line. Thankfully, crossing over the line puts us in a world where together we are able to function as communities of practice. At the heart of any community of practice are the relationships that Barth describes as collegiality. He states, "A precondition for doing *anything* to strengthen our practice and improve our school is the existence of a collegial culture in which professionals talk about practice, share their craft knowledge, and observe and root for the success of one another. Without these in place, no meaningful improvement—no staff or curriculum development, no teacher leadership, no student appraisal, no team teaching, no parent involvement, and no sustained change—is possible" (Barth, 2006:13).

In this book, a number of views of the principal will be discussed: Strategic problem solver, cultural leader, barterer, and initiator are examples. Are these the roles and images of leadership that one should follow in order to be an effective principal? Similarly, what about the motivational concepts and ideas that are central to the new principles of management and leadership that will be presented in Chapter 4, the characteristics of successful schools, the forces of leadership, strategies for bringing about change, and the dimensions of school culture discussed in other chapters? Will these ideas, if routinely applied, help one to be an effective principal? The answer is yes—well, no—actually maybe. Unfortunately, there is no guarantee that the concepts presented in this book will fit all readers or all the contexts and problems they face in the same way. Leadership is a personal thing. It comprises three important dimensions—one's heart, head, and hand. That is why different principals in the same situation so often behave differently. Leader and context defy separation.

THE HEART, HEAD, AND HAND OF LEADERSHIP

The *heart* of leadership has to do with what a person believes, values, dreams about, and is committed to—that person's *personal vision*, to use a popular term. To be sure, sharing personal conceptions of what is a good school will reveal many common qualities, but what often makes them personal statements is that they will differ, as well. The *head* of leadership has to do with the theories of practice each of us has developed over time and our ability to reflect on the situations we face in light of these theories. This process of reflection combined with our personal vision becomes the basis for our strategies and actions. Finally, the *hand* of leadership has to do with the actions we take, the decisions we make, the leadership and management behaviors we use as our strategies become institutionalized in the form of school programs, policies, and procedures. As with heart and head, how we choose to manage and lead are personal reflections not only of our vision and our practical theories but also of our personalities and our responses to the unique situations we face. In this idiosyncratic world, one-best-way approaches and cookie-cutter strategies do not work very well. Instead, diversity will likely be the norm as principals practice. Each principal must find her or his way, develop her or his approach, if the heart, head, and hand of leadership are to come together in the form of successful principalship practice.

Does that mean that the concepts presented in this book are not true? If they are not truths to be emulated and imitated, what are they? They comprise a different kind of truth. They represent a concept boutique on one hand and a metaphor repository on another. The idea is to visit the boutique, trying on one idea after another, seeking a fit here or there, and to visit the repository, seeking to create new understandings of situations one faces and new alternatives to one's practice. As boutique and repository, the role of knowledge about schooling changes from being something that principals apply uniformly to being something useful that informs the decisions they make as they practice. This is the nature of reflective practice.

THE MORAL IMPERATIVE

Although many may prefer the work of administration to be some sort of an applied science that is directly connected to a firm knowledge base of theory and research, the reality we face is that it is much more craftlike. The message from this reality is equally clear. Successful practice requires the development of craft know-how.

Yet, administering schools is no ordinary craft. Bringing together head, heart, and hand in practice; the unique nature of the school's mission; and the typically loosely structured, nonlinear, and messy context of schooling combine to make administering a *moral* craft, a fate shared with teaching (Tom, 1984) and supervision (Sergiovanni and Starratt, 1988). The reasons for this moral imperative are as follows:

1. The job of the principal is to transform the school from being an ordinary organization concerned with technical functions in pursuit of objective outcomes into an *institution*. Organizations are little more than technical instruments for achieving objectives. As instruments, they celebrate the value of effectiveness and efficiency by being more concerned with "doing things right" than with "doing right things." Institutions, however, are effective and efficient and more. They are responsive, adaptive enterprises that exist not only to get a particular job done but as entities in and of themselves. In Selznick's words:

> Organizations become institutions as they are infused with value, that is, prized not as tools alone but as sources of direct personal gratification and vehicles of group integrity. This infusion produces a distinct identity for the organization. Where institutionalization is well advanced, distinctive outlooks, habits, and other commitments are unified, coloring all aspects of organizational life and lending it a social integration that goes well beyond formal coordination and command. (Selznick, 1957:40)

Selznick's conception of institution is similar to the more familiar conception of school as learning community. To become either, the school must move beyond concerns for goals and roles to the task of building purposes into its structure and embodying these purposes in everything that it does with the effect of transforming school members from neutral participants to committed followers. The embodiment of purpose and the development of followership are inescapably moral.

2. The job of the school is to provide students with knowledge and skills and to build *character* and instill *virtue*. As Cuban (1988) points out, both technical and moral images are present in teaching and administering. "The technical image contains values that prize accumulated knowledge, efficiency, orderliness, productivity, and social usefulness; the moral image, while not disregarding such values, prizes values directed at molding character, shaping attitudes, and producing a virtuous, thoughtful person" (xvii). Technical and moral images of administration cannot be separated in practice. Every technical decision has moral implications. Emphasizing orderliness, for example, might serve as a lesson in diligence for students and might be a reminder to teachers that professional goals cannot be pursued to the extent that bureaucratic values are compromised.

3. Whether concern is for virtue or efficiency, some *standard* has to be adopted. What is efficient in this circumstance? How will virtue be determined? Determining criteria for effective teaching, deciding on what is a good discipline

policy, or coming to grips with promotion criteria standards, for example, all require value judgments. Answers to questions of how and what cannot be resolved objectively as if they were factual assertions, but must be treated as normative assertions. Normative assertions are true only because we decide that they are. "We must decide what ought to be the case. We cannot *discover* what ought to be the case by investigating what is the case" (Taylor, 1961:248). Normative assertions are moral statements.

4. Despite commitments to empowerment and shared decision making, relationships between principals and others are inherently unequal. Although often downplayed, and whether they want it or not, principals typically have more *power* than teachers, students, parents, and others. This power is in part derived legally from their hierarchical position, but for the most part it is obtained by virtue of the greater access to information and people that their position affords them. Principals are not chained to a tight schedule. They do a lot of walking around. They are the ones who get the phone calls, who are out in the streets, who visit the central office, who have access to the files, and so forth. As a result, principals function more frequently in the roles of figurehead and liaison with outside agencies. Their access to more information allows principals to decide what information will be shared with others, what information will be withheld, and frequently what information will be forgotten. Often, teachers and others in the school rely on the principal to serve as the "coordinating mechanism" that links together what they are doing with what others are doing. In teaching, where much of the work is invisible, the coordinating function is a powerful one. Furthermore, much of the information that principals accumulate is confidential. When teachers have problems, they frequently confide in the principal. Information is a source of power, and the accumulation of power has moral consequences.

Whenever there is an unequal distribution of power between two people, the relationship becomes a moral one. Whether intended or not, leadership involves an offer to control. The follower accepts this offer on the assumption that control will not be exploited. In this sense, leadership is not a right but a responsibility. Morally speaking, its purpose is not to enhance the leader's position or make it easier for the leader to get what she or he wants but to benefit the school. The test of moral leadership under these conditions is whether the competence, well-being, and independence of the follower are enhanced as a result of accepting control and whether the school benefits. Tom (1980) makes a similar argument in pointing out that "the teacher–student relationship is inherently moral because of its inequality" (317).

5. The context for administration is surprisingly loose, chaotic, and ambiguous. Thus, despite demands and constraints that circumscribe the principal's world, in actuality, *discretion* is built into the job, and this discretion has moral implications.

For example, frequently how things look is different from how things work. In their timeless research on the reality of managing schools, Morris and colleagues (1984) discovered numerous instances in which principals and schools were able to develop implicit policies and pursue courses of action that only remotely resembled officially sanctioned policies and actions. They noted that not only maintaining student enrollment levels but increasing them was often viewed as a managerial necessity by principals. However, principals were not motivated for official "educational" or "societal" reasons, but to protect or enhance the resource allocation base of their schools. Staffing patterns and budget allocations were often linked to a principal's standing among peers and were related as well to morale and productivity levels among teachers. Furthermore, principals of larger schools had more clout with the central office. Simply put, more staff and bigger budgets were viewed as being better. Schools losing resources, however, "usually suffer a decline in purposefulness, security, and confidence that goes beyond the loss of operating funds" (128).

As a result, principals tended to view monitoring, protecting, and increasing school enrollments and attendance as one of their key, albeit implicit, tasks. This led them to engage in courses of action that were at variance with the officially sanctioned definition of their tasks and roles. There was, for example, a concerted effort to change existing programs and revise the existing curriculum so they were more attractive to students and thus better able to hold their enrollment. One of the principals reported, "We may have to cut physics, for instance, and add environmental science. It's in. . . . I've got to get my faculty to see that they have to reshape the traditional curriculum of the school. Their jobs are at stake" (Morris et al., 1984:128–129). Another principal in their study worked to change his school's kindergarten program so that it was more structured and "rigorous," not for educational reasons or philosophical commitments but so that the school would be better able to compete with the neighborhood Catholic school.

Despite clear guidelines governing attendance procedures (e.g., fixed attendance boundaries and age requirements), principals became flexible by bending the rules for student admissions and taking liberties with reporting enrollment information to the central office. In the words of one principal, "In general, I'm not picky about where the students in the school live," noting further that if a child subsequently became a behavioral problem or was suspected of being a behavioral problem she always checked the home address (Morris et al., 1984:30). Some principals were inclined to look the other way even when they knew that students came from other school districts if they thought the students were "extremely bright." Some principals used leniency in enforcing attendance boundaries as the lever to extract better behavior and more achievement from students. Principals stressed that they were doing the parents and students a favor and expected good behavior in return. Not all students were treated equally. While bright students were encouraged to attend, "troublemakers" were not. In the words of one principal, "Let him go, that guy's been nothing but trouble for us" (Morris et al., 1984:131).

Although discretion can provide principals with a license for abuse, it is also a necessary prerequisite for leadership. "From choice comes autonomy. Autonomy is the necessary condition for leadership to arise. Without choice, there is no autonomy. Without autonomy, there is no leadership" (Cuban, 1988:xxii). Discretion, therefore, is necessary if principals are to function effectively. Yet, how principals handle discretion raises moral issues and has moral consequences for the school.

*N*ORMATIVE RATIONALITY

Key to understanding the moral dimension in leadership is understanding the difference between *normative rationality* (rationality based on what we believe and what we consider to be good) and *technical rationality* (rationality based on what is effective and efficient). Happily, the two are not mutually exclusive. Principals want what is good and what is effective for their schools, but when the two are in conflict, the moral choice is to prize the former over the latter. Starratt makes the point poignantly as follows: "'Organizational effectiveness' employs technical rationality, functional rationality, linear logic. Efficiency is the highest value, not loyalty, harmony, honor, beauty, truth. One can run an efficient extermination camp or an efficient monastery. The principles of efficiency are basically the same in either context" (Sergiovanni and Starratt, 1988:218).

Normative rationality provides the basis for moral leadership. Instead of just relying on bureaucratic authority to force a person to do something or a psychological authority to manipulate a person into doing something, the leader—principal or teacher, as the case may be—provides reasons for selecting one alternative over another. The reasons are open to discussion and evaluation by everyone. To pass the test of normative rationality, the reasons must embody the purposes and values that the group shares—the sacred covenant that bonds everyone in the school together as members of a learning community.

Research and reflecting on personal experience can often provide us with patterns of characteristics to which many students or teachers are likely to respond in the same way. These insights can help, and this form of knowledge is often invaluable to principals. But this knowledge cannot represent a source of authority for action that replaces moral authority. As Smith and Blase (1987) explain,

A leader in moral terms is one who fully realizes the . . . serious limitations on our ability to make accurate predictions and master the instructional process. Moreover, such a leader must encourage others to fully realize these limitations. Based on this awareness, a moral leader refuses to allow discussions of major pedagogical issues to be dominated by what the research supposedly demonstrates. . . . To do so would be to perpetuate the fiction that we have the kind of knowledge that we do not in fact possess. Rather, disagreements over how and what to teach must be played out in terms of reasoned discourse. The generalizations of educational inquiry can of course be part of these reasons, but they are not epistemologically privileged—they must share the stage with personal experience, a recounting of the experience of others, with philosophical and sociological considerations, and so on. (39)

The key is the phrase "epistemologically privileged." It is not that research findings are unimportant but that they are no more important than other sources of authority. One "so on" that might be added to Smith and Blase's list is conceptions of what is valued by the school that define it as a unique learning community.

Normative rationality influences the practice of leadership in schools in two ways. Principals bring to their job normative baggage in the form of biases and prejudices, ways of thinking, personality quirks, notions of what works and what doesn't, values that are prized, and other factors that function as personal theories of practice governing what they are likely to do and not do. School cultures are defined by a similar set of biases that represent the center of shared values and commitments that define the school as an institution. Both are sources of norms that function as standards and guidelines for what goes on in the school. As a school's culture is strengthened and its center of values becomes more public and pervasive, normative rationality becomes more legitimate. Everyone knows what the school stands for and why, and everyone can articulate these purposes and use them as guidelines for action. This in-building of purpose "involves transforming [persons] in groups from neutral, technical units into participants who have a peculiar stamp, sensitivity, and commitment" (Selznick, 1957:150).

STRENGTHENING THE HEARTBEAT

Leadership combines management know-how with values and ethics. Leadership practice, as a result, is always concerned both with what is effective and what is good; what works and what makes sense; doing things right and doing right things. As school improvement projects are considered, questions of what is good, what makes sense, and what is worth doing deserve equal billing with questions of effectiveness and efficiency. When the two sides of the ledger are in conflict, leaders will be known by the side they emphasize.

A strong heartbeat is a school's best defense against the obstacles leaders face as they work to change schools for the better. But strengthening the heartbeat of a school requires that we rethink what leadership is, how leadership works, what leadership's relationship to learning is, and why we need to practice both leadership and learning together.

When leaders are able to strengthen the heartbeat, their schools become stronger and more resilient. These qualities help leaders to share the burdens of leadership with others, to create collaborative cultures, and to be continuous learners. Leadership inevitably involves change and change inevitably involves learning. Both are easier to do better when we understand the mindscapes we bring to our practice, examine them in light of what we want to do, and change them. Change begins with us—with our hearts, our heads, and our hands that drive our leadership practice.

Lots of words could be used to capture the meaning of *heartbeat*. Three cousins—*social capital, community,* and *relational trust*—are good examples. Each of the cousins is a little different. Social capital provides the support students and teachers need (Coleman, 1988). Community provides the caring that students and teachers need (Sergiovanni, 1994). And relational trust provides the basis for developing deep reciprocal roles and role relationships with strong moral overtones (Bryk and Schneider, 2002). Reciprocal roles and role relationships can transform schools from ordinary to sacred places. They are essential, for example, in building community in schools. Taken together the three cousins enrich leadership and show how a strengthened school heartbeat can provide support for deep learning for both teachers and students.

Conventional wisdom tells us that leadership is about finding solutions to the problems that people face. But in reality leadership is more about helping people gain an understanding of problems they face and about helping them manage these problems and even learn to live with them. Even in the best of circumstances leadership is not easy. Community is a good example. Few leaders find their efforts at community building to be models of perfect harmony. Important differences exist among any faculty that is alive and well. But the wise leader knows that schools need centers of harmony that contain enough of what is important and shared to hold things together. At the same time they encourage differences in how this center of ideas is embodied in practice. Community for them is like a mosaic (see, e.g., Etzioni, 1996/1997) composed of many different elements held together by a common frame and glue.

Few leaders have all the competence, all the time, and all the information needed at any one time to get the job done. The wise among them try hard to rely on others and to build up the leadership capacity in others. Leaders have funds of knowledge and funds of skills that need constant replenishment. An important part of their job is to cultivate and amass the intellectual capital needed for the school's organizational IQ to increase. No doubt smart leaders help, but it is smart schools that will make the difference over time. That is why leadership and learning together are so important. We can have leadership and we can have learning. We can focus on individuals and we can focus on the school. We can view learning as a private good that serves individual interests but has little to do with pursuing school goals. And we can view learning as something individuals feel compelled to do because it is a public good that helps schools achieve their goals (Elmore, 2002). In each case, effects multiply when these dimensions are brought together.

ℋHE EIGHT COMPETENCIES

Normative rationality and the moral imperative point to eight basic competencies that are key to success in today's principalship. Once the competencies are mastered, capacity building, community building, and leading with ideas move to the center of the principal's work. Four of the competencies—the management of attention, the management of trust, the management of meaning, and the management of self—are borrowed from Warren Bennis (1989). The remaining four competencies are the management of paradox, the management of effectiveness, the management of follow-up, and the management of responsibility. To be successful as developers and community builders, leaders will need to back up their leadership with ideas. And for leading with ideas to be successful, leaders will have to master the eight basic competencies (Sergiovanni, 2001).*

The management of *attention* is the ability to focus others on values, ideas, goals, and purposes that bring people together and that provide a rationale—a source of authority for what goes on in the school. Leaders manage attention by what they say, what they reward, how they spend time, the behaviors they emphasize, and the reasons they give for the decisions they make.

Leaders practice *purposing,* defined as that continuous stream of action that induces clarity, consensus, and commitment regarding schools' purposes (Vaill, 1984). Purposing involves both the vision of the leader and the covenant that the school shares. In successful schools consensus runs deep. It is not enough to have worked out what people in the school stand for and what they expect to accomplish. Leaders continuously struggle to develop a binding and solid agreement that represents a value system for living together and forms the basis for decisions and actions (Sergiovanni, 1992).

The management of *meaning* is the ability to connect teachers, parents, and students to the school in such a way that they find their lives useful, sensible, and valued. Even the mundane routines of schools are valued and are connected to the larger purposes and meanings that define who people are, why they are in the school, why the school needs them, and why their participation with the school is worthwhile. Together the management of attention and the management of meaning answer these questions: What are our priorities? What are our commit-

*"The Eight Basic Competencies" by Thomas J. Sergiovanni is drawn from *Leadership: What's in It for Schools?* by Thomas J. Sergiovanni (London: Routledge/Falmer, 2001), pp. 47–54. © Thomas J. Sergiovanni. This version is from Thomas J. Sergiovanni, *Rethinking Leadership: A Collection of Articles,* 2nd ed., published jointly by Corwin Press in Thousand Oaks, CA, and the National Staff Development Council (2007), pp. 134–139.

ments to each other? Why are they important? How do they link to the ordinary things that we do? The answers to these questions help people become connected to each other and to the school, building hope and commitment and raising levels of civility and academic engagement.

The management of *trust* is the ability to be viewed as credible, legitimate, and honest. Bennis (1989:21) uses the term *constancy* to communicate that whether parents, teachers, and students like what a leader does or not, they always know where that leader is coming from, what that leader stands for, and why that leader is doing things. It is not enough to make decisions; leaders have to explain them and show how they are linked to the heartbeat of the school as well.

But trust has more than personal qualities. It is a key ingredient in the development of social capital. Coleman (1988) found that social capital correlates with the development of human capital (more learning in a school, for example), a finding confirmed by Putnam (2000) and more recently by Bryk and Schneider (2002). These latter researchers provide a compelling case for strong links between the amount of "relational trust" found in a school and made available to students and the students' subsequent academic performance. Not only does social capital seem related to learning, it is also a social need of students and others. If social capital is not available to students, they create it for themselves by turning more and more to the student subculture and its norms. Too often, however, student norms stand in the way of student achievement.

The management of *self* is the ability to know who you are, what you believe, and why you do the things you do. When a leader's behavior can be defended in such a way that others at least understand and respect that behavior, then self-knowledge has been achieved. Despite the importance of the management of self, too often this competency is neglected. The management of self is an art worth developing—though one not easily achieved without a measure of practical intelligence. Practical intelligence is the ability to know how things work and the ability to make things work. The cultivation of keen insight into human nature and the use of this knowledge in some practical way are examples (Sternberg, 1996).

The management of *paradox* is the ability to bring together ideas that seem to be at odds with each other. Combining an emphasis on rigorous standards with a refusal to impose standardization or compromise local discretion; expecting a great deal from teachers while empowering them to take control of their professional lives; responding to adolescent needs for independence while providing the disciplined safe havens they need; involving parents without compromising professional autonomy; and bringing everyone together in a common quest united by shared values while honoring diversity and promoting innovative ideas are examples. When implemented, these seemingly contradictory ideas can actually bring us together, make us brighter and stronger, and help us achieve larger purposes. The management of paradox is easier when leaders look to ideas, values, and visions of the common good as a moral sense of authority for what they do.

The management of *effectiveness* is the ability to focus on the development of capacity in a school that allows it to improve performance over time. Key to the management of effectiveness is how school success is understood and measured. When effectiveness is managed well, school success involves getting results and more. School success also involves learning and cultivating relationships. Learning builds the capacity of teachers to know more about their work, to figure out how to create better pathways to success, and to improve practice as a result. Relationships, as pointed out earlier, provide the support that teachers need to come together as a community of learners and a community of practice. Thus, determining the success of any initiative requires answers to three sets of questions:

1. What is being accomplished? Are the results of high quality? Does what is being done make sense to parents and other constituencies?
2. What are they learning about their work? Are they likely to be more effective the next time around as a result? How are they sharing what they are learning?
3. Is everyone working together as a community of practice? Is everyone supporting each other and helping each other? Is the community proud of what they are doing and do they enjoy working together?

Trust first and then vision. Next comes strategy followed by action plans. But success requires that we go to the next step. Strategies and action plans need day-to-day planning and execution. Who will do what, by when, and with whom? What specific training will be needed that will enable us to be successful? A system of supervision needs to be in place to monitor what is going on and to provide in-class and on-call professional development. If teachers need help, for example, they ought to be able to get it on the spot—when they need it. Other questions to ask: What kinds of assessments will be needed? Who will be responsible for all the little day-to-day things that need to be done for our action plans to become realities? Leaders, in other words, need to be competent in the management of *follow-up*.

Too often leaders seem to tire when it gets down to details, preferring to delegate these responsibilities to others. But without follow-up by the full complement of a school's leadership and the full complement of a school district's leadership, the job rarely gets done to standard. Execution of plans takes detailed, careful, and continuous supervision, support, and assessment.

The management of follow-up is more likely to be accomplished when principals are involved in the day-to-day struggle of implementation. Principals, for example, should participate in professional development training. Learning walks or walk-throughs should become a part of their weekly routine as they visit classrooms to examine firsthand what is going on and what progress is being made. Responsibility for follow-up can be shared but not delegated. Unless principals are in the midst of the implementation process and unless they play key roles in its management and assessment, implementation of any quality and for any length of time is likely to evaporate. Teacher leadership, too, is critical to successful follow-up. Without teacher leadership we change how things look but not how things work.

The management of *responsibility* involves the internalization of values and purposes that obligate people to meet their commitments to each other and to the school. Professionals have long known the power of both extrinsic rewards and intrinsic rewards in motivating people. Extrinsic and intrinsic rewards comprise two widely accepted motivational rules: *what is rewarded gets done* and *what is rewarding gets done.* But in reality people are motivated by three motivational rules, with the third being *what one feels a duty or obligation to do, gets done.* When people feel obligated to do something, they not only do it well but also do it even when the going gets tough. They do it whether it is pleasant or not and whether they want to or not. This third motivational rule is important because duty and obligation are not only stronger than gain or pleasure, but also sustain themselves over time.

Thus, the best way to manage responsibility is to evoke duty and obligation as motivators. This is done when schools are helped to become not just learning and caring communities but communities of responsibility. In communities of responsibility leadership is based on a different kind of authority—one embedded in the ideas that encourage us to respond from within, to become self-managing. Instead of following the leader, the emphasis is on following commitments, promises, obligations, validated research, sound principles, agreed-upon standards, and other ideas. In communities of responsibility it is norms, values, beliefs, purposes, goals, standards, hopes, and dreams that provide the ideas for morally based leadership. These ideas are not mandated scripts that require carbon-copy conformity. They are instead more like frameworks that provide people with a heightened sense of understanding, meaning, and significance. When leadership is morally based, its effect on spirit, commitment, and results is not only strong but obligatory, allowing the school to function with commitment and determination.

In sum, the eight basic competencies are the basis for developing and using an idea-based leadership. This use changes the sources of authority for leadership from bureaucratic requirements and from the leader's personal charm quotient to purposes, values, theories, and other cognitive frameworks. These distinctions will be explained throughout this book. Though bureaucratic and personal requirements may be helpful, they should not be placed at the center in deciding what to do. Richard Elmore (2003) sums up the importance of substance in leadership to school improvement as follows:

> The U.S. fetish for leadership leads to an overemphasis on the personal attributes of school leaders and a correspondingly weak focus on the technical, cognitive demands of instructional practice and the affective and behavioral responses of those demands. Successful leaders have an explicit theory of what good instructional

practice looks like. They model their own learning and theories of learning in their work, work publicly on the improvement of their own practice, and engage others in powerful discourse about good instruction. These leaders understand that improving school performance requires transforming a fundamentally weak instructional core, and the culture that surrounds it, into a strong, explicit body of knowledge about powerful teaching and learning that is accessible to those who are willing to learn it. (10)

Leadership is strengthened and leadership initiatives succeed best when we recognize that process is usually trumped by substance. Successful school leaders, for example, bring both to their practice but in the end these leaders know that while how we do things is important, what we do is even more important. This is the leadership theme that is discussed below.

$\mathcal{F}$OLLOWERSHIP IS THE GOAL

The importance of purposing to leadership changes how it is understood and practiced. With purposing in place in a school, one cannot become a leader without first becoming a follower. The concept of followership will be discussed further in Chapters 6, 7, and 8. What it means to be a follower and what it means to be a subordinate are very different. Subordinates respond to bureaucratic authority and sometimes to personal authority. Followers, by contrast, respond to ideas. You can't be a follower unless you have something to follow. Furthermore, as Zaleznik (1989) suggests, subordinates may cooperate with the management system but are rarely committed to it. By contrast, one of the hallmarks of being a follower is commitment. As Kelly (1988) points out, followers "are committed to the organization and to a purpose, principle, or person outside themselves. . . . [And as a result, they] build their competence and focus their efforts for maximum impact" (144). Followers, by definition, are never constrained by minimums but are carried by their commitment to performance that typically exceeds expectations. Subordinates, by contrast, do what they are supposed to; they tend not to do more.

When subordinateness is transcended by followership, a different kind of hierarchy emerges in the school. Principals, teachers, students, parents, and others find themselves equally "subordinate" to a set of ideas and shared conceptions to which they are committed. As a result, teachers respond and comply not because of the principal's directives but out of a sense of obligation and commitment to these shared values. That's what it means to be a follower.

The principal's job is to provide the kind of purposing to the school that helps followership to emerge. The principal then provides the conditions and support that allow people to function in ways that are consistent with agreed-upon values. At the same time, the principal has a special responsibility to continually highlight the values, to protect them, and to see that they are enforced. The true test of leadership under these conditions is the principal's ability to get others in the school to share in the responsibility for guarding these values. This litany of roles will be discussed in the text as leadership by purposing, empowerment and enablement, outrage, and finally, kindling outrage in others.

One of the persistent problems of administration is obtaining compliance, which is at the heart of the principal's role. Invariably, compliance occurs in response to some sort of authority, but not all sources of authority are equally powerful or palatable. In this book, four sources of authority will be discussed: bureaucratic, personal, professional, and moral. All four have a role to play if schools are to function effectively; however, the four compete with each other. When principals use bureaucratic authority, they rely on rules, mandates, and regulations in efforts to direct thought and action. When principals use personal authority, they rely on their own interpersonal style, cleverness, guile, political know-how, and other forms of managerial and psychological skill in order to direct thought and action. When principals rely on professional authority, they appeal to expertness, expecting everyone to be subordinate to a form of technical rationality that is presumably validated by craft notions of what constitutes best educational practice or scientific findings from educational research. When principals rely on moral authority, they bring to the forefront a form of normative rationality that places everyone subordinate to a set of ideas, ideals, and shared values and asks them to respond morally by doing their duty, meeting their obligations, and accepting their responsibilities. All of the sources of authority are important, but the art of administration is balancing the four in such a way that moral and professional authority flourish without neglecting bureaucratic and personal authority.

THE CHALLENGE OF LEADERSHIP

In the principalship, the challenge of leadership is to make peace with two competing imperatives: the managerial and the moral. The two imperatives are unavoidable, and the neglect of either creates problems. Schools must be run effectively and efficiently if they are to survive. Policies must be in place. Budgets must be set. Teachers must be assigned. Classes must be scheduled. Reports must be completed. Standardized tests must be given. Supplies must be purchased. The school must be kept clean. Students must be protected from violence. Classrooms must be orderly. These are essential tasks that guarantee the survival of the school as an organization. Yet, as Selznick (1957) reminds us, for the school to transform itself from an organization into an institution, a learning community must emerge. Institutionalization is the moral imperative that principals face.

Discussing the moral imperative in administration; proposing such leadership values as purposing, empowerment, outrage, and kindling outrage in others; and arguing for the kind of balance among bureaucratic, psychological, professional, and moral sources of authority in schools that noticeably tilts toward professional and moral all challenge the "professional manager" conception of the principal-ship by placing concerns for substance firmly over concerns for process.

On the upside, the development of school administration as a form of man-agement technology brought with it much needed attention to the development of better management know-how and of organizational skills badly needed to deal with an educational system that continues to grow in technical, legal, and bureau-cratic complexity. On the downside, professionalism has too often resulted in prin-cipals thinking of themselves less as statespersons, educators, and philosophers, and more as organizational experts who have become absorbed in what Abraham Zaleznik (1989) refers to as the *managerial mystique*. "As it evolved in practice, the mystique required managers to dedicate themselves to process, structures, roles, and indirect forms of communication and to ignore ideas, people, emotions, and direct talk. It deflected attention from the realities [of education] while it reassured and rewarded those who believed in the mystique" (2). The managerial mystique holds so strongly to the belief that "the right methods" will produce good results that the methods themselves too often become surrogates for results, and to the belief that management and bureaucratic controls will overcome human short-comings and enhance human productivity that controls become ends in them-selves. School improvement plans, for example, become substitutes for school improvements; scores on teacher appraisal forms become substitutes for good teaching; accumulating credits earned in courses and required inservice work-shops become substitutes for changes in school practice; discipline plans become substitutes for student control; leadership styles become substitutes for purpose and substance; congeniality becomes a substitute for collegiality; cooperation becomes a substitute for commitment; and compliance becomes a substitute for results.

Zaleznik (1989) maintains that the managerial mystique is the antithesis of leadership. The epitome of the managerial mystique is the belief that anyone who can manage one kind of enterprise can also manage any other kind. It is the ge-neric management techniques and generic interpersonal skills that count rather than issues of purpose and substance. Without purpose and substance, Zaleznik argues, there can be no leadership. "Leadership is based on a compact that binds those who lead and those who follow into the same moral, intellectual and emo-tional commitment" (15).

THE LIFEWORLD OF SCHOOLING

Everyone wants good schools—an aspiration shared by people in all walks of life. Few would disagree that we should be able to identify the good schools we have now, to learn from them, and to increase their number. Further, most people believe that providing schools and their publics with information as to where they are now, given their own goals and aspirations and the goals and aspirations of the state, is a reasonable idea. Schools need this information to plan the next steps, new directions, and other initiatives on the road to improvement. But it is not likely that any of these things will happen unless our schools are involved at the ground floor in standards and assessment. Ground-floor involvement of each school means having a good, practical, broad, realistic, and lifeworld-serving definition of what is a good school in the first place.

The term *lifeworld* needs some explaining (see, e.g., Sergiovanni, 2000). Borrowing from the philosopher and sociologist Jurgen Habermas (1987), we might think of the lifeworld as a school's local values, traditions, meanings, and purposes. In the best of circumstances the lifeworld determines and legitimizes local initiatives aimed at achieving a school's own destiny (Sergiovanni, 2000). The lifeworld includes the traditions, rituals, and norms that define a school's culture. Lifeworlds differ as we move from school to school, and these differences lay the groundwork for developing a school's unique character. As character builds, the capacity of a school to serve the intellectual, social, cultural, and civic needs of its students increases. School character helps schools be more effective. *Effectiveness* is broadly defined as achieving higher levels of pedagogical thoughtfulness, developing relationships characterized by caring and civility, and achieving increases in the quality of student performance on both conventional and alternative assessments.

The evidence from a wide variety of sources (i.e., Bryk, Lee, and Holland, 1993; Coleman and Hoffer, 1987; Hill, Foster, and Gendler, 1990) leads to the conclusion that schools that function as focused communities where unique values are important, schools where caring for each other is the norm, schools where academic matters count, and schools where social covenants are established that bring parents, teachers, students, and others together in a shared commitment to the common good are able to use the values of the lifeworld and to get surprisingly good results. This link between the lifeworld of a school and that school's effectiveness establishes local authority as a necessary ingredient in any school effectiveness equation.

MORE THAN EFFECTIVE

It is much easier to identify what is an "effective" school than to struggle with a deeper definition of what is a "good" school. Sara Lawrence Lightfoot's research, reported in her book *The Good High School* (1983), is an example of searching for a more meaningful and expansive definition of effectiveness. She provided portraits of six very different but very good high schools. What emerges from her seminal study is that a single list of indicators for a good school is not so easily achieved. She found that good schools have invented ways to effectively serve different neighborhoods, contain a diverse mix of goals and purposes, and use unique ways to achieve these goals and purposes. Further, good schools have principals who provide a unique blend of leadership strategies and styles. Goodness is about the kind of wholeness and purpose and the kind of responsiveness to unique characteristics and needs that contribute to school character. Goodness builds from and grows from what a particular school and its community values. The lifeworld of a school, not externally imposed organizational structures or outside mandates, is the key to this broader view of effectiveness.

BUILDING THE CHARACTER OF YOUR SCHOOL

One of the major themes of this book is the importance of a school's culture. For better or for worse, culture influences much of what is thought, said, and done in a school. Character is a concept similar to culture but much less neutral. A school's character is known by how the school is viewed by members and outsiders in ethical and moral terms. Building and enhancing the school's character is the key to establishing its credibility among students, teachers, parents, and administrators and externally in the broader community. Wilkins (1989) notes that the components of an organization's character are its common understandings of *purpose* and identity that provide a sense of "who we are"; faith of members in the fairness of the leadership and in the ability of the organization to meet its commitments and to get the job done; and the distinctive cultural attributes that define the tacit customs, networks of individuals, and accepted ways of working together and of working with others outside of the organization. How reliable are the actions of the school? How firm is the school in its convictions? How just is its disposition? Wilkins points out that purpose, faith, and cultural attributes "add up to the collective organizational competence" (1989:27). To him, faith is a particularly important component of an organization's character, and loss of faith in either the organization or its leadership results in loss of character. Building faith restores character. Enhancing faith increases character. Without faith and character the organization and its members are not able to move beyond the ordinary to extraordinary performance. With faith such a transformation is possible. No matter how relentlessly principals pursue their managerial imperative, reliability in action, firmness in conviction, and just disposition are the consequences of the moral imperative. Without tending to the moral imperative there can be no organizational character, and without character a school can be neither good nor effective (Sergiovanni, 2000, 2005).

A COMMITMENT TO DEMOCRATIC VALUES

The inescapable moral nature of administrative work and in particular seeking to establish moral authority embodied in the form of purposing and shared values and expressed as "cultural leadership" raises important questions of manipulation and control. Cultural leadership can provide principals with levers to manipulate others that are more powerful than the levers associated with bureaucratic and psychological authority. Lakomski (1985) raises the question squarely:

> To put the objection more strongly, it may be argued that if all cultural analysis does is to help those in power, such as principals and teachers, to oppress some students more effectively by learning about their views, opinions, and "student cultures," then this method is just another and more sophisticated way to prevent students (and other oppressed groups) from democratic participation in educational affairs. (15)

Her comments apply as well to teachers and others. Furthermore, cultural leadership can become a powerful weapon for masking the many problems of diversity, justice, and equality that confront schools. There is nothing inherently democratic about cultural leadership, and, indeed, depending on its substance this kind of leadership can compromise democratic values. Consensus building and commitment to shared values can often be little more than devices for maintaining an unsatisfactory status quo and for discouraging dissent. Finally, not all covenants are equal. The values that define the "center" of different school communities are not interchangeable.

Cultural leadership can be understood and practiced as a technology available to achieve any goal and to embody any vision or as a means to celebrate a particular set of basic values that emerge from the American democratic tradition. It makes a difference, for example, whether the basic values that define a school community revolve around themes of efficiency, effectiveness, and excellence or whether these are considered to be mere means-values in service to such ends-values as justice, diversity, equality, and goodness. In the spirit of the latter point of view, Clark and Meloy (1984) propose the Declaration of Independence as a metaphor for managing schools to replace bureaucracy. This metaphor guarantees to all persons that school management decisions will support such values as equality, life, liberty, and the pursuit of happiness based on the consent of the governed.

Discussion of democracy in schools typically wins nods from readers. However, as Quantz, Cambron-McCabe, and Dantley (1991) point out, democracy is not always understood as both process and substance:

> There is often a confusion of democracy with pure process—the belief that as long as there is some form of participatory decision-making that democracy has been achieved. We argue, however, that democracy implies both a process and a goal, that the two, while often contradictory, cannot be separated. We believe that democratic processes cannot justify undemocratic ends. For example, we cannot justify racial and gender inequity on the basis that the majority voted for it. While this dual-reference test for democracy is not simple or clean, while it often requires us to choose between two incompatible choices, both in the name of democracy, we

can conceive of no other way to approach it. In other words, even though an appeal to democratic authority cannot provide a clear and unequivocable blueprint for action in every particular instance, it can provide a general and viable direction for intelligent and moral decision-making by school administrators. (6)

One of the challenges of moral leadership in schools is to engage oneself and others in the process of decision making without thought to self-interest. Can we discuss and decide our grading policies, discipline procedures, student grouping practices, supervisory strategies, and so forth without regard to whether we will be winners or losers? Sending children routinely to the principal's office for discipline, for example, or favoring homogeneous grouping of students may be in the interest of teachers but not students. Requiring all teachers to teach the same way may make it easier for the principal to hold teachers accountable, but not for teachers who want to teach in ways that make sense to them. Discouraging parental involvement in school governance makes for fewer headaches for school people but disenfranchises the parents. What is just under these circumstances? John Rawls (1971) has suggested that decisions such as these should be made by people choosing in a hypothetical position of fairness under what he called "a veil of ignorance." The idea is to pretend that we don't know anything about ourselves—our sex, our race, our position in the school, our talents, and so forth. We don't know, in other words, whether we are black or white, principal or teacher, student or custodian, parent or teacher aide. Our identities are only revealed when the veil of ignorance is lifted. Rawls maintains that in this way we are likely to fashion our principles and make decisions regardless of who we turn out to be. With bias diminished, chances are that the principles would be fairer and the decisions more just.

*T*IME, FEELING, FOCUS

Anyone aspiring to the principalship had better have a strong commitment to work. This assertion should perhaps be modified as follows: Anyone who is aspiring to be a *successful* principal had better have a strong commitment to work. Success has its price. Consider, for example, the following statement:

> A passion for excellence means thinking big and starting small: excellence happens when high purpose and intense pragmatism meet. This is almost, but not quite, the whole truth. We believe a passion for excellence also carries a price, and we state it simply: the adventure of excellence is not for the faint of heart.
>
> Adventure? You bet. It's not just a job. It's a personal commitment. Whether we're looking at a billion dollar corporation or a three-person accounting department, we see that excellence is achieved by people who muster up the nerve (and the passion) to step out—in spite of doubt, or fear, or job description—to maintain face-to-face contact with other people, namely customers and colleagues. They

won't retreat behind office doors, committees, memos or layers of staff, knowing this is the fair bargain they make for extraordinary results. They may step out for love, because of a burning desire to be the best, to make a difference, or perhaps, as a colleague recently explained, "because the thought of being average scares the hell out of me. (Peters and Austin, 1985:414)

In his studies of high-performing leaders, Vaill (1984) found that "(1) Leaders of high-performing systems put in extraordinary amounts of *time*; (2) Leaders of high-performing systems have very strong *feelings* about the attainment of the system's purposes; and (3) Leaders of high-performing systems *focus* on key issues and variables" (94). Vaill notes that "there are of course many nuances, subtleties, and local specialties connected with the leadership of many high-performing systems, but over and over again, Time, Feeling, and Focus appear no matter what else appears" (94). The three go hand in hand. Vaill states, for example, that administrators who put in large amounts of time without feeling or focus are exhibiting "workaholism." Time and feeling without focus, however, often lead to dissipated energy and disappointment. Finally, time and focus without feeling seem to lack the necessary passion and excitement for providing symbolic and cultural leadership. Successful leaders—principals among them—are not afraid of hard work. By putting in large amounts of time, they demonstrate that they are not afraid of hard work; however, they don't dissipate this time by taking on everything. Instead, they concentrate their efforts on those characteristics and values that are clearly more important to the success of their organization than are others. Furthermore, unlike cold, calculated, objective, and uninvolved managers, they bring to their enterprises a certain passion that affects others deeply.

As a result of his extensive studies of the principalship and school leadership, Greenfield (1985) concludes that principals need to be more passionate about their work, clearer about what they seek to accomplish, and more aggressive in searching for understandings that lead to improved schooling. Greenfield speaks of passion as "believing in the worth of what one seeks to accomplish and exhibiting in one's daily action a commitment to the realization of those goals and purposes" (17). He maintains that clarity about goals and outcomes should be accompanied by a commitment to flexibility regarding processes, procedures, and other means to attain ends.

Finally, anyone who is aspiring to be a good principal needs to have some sense of what she or he values, something to be committed to, a compass to help navigate the way—a personal vision. Barth (1990) points out:

Observers in schools have concluded that the lives of teachers, principals, and students are characterized by brevity, fragmentation, and variety. During an average day, for instance, a teacher or principal engages in several hundred interactions. So do many parents. A personal vision provides a framework with which to respond and to make use of the many prescriptions and conceptions of others. But more important, these ideas centered around schools as communities of learners and leaders have provided me with a road map which has enabled me to respond to the hundreds of daily situations in schools . . . in a less random and more thoughtful way. Without a vision, I think our behavior becomes reflexive, inconsistent, and shortsighted as we seek the action that will most quickly put out the fire so we can get on with putting out the next one. In five years, if we're lucky, our school might be fire free—but it won't have changed much. Anxiety will remain high, humor low, and leadership muddled. Or as one teacher put it in a powerful piece of writing, "Without a clear sense of purpose we get lost, and our activities in school become but empty vessels of our discontent." Seafaring folk put it differently: "For the sailor without a destination, there is no favorable wind." (211)

SERVANT LEADERSHIP

One of the great secrets of leadership is that, before one can command the respect and followership of others, she or he must demonstrate devotion to the organization's purposes and commitment to those in the organization who work day by day on the ordinary tasks that are necessary for those purposes to be realized. As Greenleaf (1977) points out, people "will freely respond only to individuals who are chosen as leaders because they are proven and trusted as servants" (10). This perspective has come to be known as *servant leadership* (Greenleaf, 1977), with its basic tenets found in the biblical verse: "Ye know that the rulers of the Gentiles lorded over them, and that their great ones exercised authority over them. Not so shall it be among you: but whosoever would become great among you shall be your minister and whosoever would be first among you shall be your servant" (Matthew 20:25–27).

Servant leadership describes well what it means to be a principal. Principals are responsible for "ministering" to the needs of the schools they serve. The needs are defined by the shared values and purposes of the school's covenant. They minister by furnishing help and being of service to parents, teachers, and students. They minister by providing leadership in a way that encourages others to be leaders in their own right. They minister by highlighting and protecting the values of the school. The principal as minister is one who is devoted to a cause, mission, or set of ideas and accepts the duty and obligation to serve this cause. Ultimately, her or his success is known by the quality of the followership that emerges. Quality of followership is a barometer that indicates the extent to which moral authority has replaced bureaucratic and psychological authority. When moral authority drives leadership practice, the principal is at the same time a leader of leaders, follower of ideas, minister of values, and servant to the followership.

SOME REFLECTIONS

1. How committed are you to becoming a successful school principal? Generally speaking, commitment to your present job provides a good idea of one's over-

exhibit
1.1

Job Commitment Index

Responses: 4—Strongly Agree, 3—Agree, 2—Disagree, 1—Strongly Disagree

	1	2	3	4
1. Most of the important things that happen to me involve my work.	—	—	—	—
2. I spend a great deal of time on matters related to my job, both during and after hours.	—	—	—	—
3. I feel badly if I don't perform well on my job.	—	—	—	—
4. I think about my job even when I'm not working.	—	—	—	—
5. I would probably keep working even if I didn't have to.	—	—	—	—
6. I have a perspective on my job that does not let it interfere with other aspects of my life.	—	—	—	—
7. Performing well on my job is extremely important to me.	—	—	—	—
8. Most things in my life are more important to me than my job.	—	—	—	—
9. I avoid taking on extra duties and responsibilities in my work.	—	—	—	—
10. I enjoy my work more than anything else I do.	—	—	—	—
11. I stay overtime to finish a job even if I don't have to.	—	—	—	—
12. Sometimes I lie awake thinking about the next day's work.	—	—	—	—
13. I am able to use abilities I value in doing my job.	—	—	—	—
14. I feel depressed when my job does not go well.	—	—	—	—
15. I feel good when I perform my job well.	—	—	—	—
16. I would not work at my job if I didn't have to.	—	—	—	—

Source: The Job Commitment Index is generally adapted from the Occupational Commitment Scale developed by Becky Heath Ladewig and Priscilla N. White, Department of Human Development and Family Life, University of Alabama.

all commitment to work. For an indication of your present job commitment, respond to the Job Commitment Index in Exhibit 1.1. This index contains 16 items about how people feel about their jobs. Indicate the extent to which you agree or disagree with each item. As you count your score, reverse-score items 6, 8, 9, and 16. Your score will range from a low of 16 to a high of 64, with 64 representing the highest level of commitment. Keep in mind that there is always the chance that a person's commitment to work may be high, but that her or his present job presents such unusual difficulties that low commitment and a low score result. How would your principal respond to this index?

2. Teachers too share responsibility for the moral imperative, and virtually every action they take under loosely structured conditions has moral overtones. As Cuban (1988) notes, "Teachers stand between what policymakers intend, what administrators direct, what students and parents expect, and what occurs in classrooms. By their decisions and actions, teachers determine the degree to

which a policy is implemented faithfully, transformed to fit the classroom, or ignored. Within classrooms, then, teachers engage in political acts" (33). And for this reason "teaching itself is a moral act" (32). To what extent do you agree with these assertions? Provide examples to support your views.

3. If leadership is a craft, then what role does science play? One response is that the purpose of science is to inform the decisions that leaders make, not to make decisions for them. Informed intuition drives craft decision making. What is your reaction to this response? In your practice as a teacher, does research tell you what to do, or does research inform the decisions that you make about your practice? Give examples. What about the practices of your principal?

4. Vaill says that administrators who put in large amounts of time without feeling or focus are exhibiting "workaholism." Do you agree with his assertion? Bring to mind a principal who is a "workaholic" and a principal who works hard but is not. How are they different?

ℛEFERENCES

Barth, Roland S. 1990. *Improving Schools from Within.* San Francisco: Jossey-Bass.

Barth, Roland S. 2006, March. "Improving Relationships Within the Schoolhouse," *Educational Leadership* 63(6), 8–13.

Bennis, Warren. 1989. *Why Leaders Can't Lead: The Unconscious Conspiracy Continues.* San Francisco: Jossey-Bass.

Bryk, Anthony S., and Barbara Schneider. 2002. *Trust in Schools: A Core Resource for Improvement.* New York: Russell Sage Foundation.

Bryk, Anthony S., Valerie E. Lee, and Peter B. Holland. 1993. *Catholic Schools and the Common Good.* Cambridge, MA: Harvard University Press.

Clark, David L., and Judith M. Meloy. 1984. "Renouncing Bureaucracy: A Democratic Structure for Leadership in Schools," in T. J. Sergiovanni and J. H. Moore (Eds.), *Schooling for Tomorrow: Directing Reforms to Issues That Count.* Boston: Allyn and Bacon.

Coleman, J. S. 1988. "Social Capital in the Creation of Human Capital," *American Journal of Sociology* 94 (Supplement), S95–S120.

Coleman, James S., and Thomas Hoffer. 1987. *Public and Private High Schools: The Impact of Communities.* New York: Basic Books.

Cuban, Larry. 1988. *The Managerial Imperative and the Practice of Leadership in Schools.* Albany: State University of New York Press.

Elmore, Richard F. 2002. *Bridging the Gap Between Standards and Achievement: The Imperative for Professional Development in Education.* Washington, DC: Albert Shanker Institute.

Elmore, Richard F. 2003. "A Plea for Strong Practice," *Educational Leadership* 61(3), 6–10.

Etzioni, Amitai. 1996/1997. "The Community of Communities," *The Responsive Community* 7(1), 21–32.

Fullan, Michael. 2003. *The Moral Imperative of School Leadership.* Thousand Oaks, CA: Corwin Press.

Greenfield, William D. 1985, June 29. "Instructional Leadership: Muddles, Puzzles, and Promises." The Doyne M. Smith Lecture. Athens: University of Georgia.

Greenleaf, Robert K. 1977. *Teacher as Servant.* New York: Paulist Press.

Habermas, Jurgen. 1987. *The Theory of Communicative Action.* Vol. 2: *Lifeworld and System: A Critique of Functional Reason.* Trans. T. McCarthy. Boston: Beacon Press.

Hill, Paul T., Gail E. Foster, and Tamar Gendler. 1990. *High Schools with Character.* Santa Monica, CA: RAND Corporation.

Kelly, Robert E. 1988, November–December. "In Praise of Followers," *Harvard Business Review.*

Lakomski, Gabriele. 1985. "The Cultural Perspective in Educational Administration," in R. J. S. Macpherson and Helen M. Sungaila

(Eds.), *Ways and Means of Research in Educational Administration.* Armidale, New South Wales: University of New England.

Lightfoot, Sara Lawrence. 1983. *The Good High School: Portraits of Character and Culture.* New York: Basic Books.

Morris, Van Cleave, Robert L. Crowson, Cynthia Porter-Gehrie, and Emanual Hurwitz, Jr. 1984. *Principals in Action.* Columbus, OH: Merrill.

Peters, Tom, and Nancy Austin. 1985. *A Passion for Excellence.* New York: Random House.

Putnam, Robert D. 2000. *Bowling Alone.* New York: Simon & Schuster.

Quantz, Richard A., Nelda Cambron-McCabe, and Michael Dantley. 1991. "Preparing School Administrators for Democratic Authority: A Critical Approach to Graduate Education," *The Urban Review* 23(1), 3–19.

Rawls, John. 1971. *A Theory of Justice.* Cambridge, MA: Harvard University Press.

Selznick, Philip. 1957. *Leadership in Administration: A Sociological Interpretation.* New York: Harper & Row. California Paperback Edition 1984. Berkeley: University of California Press.

Sergiovanni, Thomas J. 1992. *Moral Leadership.* San Francisco: Jossey-Bass.

Sergiovanni, Thomas J. 1994. *Building Community in Schools.* San Francisco: Jossey-Bass.

Sergiovanni, Thomas J. 2000. *The Lifeworld of Leadership: Creating Culture, Community and Personal Meaning in Our Schools.* San Francisco: Jossey-Bass.

Sergiovanni, Thomas J. 2001. *Leadership: What's in It for Schools?* London: Routledge/Falmer.

Sergiovanni, Thomas J. 2005. *Strengthening the Heartbeat: Leading and Learning Together in Schools.* San Francisco: Jossey-Bass.

Sergiovanni, Thomas J., and Robert J. Starratt. 1988. *Supervision: Human Perspectives.* New York: McGraw-Hill.

Smith, John K., and Joseph Blase. 1987. *Educational Leadership as a Moral Concept.* Washington, DC: American Educational Research Association.

Sternberg, Robert J. 1996, November 13. "What Is Successful Intelligence?" *Education Week,* 48.

Taylor, Paul W. 1961. *Normative Discourse.* Englewood Cliffs, NJ: Prentice-Hall.

Tom, Alan. 1980. "Teaching as a Moral Craft: A Metaphor for Teaching and Teacher Education," *Curriculum Inquiry* 10(3).

Tom, Alan. 1984. *Teaching as a Moral Craft.* New York: Longman.

Vaill, Peter B. 1984. "The Purposing of High-Performing Systems," in Thomas J. Sergiovanni and John E. Corbally (Eds.), *Leadership and Organizational Culture.* Urbana: University of Illinois Press.

Wilkins, Alan L. 1989. *Developing Corporate Character.* San Francisco: Jossey-Bass.

Zaleznik, Abraham. 1989. *The Managerial Mystique: Restoring Leadership in Business.* New York: Harper & Row.

Part Two

TOWARD A NEW THEORY

2

THE PRINCIPAL'S JOB TODAY AND TOMORROW

*L*et's begin our examination of the principal's job with your perceptions of the tasks and functions that should make up this role and of their relative importance.

Imagine yourself as a candidate for the principalship of an 800-student middle school in a community close to Philadelphia. Your overall credentials as an administrator and your background as a successful teacher are sufficiently impressive that the search committee considers you one of its top three candidates. You have been invited to visit the school and to be interviewed by the committee and the superintendent for this job. To help you prepare for your visit, the committee informs you of a number of areas that they wish to explore and a number of issues that they wish to discuss. Among these are:

What do you consider to be the major tasks of a principal?
Which of these tasks do you believe to be most important?
As you plan your daily and weekly schedule, what proportion of time would you allocate to each of these tasks?

You want to be as prepared as possible for your interview. Therefore, consider these questions and write down some of your ideas. Start by writing a brief general description of your perception of the role of the principal and her or his prime reasons for existing as part of the structure of schooling. Follow this general description with a listing of roles and task areas that you believe should define the principal's responsibilities. Curriculum and program development, supervision and evaluation, and student discipline are examples of task areas that might come to mind. As you examine your list, rank the tasks in order of their importance to you. Then, using 100 percent of the time available to you in an average work week, allocate percentages of time that you would try to spend in each area if you were to obtain this principalship.

In your deliberations about principalship responsibilities, roles, and tasks, you have probably been thinking in terms of the school in the ideal. You have been describing your perceptions of what is important and what you think the principal *ought* to do.

*I*DEAL CONCEPTIONS OF THE PRINCIPALSHIP

Definitions of the principal's roles and responsibilities have changed over time. Traditional definitions focused on the administrative processes and functions that must be emphasized for schools to work well. Effective principals, for example, are responsible for planning, organizing, leading, and controlling. *Planning* means setting goals and objectives for the school and developing blueprints and strategies for implementing them. *Organizing* means bringing together the necessary human, financial, and physical resources to accomplish goals efficiently. *Leading* has to do with guiding, motivating, and supervising subordinates. *Controlling* refers to the principal's evaluation responsibilities and includes reviewing and regulating performance, providing feedback, and otherwise tending to standards of goal attainment.

Gradually, lists of tasks and roles have given way to lists of competencies and proficiencies as the favored way to map out the territory of educational administration. For example, in 1997, the National Association of Elementary School Principals (NAESP) issued the document *Elementary and Middle School Proficiencies for Principals,* which contained a list of 96 proficiencies grouped into eight categories that define *expertness* in the principalship. The first three of the eight categories and the first three proficiencies listed for each category follow:

- *Leadership Behavior.* The schools of proficient principals are marked by collegiality and a sense of common purpose. In the exercise of leadership, the proficient principal:
  —Demonstrates vision and provides leadership that appropriately involves the school community in the creation of shared beliefs and values.
  —Demonstrates moral and ethical judgment.
  —Demonstrates creativity and innovative thinking.

- *Communication Skills.* The image the principal projects affects how students, staff, parents, and the community perceive the school. In using communication skills, the proficient principal:
  —Articulates beliefs persuasively, effectively explains decisions, checks for understanding, and behaves in ways that reflect these beliefs and decisions.
  —Writes and speaks clearly and concisely so the message is understood by the intended audience.
  —Conveys opinions succinctly and distinguishes between facts and opinions when communicating priorities.
- *Group Processes.* The proficient principal mobilizes others to collaborate in solving problems and accomplishing school goals. In facilitating group processes, the proficient principal:
  —Understands group dynamics and applies effective group process skills.
  —Establishes a framework for collaborative action and involves the school community in developing and supporting shared beliefs, values, mission, and goals for the school.
  —Uses appropriate team-building skills. (6–18)

The remaining five categories of competencies are the following:

- Curriculum and Instruction
- Assessment
- Organizational Management
- Fiscal Management
- Political Management

In recent years, more emphasis is being given to what principals in schools are supposed to accomplish as a way of defining the job. The idea behind this trend is to determine the outcomes that schools should pursue and students should achieve. Much less attention is given to pointing out the processes that must be used. Presumably, principals in schools are expected to do whatever is necessary to achieve the outcomes. Defining the job this way has the advantage of freeing principals and others with whom they work from bureaucratic restrictions and constraints. Few scripts for the principal to follow are provided. Lists of things principals must do are kept to a minimum. This focus on results leads to the development of measurable improvement goals that are aligned to school and district goals and sometimes to standards. With these in place events are assessed on the basis of results rather than intents (DuFour et al., 2006:5; Schmoker, 1999).

Defining the role of the principal in terms of outcomes, however, increases the likelihood that means will be separated from ends. Separating the two is risky business and can be troublesome in schools. For example, it is hard to specify all the important outcomes in advance. A tendency exists to specify outcomes that are easy to understand and easy to evaluate. As a result, many other outcomes that may be more important are overlooked. Furthermore, a difference exists between effective practices and good practices. What principals and teachers may do, for example, may work but may not be right. The outcomes approach tends to define effectiveness more in terms of what works than what is right, and this tendency raises important moral questions. Still, this new approach brings to school leadership a degree of instructional coherence that many feel is long overdue. Newmann and colleagues define instructional coherence as "a set of interrelated programs for students and staff that are guided by a common framework for curriculum, instruction, assessment, and learning climate and that are pursued over a sustained period" (2001:297). The acceptance and use of a common framework is critical to the success of this approach.

$\mathcal{T}$HICK VISIONS: A VALUES APPROACH

One way to capitalize on the advantages of an outcomes-based approach to defining the role of the principal, while avoiding some of the disadvantages, is to adopt a values-based approach. When using this approach, assumptions and beliefs presumed to be important are specified and used as a basis for deciding what it is that principals and others should do. The specification of assumptions and beliefs provides a standard for determining what is good and bad, effective and ineffective, and acceptable and unacceptable. Sometimes the standards are backed up by hard research; other times they are backed up by informed and respected craft knowledge; and still other times they are reasoned expressions of philosophical positions, assumptions, and judgments. Using a values-based approach for defining the role of the principal not only ensures that what principals decide to do meets acceptable standards but it also provides the school with a set of indicators that defines its educational and moral health.

A values approach seeks to identify *thick* visions and then translate these visions into images of what we want the school to be like. Thick visions are more than mission statements, more than catchy prose, and more than inspirational words. They are working documents that state publicly what is important, why it is important, what our obligations are, and how we get where we want to go. Thick visions are contracts, even covenants, that spell out our roles and responsibilities to the school and its vision. These images include goals and pathways that help a school calibrate its direction and help that school create the frameworks, structures, norms, and other means to succeed. Thick visions are accompanied by a set of promises that principals must make and a set of promises that they ask others to make (teachers, students, and parents, for example). Promises detail what each of these constituent groups must do to bring the school closer to its vision. For thick visions to be practical and effective, not only must they obligate constituent groups to embody the vision in what they do, but they must also assemble the research, review respected craft knowledge, and inventory the values that will be needed to inform the work of principals. Thick visions provide vivid images of what we seek and provide insights into how to get there. They do this by stating what it is that principals must do, that schools must do, and that various constituent groups must do for the visions to be realized (see, e.g., DuFour and Eaker, 1998).

BREAKING RANKS

In 1996, the National Association of Secondary School Principals (NASSP), working cooperatively with the Carnegie Foundation for the Advancement of Teaching, published a report titled *Breaking Ranks: Changing an American Institution*. This report provides an example of using a values-based approach to define educational standards. *Breaking Ranks* provides a list of over 80 implementing recommendations for changing the American high school. The report is based on the belief that

> if one theme could be extracted that is overarching and paramount, it is a message that the high school of the 21st century must be much more student-centered and above all much more personalized in programs, support services, and intellectual rigor. These seven recommendations are illustrative of what we envision: Every student will have a personal adult advocate; the Carnegie unit must be replaced or redefined; student anonymity must be banished; teachers should meet no more than 90 students per day; every student should have a Personal Plan of Progress; imaginative flexible scheduling must be the order of the day; every principal and teacher will have a Personal Learning Plan. (NASSP, 1996:vi)

Breaking Ranks II: Strategies for Leading High School Reform, published in 2004 by the NASSP in partnership with the Education Alliance at Brown University, is also an example of a values approach to identifying principal roles and responsibilities. In this document not only are thick visions for changing the American high school discussed but the implementation strategies that make them thick are also discussed.

Breaking Ranks II provides 31 recommendations for changing the high school with each recommendation assigned to one of three core areas:

1. Collaborative leadership and professional learning communities
2. Personalization
3. Curriculum, instruction, and assessment

The same ground is covered by both reports, but *Breaking Ranks II* differs in several important ways. Many of the original 82 *Breaking Ranks* recommendations have been combined. Recommendations that are beyond the control of principals have been deleted. And the emphasis is not just on what must be done to improve the high school but on how to do it. For example, a number of extended profiles of schools that are on the road to implementing the 31 recommendations are included.* Each of the profiles was written by a member of that school's improvement team responsible for leading reform efforts.

In sum, a values approach reminds principals of their responsibilities and defines for them their success in terms of a vision of what their school should look like. This is followed by a public commitment to pursue that vision and by promises that must be made and obligations that must be assumed by various constituents in order to enable that vision.

As *Breaking Ranks II* describes it,

> Defining a vision for your school should be a product of many thoughtful conversations within your school and within your community. There is no template of what a *Breaking Ranks* school might look like because school values differ from community to community. However, in the interest of spurring conversation within your school, the letter below from a fictional principal attempts to paint a picture for students, school board members, school staff, the superintendent, and the larger community—and thereby get them involved. It details what the school might look like when the reforms have been implemented. This text may form the basis of a conversation among your leadership team and beyond about the vision for your own school.
>
> > Our Breaking Ranks high school will be a learning community that reflects a culture born of respect and trust, where the spirit of teaching and learning is driven by student inquiry, reflection, and passion. Our efforts to cultivate that spirit will begin well before students enter freshman year or before they transfer into our school with a feeder schools–to–high school transition program—so that when students join us, they understand that each of them is expected to achieve to his or her highest potential. Before walking in the door the first day of school, each will have investigated the opportunities available and each will have already met with a teacher or other member of the staff to lay the groundwork for building a personal connection to the school.
> >
> > Rather than leave a student's high school experience and the outcome of that experience to pure chance, we believe we have the obligation to understand a teenager's personal needs and to challenge them by meeting those needs intellectually, socially, and personally. While some students have little problem finding a voice, others struggle well into adulthood to find a productive voice. By providing a variety of structured experiences in which students can be actively engaged, we believe we can address a student's need to

---

*The schools are Noble High School, a rural school in North Berwick, Maine; Wyandotte High School, an urban school in Kansas City, Kansas; and Littleton High School, a suburban school in Colorado.

- Express personal perspectives
- Create individual and group identities
- Examine options and choose his or her own path
- Take risks and assess the effects
- Use his or her imagination
- Demonstrate mastery

Chance is not a game that should be played with a student's life. High schools have been able to address *some* of these needs for *some* of their students since schooling began. We endeavor to entice *each* student to fulfill *each* of those needs.

How often is it that only a few students express themselves—even though in theory all are "allowed"? Does that mean others don't want to? Are afraid to? Some would say, "part of growing up is finding the ability to express oneself, and if someone can't, then that's life." But what happens if one never learns that skill? Is that life? We think not! We will provide several arenas in which each student can express himself or herself in one-on-one and group settings—through our advisory program, our activities program, student exhibitions and presentations, and within each classroom.

How often do students fall into the wrong cliques only because they want to belong to something? While we cannot dictate friendships, clearly we have an opportunity to provide groups (project groups, advisories, etc.) in which each student feels a sense of belonging and perhaps where friendships will be fostered.

How often does each student have the opportunity to demonstrate mastery of a subject, a concept, an instrument, a sport? The "A" students, the valedictorian, the lead in the play or the band, the star on the football team all have those opportunities—and well deserved at that. But what about the students who haven't been working on a skill for as long, or who try just as hard and don't quite "make the cut"? We're not talking here about equality of rewards or giving everyone a star, but rather that each student should be encouraged to excel and should receive recognition for it—individually and, if appropriate, in a group setting. Our school has designed the practices to make this a reality in the classroom, in advisory settings, and through our student activities program. Students will be creating, developing, and publicly exhibiting projects that demonstrate their mastery of learning on a regular basis and will also be able to demonstrate their unique talents through a student activities program and a service-learning program tied directly to skills and knowledge needed to meet the larger learning goals for each student.

Our efforts to meet the needs of students are not simply so we can develop friendships with students and make them feel better about themselves. The business of education is about learning and achievement for each student. We believe that without these personal connections and our understanding of the motivations, aspirations, and learning styles of students, most students will never become engaged in their own learning and never really achieve their potential. The statistics about students who never complete high school—at least a quarter of all students—tell only a small part of the tale. What about those students who graduate, never having been challenged, and then go on to college only to drop out? Or those students who are bored day in and day out? Or those top notch students who could have been seriously challenged by taking more challenging courses, or pursuing an internship or in-depth research project, or being mentored by an expert in the "field of their dreams," or taking courses at the nearby college or online, but instead are left to stare out the window and wait for the bell to ring while the teacher reviews materials the student has already mastered?

We need to reach each of these students their first day, their first week, their first month, and throughout high school. We can't wait until graduation to say, "she has a lot of potential—I hope she has an opportunity to use it in college." Our school will get to know the potential of each student through our Personal Adult Advocate program. Our emphasis on decreasing the total number of students per teacher will allow teachers more time to confer with parents and mentors to personalize each student's educational experience, and to be able to effectively advise a small group of students. Each advocate will work with students to develop and monitor individual Personal Plans for Progress that will detail the academic, social, and other aspirations and needs of students. The adult advocate will work with students, their parents, and their teachers to ensure that each student's potential is being realized in the classroom, on the field, in the community, and, most important, in the mind of the student.

Academic achievement in our school will be driven by students being engaged in classes, seminars, and lessons designed by teams of teachers that integrate the curriculum. Students will be encouraged to write in all classes and to attack challenges from various perspectives using their own strengths while addressing their weaknesses. There will be no tracking of students. Instead, students will be grouped heterogeneously and include educationally challenged and culturally diverse students in all classes, and students will have multiple opportunities to redo their work until the work meets the established standards. The school will support personal drive and aspiration by providing a rigorous curriculum, AP courses, the International Baccalaureate (IB) program, college-credit courses, internships, and service-learning opportunities to all who are willing to take on the challenge. All students will have access to honors programs, and students will earn honors credit by their distinctive performance.

Our school will be dramatically different from the traditional American high school, and that difference will be obvious to even the casual observer. Upon entering our "Breaking Ranks" high school, the level and intensity of questioning and listening by students and the teachers who are encouraging more questioning and listening will set our school apart from others.

At graduation, the teachers and administrators who joined the profession and have made their own sacrifices to make a difference in the lives of young people, the parents who have supported, cajoled and inspired their sons and daughters—now young men and women—and the students who have spent four years of their lives and are now preparing to leave home for perhaps the first time should never have to say, "We missed an opportunity to challenge ourselves." At our school, those words will never be uttered because the work of each student and his or her portfolio will be the proof for everyone at graduation to see that, at every step of the way, each student was challenged. (2–5)*

To realize this image of success and to realize the things that must be done to make that success yours, the core recommendations must be viewed as both role definitions and pathways to be traveled. The core recommendations appear in Exhibit 2.1. Note that the recommendations are grouped into the three main task areas discussed earlier: helping to develop and then supporting collaborative leadership and professional learning communities; helping to develop a culture of caring in the school that provides students with the personalization they need to be accepted and to succeed; and leading new initiatives in curriculum, instruction, and assessment reforms. The three get nods of approval that are not likely to lead to action. When the recommendations, and the pathways needed to implement them, are added to the task areas, they become part of a thick vision that leads to action. When visions are thick, each of the task areas becomes connected to concrete pathways that map the territory and point the way for principals and others who share responsibility for leading change. And when visions are thick the responsibilities that teachers, parents, principals, and others have for traveling the pathways and implementing the vision are delineated.

A STANDARDS-BASED APPROACH

The use of standards is the latest attempt to define and describe what school principals and other administrators should do. Standards can be intimidating. They project a "gold standard" kind of image imbued with objectivity and scientific validity. But, as is the case with most prescriptions of what ought to be, standards are not objective. They represent the judgments of committees of experts, policy makers, and others. These judgments are influenced and informed by what research says. This posture leaves plenty of room for subjectivity. That is why different committees often come up with different standards. Still, the standards movement in educational administration seems grounded in what some research traditions

exhibit
2.1

Breaking Ranks II Core Recommendations

Collaborative Leadership & Professional Learning Communities	Personalization and the School Environment	Curriculum, Instruction, & Assessment
• The principal will provide leadership in the high school community by building and maintaining a vision, direction, and focus for student learning. • Each high school will establish a site council and accord other meaningful roles in decision making to students, parents, and members of the staff in order to promote student learning and an atmosphere of participation, responsibility, and ownership. • A high school will regard itself as a community in which members of the staff collaborate to develop and implement the school's learning goals. • Teachers will provide the leadership essential to the success of reform, collaborating with others in the educational community to redefine the role of the teacher and to identify sources of support for that redefined role.	• High schools will create small units in which anonymity is banished. • Each high school teacher involved in the instructional program on a full-time basis will be responsible for contact time with no more than 90 students during a given term so that the teacher can give greater attention to the needs of every student. • Each student will have a Personal Plan for Progress that will be reviewed often to ensure that the high school takes individual needs into consideration and to allow students, within reasonable parameters, to design their own methods for learning in an effort to meet high standards.	• Each high school will identify a set of essential learnings—above all, in literature and language, writing, mathematics, social studies, science, and the arts—in which students must demonstrate achievement in order to graduate. • Each high school will present alternatives to tracking and to ability grouping. • The high school will reorganize the traditional department structure in order to integrate the school's curriculum to the extent possible and emphasize depth over breadth of coverage. • The content of the curriculum, where practical, should connect to real-life applications of knowledge and skills to help students link their education to the future. • The high school will promote service programs and student activities as integral to an education, providing opportunities for all students that support and extend academic learning.

exhibit *2.1* **Continued**

Collaborative Leadership & Professional Learning Communities

- Every school will be a learning community for the entire community. As such, the school will promote the use of Personal Learning Plans for each educator and provide the resources to ensure the principal, teachers, and other staff members can address their own learning and professional development needs as they relate to improved student learning.
- The school community will promote policies and practices that recognize diversity in accord with the core values of a democratic and civil society and will offer substantive ongoing professional development to help educators appreciate issues of diversity and expose students to a rich array of viewpoints, perspectives, and experiences.

Personalization and the School Environment

- Every high school student will have a Personal Adult Advocate to help him or her personalize the educational experience.
- Teachers will convey a sense of caring so that students feel that their teachers share a stake in student learning.
- High schools will develop flexible scheduling and student grouping patterns that allow better use of time in order to meet the individual needs of students and to ensure academic success.
- The high school will engage students' families as partners in the students' education.

Curriculum, Instruction, & Assessment

- The academic program will extend beyond the high school campus to take advantage of learning opportunities outside the four walls of the building.
- Teachers will design high-quality work and teach in ways that engage students, encourage them to persist, and, when the work is successfully completed, result in student satisfaction and their acquisition of knowledge, critical thinking and problem solving skills, and other abilities valued by society.
- Teachers will know and be able to use a variety of strategies and settings that identify and accommodate individual learning styles and engage students.
- Each high school teacher will have a broad base of academic knowledge with depth in at least one subject area.
- Teachers will be adept at acting as coaches and facilitators to promote more active involvement of students in their own learning.

(continued)

exhibit *2.1* **Continued**

Collaborative Leadership & Professional Learning Communities	Personalization and the School Environment	Curriculum, Instruction, & Assessment
• High schools will build partnerships with institutions of higher education to provide teachers and administrators at both levels with ideas and opportunities to enhance the education, performance, and evaluation of educators. • High schools will develop political and financial relationships with individuals, organizations, and businesses to support and supplement educational programs and policies. • At least once every five years, each high school will convene a broad-based external panel to offer a Public Description of the school, a requirement that could be met in conjunction with the evaluations of state, regional, and other accrediting groups.	• The high school community, which cannot be value-neutral, will advocate and model a set of core values essential in a democratic and civil society. • High schools, in conjunction with agencies in the community, will help coordinate the delivery of physical and mental health and social services for youth.	• Teachers will integrate assessment into instruction so that assessment is accomplished using a variety of methods and does not only measure students, but becomes part of the learning process. • Recognizing that education is a continuum, high schools will reach out to elementary and middle-level schools as well as institutions of higher education to better serve the articulation of student learning and to ensure that, at each stage of the continuum, stakeholders understand what will be required of students at the succeeding stage. • Schools will develop a strategic plan to make technology integral to curriculum, instruction, and assessment, accommodating different learning styles and helping teachers to individualize and improve the learning process.

Source: Breaking Ranks II: Strategies for Leading High School Reform (pp. 17–18) by National Association of Secondary School Principals, 2004, Reston, VA: The Association. Copyright © 2004 by NASSP. Used with permission. For more information on NASSP products and services to promote excellence in middle level and high school leadership, visit www.principals.org.

(but not all) say are the principalship behaviors that contribute to effective schools. For this reason, they should not be taken lightly.

In 1996, the Council of Chief State School Officers adopted the list of standards for school leaders provided by the Interstate School Leaders Licensure Consortium (ISLLC). Neil Shipman, an assessment expert and director of ISLLC, and Joseph Murphy, a highly respected professor of educational administration and chair of ISLLC, describe the two-year effort as follows:

> Forged from research on productive educational leadership and the wisdom of colleagues, the standards were drafted by personnel from 24 state education agencies and representatives from various professional associations. The standards present a common core of knowledge, dispositions, and performances that will help link leadership more forcefully to productive schools and enhanced educational outcomes. Although developed to serve a different purpose, the standards were designed to be compatible with the new National Council for the Accreditation of Teacher Education (NCATE) *Curriculum Guidelines* for school administration—as well as with the major national reports on reinventing leadership for tomorrow's schools. As such, they represent another part of a concerted effort to enhance the skills of school leaders and to couple leadership with effective educational processes and valued outcomes. (Council of Chief State School Officers, 1996:3)

Beginning in 2003, new NCATE standards are being used to assess the preparation program of universities seeking accreditation. Although covering most of the same territory found in the standards previously used (they are largely a reformatting of the ISLLC standards), the new standards differ by being performance based. Not only must universities show they are addressing the right content, they must provide compelling evidence that their students are able to perform in each of the standards areas at a required level of competence. Members of the Educational Leadership Constituent Council (ELCC) include NAESP, NASSP, and the Association for Supervision and Curriculum Development (ASCD).

The new standards appear as Appendix 2.1. Note that, although the standards for principals and central office administrators are the same, they are expected to be mastered at a higher level by central office administrators. This feature may raise several important questions: Should we assume that those higher up in the hierarchy should also know more about teaching and learning and other standards than those lower? Does this matching of competence through hierarchy apply as well to teachers? Although it is safe to assume principals should know more about many of these standards, should we assume that principals should know more than teachers do about those aimed to teaching and learning? If the answer is yes, then principals may require massive doses of ongoing professional development for them to keep up with teachers. By and large many principals do indeed know more about teaching and learning than do many teachers. Today's principals move into that position because of their accomplishments as teachers, and most are prepared to assume instructional leadership roles all the way into the classroom itself. In recent years principals have taken more seriously their role as principal teacher, and increasingly instructional leadership is moving to the center of their practice—a theme we will discuss later in this chapter.

PAROCHIAL SCHOOLS

For parochial school principals, the religious dimension must be added to any array of roles and responsibilities that define the principalship. For example, in his analysis of the socialization of Catholic school principals, Augenstein (1989; Augenstein and Konnert, 1991) defines the role requirements of the religious dimension as knowing about and making available church documents and other religious resources, providing for spiritual development, being a leader of prayer, creating an environment for religious education, integrating gospel values and other religious principles into the curriculum, and providing services to the parish and civic community. Other types of Christian schools, as well as Jewish schools and Muslim schools, would have similar lists of added roles, responsibilities, and proficiencies that reflect their uniqueness. Modern lists of proficiencies provide a rendering of tasks and roles that are considerably more descriptive than the generic lists of the past and that emphasize much more the specific context of schooling, teaching, and learning.

The Sydney Catholic Schools in New South Wales, Australia, have developed a Catholic School Leadership Framework as shown in Figure 2.1 (Canavan, 2003:159). Six dimensions of leadership are identified and grouped into three main categories: purposes, support, and personal dimensions. Religious leadership is at the heart of the framework. Without it Catholic schools, and other parochial schools, place their unique focus at risk. Should this focus be lost, each of the other leadership dimensions is weakened. In reporting their research that compared achievement levels of students in focused Catholic schools and in public schools with more comprehensive public schools, Hill, Foster, and Gendler note, "Focus schools resemble one another, and differ from zone comprehensive public schools in two ways. First, focus schools have clear uncomplicated missions centered on the experiences [they intend] to provide [their] students and on the [way they intend] to influence [their] student performance, attitudes, and behavior. Second, focus schools are strong organizations with a capacity to initiate action in pursuit of their missions, to sustain themselves over time, to solve their own problems, and to manage their external relationships" (1990:vii). They note further that "their distinct characters set them apart, in the minds of their staff, students, and parents from other schools. . . . Each has a special identity that inspires a sense of loyal and common commitment. They are committed to education in its broadest sense, the development of whole students. They induce values, influence attitudes, and integrate diverse sources of knowledge. They also transmit facts and impart skills, but mainly they try to mold teenagers into responsible, productive

Core Purpose

The core purpose of the Catholic school is to take forward the mission of Jesus and the Church in partnership with parents and parish for the formation, education, and development of the students entrusted to the school.

Religious Leadership	Leadership for Learning
Mission of the contemporary Catholic Church	Educational vision
Religious Education curriculum	Learning culture
Catholic life/integration of values	Student learning outcomes
Parish/schools/parents partnership	Student needs
Ritual/celebration/liturgy/prayer/retreats	Curriculum
Sacramental/eucharistic/scriptural life	Teaching practice
Pastoral care	Assessment and reporting
Service to community	Quality assurance
Social justice	Learning resources
Christian leadership	

Personal Dimensions

The personal dimensions of leadership underpin and relate to all areas of the Leadership Framework

Personal Dimensions of Leadership

Faith/spirituality

Human/personal dimension

Relationships/communication

Ethical/moral dimension

Cognitive/emotional dimension

Decision making/responsibility

Leadership

Leader as learner

Supporting Processes

The core purpose is served by the support processes—Human Resources, Strategic, and Organizational Leadership. It is important that these processes do not become ends in themselves, but that they are always seen to serve the core purpose.

Human Resources Leadership	Strategic Leadership	Organizational Leadership
Employment processes/perspective	Leadership of vision/mission/goals	Coordination of school processes and activities
Deployment of staff/workplace practices	Archdiocesan context	Legal/statutory requirements
Performance management and review	Strategic direction	Technology
Employee relations	Culture of change	Records management
Development of staff	Annual cycle of implementation	Financial management
Succession planning	Culture of reflection, review, and improvement	Risk management
Support staff	Community leadership	Property and facilities
Relationship with unions	School marketing	Enrollments/forward planning

figure **2.1** **Catholic School Leadership Framework, Sydney Catholic Schools, New South Wales, Australia**

Source: "Building Strategic Leadership and Management Capacity to Improve School Effectiveness" by Kelvin Canavan, 2003, in *Catholic Education: A Journal of Inquiry and Practice* 7(2), 159.

adults" (1990:55–56). The focus schools had strong social contracts that defined reciprocal responsibilities of teachers, students, parents, and administrators. It is clear to everyone what the benefits are in fulfilling this contract faithfully. They had a strong commitment to parenting and worked hard to mold students' values. They had "centripetal curricula" that brought students together toward learning a common set of course skills and perspectives.

The dimensions above are the DNA of organizational character. They are easier to develop in schools with explicit, unique, and meaningful purposes that are widely accepted. Sure, leadership for learning is important too. But it is the religious theme that provides an enriched core of purposes that include values, traditions, rituals, and norms that not only provide focus but serve as a source of authority for what these schools do.

In a general way, the Educational Leadership Constituent Council list of standards applies to parochial school principals, too. But, as suggested above, there are important differences. In addition to being educational and managerial leaders, principals of religious-affiliated schools are expected to be spiritual leaders responsible for building a community of faith within the school that is embedded with pastoral qualities. Appendix 2.2, "Profile of an ICEL Graduate," provides an example of standards used by the Institute for Catholic Educational Leadership (ICEL) at the University of San Francisco to define the characteristics they expect of their graduates.

THE COMPLEX NATURE OF MANAGERIAL WORK

To what extent do statements of standards, recommendations, and needed proficiencies agree with reports from the "real world" that tell us what principals actually do and how they actually spend their time? We might think of such reports as descriptive studies of the principal's job. The 1973 publication of Henry Mintzberg's book *The Nature of Managerial Work* sparked a great deal of interest in descriptive studies of administration in education. Descriptive studies attempt to map out the actual roles and tasks of principals by focusing on what administrators actually do. The complex nature of administrative work is ingrained in the school's DNA and defies simplifying. Even a cursory shadowing of your principal at work will reveal this complexity. Thus, though Mintzberg's findings are not recent, today's administrators experience a similar world and respond in much the same way.

Mintzberg, for example, found that the work of administrators was characterized by brevity, variety, and fragmentation, and that the majority of administrative activities were of brief duration, often taking only minutes. Activities were not only varied but also patternless, disconnected, and interspersed with trivia; as a result, the administrator often shifted moods and intellectual frames. These findings suggest a high level of *superficiality* in the work of administration. Mintzberg noted further that, because of the open-ended nature of administrative work, the administrator is compelled to perform a great number of tasks at an unrelenting pace. This contributes further to superficiality. Free time is only rarely available, and job responsibilities seem inescapable.

The administrators in Mintzberg's study demonstrated a preference for live action and for oral means of handling this action. They favored the job's current and active elements over abstract, technical, and routine elements. They preferred to visit with others personally, to talk on the telephone, and to conduct formal and informal conferences, rather than to rely on written means of communication. Because of this propensity for oral action, most of the business of the organization remained unrecorded and was stored in the administrator's memory. This, in turn, made delegation and shared decision making difficult. Mintzberg found that administrators are overloaded with *exclusive* knowledge about the organization and overburdened, as well, with incursions on their time as others seek this information. He observed further that administrators had difficulty in keeping on top of events and that no mechanisms existed to relieve them of minor responsibilities. Faced with the apparent requirement that one be involved in almost everything, the recourse was to treat work activities in a distinctly superficial manner.

Echoing Mintzberg's findings, Sproul (1976) found that such words as *local, verbal, choppy,* and *varied* were most often used to describe the typical administrative workday. Choppiness, for example, was evidenced by the presence of many activities of brief duration. A composite administrator in Sproul's study engaged in 56 activities daily, each averaging about nine minutes, and participated in 65 events, each averaging six minutes. Events were described as periods of time one minute or longer during which administrators used one medium of communication such as the phone, a conversation, or a memo.

School principals, too, often must deal with aspects of work superficially. The reasons for this can be understood as one examines the full range of responsibilities that principals have. Barth (1980) describes the extent of such responsibilities as follows:

> The principal is ultimately responsible for almost everything that happens in school and out. We are responsible for personnel—making sure that employees are physically present and working to the best of their ability. We are in charge of program—making sure that teachers are teaching what they are supposed to and that children are learning it. We are accountable to parents—making sure that each is given an opportunity to express problems and that those problems are addressed and resolved. We are expected to protect the physical safety of children—making sure that the several hundred lively organisms who leave each morning return, equally lively, in the afternoon.
>
> Over the years principals have assumed one small additional responsibility after another—responsibility for the safe passage of children from school to home, responsibility for the safe passage of children from home to school, responsibility for making sure the sidewalks are plowed of snow in winter, responsibility

for health education, sex education, moral education, responsibility for teaching children to evacuate school buses and to ride their bikes safely. We have taken on lunch programs, then breakfast programs; responsibility for the physical condition of the furnace, the wiring, the playground equipment. We are now accountable for children's achievement of minimum standards at each grade level, for the growth of children with special needs, of the gifted, and of those who are neither. The principal has become a provider of social services, food services, health care, recreation programs and transportation—with a solid skills education worked in somehow. (4–6)

Recent Studies

As suggested above, though Mintzberg's study was published in 1973 and Barth's description appeared in a 1980 publication there is no reason to believe the job of principals has become less complex, requires less time, or allows for leisurely reflection. Indeed a 2001 study conducted by the NASSP finds that the mean number of hours a principal works during a typical week is 62.21. Women principals reported working 69.67 hours and men principals 60.51 hours. Not enough time, too much paperwork, and inadequate financial resources were major problems for principals, having been mentioned as impediments by 70.3 percent, 69 percent, and 50.8 percent of the principals. Twenty-eight percent of the principals mentioned burnout as a problem.

A 2003 study conducted by Public Agenda for the Wallace Foundation (Farkas, Johnson, and Duffett, 2003) found that 58 percent of the principals surveyed cited insufficient funding and implementation of No Child Left Behind as the most pressing problems they were facing. Sixty-three percent of the principals agreed that "Administrators are obliged to spend a disproportional amount of money and other resources on special education" (13). Eighty-one percent of them agreed that "The volume and complexity of federal and state regulations regarding special education has gotten worse in recent years" (13). Forty-five percent of the principals responded that "Daily emergencies rob me of time that would be better spent in the classroom or on teaching issues" was somewhat close to their own situation, and 29 percent reported that this statement was very close, for a total of 74 percent (15).

No CHILD LEFT BEHIND

According to the 2003 Public Agenda survey, a broad consensus exists among principals that the landmark federal initiative No Child Left Behind (NCLB) has its merits but at the same time is a challenge to implement. Among the major complaints is that NCLB is an unfunded mandate (88 percent agree). One in three principals says implementation of NCLB is the most pressing issue he or she is facing.

Among the concerns expressed by the principals in the Public Agenda survey was that NCLB relied too heavily on standardized tests (73 percent agree); it is an intrusion by the federal government into areas that have normally been left to state and local governments (53 percent agree); and that consequences for schools that do not measure up are unfair (57 percent).

On a positive note, 57 percent of the principals thought it was realistic for teachers to be highly qualified; 53 percent said testing students annually helps show where improvement is necessary; and perhaps most important, 37 percent said that aggregating testing and other information by race and other groupings has helped in forcing schools to deal with the gaps in achievement. The Public Agenda/Wallace Report concludes that "There are doubts and misgivings—even a degree of suspicion—among school leaders toward No Child Left Behind. But there is no revolution in the offing and, even more important, no hard-core resistance to the basic assumptions of the act" (28). It remains to be seen what the future holds for NCLB. So far parents have been sitting on the sidelines, and school leaders have been doing their best to make this law work. If either group becomes unbearably unhappy with the law's implementation, we can expect significant changes. But whether the law changes or not, the increased emphasis now being placed on closing the achievement gap among different groups of students will continue.

An Optimistic View

Despite the pressures and despite the dim view that most principals have about school bureaucracy they remain optimistic and hopeful. In a 2006 update of the 2003 Public Agenda survey, principals reported that they were generally pleased with how well their school was doing. Ninety percent of the principals in the 2006 survey said that the public schools in their community are doing an excellent or good job. Eighty percent said that the education children are getting today is better than the education that they got when they were students. When the principals were asked, "Which of the following do you think is a pressing issue facing your school district these days," 41 percent of the principals said insufficient funding; 22 percent said meeting the requirements of NCLB; 16 percent said bureaucracy and paperwork; and 12 percent said a shortage of really effective teachers. Twenty-eight percent of the principals said that the statement "Daily emergencies rob me of time that would be better spent on academic and teaching issues" comes very close to describing their experiences as a principal; 40 percent said somewhat close.

Regarding NCLB, principals in the survey were asked if they thought it realistic or unrealistic to expect their district to meet the requirements that "by the end of the 2005–2006 year all teachers of the core academic subjects must be highly qualified—that is fully certified and have an academic major or pass a subject-matter test in the subject they teach." Seventy-one percent of the principals responded that this was a realistic goal and 29 percent of the principals responded that this was an unrealistic goal.

And finally, the principals in the 2006 survey were asked to assess the amount of decision-making authority that they had. Six percent responded that they have too little to be effective; 38 percent responded that they do not have enough to be ~~effective; an~~d 55 percent responded that they have the amount of authority ~~to do~~ their jobs well. This response pattern acknowledges that about ~~55 percent of princi~~pals said they are fully resourced to lead. Still, too many princi-pals are underutilized and until this pattern changes progress will be slow-going.

[handwritten margin note: very important model (D + C) frame for prin. interview]

DEMANDS, CONSTRAINTS, AND CHOICES

In another classic study, Rosemary Stewart (1982) describes managerial jobs "as consisting of an inner core of *demands,* an outer boundary of *constraints,* an in-between area of *choices*" (14). Demands are the things that principals must do. If they fail to do these things, sanctions are invoked, and often these sanctions are serious enough to endanger one's job. Demands are determined by school out-come specifications, legal requirements, bureaucratic rules and regulations, and the array of role expectations of important others such as superintendents, school board members, teachers, and parents. Constraints are determined by norms and values that exist in the community or school, availability of human and mate-rial resources, union contracts, space limitations, and the capability limitations of teachers and others with whom the principal must work. As with demands, prin-cipals who ignore constraints face the likelihood of threatened job security.

Although two principals may be subjected to the same demands and con-straints, their leadership practices nonetheless typically vary. Within any demand-and-constraint set there are always choices in the form of opportunities to do the same things differently and to do other things that are not required or prohibited. It is in this area of choices that the opportunities for excellence exist. Whether these opportunities flourish depends on the latitude that principals are able to make for themselves. One hallmark of a successful principal is her or his ability to expand the area of choices and thus reduce demands and constraints. This extra margin of latitude makes an important difference in enhancing the overall effec-tiveness of the school.

THE CHANGING ROLE

The National Association of Elementary School Principals (NAESP) 1998 study of the principalship (Doud and Keller, 1998:2) noted that the role of principals changed dramatically over the previous decade. Principals, for example, reported significant increases in responsibility (increases over 55 percent) in the following areas:

Areas of Responsibility	Percentage of Increase
1. Marketing/politics, and so on, to generate supports for school and education	70.0%
2. Working with social agencies	66.0%
3. Planning/implementing of site-based staff development	65.5%
4. Development of instructional practice	63.5%
5. Curriculum development	62.4%
6. Working with site-based councils/other constituencies	61.6%
7. Attention to issues related to potential legal liabilities	58.1%

The three leading responsibility indicators represent a cluster that is directly related to themes of increased autonomy at the local school site, increased emphasis on school choice, the need to market one's school effectively, and dealing with the politics involved. Curriculum development and instructional practice areas suggest the increased emphasis that is now being placed on individual schools to perform and to be held accountable to state standards.

The 2008 NAESP study will be published at about the same time the sixth edition of this book is published. Use the website www.naesp.org (or a current website) to access the 2008 study. What does the 2008 survey say about current principals' responsibilities? How do these responsibilities compare? Has there been a shift away from the school site to the central office as the place where school improvement is now being developed and managed? Or is authority still pretty much at the local school site as was the case in 1998?

Figure 2.2 shows the percentage of principals in the 1998 NAESP study who list the areas provided as one of the three in which they spend the most time. Despite dramatic increases in responsibility in dealing with marketing, choice, school-based management, curriculum, and teaching, it is the daily and continuous interaction with teachers, other staff, and students that consumes the lion's share of a principal's time. Much of this interaction, of course, is consistent with the reported areas of increased responsibility. But much of it is not. As Doud and Keller point out, "Perhaps the biggest surprise among these rankings was the relatively low priority given to planning/conducting staff development. Despite the call of most site-based school management proponents and the priority given to staff development within many site-based school improvement planning processes, this finding clearly suggests that—within the prioritization of responsibility areas—staff development receives relatively little of the principal's time" (1998:12). Since the 1998 survey a great deal of attention has been given to staff development in the national debate about effective school improvement strategies.

In the fifth edition of this book we asked, Will this greater emphasis on professional development be the case in your school? Use the 1998 NAESP data and format that appears in Figure 2.2 to develop an instrument to assess how principals today use time. Ask principals to identify the three areas from Figure 2.2 on which

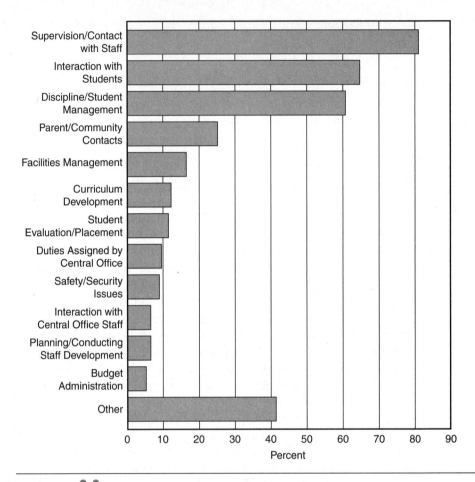

figure **2.2**   **Percentage of Respondents Listing the Area as One of the Three on Which They Spent the Most Time**

Source: A Ten-Year Study: The K–8 Principal in 1998 (p. 10) by James L. Doud and Edward P. Keller, 1998, Alexandria, VA: National Association of Elementary School Principals. Reprinted with permission. National Association of Elementary School Principals. All rights reserved.

they spend the most time. To gather a sample of respondents, ask 10 teachers to each identify two principals and invite the two to respond. Compare your findings in this 20-principal study with those of the larger 1998 survey.

Although some progress has been made in viewing the principal as a leader of leaders and the school as a community of leaders, the burdens of leadership continue to remain squarely on the shoulders of the principal. Citing Schiff (2002), Cooley and Shen (2003) note that "an average work week for principals is 62 hours with less than one-third of the time spent on curriculum and instructional activities" (12).

An important question is, Can new role definitions and responsibilities be effectively assumed by principals and schools without thinking through the question of redistributing the burdens of responsibility that now exist? If teachers were to accept more responsibility in the areas of supervision and evaluation by developing communities of practice and engaging in peer review, then principals would have more time for the emerging demands that they face in today's schools. Not only would such a redistribution of responsibilities be efficient, but it would represent a giant step toward increasing professionalism and enhancing capacity building among teachers. Indeed, many experts believe that distributed leadership is key to improving schools (Spillane, Halverson, and Diamond, 2001).

*P*RINCIPALS' PRIORITIES: COMPARING PERCEPTIONS

This section examines two perception sets. One set compares the perception of principals on the aspects of schooling that they consider to be most important (principals' priorities) with the opinions of teachers and parents as to what the principal's priorities are. The other set compares the tasks that principals think are most important with the tasks that teachers, parents, and students perceive that the principal thinks are most important. This kind of comparison can reveal blind spots that principals may have. They may feel, for example, that paying attention to students is important, but teachers, parents, and students may not agree. Blind spots are obstacles to change. Unless one can see things as they are it is not likely that changes will occur.

In the first comparison (see Figure 2.3), principals were asked which aspects of their schools were most important to them. They were to select up to three aspects from a list of eight. Seventy-five percent of the principals who responded chose "motivation of students and teachers to succeed" as one of their three choices. "School morale," "test scores," and "parental involvement" were aspects selected by 45 percent, 42 percent, and 41 percent of the principals. By contrast, "discipline" was selected as one of three priorities by only 18 percent of the principals. When teachers and parents were asked to select up to three aspects they thought best represented the principal's priorities, 61 percent of the teachers and 45 percent of the parents selected motivating students and teachers to achieve. But 61 percent of the teachers also selected test scores as one of the principal's top priorities. Indeed, teachers felt that the emphasis on test scores exceeded the emphasis on motivating students and teachers to achieve. When the two are viewed together, it might suggest that motivating students and teachers to achieve may be focused almost exclusively on the preparation for and passing of tests.

Though 61 percent of the teachers perceived that the principal's top priority was good test scores, only 42 percent of the principals actually chose tests, for a difference of 19. This difference suggests that either teachers overestimate the extent to which principals consider test scores a priority or principals underestimate

Q: Which of the following aspects of schooling are most important? Select up to 3.

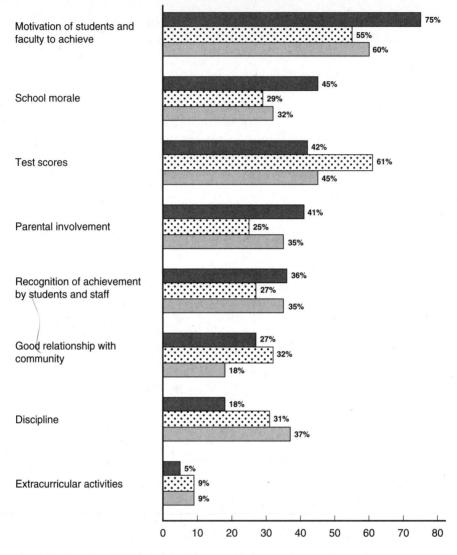

Principal's Priorities: Which aspects of your school are most important to you?

n=800

Teachers' Perception: Which aspects are most important to your principal?

n=1017

Parents' Perception: Which aspects are most important to your child's principal?

n=1107

figure **2.3** **Principals', Teachers', and Parents' Views of the Principal's Priorities**

Source: This figure is assembled from data included in pages 23 and 24 of the *MetLife Survey of the American Teacher: An Examination of School Leadership,* 1 Madison Ave., New York, NY 10010. © 2003 Harris Interactive, Inc.

the extent to which they consider test scores a priority. Forty-five percent of parents chose test scores as one of the principal's three responses, representing a difference of three. When compared with the 42 percent figure for principals this discrepancy seems to suggest that parents do not view the principal as seriously underestimating the importance of test scores. Only 18 percent of the principals chose discipline as one of their priorities. This compared with 31 percent of the teachers and 37 percent of the parents choosing discipline as one of the principal's priorities. Parents, for example, may in effect be saying that from their vantage point discipline was indeed a priority of the principals.

There is a relationship between participation in extracurricular activities and student engagement and participation in extracurricular activities and student achievement. Yet, many principals seem to think that extracurricular activities are not very important. Their advice seems to be if you want to get ready for the tests don't do anything that will distract from the old "drill and kill." Teachers agree with this perception of the principal, as do parents.

Table 2.1 compares the opinions of principals, teachers, parents, and students as to which tasks provided in a list of 12 were the most important parts of a principal's job. Respondents were asked to select all that applied. All four respondent groups agreed that making the school safe and encouraging teachers and students to do their best were the most important parts of a principal's job. For both items, the percentages for principals, teachers, and parents were 87, 83, and 86. This compared with only 55 percent and 37 percent of the students. The 11th- and 12th-ranked tasks, which students chose as the least important parts of the principal's job, were for the principal to know all students and to let people in the community know about the school. The least important tasks as selected by principals were to make sure students got along and knowing all students.

The sum of differences in rank for principals and students was 23. This compared with a difference of only 9 for principals and teachers and a difference of only 6 for principals and parents. By and large teachers and parents agreed on what should be the most important part of a principal's job. But principals and students disagree.

A LOOK AHEAD

Despite the complexities involved in identifying tasks and comparing the opinions of principals with teachers, parents, and students, it seems evident that instructional leadership roles have grown in importance. The emphasis on instructional leadership may not be reflected in surveys of principals as to what is important. But the expectation is there, nonetheless, whether principals like this emphasis or not.

In their classic study of how principals make a difference in promoting quality schooling, Smith and Andrews (1989:8) concluded that strong principals functioned as forceful and dynamic leaders who brought to their practice high energy, initiative, tolerance for ambiguity, a sense of humor, analytical ability, and table **2.1**   **Principals', Teachers', Parents', and Students' Opinions on the Principal's Most Important Tasks**

Q. What are the most important parts of the school principal's job? Select all that apply.

Base	Principals Total 800		Teachers Total 1,017		Parents Total 1,017		Students Total 919	
	%	Rank	%	Rank	%	Rank	%	Rank
To make sure the school is safe	87	1	83	1	86	1	55	1
To encourage teachers and students to do their best	87	1	83	1	86	1	37	2
To help teachers do their jobs well	85	3	79	3	75	4	21	7
To be the leader of the school	78	5	77	4	78	3	34	3
To help students get a good education	83	4	66	5	75	4	31	4
To let people in the community know about the school	74	7	59	6	48	8	4	12
To make teachers and students proud of the school	74	7	57	7	56	7	12	9
To make sure teachers do a good job	75	6	56	8	71	6	29	5
To make sure students behave well	68	10	50	9	40	10	23	6
To keep kids from bullying and teasing	70	9	46	10	46	9	16	8
To know all the students	64	12	40	11	28	11	8	11
To make sure students get along with each other	66	11	34	12	27	12	12	9

This table is assembled from data included in pages 26 and 27 of the *MetLife Survey of the American Teacher: An Examination of School Leadership,* 1 Madison Ave., New York, NY 10010. © 2003 Harris Interactive, Inc.

a practical stance toward life. They identified four broad areas of strategic role interaction between principal and teachers: (1) resource provider, (2) instructional resource, (3) communicator, and (4) visible presence. Their research reveals important differences in the ways teachers viewed strong, average, and weak principals across these four role dimensions. In every case, strong principals received more positive ratings than average and weak, and average principals more positive ratings than weak. Their findings are summarized in Exhibit 2.2. The Smith

How Teachers Rate Their Principals: A Comparison of Strong, Average, and Weak Leaders

exhibit
2.2

	Percentage of Positive Ratings			
	Strong Leader (n=800)	Average Leader (n=2,146)	Weak Leader (n=300)	Difference*
Principal as Resource Provider				
1. My principal promotes staff development activities for teachers.	95	68	41	54
2. My principal is knowledgeable about instructional resources.	90	54	33	57
3. My principal mobilizes resources and district support to help achieve academic achievement goals.	90	52	33	57
4. My principal is considered an important instructional resource person in the school.	79	35	8	71
Principal as Instructional Resource				
1. My principal encourages the use of different instructional strategies.	89	78	75	14
2. My principal is sought out by teachers who have instructional concerns or problems.	72	47	25	47
3. My principal's evaluation of my performance helps improve my teaching.	78	46	17	61
4. My principal helps faculty interpret test results.	54	35	9	45
Principal as Communicator				
1. Improved instructional practice results from interactions with my principal.	80	49	25	55
2. My principal leads formal discussions concerning instruction and student achievement.	85	41	17	68
3. My principal uses clearly communicated criteria for judging staff performance.	90	63	17	73
4. My principal provides a clear vision of what our school is all about.	90	49	17	73
5. My principal communicates clearly to the staff regarding instructional matters.	92	50	17	75
6. My principal provides frequent feedback to teachers regarding classroom performance.	68	29	18	50

(continued)

exhibit **2.2** **Continued**

	Percentage of Positive Ratings			
	Strong Leader (n=800)	Average Leader (n=2,146)	Weak Leader (n=300)	Difference*
Principal as Visible Presence				
1. My principal makes frequent classroom observations.	72	31	17	55
2. My principal is accessible to discuss matters dealing with instruction.	94	68	66	28
3. My principal is a "visible presence" in the building to both staff and students.	93	75	46	47
4. My principal is an active participant in staff development activities.	97	64	50	47

*Difference in percentage of strong and weak leaders. The higher the difference, the more important is this characteristic or behavior and the more active and focused on teaching and learning is the leadership.

Source: Instructional Leadership: How Principals Make a Difference (pp. 32–37) by Wilma F. Smith and Richard L. Andrews, 1989, Alexandria, VA: Association for Supervision and Curriculum Development. Copyright © 1989 by ASCD. Reprinted by permission. All rights reserved. This exhibit combines data from figures 2.4, 2.5, 2.6, and 2.7 in the original.

and Andrews research demonstrates the importance of principals giving prime attention to the schools' *core technology,* teaching and learning—a finding now well established in the literature (Teddlie, Kirby, and Stringfield, 1989).

Note also that the larger the difference between percentages for strong and weak leaders, the more focused is teaching and learning and the more active is leadership behavior. Strong leaders, for example, are more likely to and much more able to provide clearly communicated criteria for judging staff performance, provide a clear vision of what their school is all about, provide clear communications about instructional matters, be considered an instructional support person, lead formal discussions concerning instruction and student achievement, provide evaluation of teacher performance that improves teaching, be accessible to discuss matters concerned with instruction and student achievement, be knowledgeable about instructional resources, and mobilize district support to help achieve academic goals. By contrast, being a visible presence, encouraging the use of many instructional strategies, and being sought out by teachers who have instructional concerns are characteristics that do not discriminate very much between strong and weak leaders. They both engage in these activities, suggesting that these activities are not indicators of instructional leadership effectiveness.

*N*EW EMPHASIS ON INSTRUCTIONAL LEADERSHIP

Instructional leadership has always played a prominent role in surveys of what principals consider to be important and how they would like to spend their time. Ideally principals should be instructional leaders who focus on improving student achievement. But in studies of how principals actually spend their time, they rarely measure up to this ideal.

The evidence suggests, however, that things may be changing. Thanks to NCLB, the standards movement, and pressure from superintendents, principals are beginning to "walk their talk" more frequently. This is particularly true in large urban school districts that have committed to whole district initiatives as a way to improve schools and to measurable increases in the amount of student learning.

Emphasizing whole-district change rather than concentrating on improving one school at a time requires a more focused sense of the common good, a more common definition of "what students should know and be able to do," a more common view of teaching and learning strategies, and common assessments.

Among the cities with school districts that are following this path are Boston, Providence, New York, and San Diego. One key development is that to be successful this approach requires that superintendents, too, be instructional leaders. No longer content to sit on the sidelines, superintendents are taking a direct hand in laying out expectations for building the capacity of teachers and developing monitoring systems to ensure that principals are indeed committed to instructional leadership, are following through in providing it, and have the data and other information to confirm that their efforts are paying off. This new role of superintendents adds a measure of pressure for principals to show progress, increasing even more their emphasis on instructional leadership.

Though whole district change does not necessarily lead to overstandardization of what principals and schools are doing and how they are assessed, often it does. And when it does, principals can find themselves without the discretion they need and without the authority they need to get the job done. In the four urban districts mentioned earlier, the emphasis for the most part is on teaching and learning by building the capacity of schools to improve rather than on providing scripts that everyone must religiously follow. The emphasis on capacity building serves as a moderating buffer against standardization.

Boston, for example, has adopted Six Essentials of Whole School Improvement to guide their efforts. It is the principals who have primary and day-by-day responsibility for ensuring that the essentials are embodied in the practices of their schools. Leadership looms large in each of the six essentials, allowing for the roles of principals to increasingly focus on instructional leadership. The essentials are as follows:

Essential 1: Effective instructional practice and a collaborative school climate lead to improved student learning.

Essential 2: Student work and data drive instruction and professional development.

Essential 3: Investments in professional development improve instruction.

Essential 4: Shared leadership sustains instructional improvement.

Essential 5: Resource use supports instructional improvement and improved student learning.

Essential 6: Schools partner with families and community to support student learning.

DIRECT AND INDIRECT LEADERSHIP

Despite the importance of instructional leadership, principals must be careful that they assume not only a direct role in improving the learning of their students, but an indirect role as well. Clearly the direct instructional leadership role of principals makes a difference. But over the long haul it may be that indirect leadership is more important.

A series of important papers published by Hallinger and Heck (1996a, 1996b, 1999) provides support for the importance of the principal's indirect leadership in improving student achievement. Their conclusion is that the behavior of principals does not provide a measurable direct effect on school effectiveness or on student achievement, but does provide a measurable indirect effect. It will be interesting to examine how this emphasis on direct versus indirect leadership plays itself out as educational administration strives to become a profession anchored more to teaching and learning than has been the case before.

Perhaps what is more important than the direct versus indirect question is the content and focus of principal leadership. A 2001 survey of high school principals and how they spend their time found that, although the rhetoric is right, gaps exist between what principals want to do and ought to do and what they wind up doing. According to the NASSP (2001) report,

> Although high school principals are hard working, highly committed, and dedicated to the business of teaching and learning, they report spending much of their time and energy carrying out functions that have little to do with student learning, effective teaching, or creating a climate conducive to both of these. The role of the principal, as presently structured, is reported by the survey respondents to be that of a manager mostly engaged in urgent activities. Principals need help extinguishing the "fires" that flare up continuously throughout the 13-hour days principals regularly work. (31)

In the report the NASSP combines indirect and direct leadership by defining instructional leadership as follows:

> Being an instructional leader requires the purposeful and intentional action of principals spending significant time doing those things that are important, but often not urgent: planning, team building, teacher development, and relationship

building. For principals to decrease their time as managers and increase their time in instructional leadership, the following must be available: relevant preparation and preservice and inservice professional development; organizational structures and personnel to assist with school management tasks; and resources to support staff professional development. Leadership will vary from school to school, depending upon the experience, the skills, and the will of the principal as well as the support available in the community. But the focus of the leader of every high school must be student learning and instruction. (NASSP, 2001:31)

Despite the difficulties, it is clear that, when principals work to provide the conditions and means for teacher learning, student achievement increases (Darling-Hammond, 1997). When principals emphasize the building of effective learning and caring communities for teachers within the school, teacher learning improves, and student achievement benefits as a result (Sergiovanni, 1994). When principals work to provide a safe, respectful, and caring environment for students, student achievement improves (Sebring et al., 1995, 1996). School culture counts, and every effort that principals give to building strong and effective cultures is an investment in student learning.

Resnick (2001/2002) believes that, given what we know about effective teaching and learning, principals must know and engage in matters of instruction to a greater extent and with greater depth than is now the case. She suggests the following as examples of things that principals who are instructional leaders might do regularly:

- Lead faculty in analyzing classroom-by-classroom test data, disaggregated by socioeconomic status, race, ethnicity, and language group
- Lead a grade-level group of teachers in analyzing examples of student work from their classes with reference to benchmark work that meets state or district standards
- Lead a faculty committee in aligning textbook or other teaching materials to standards
- Visit classrooms daily to observe teaching—after developing with teachers descriptions of criteria of good teaching
- Build professional development plans with individual teachers, based on classroom observations, student data, and characteristics of the adopted instructional program
- Plan details of professional development activities with content coaches and mentors who are available to work with teachers in the school (Resnick, 2001/2002:2)

For those who argue that principals are not now prepared for this kind of practice, Resnick responds by stating it is reasonable to expect principals to learn these and other instructional leadership competencies. The key, nonetheless, will be one of balance. And that balance is found not by exclusively claiming the instructional leadership role but by being a leader of leaders. Teachers, too, must become instructional leaders and take much more responsibility than is now the case for the success of their schools.

$\mathcal{S}$OME REFLECTIONS

1. Resnick offers six examples of things that instructional leaders do daily. Provide two more examples. Divide the eight examples into two groups: more direct leadership and more indirect leadership. How often does your principal engage in these activities? Would you say usually, often, sometimes, not often, rarely? What other instructional leadership activities does your principal often or usually engage in?

2. As you review the sample letter from *Breaking Ranks II:*
   - Describe the roles principals will have to emphasize to make this description of what could be a reality. How do these roles measure up to the roles that principals not involved in leading change now emphasize?
   - Assume you are interested in starting conversations about reforms that will be needed in your school for students to be more connected and to improve levels of student achievement. What kind of picture would you paint in an open letter to students, teachers, and parents of your school?
   - As principal what is the first thing you would do to get started? List two or three other steps you would then take.
   - The evidence suggests that changing structures and changing programs may be helpful but will not be effective over the long haul unless school cultures change. Why is this so?

3. How is the challenge of superficiality in administrative work met by those who prescribe how administrators should behave? The well-known management consultant and theorist Peter Drucker (1967) recommended that principals set and stick to priorities. This is good advice, when it can be followed. Another well-known theorist, Chester Barnard (1938), suggested that administrators be more selective in the questions they address. In his words: "The fine art of executive decision-making consists of not deciding questions that are not pertinent, in not deciding prematurely, in not making decisions that cannot be made effectively, and in not making decisions that others should make" (194). How realistic are these prescriptions? When is it not possible to follow them? What gets in the way of following them? How might practicing principals react to them?

4. Studies of principals at work indicate that the real world of school administration is often quite different from the world described in the theoretical literature and in principals' preferences. Appendix 2.3 is a portrait of one day in the life of an urban elementary school principal. How does this description of actual administrative work contrast with the views you had of the principal's job at the beginning of this chapter? Based on what this principal actually

does and how she actually spends her time, write a brief job description for the principalship. How does this job description compare with that found and used in your school district? Does this description meet the standards set by the Educational Leadership Constituent Council? Give examples. See Appendix 2.1 for a list of these standards.

5. Think about the demands, constraints, and choices that your principal faces. List five things that your principal must do. Now list five things that your principal may not do. How big is the area of choices? What are some examples of the choices your principal has? Does your principal take advantage of this area of choices? Give an example.

REFERENCES

Augenstein, John J. 1989. "Socialization Differences among Principals in Catholic Schools," *The Living Light* 25(3), 226–231.

Augenstein, John J., and W. William Konnert. 1991. "Implications of Informal Socialization Process of Beginning Elementary School Principals for Role Preparation and Initiation," *Journal of Educational Administration* 29(1), 39–50.

Barnard, Chester. 1938. *The Functions of an Executive.* Cambridge, MA: Harvard University Press.

Barth, Roland S. 1980. "Reflections on the Principalship," *Thrust for Educational Leadership* 9(5).

Canavan, Kelvin. 2003. "Building Strategic Leadership and Management Capacity to Improve School Effectiveness," *Catholic Education: A Journal of Inquiry and Practice* 7(2), 150–164.

Cooley, Van E., and Jianping Shen. 2003, March. "School Accountability and Professional Job Responsibilities: A Perspective from Secondary Principals," *NASSP Bulletin* 87(634), 10–25.

Council of Chief State School Officers. 1996. *Interstate School Leaders Licensure Consortium: Standards for School Leaders.* Washington, DC: Author.

Darling-Hammond, Linda. 1997. *The Right to Learn: A Blueprint for Creating Schools That Work.* San Francisco: Jossey-Bass.

Doud, James L., and Edward P. Keller. 1998. *A Ten-Year Study: The K–8 Principal in 1998.* Alexandria, VA: National Association of Elementary School Principals.

Drucker, Peter. 1967. *The Effective Executive.* New York: Harper & Row.

DuFour, Richard, Rebecca DuFour, Robert Eaker, and Thomas Many. 2006. *Learning by Doing: A Handbook for Professional Learning Communities at Work.* Bloomington, IN: Solution Tree.

DuFour, Richard, and Robert Eaker. 1998. *Professional Learning Communities at Work: Best Practices for Enhancing Student Achievement.* Bloomington, IN: Solution Tree.

Farkas, Steve, Jean Johnson, and Ann Duffett. 2003. *Rolling Up Their Sleeves: Superintendents and Principals Talk about What's Needed to Improve Public Schools.* Report from Public Agenda for the Wallace Foundation. New York: Public Agenda.

Hallinger, Philip, and Ronald H. Heck. 1996a. "Reassessing the Principal's Role in School Effectiveness: A Review of Empirical Research 1980–1995," *Educational Administration Quarterly* 32(1), 5–44.

Hallinger, Philip, and Ronald H. Heck. 1996b. "The Principal's Role in School Effectiveness: A Review of Methodological Issues, 1980–1995," in Kenneth Leithwood et al. (Eds.), *The International Handbook of Research in Educational Administration.* New York: Kluwer.

Hallinger, Philip, and Ronald H. Heck. 1999. "Can Leadership Enhance School Effectiveness?" in Tony Bush, Les Bell, R. Bolan, Ron Glatter, and P. Ribbens (Eds.), *Educational Management: Redefining Theory, Policy and Practice.* London: Paul Chapman.

Hill, Paul T., Gail E. Foster, and Tamar Gendler. 1990. *High Schools with Character*. Santa Monica, CA: RAND Corporation.

Mintzberg, Henry. 1973. *The Nature of Managerial Work*. New York: Harper & Row.

National Association of Elementary School Principals. 1997. *Elementary and Middle Schools: Proficiencies for Principals* (3rd ed.). Alexandria, VA: Author.

National Association of Secondary School Principals. 1996. *Breaking Ranks: Changing an American Institution*. Report of the Secondary School Principals Association on the High School for the 21st Century. Reston, VA: Author.

National Association of Secondary School Principals. 2001. *Priorities and Barriers in High School Leadership: A Survey of Principals*. Reston, VA: Author.

National Association of Secondary School Principals. 2004. *Breaking Ranks II: Strategies for Leading High School Reform*. Reston, VA: Author.

Newmann, Fred M., BetsAnn Smith, Elaine Allensworth, and Anthony S. Bryk. 2001. "Instructional Program Coherence: What It Is and Why It Should Guide School Improvement Policy," *Educational Evaluation and Policy Analysis* 23(4), 297–321.

Public Agenda. 2006. "Reality Check 2006: The Insiders." Selected Survey Results at www.publicagenda.org/research/pdfs/rc0604_questionaire.pdf accessed October 5, 2006.

Resnick, Lauren. 2001/2002, Fall/Winter. "Learning Leadership on the Job," *Wallace-Readers Digest Funds Leaders Count Report* 1(2).

Schiff, T. 2002. "Principals Readiness for Reform: A Comprehensive Approach," *Principal Leadership* (High School ed.) 2(5), 21–26.

Schmoker, Mike. 1999. *Results: The Key to Continuous Improvement* (2nd ed.). Alexandria, VA: Association for Supervision and Curriculum Development.

Sebring, Penny Bender, Anthony S. Bryk, John Q. Eston, Stuart Luppescu, Y. M. Thum, W. Lopez, and B. Smith. 1995. *Charting Reform: Chicago Teachers Take Stock*. Chicago: Consortium on Chicago School Research.

Sebring, Penny Bender, Anthony S. Bryk, Melissa Roderick, E. Camburn, Stuart Luppescu, Y. M. Thum, B. Smith, and J. Kahne. 1996. *Charting Reform in Chicago: The Students Speak*. Chicago: Consortium on Chicago School Research.

Sergiovanni, Thomas J. 1994. *Building Community in Schools*. San Francisco: Jossey-Bass.

Smith, Wilma A., and Richard L. Andrews. 1989. *Instructional Leadership: How Principals Make a Difference*. Alexandria, VA: Association for Supervision and Curriculum Development.

Spillane, James P., Richard Halverson, and John B. Diamond. 2001. "Investigating School Leadership Practice: A Distributed Perspective," *Educational Researcher* 30(3), 24.

Sproul, Lee S. 1976, November 13–14. "Managerial Attention in New Educational Systems." Seminar on Organizations as Loosely Coupled Systems, Urbana: University of Illinois.

Stewart, Rosemary. 1982. "The Relevance of Some Studies of Managerial Work and Behavior to Leadership Research," in James G. Hunt, Uma Sekaran, and Chester A. Schriesheim (Eds.), *Leadership beyond Establishment Views*. Carbondale: Southern Illinois University.

Teddlie, Charles, Peggy D. Kirby, and Sam Stringfield. 1989. "Effective versus Ineffective Schools: Observable Differences in the Classroom," *American Journal of Education* 97(3).

New Standards for Advanced Programs in Educational Leadership. Prepared by the NPBEA for the Educational Leadership Constituent Council

Standard 1.0 Candidates who complete the [university-based preparation] program are educational leaders who have the knowledge and ability to promote the success of all students by facilitating the development, articulation, implementation, and stewardship of a school or district vision of learning supported by the school community.

Elements	Meets Standards for School Building Leadership
1.1 Develop a Vision	**a.** Candidates develop a vision of learning for a school that promotes the success of all students. **b.** Candidates base this vision on relevant knowledge and theories, including but not limited to an understanding of learning goals in a pluralistic society, the diversity of learners and learners' needs, schools as interactive social and cultural systems, and social and organizational change.
1.2 Articulate a Vision	**a.** Candidates demonstrate the ability to articulate the components of this vision for a school and the leadership processes necessary to implement and support the vision. **b.** Candidates demonstrate the ability to use data-based research strategies and strategic planning processes that focus on student learning to inform the development of a vision, drawing on relevant information sources such as student assessment results, student's and family demographic data, and an analysis of community needs. **c.** Candidates demonstrate the ability to communicate the vision to staff, parents, students, and community members through the use of symbols, ceremonies, stories, and other activities.
1.3 Implement a Vision	**a.** Candidates can formulate the initiatives necessary to motivate staff, students, and families to achieve the school's vision. **b.** Candidates develop plans and processes for implementing the vision (e.g., articulating the vision and related goals, encouraging challenging standards, facilitating collegiality and teamwork, structuring significant work, ensuring appropriate use of student assessments, providing autonomy, supporting innovation, delegating responsibility, developing leadership in others, and securing needed resources).
1.4 Steward a Vision	**a.** Candidates demonstrate an understanding of the role effective communication skills play in building a shared commitment to the vision.

Elements	Meets Standards for School Building Leadership
1.4 Steward a Vision *(continued)*	**b.** Candidates design or adopt a system for using data-based research strategies to regularly monitor, evaluate, and revise the vision.
	c. Candidates assume stewardship of the vision through various methods.
1.5 Promote Community Involvement in the Vision	**a.** Candidates demonstrate the ability to involve community members in the realization of the vision and in related school improvement efforts.
	b. Candidates acquire and demonstrate the skills needed to communicate effectively with all stakeholders about implementation of the vision.

Standard 2.0   Candidates who complete the program are educational leaders who have the knowledge and ability to promote the success of all students by promoting a positive school culture, providing an effective instructional program, applying best practice to student learning, and designing comprehensive professional growth plans for staff.

Elements	Meets Standards for School Building Leadership
2.1 Promote Positive School Culture	**a.** Candidates assess school culture using multiple methods and implement context-appropriate strategies that capitalize on the diversity (e.g., population, language, disability, gender, race, socioeconomic) of the school community to improve school programs and culture.
2.2 Provide Effective Instructional Program	**a.** Candidates demonstrate the ability to facilitate activities that apply principles of effective instruction to improve instructional practices and curricular materials.
	b. Candidates demonstrate the ability to make recommendations regarding the design, implementation, and evaluation of a curriculum that fully accommodates learners' diverse needs.
	c. Candidates demonstrate the ability to use and promote technology and information systems to enrich curriculum and instruction, to monitor instructional practices and provide staff the assistance needed for improvement.
2.3 Apply Best Practice to Student Learning	**a.** Candidates demonstrate the ability to assist school personnel in understanding and applying best practices for student learning.

appendix 2.1 Continued

Elements	Meets Standards for School Building Leadership
2.3 Apply Best Practice to Student Learning *(continued)*	**b.** Candidates apply human development theory, proven learning and motivational theories, and concern for diversity to the learning process. **c.** Candidates demonstrate an understanding of how to use appropriate research strategies to profile student performance in a school and analyze possible differences among subgroups of students to promote an environment for improved student achievement.
2.4 Design Comprehensive Professional Growth Plans	**a.** Candidates design and demonstrate an ability to implement well-planned context-appropriate professional development programs based on reflective practice and research on student learning consistent with the school vision and goals. **b.** Candidates demonstrate the ability to use observations, collaborative reflection, and adult learning strategies to form comprehensive professional growth plans with teachers and other school personnel. **c.** Candidates develop and implement personal professional growth plans that reflect a commitment to lifelong learning.

Standard 3.0   Candidates who complete the program are educational leaders who have the knowledge and ability to promote the success of all students by managing the organization, operations, and resources in a way that promotes a safe, efficient, and effective learning environment.

Elements	Meets Standards for School Building Leadership
3.1 Manage the Organization	**a.** Candidates demonstrate the ability to optimize the learning environment for all students by applying appropriate models and principles of organizational development and management, including research and data driven decision-making with attention to indicators of equity, effectiveness, and efficiency. **b.** Candidates develop a plan of action for focusing on effective organization and management of fiscal, human, and material resources, giving priority to student learning, safety, curriculum, and instruction. **c.** Candidates demonstrate an ability to manage time effectively and deploy financial and human resources in ways that promote student achievement.

Elements	Meets Standards for School Building Leadership
3.2 Manage Operations	**a.** Candidates demonstrate the ability to involve staff in conducting operations and setting priorities using appropriate and effective needs assessment, research-based data, and group process skills to build consensus, communicate, and resolve conflicts in order to align resources with the organizational vision.
	b. Candidates develop communications plans for staff that include opportunities for staff to develop their family and community collaboration skills.
	c. Candidates demonstrate an understanding of how to apply legal principles to promote educational equity and provide safe, effective, and efficient facilities.
3.3 Manage Resources	**a.** Candidates use problem-solving skills and knowledge of strategic, long-range, and operational planning (including applications of technology) in the effective, legal, and equitable use of fiscal, human, and material resource allocation and alignment that focuses on teaching and learning.
	b. Candidates creatively seek new resources to facilitate learning.
	c. Candidates apply and assess current technologies for school management, business procedures, and scheduling.

Standard 4.0   Candidates who complete the program are educational leaders who have the knowledge and ability to promote the success of all students by collaborating with families and other community members, responding to diverse community interests and needs, and mobilizing community resources.

Elements	Meets Standards for School Building Leadership
4.1 Collaborate with Families and Other Community Members	**a.** Candidates demonstrate an ability to bring together the resources of family members and the community to positively affect student learning.
	b. Candidates demonstrate an ability to involve families in the education of their children based on the belief that families have the best interests of their children in mind.
	c. Candidates demonstrate the ability to use public information and research-based knowledge of issues and trends to collaborate with families and community members.

Elements	Meets Standards for School Building Leadership
4.1 Collaborate with Families and Other Community Members *(continued)*	**d.** Candidates apply an understanding of community relations models, marketing strategies and processes, data-based decision-making, and communications theory to craft frameworks for school, family, business, community, government, and higher education partnerships. **e.** Candidates develop various methods of outreach aimed at business, religious, political, and service organizations. **f.** Candidates demonstrate the ability to involve families and other stakeholders in school decision-making processes, reflecting an understanding that schools are an integral part of the larger community. **g.** Candidates demonstrate the ability to collaborate with community agencies to integrate health, social, and other services. **h.** Candidates develop a plan for a comprehensive program of community relations and effective relationships with the media.
4.2 Respond to Community Interests and Needs	**a.** Candidates demonstrate active involvement within the community, including interactions with individuals and groups with conflicting perspectives. **b.** Candidates demonstrate the ability to use appropriate assessment strategies and research methods to understand and accommodate diverse school and community conditions and dynamics. **c.** Candidates provide leadership to programs serving students with special and exceptional needs. **d.** Candidates demonstrate the ability to capitalize on the diversity (cultural, ethnic, racial, economic, and special interest groups) of the school community to improve school programs and meet the diverse needs of all students.
4.3 Mobilize Community Resources	**a.** Candidates demonstrate an understanding of and ability to use community resources, including youth services, to support student achievement, solve school problems, and achieve school goals. **b.** Candidates demonstrate how to use school resources and social service agencies to serve the community.

Elements	Meets Standards for School Building Leadership
4.3 Mobilize Community Resources *(continued)*	**c.** Candidates demonstrate an understanding of ways to use public resources and funds appropriately and effectively to encourage communities to provide new resources to address emerging student problems.

Standard 5.0 Candidates who complete the program are educational leaders who have the knowledge and ability to promote the success of all students by acting with integrity, fairly, and in an ethical manner.

Elements	Meets Standards for School Building Leadership
5.1 Acts with Integrity	**a.** Candidates demonstrate a respect for the rights of others with regard to confidentiality and dignity and engage in honest interactions.
5.2 Acts Fairly	**b.** Candidates demonstrate the ability to combine impartiality, sensitivity to student diversity, and ethical considerations in their interactions with others.
5.3 Acts Ethically	**c.** Candidates make and explain decisions based upon ethical and legal principles.

Standard 6.0 Candidates who complete the program are educational leaders who have the knowledge and ability to promote the success of all students by understanding, responding to, and influencing the larger political, social, economic, legal, and cultural context.

Elements	Meets Standards for School Building Leadership
6.1 Understand the Larger Context	**a.** Candidates act as informed consumers of educational theory and concepts appropriate to school context and can demonstrate the ability to apply appropriate research methods to a school context.
	b. Candidates demonstrate the ability to explain how the legal and political systems and institutional framework of schools have shaped a school and community, as well as the opportunities available to children and families in a particular school.
	c. Candidates demonstrate the ability to analyze the complex causes of poverty and other disadvantages and their effects on families, communities, children, and learning.
	d. Candidates demonstrate an understanding of the policies, laws, and regulations enacted by local, state, and federal authorities that affect schools, especially those that might improve educational and social opportunities.

appendix **2.1** **Continued**

Elements	Meets Standards for School Building Leadership
6.1 Understand the Larger Context *(continued)*	**e.** Candidates demonstrate the ability to describe the economic factors shaping a local community and the effects economic factors have on local schools. **f.** Candidates demonstrate the ability to analyze and describe the cultural diversity in a school community. **g.** Candidates can describe community norms and values and how they relate to the role of the school in promoting social justice. **h.** Candidates demonstrate the ability to explain various theories of change and conflict resolution and the appropriate application of those models to specific communities.
6.2 Respond to the Larger Context	**a.** Candidates demonstrate the ability to communicate with members of a school community concerning trends, issues, and potential changes in the environment in which the school operates, including maintenance of an ongoing dialogue with representatives of diverse community groups.
6.3 Influence the Larger Context	**a.** Candidates demonstrate the ability to engage students, parents, and other members of the community in advocating for adoption of improved policies and laws. **b.** Candidates apply their understanding of the larger political, social, economic, legal, and cultural context to develop activities and policies that benefit students and their families. **c.** Candidates advocate for policies and programs that promote equitable learning opportunities and success for all students, regardless of socioeconomic background, ethnicity, gender, disability, or other individual characteristics.

Source: National Policy Board for Educational Administration on behalf of the Educational Leadership Constituent Council, 2002, reprinted by permission. The standards presented here are those for school building–level administrators only. The standards are used as part of the NCATE accreditation process. Other members of the ELCC include American Association of School Administrators, National Association of Elementary School Principals, National Association of Secondary School Principals, and Association for Supervision and Curriculum Development.

Profile of an ICEL Graduate

A graduate of the Institute for Catholic Educational Leadership is:

- OPEN TO GROWTH and, therefore, should be:
  - A visionary leader who articulates clearly the school's philosophy and mission to the various publics;
  - An educational leader who is cognizant of the lifelong process of learning and communicates this to colleagues and students.

- ACADEMICALLY AND PROFESSIONALLY COMPETENT, and, therefore, should be:
  - A scholar who has demonstrated academic competence in all coursework;
  - A researcher who is knowledgeable of the latest findings in Catholic education and the field of education in general;
  - An educator who is aware of current methodologies and is able to apply them effectively when assessing the local school site;
  - A leader who is economically astute and possesses financial skills.

- A RELIGIOUS LEADER, and, therefore, should be:
  - A person who has an understanding of Catholic education as an integral part of the Church's teaching mission;
  - A person of faith who is able to communicate this faith with others;
  - A person whose lifestyle is founded upon Gospel values and who is a role model for students, parents, and faculty;
  - A moral educator and leader.

- A COMMUNITY BUILDER and, therefore, should be:
  - An astute and sensitive leader who is able to assess the school climate and to foster a sense of community among all facets of the school;
  - A leader who builds a school's Catholic identity based upon its history, tradition, and rituals;
  - A collaborator who works well with other professionals in the Catholic, private, and public sectors;
  - A leader who stimulates the involvement of students, parents, and faculty in community service as a natural outgrowth of the school's mission;
  - A person of compassion and justice whose decisions respond to the needs of the individual as well as to the good of the entire community.

- COMMITTED TO DOING JUSTICE and, therefore, should be:
  - An educator who integrates faith into culture and life in order to promote justice and service to others;
  - An educator who encourages those within the school community to focus attention on local, national, and global needs;
  - A leader who works to ensure the integrity of each individual within the school community.

Source: "Ensuring the Catholicity of the Church's Schools: The University of San Francisco Responds to the Challenge" by Mary Peter Traviss and Gini Shimabukuro, March 1999, *Catholic Education: A Journal of Inquiry and Practice* 2(3), 338–339. Reprinted by permission.

A Day in the Life of an Urban Elementary Principal

When Mary Stewart arrived at Blaire Elementary School at 8:15 A.M., the teachers were stopping by the office to sign in on their way to their classrooms. Stewart removed her coat and boots, hanging them in the closet outside her office. She put on a pair of medium-heeled shoes, explaining to the researcher, ". . . the children like to see the principal a little dressed up." Joining her clerk in the outer office, the two of them reviewed the list of teachers who would be absent and the steps to be taken to secure substitutes. One substitute, sent by the central office "Sub Center," had already arrived, and Stewart asked the clerk to give her the regular teacher's file containing a class seating chart and lesson plans.

Returning to her desk, Stewart's eyes drifted to the Continuous Progress Program packet and accompanying memorandum from district offices that had arrived the previous afternoon. It was a reminder that the next reporting period was imminent and that all forms must be filed this coming Friday before the close of business. This meant that Stewart would be spending part of each of the next three days buttonholing the teachers to get their reports to her on each child, and then summarizing these figures in an all-school report. Stewart anticipated that she would have to divert some time from other managerial duties to get this paperwork finished on time.

As she reviewed her calendar, Stewart mentally prepared for a meeting with faculty representatives of the Professional Problems Committee. The Union contract provided that this group, elected by the teachers, must meet regularly with the principal. At 8:30, Stewart left her office for the short walk to the school library, where the committee members were gathering. Stewart called the meeting to order about 8:35. High on her list of items was the matter of selecting textbooks for next year. But before this discussion got underway, the teachers wanted to relay questions to Stewart that individual teachers had raised with them: a problem in supervising the third floor washrooms, a question about how next year's faculty advisor to the eighth grade graduating class was to be selected, and a problem in getting supplies during a particular free period when the office clerk was often not available. After promising to work on these problems, Stewart spent most of the remaining time discussing plans with the teachers to host upcoming meetings with publisher representatives. Together they also reviewed plans to form faculty textbook review committees, and procedures for selecting a common textbook for each grade level.

After the meeting, Stewart was approached by two teachers with individual questions. Miss La Pointe wanted to know whether Stewart would be available during eighth period. Stewart nodded and invited her to stop by the office at that time. Mr. Fields, the gym teacher, informed her that the basketball team did well at yesterday's game. They came close to beating Doyle, which is one of the best teams in the district. Stewart congratulated him, and took the opportunity to ask how Marvin Goth was behaving in class lately. Fields said that Marvin still got "edgy," but in general was "doing a lot better."

As Stewart walked through the hallway back to her office, Mrs. Noyes motioned to her from inside the classroom. The students were already in their classrooms or moving quickly through the halls in the last moments before the class bell rang. Noyes told Stewart that she was scheduled to take the students on a field trip this morning, but that one of the parents had called at the last moment to say that she would not be able to come. This left Noyes one parent volunteer short. Should she cancel the trip? Stewart remembered that Mrs. Case would be volunteering in the reading center this morning. She offered to ask her if she would fill in.

On the way to the reading center, Stewart peeked into several classrooms. As she passed the student washrooms she quickly looked into each, checking to see that no students were present and that the rooms were in order. As one student hurried past her, she asked him why he was not in class. He said that he had arrived late. She checked to see that he had a late admittance slip, and then urged him to get to school on time in the future.

When she entered the reading center, she nodded in the direction of the reading teacher and motioned that she wanted to speak with Mrs. Case. Mrs. Case quickly joined her and agreed to help with the field trip. On her way out the door, Stewart complimented the reading teacher on a bulletin board entitled "Read for Experience."

Instead of returning to her office, Stewart continued to walk the halls on the second and third floors. On the third floor, she spent a few minutes studying the washroom situation. Then, stopping briefly at each classroom, she asked the teachers to be sure that only one student at a time was excused to use them. On her way back down the stairs, she detoured for a moment on the second floor to swing by a classroom with a substitute teacher, "just to see how he's doing." Finding the students somewhat unruly, she stepped into the classroom, fixing the well-known principal's stare on the children. As expected, her presence quieted the room. She greeted the substitute and inquired whether the regular teacher's substitute file was in order. He said that everything seemed fine, "they're just testing a little bit."

When Stewart returned to the office, she spoke briefly with the clerk, reviewing the arrival and assignment of substitute teachers. Stewart asked the clerk to inform the librarian that she would have to cover one of the classes during second period, if the substitute teacher did not arrive by then. Then Stewart picked up the mail that had arrived via the school system's delivery service. She asked the clerk to inform Mrs. Noyes that Mrs. Case would come on the field trip. She also asked the clerk to be sure that a teacher aide was available during seventh period to give out teaching supplies. As they talked, the clerk handed her two telephone messages.

Stewart entered her office, leaving the door to the outer office open. (A second door connecting directly to the hallway was kept closed. In this way, anyone who wanted to see Stewart had to go through the clerk. Stewart, herself, usually passed through the outer office in order to exchange information with the clerk on the way in or out of her own private office.) She quickly e-mailed a note to Mrs.

Reynolds, on the second floor, informing her that the teacher aide would be available during seventh period to give out supplies. She also e-mailed a bulletin to all teachers: "Teachers: It appears that students from different classes are meeting at pre-arranged times in the third floor washrooms again. When excusing students to the washrooms, please be sure they use the nearest washroom, only. Thank you."

Stewart next placed a call to another principal who had left a message. The principal told her that he was calling a meeting of the district's science fair committee and would appreciate knowing when a convenient time would be for Stewart. They agreed to meet at 10:00 A.M. the following day at Blaire School. After the phone conversation, Stewart sent an e-mail to the cafeteria director, asking that coffee and some rolls be available the next morning in the conference room adjoining her office. She consulted the teachers' schedule and then also e-mailed a note to Mrs. St. Antoine, asking her to come to her office during seventh period.

Stewart once again picked up the telephone and dialed the number of a representative from a photography company that took students' yearly pictures. No answer, so Stewart left a message that she called. She set the phone message at the corner of her desk, so that she "would remember his name when he calls again."

She then began to look at the morning mail and some items the clerk had placed in her in-box:

- A personnel bulletin listing several openings in the system for teachers and administrators.
- An announcement of a conference for reading teachers.
- A set of rating cards to be completed for each teacher; these teacher rating cards were filled out each year by the principal and placed in the teachers' personal files.

Stewart placed the rating cards to one side on her desk, then got up, taking the other items to the outer office with her. She placed the conference announcement in the reading teacher's mailbox and tacked the personnel bulletin to the teacher's bulletin board. As she did so, the clerk informed her of an incoming telephone call.

Returning to her desk, she picked up the phone and heard the voice of the photographer's representative, glancing in recognition at the name on the earlier phone message. After some preliminary pleasantries, this: "Mr. Haskins, every year we make a selection from among several school photographers to take school pictures. You say you'd like to be considered this year? Fine, I'll be glad to include you in the group. Could you send me some materials—a list of the size and kind of photo to be included in each student's packet . . . maybe a sample packet, OK? Also the cost to the student, and the amount the school keeps for each packet sold. Also any other items that you make available, such as class pictures and teacher photographs."

appendix *2.3*   **Continued**

Stewart went on to explain to the photographer that the eighth grade faculty sponsor participated in the selection. However, the sponsor for the following year had not yet been picked out. "I'll make sure that you get the information on the selection process and the date and time of the meeting when we ask all photographers to come to the school to demonstrate their work. However, I'd appreciate it if you would not meet directly with the faculty sponsor, except of course at the demonstration session. I look forward to seeing your materials, and thanks for your interest in the school."

Stewart put down the phone and turned to the researcher: "You know, it's a pleasure dealing with these photographers. They really enjoy coming to the school, and I must say, the kids get a kick out of these sessions too." Then, turning to another subject, Stewart explained to the researcher that she had gotten a hurry-up phone call from downtown headquarters a day or so ago calling her to a special meeting on the Access to Excellence program. "It's scheduled for Friday at eleven, and that's just when I'll be putting the finishing touches on the Continuous Progress materials. I hope I can get them done in time. But, you know, these meetings . . . they're having more and more of them. They want to turn this school into an 'academy,' whatever that is. And we've got to go downtown and sit around for a couple hours to be told what it is. Then, no doubt, there'll be more meetings at district (headquarters) setting it up. Seems as if I spend more and more of my time away from here, going to meetings, meetings. Hard to keep on top of things here when I'm not around."

The researcher listened intently, and the two of them discussed the possibility of "academy" status and what that would mean for the school and for the community.

After a discussion of 15 minutes, Stewart looked at her watch and saw that it was nearly time for the primary grades recess. Breaking off the conversation with the researcher, she got up, walked through the outer office, and went to stand by the exit doors to the primary play area. When the bell sounded, the children were escorted through the building toward the exit. In the ensuing commotion, Stewart spoke sharply to a few boisterous children, telling them to "walk, don't run," and to "move slowly down the stairs."

She explained in an aside to the researcher that her customary practice was to accompany the youngsters out onto the playground where she and the teachers could supervise their play. However, today, she had to get back to the office to prepare a schedule for teacher rating conferences with each teacher. Returning to her desk, she assembled the teacher evaluation materials and accessed the teachers' daily schedules. Allowing 20 minutes for each teacher, she began making up a conference schedule. In the middle of this activity, she was interrupted by three boys entering the outer office, with a teacher aide following close behind. One of the boys was crying and holding the back of his head. The aide explained that the injured boy had fallen and hit his head on a patch of ice near the rim of the play area. The other two boys, she reported, had been chasing the injured boy.

Stewart moved to the outer office and told the two chasers to sit down on a bench inside the hallway door. She inspected the head injury and found that it was beginning to swell at the point of impact. Sending a student helper to the cafeteria to fetch some ice, she asked the injured boy for his name, his home telephone number, and his mother's name. She then dialed the number and spoke with the mother. After hearing what had happened, the mother said that she would come pick him up as soon as she could get a neighbor to drive her to the school. The helper soon arrived back with the ice, and Stewart wrapped it in a paper towel and gave it to the boy to place on the bump. She told him to sit down on the bench and wait for his mother, whereupon she invited the two chasers into the inner office and closed the door. "Now look, you know you're not supposed to run where there is ice. . . . It's too dangerous. Now that someone's hurt, the matter is serious. I want your parents to know about this." She filled out a form that requested a parent to come to school with the boys the following morning. With the boys still at her desk, she telephoned their homes and orally requested that a parent come to see her the next morning. She explained to the boys' mothers, "There's been an injury and your son was involved. Something must be done about their wild behavior during recess." She then sent the boys back to their classrooms, explaining that she would see them again in the morning.

As she gave them their hall passes, the injured boy's mother arrived. Stewart explained to her that two other boys had been involved and that she would be meeting with their parents in the morning. The mother asked her son, "Who did it?" and he replied it was "Jeff and Michael." "Those boys," the mother said, "why do they pick on him so much? Last week they pushed him in the bushes on the way home from school. Now they've gone too far." Stewart asked the mother to "Let me see if I can't work something out." She promised to call her back in the morning, after she met with the other parents.

As the boy and his mother left, Stewart looked up and saw that it was beginning to snow heavily. She went to the public address system and announced that students eating lunch at school would remain inside the building during the lunchtime recess.

Stewart returned to her desk and worked on the conference schedule, but was shortly interrupted by two phone calls. One concerned the placement of a student teacher in the school. The other was from her husband, asking if she would like to meet him downtown for dinner. As Stewart was finishing the schedule, the clerk brought in a master copy of the parents' bulletin for her to approve before it was duplicated. She set aside the schedule and read through the bulletin as the clerk waited to one side. She pointed out two typos and then placed her signature on the copy master. The clerk took it and left. A moment later she returned with the U.S. mail. Stewart took a quick glance at the envelopes before setting them to one side and continuing to finish the schedule. Stewart e-mailed the final schedule to each teacher.

Stewart then headed toward the cafeteria, speaking with students in the hall on the way, telling them to "slow down" and "go to your recess areas." She took a tray and moved through the lunch line. Instead of going to the faculty room, she returned to her office to eat. There, she was available for teachers who might want to stop by. As she ate, she looked through the U.S. mail: promotional material for textbooks, school administration booklets, and instructional supplies. Also an announcement of a tea at a local Catholic High School for the eighth-graders. Stewart set this aside and threw out the rest.

A student asked to see Stewart. As student council president, she wanted to know when the next student council meeting would be (the last meeting had been cancelled because of snow). They picked a date, and the student said that she would inform the council members. Stewart chatted for a few minutes with the girl about her plans for high school.

Getting up from her desk, Stewart carried her tray and the tea announcement to the outer office. She left the announcement in the eighth-grade class sponsor's mailbox and returned her tray to the cafeteria. Then she began her tour of the hallways, inspecting the building as the students returned to their classes to settle down for the afternoon's course work.

When she returned to her office, the clerk handed her a phone message. Stewart dialed the phone for an in-house call and reached the building engineer. He told her that a small window at the back of the building had been broken during the lunch hour by some loitering high school students. He said he had covered it with some heavy cardboard, "but I thought you should know about it. Also, you know the art room . . . the shades in there have been damaged. The (art) teacher just lets the kids go wild in there during seventh and eighth periods. I think you should talk to him." Stewart agreed to check on it.

Miss La Pointe arrived. She had agreed to start a dramatic program in the school and wanted to report to Stewart the plans she was making for a spring production. They discussed use of the auditorium, rehearsal schedules, the play La Pointe had selected, and the tryout announcement La Pointe had prepared. Toward the end of the seventh period, the conference was concluded, and La Pointe left to return to her classroom. Stewart got up and, checking to make sure that the teacher's aide was on station in the outer office to give out supplies, headed for the art room to see the damaged shades and to make sure the students were under control.

When she returned to the office, Stewart found Mrs. St. Antoine waiting for her in the outer office. Stewart invited her into her own office and asked for an update about the plans for the eighth grade tea, dinner, and other graduation festivities. St. Antoine discussed with her the results of faculty and student committee meetings to that point. Then Stewart asked St. Antoine whether she was thinking about remaining eighth grade sponsor next year. St. Antoine seemed a bit embarrassed. She said that she enjoyed working with the students very much, but that there was some jealousy from some of the other eighth-grade teachers who felt excluded. They discussed how some of the other eighth-grade teachers might be brought more closely into the planning, and St. Antoine left agreeing that she would try to mend some of the fences that had been neglected.

Seeing that it was near the end of the day, Stewart checked her desk to see what remained to be done. Noting the stack of material in the in-box, she looked through it. It contained several forms that required signing; they pertained to the ordering of supplies, teacher absences, and a field trip permission. Stewart signed all of the forms but one. It was a request to order a film. Stewart was unfamiliar with the film and wanted to discuss its nature and use with the teacher before signing.

Stewart put on her hat and coat and walked to the main exit doors just as the students were beginning to leave. Stationed just outside the exit, she called to the students inside the hallway and out on the playground to "slow down" and "watch out, it's slippery." When the students were gone she returned to her office to find a tiny kindergartner sitting with tear-filled eyes next to the teacher aide. The aide explained that the girl's father was supposed to pick her up from school, but had not arrived. They tried to make some phone calls to find out who was coming for the girl, but could not get an answer. The girl suggested that they call her aunt, which they did. The aunt agreed to take the girl, but said no one could come and get her right now. Stewart agreed to bring the girl by the aunt's house. "There now," the aide told the girl, "the principal will take you to your aunt's house." Stewart placed a few items in a small brief case and was ready to leave. She waited as the aide and clerk prepared to leave also. As they put on their coats, she checked the teachers' sign-in sheets to be sure that they were all out of the building. Then she locked the office as they left together. Stewart reached for the small girl's hand and helped her down the slippery steps. Before going to her car, she muttered to the researcher, "I suppose I shouldn't be doing this . . . liability and all. But someone has to."

Source: The Urban Principal: Discretionary Decision-Making in a Large Educational Organization (pp. 40–47) by Van Cleve Morris, Robert L. Crowson, Emanuel Hurwitz, Jr., and Cynthia Porter-Gehrie, 1981, Washington, DC: National Institute for Education, NIE-G-79-0019. The version of the urban principal case that appears here closely follows the original.

3

THE LIMITS OF TRADITIONAL
MANAGEMENT THEORY

*I*t is not by chance that some principals are more effective than others, even
when all are faced with the same demands and constraints. Effective principals have a better understanding of how the world of schooling and school
leadership works. They base their practice on a different theory, and this enables
them to create a more effective practice.

Principals are faced with an important choice. On the one hand, they can base
their practice on the assumption that predetermined solutions exist for most of the
problems they face, solutions that are directly linked to research-based theories
and techniques. On the other hand, they can base their practice on the assumption
that few of the problems they face lend themselves to predetermined solutions.
They can resign themselves to the difficult task of having to create knowledge in
use as they practice. Principals who make the second choice realize that despite
the attractiveness of the first, predetermined solutions can only be trusted to work
for the few problems that are fixed and located in stable environments. They realize that the majority of problems and situations they face are characterized by
ambiguity and confusion. These are problems located in a turbulent environment
where practice is largely indeterminate. They would argue, as does Donald Schön,
that the most important problems principals face are beyond the reach of technical, rational solutions. In Schön's words: "The practitioner must choose. Shall he

remain on the high ground where he can solve relatively unimportant problems according to prevailing standards of rigor, or shall he descend to the swamp of important problems and nonrigorous inquiry?" (1987:3).

Mindscapes of Practice

The choice that a principal makes is largely dependent on her or his theory or "mindscape" of practice. Mindscapes influence what we see, believe, and do. Two distinct views of schooling and administering can be identified, are worth describing and understanding, and can be evaluated for good fit with the real landscape of practice. They are the mindscapes of the "Neats" and of the "Scruffies." Principals and researchers who are Neats or Scruffies have widely different conceptions of the nature of practice and of the relationships between this practice and knowledge from theory and research. For Neats, theoretical knowledge is superordinate to practice; for Scruffies, theoretical knowledge is subordinate to practice. Their respective views can be summarized as follows:

- *Neats* hold the view that educational administration resembles an applied science within which theory and research are directly and linearly linked to practice. The former always determine the latter, and thus knowledge is superordinate to the principal and designed to prescribe practice.
- *Scruffies* hold the view that educational administration resembles a craftlike science within which practice is characterized by interacting reflection and action episodes. Theory and research are only one source of knowledge. This knowledge is subordinate to the principal and is designed to inform but not to prescribe practice. Tacit knowledge and intuition develop and strengthen as they are informed by theory, research, experience, and the craft knowledge of others.

The Neats

Neats believe it is both possible and desirable to identify the one best way to practice. They search for the one best list of standards that specifies what everyone everywhere must learn. They adopt the one best list of school characteristics or the one best model of schooling in order to make schools effective. The Neats believe that a generic set of teaching effectiveness behaviors exists that can be applied by all teachers in all situations to all students without regard for contexts, values, purposes, and other "it depends" variables. The research on effective schools, leadership styles, and conflict-management strategies are viewed similarly as truths to be accepted and applied. Principalship practice is considered to be a research-based technology that can be directly learned and routinely applied. To the Neats, the principal is presumed to function as a highly trained technician.

How does the view of the Neats fit the real world of practice? Not very well. Patterns of school practice are actually characterized by a great deal of uncertainty, instability, complexity, and variety. Value conflicts and uniquenesses are accepted aspects of educational settings. According to Schön (1983), these characteristics are perceived as central to the world of professional practice in all the major professions, including medicine, engineering, management, and education. He concludes, "Professional knowledge is mismatched to the changing characteristics of the situation of practice" (14). Although one may be comfortable in viewing the principalship as a logical process of problem solving with the application of standard techniques to predictable problems, a more accurate view may be a process of "managing messes" (16).

In the actual world of schooling, the task of the principal is to make sense of messy situations by increasing understanding and discovering and communicating meanings. Situations of practice are typically characterized by unique events; therefore, uniform answers to problems are not likely to be helpful. Teachers, supervisors, and students bring to their classrooms beliefs, assumptions, values, opinions, preferences, and predispositions. Thus, objective and value-free administrative strategies are not likely to address issues of importance. Uncertainty and complexity are normal aspects in the process of schooling. Intuition becomes necessary to fill in the gaps of what can be specified as known and what cannot. Yet, ordinary intuition will not do. Intuition must be informed by theoretical knowledge and current research on one hand and adept understandings of the situation on the other.

REFLECTIVE PRACTICE: THE PARADIGM OF THE SCRUFFIES

The Scruffies' view of the principalship is that of a science of the practical—a science that stems from theories of practice and that provides principals with practical as well as theoretical mindscapes from which to work. The concept of *reflective practice* is critical to this new science.

Reflective practice is based on the reality that professional knowledge is different from scientific knowledge. Professional knowledge is created in use as professionals who face ill-defined, unique, and changing problems decide on courses of action. The well-known educational statesman Ralph Tyler maintained that researchers don't have a full understanding of the nature of professional knowledge in education. He stated:

> Researchers and many academics also misunderstand educational practices. The practice of every profession evolves informally, and professional procedures are

not generally derived from systematic design based on research findings. Professional practice has largely developed through trial and error and intuitive efforts. Practitioners, over the years, discover procedures that appear to work and others that fail. The professional practice of teaching, as well as that of law, medicine, and theology, is largely a product of the experience of practitioners, particularly those who are more creative, inventive, and observant than the average. (cited in Hosford, 1984:9)

Scientific studies in the various professions are important. But science, according to Tyler, "explains phenomenon, it does not produce practices" (cited in Hosford, 1984:10). Professionals rely heavily on informed intuition as they create knowledge in use. Intuition is informed by theoretical knowledge on the one hand and by interacting with the context of practice on the other. When teachers use informed intuition, they are engaging in reflective practice. When principals use informed intuition, they too are engaging in reflective practice. Knowing is in the action itself, and reflective professionals become students of their practice. They research the context and experiment with different courses of action. Schön (1983) suggests:

> They may ask themselves, for example, "what features do I notice when I recognize this thing? What are the criteria by which I make this judgment? What procedures am I enacting when I perform this skill? How am I framing the problem that I'm trying to solve?" Usually, reflection on knowing-in-action goes together with reflection on the stuff at hand. There is some puzzling, or troubling or interesting phenomenon with which the individual is trying to deal. As he tries to make sense of it, he also reflects on the understandings which have been implicit in his action, understandings which he surfaces, criticizes, re-structures and embodies in further action.
>   It is this entire process of reflection-in-action which is central to the "art" by which practitioners sometimes deal with situations of uncertainty, instability, uniqueness, and value conflicts. (50)

To Schön (1984), reflection-in-action involves "on-the-spot surfacing, criticizing, re-structuring and testing of intuitive understandings of experienced phenomenon; often, it takes the form of a reflective conversation with the situation" (42). Reflection-in-action captures the principal at work as she or he makes judgments in trying to manage a very messy work context.

Life would be simpler if accepting the paradigm of the Scruffies meant the position of the Neats was false. The reality is that both are true. For simple problems that exist in stable environments under determinate conditions, thinking like a Neat serves principals well. However, for complex problems that exist in turbulent environments under indeterminate conditions, thinking like a Scruffie makes more sense.

Take leadership, for example. For Scruffies, managing and leading resemble a game of golf in which the distance to the hole is always changing. You know the hole is straight ahead, but you can never be sure just how far away it is. You have a pretty good understanding of the distances that you can get from each club (club payoff), but you cannot choose a club based on where the hole is at the moment. You must guess where the hole will be after you swing. Knowledge of club pay-off remains important in this context, but it cannot be used directly. Instead, this knowledge becomes part of one's conceptual framework for making an educated guess in choosing the right club for an assumed distance. In this game, laws exist that determine where the hole will be next, but they cannot be fully understood.

The better golfers are those who develop an intuitive feel for past, current, and likely patterns of appearance of the hole as the game is played. Their play is neither whimsical nor random. Instead, they make mature, educated guesses (in the case of principals, informed professional judgments). These guesses combined with knowledge of club payoff helps them to win. Being familiar with the topographical features of each of the holes to be played, the play of the greens, the texture of the grass and rough, and the idiosyncrasies of each of the sand traps yields other pieces of information that might or might not come in handy should a hole pop up here rather than there. Having a firm fix on topography and club payoff is not enough if one cannot develop a feel for the patterns that are likely to emerge. However, and equally as important, being pretty good at predicting the patterns but having little understanding of course topography or club payoff will not be of much help.

The key to reflective practice can be found in William James's 1892 message to the teachers of Cambridge, Massachusetts. He pointed out the importance of "an intermediary inventive mind" in making practical application of scientific knowledge. In his words:

> The science of logic never made a man reason rightly, and the science of ethics . . . never made a man behave rightly. The most such sciences can do is to help us catch ourselves up and check ourselves, if we start to reason or behave wrongly; and to criticize ourselves more articulately after we have made mistakes. A science only lays down lines within which the rules of the art must fall, laws which the follower of the art must not transgress; but what particular thing he shall positively do within those lines is left exclusively to his own genius. (8)

The idea of reflective practice is still relatively new, and much more thinking needs to be given to its development and use in educational administration. It seems clear, nonetheless, that reflective principals are in charge of their professional practice. They do not passively accept solutions and mechanically apply them. They do not assume that the norm is the one best way to practice, and they are suspicious of easy answers to complex questions. They are painfully aware of how context and situations vary, how teachers and students differ in many ways, and how complex school goals and objectives actually are; they recognize that, despite difficulties, tailored treatments to problems must be the norm. At the same time, reflective professional practice requires that principals have a healthy respect for, be well informed about, and use the best available theory and research and accumulated practice wisdom. All these sources of information help increase understanding and inform practice. The rub is that no matter how reflective a principal tries to be, effectiveness will remain elusive if still based on traditional management theory. Management theory itself needs to be reinvented.

CHANGING MINDSCAPES

Traditional management enjoys official sanction in many state capitals and in many university preparation programs for school administrators. It is also the mindscape that dominates much of the literature on school improvement. It's no surprise, therefore, that this mindscape is entrenched in the thinking of many school principals and is difficult to change.

Consider, for example, the case of elementary school principal Jane. Jane now spends from one-third to one-half of her time trying to be an "instructional leader" as prescribed by a recent state law. This law requires that she evaluate every teacher in her building two times a year, using a state assessment instrument composed of a generic list of 50 teaching behaviors gleaned from dozens of independent research reports on "effective teaching." She is required as well to take into account the scores of students on the state's mandated standardized skills test as part of this evaluation. The instrument is several pages long and involves a good deal of paperwork in addition to one hour of classroom observation for each evaluation. Jane takes her responsibilities seriously and estimates that a conscientious job takes about three hours for each evaluation.

Teachers are required to develop "growth plans," which Jane must monitor as well. The growth plans indicate how each teacher intends to improve her or his teaching and thus earn higher evaluation scores. Jane estimates that she spends 180 hours, or 22 days, a year just conducting the required evaluations. She dreads the many hours it takes to collect, study, and comment on the growth plans and then figure out sensible, albeit efficient, ways to follow up what teachers claim they will do. She notices that the growth plans are often perfunctory in tone, and this bothers her.

Among Jane's other instructional leadership responsibilities are daily monitoring of teachers to ensure that they follow the state-mandated standards for each of the subjects or courses taught and that they adhere to the proper time allocations as provided by the mandated schedule. Jane can keep tabs on this process by practicing "management by walking around," but is not able by relying on this process alone to demonstrate concretely to her superiors that her school is in compliance. Seeking to avoid a poor evaluation from her supervisors, Jane requires that teachers indicate the standards they are teaching to on their daily lesson plans, as well as the amount of time they spend teaching each of these objectives. She dutifully collects these lesson plans each Friday and examines them to be sure that teachers are in compliance. As time permits, Jane tries to write comments on the plans that might result in teachers thinking about their lessons more effectively and teaching better.

In Jane's school district, heavy emphasis is given to the state tests that are closely linked to the required standards. The results of these tests must be submitted to the school district's central office and by that office to the state department of education. The results are then published in the newspaper, with statewide comparisons made district by district and district comparisons made school by school. There is enormous pressure for schools to do well on the **test comparisons**. If the test scores in her school are not high enough, she hears **about it** from the superintendent's office. As part of her evaluation, for example, she must report to her supervisor the current year's test results and note progress (or lack of progress) made by comparing these results with test scores for the two previous years.

Sometimes Jane gets the impression that the superintendent wants the scores up at any cost and that all that counts is the bottom line. In turn, she puts enormous pressure on her teachers to be sure that the students do well on the tests. All teachers, for example, have been "inserviced" so that their day-by-day teaching should now be based on a popular teaching model made up of a series of specific steps thought to result in better student achievement. In addition to the evaluation system that is now in place and the monitoring of lesson plans and test scores, Jane spends much of her time coaching and monitoring the teachers to be sure that they are using the required teaching techniques.

In her school, Jane supervises a tightly connected "instructional management system" that seeks to link together measurable objectives, a highly specific curriculum, and required, detailed time schedules with a monitoring system of controls to ensure that teachers are doing what they are supposed to be doing and at the right time. Despite this management system, the results have been frustrating. Although there have been modest gains in test scores, particularly with respect to lower-level skills, a number of problems have emerged. The curriculum is becoming increasingly narrow, absentee rates are up, and Jane worries that teachers are using fewer and fewer of their talents and skills. She shudders at the harshness of the term *deskilled* that some people use to describe what is happening to teachers in her school, but is haunted by its imagery nonetheless.

A number of other "unanticipated consequences" from using this particular instructional management system are emerging. Teachers seem to be teaching more and more to the test. Furthermore, Jane is convinced that they are "showboating" the indicators that appear on the required teacher evaluation instrument when she is present and observing, but not using them at other times. She suspects that she is often observing staged lessons that allow for easy display of the indicators in the teachers' efforts to get higher evaluation scores.

Jane wonders what is wrong. Could Murphy's Law be true? Although from a traditional management perspective Jane can provide evidence that she is doing what she is supposed to, that the required instructional management system is in place, and that (at least overtly) teachers are doing what they are supposed to, Jane feels that appearances do not match reality and that things are just not working well. After much painful soul searching, she reaches the conclusion that something different must be done.

This conclusion is very disconcerting for Jane. She feels that she is on the verge of experiencing a professional career crisis that resembles the proverbial "midlife crisis." After all, Jane was an outstanding student during her years of graduate study in educational administration. She took the required workshops offered by the state-sponsored Leadership Development Academy and did so well that last summer she was asked to be an academy trainer. She knows how important such management ideas as POSDCoRB are to providing the kind of rational and efficient management needed for schools to work well. She knows how to demonstrate the leadership behaviors learned in a recent workshop, and last summer she developed workshops of her own on conflict management and on how to conduct a successful conference. She has earned a reputation for knowing how to handle people.

On the walls of Jane's office are displayed several plaques containing sayings of widely accepted management principles. Each of the plaques was given to her as an award for completing one of the Leadership Development Academy's workshops. One says, "If you can't measure it, you can't manage it." Another says, "What gets rewarded gets done." And a third says, "What gets measured gets taught"—a saying often repeated by her State Commissioner of Education as she shares her vision for schools in speeches throughout the state. Still other plaques remind Jane of the importance of having clear objectives, letting people know exactly what is expected of them, and being a rational and objective manager.

Jane is surrounded by the dimensions, principles, and expressions of traditional management theory—the theory of the Neats. Furthermore, this theory matches well her own mindscape of what management is, how schools are to operate if they are to function well, and the kind of leadership she should provide as a school principal. Finally, this mindscape is nurtured by the system of rewards in place in her school district. The more her practice reflects traditional management theory, the more successful she is assumed to be. It is no wonder Jane experiences dissonance and anxiety from the realization that it doesn't work very well. Changing one's mindscape is a little like changing one's religion.

In recent months, Jane has come to realize that, for traditional management to work, schools need to be more tightly structured and predictable than is typically the case and people need to be more passive and uniform than is typical. At first, she responded to this awareness by continuing to do the same things, only doing them better. But gradually she accepted the reality that when the world cannot be changed to fit your theory, you had better change your theory to fit the world. This thought made more sense when she read somewhere about the differences between management and leadership. Management is concerned with doing things right, she remembered. Leadership is concerned with doing right things.

Jane realizes that successful principals are both effective managers and effective leaders. But if one has to choose between the two, the only sensible choice is to do right things, even if it means that you are not doing them in the way specified by the system. Arriving at this decision was an important and courageous milestone for Jane. Although anxious at first, she now feels comfortable with the idea that when bureaucratic and moral authority are in conflict, moral authority must always take precedence.

Jane was not known as a reckless person. Indeed, if anything, she was considered to be quite conventional and conservative in the way she did things. Thus, she began to respond to the looseness she found in the structure of schooling by bending rules and interpreting issues in a fashion that always reflected the spirit of the rule but not the letter. When Jane encountered the system tightening up because her supervisors practiced close supervision, or when she was forced by the system to ignore individual differences in people and situations, she would follow the opposite tack by emphasizing the letter of the rule but not the spirit. Perfunctory execution became part of her management repertoire—a skill she realized that teachers often used to advantage when locked into the same predicament.

During the evaluation of teachers using the standardized system, for example, Jane took liberties with the required procedures by not insisting that all the listed teaching behaviors be displayed by teachers, but only the ones that made sense, given the lessons or units they were teaching, the objectives they set, and the learning needs of their students. She would talk to teachers about what they wanted to accomplish in their lessons and how. She was sensitive to and respectful of the differences in personality that determined their teaching styles. She realized, for example, that reticent teachers had a harder time providing the kind of bubbling reinforcement and feedback that "win points" than did their more outgoing counterparts. Together, Jane and the teachers would look over the four-page list of required teaching behaviors, deciding on the 8 or 10 behaviors that seemed to make the most sense for the particular teaching episode to be evaluated and in light of particular teaching problems identified. The evaluation was then based on this shorter but more meaningful version.

Jane frequently found herself in the middle of two conflicting sources of authority—what the bureaucracy wanted and what research and other informed practice said. The bureaucracy, for example, wanted her to use tight alignment strategies that required breaking down the mandated standards into small pieces, to teach these pieces directly, and to use practiced assessments that measured the extent to which these pieces had been learned. Luckily Jane was a member of a local principals' center study group that was examining the use of student work samples to help make decisions about teaching and learning. The group had been discussing the research of Fred M. Newmann, Anthony S. Bryk, and Jenny K. Nagaoka (2001) on the relationship between authentic intellectual work and scores on standardized tests. The sum of their findings was that Chicago teachers who gave more powerful assignments that required students to use their minds well got better results on the district's standardized tests than teachers who gave assignments that only required concentrated use of basic skills. This second group of teachers taught the required skills directly. In the words of the researchers, "We conclude, therefore, assignments calling for more authentic intellectual work actually improve student scores on conventional tests. The results suggest that if teachers, administrators, policy makers, and the public at-large place more emphasis on authentic intellectual work in classrooms, yearly gains on standardized tests in Chicago could surpass national norms"(2). After sharing the findings with the faculty there was a shift in strategy from using a tight alignment approach that required "teaching to the test" to crafting more powerful lessons. Once test scores improved the faculty was hooked, and this topic became the central school professional development theme. From examining the assignments that teachers gave, the faculty then focused on examining student work, asking a variety of questions including "Was the work good enough?" and, if the answer was no, "What needed to be done?"

Jane was also involved with the "learning walk" as a way for teachers to take turns spending a half day with her walking through each of the classrooms in the school. Jane and her teaching partner were looking for examples in practice of the school's "this we believe" principles about good teaching. Learning walks were always followed by a conversation about the experience with teachers. Whether teachers were being visited or were visiting with Jane, they seemed to enjoy the learning walk experience. Learning walks soon led to Jane and her faculty experimenting with coaching. So far the introduction of coaching is going well, and teachers have been talking with Jane about setting up a program of coaching that would model the idea for other schools in the district. They plan to seek funding from the central office and have been talking with the district's director of professional development.

Whenever Jane's supervisors got wind of what was going on and cracked down on her to comply more specifically with the system, Jane shifted her stratagem by routinely evaluating people with dispatch to save as much time as possible for other things. Once the evaluations were complete and the paperwork filed, Jane and her teachers were able to work more meaningfully and in better ways on the improvement of teaching. Jane is learning fast how to provide leadership in the complex, messy, and nonlinear scruffy world. Her mindscapes of management and leadership theory are changing to match the actual landscapes she encounters in practice.

THE LIMITS OF TRADITIONAL MANAGEMENT THEORY

It would be a mistake for Jane to believe that traditional management theory is useless. She should not abandon it but should, rather, learn how to use it to her best advantage. Traditional management theory has its merits and limitations, and it is important for principals to know the difference.

- Traditional management theory is suited to situations of practice that are characterized by linear conditions. However, the usefulness of this theory ends where nonlinear conditions begin.

- Traditional management theory is suited to situations of practice that can be tightly structured and connected without causing unanticipated harmful effects. However, the usefulness of this theory ends where loosely structured conditions begin.
- Traditional management theory is suited to situations in which the need exists to bring about a routine level of competence and performance. However, the usefulness of this theory ends when the goal is to bring about extraordinary commitment and performance. Traditional management theory works when a measure of standardization is needed to improve efficiency and when a measured amount of common understandings are prerequisites for higher-order learning.

Linear and Nonlinear Conditions

When deciding on management and leadership strategies, it is important to take into account the extent to which conditions are or are not linear. Linear conditions are characterized by the following:

- Stable, predictable environments
- Tight management connections
- Loose cultural connections
- Discrete goals
- Structured tasks
- Single solutions
- Easily measured outcomes
- Established operating procedures
- Determinate consequences of action
- Clear lines of authority

Under linear conditions, simplicity, clarity, order, and predictability are present. Examples of administrative tasks that typically fit linear conditions include the routing of bus schedules, purchasing books, planning conference times, and other events and activities in which human interactions are simple, incidental, or nonexistent. Yet, even these tasks can quickly become nonlinear—for instance, an eight-inch snowstorm can create havoc with a bus schedule.

By contrast, nonlinear conditions are characterized by the following:

- Dynamic environments
- Loose management connections
- Tight cultural connections
- Multiple and competing goals
- Unstructured tasks
- Competing solutions
- Difficult-to-measure outcomes

- Unestablished operating procedures
- Indeterminate consequences of action
- Unclear and competing lines of authority

The vast majority of human interactions that take place in schools can be described as nonlinear. Gleick writes in *Chaos: Making a New Science:* "Nonlinearity means that the act of playing the game has a way of changing the rules" (1987:24). In nonlinear situations, every decision that is made in response to conditions at the base time (time 1) changes these conditions in such a way that successive decisions also made at time 1 no longer fit. It is difficult, therefore, for a principal to plan a series of steps, commit to a set of stepwise procedures, or otherwise make progressive management and leadership decisions based on the initial assumptions. When the context changes, the original sequence no longer makes sense. One cannot predict the conditions of time 2 until the conditions are experienced.

Under nonlinear conditions, management resembles following a compass when the position of north changes with each step you take. As Cziko (1989) phrases it: "A process demonstrating chaos is one in which strict deterministic causality holds at each *individual* step in an unfolding process, and yet it is impossible to predict the outcome over any *sequence* of steps in the process." In summary, nonlinear relationships between two events lead to consequences that are unpredictable. Furthermore, if the context for action changes, as is often the case in managing, leading, and teaching, the original sequence no longer makes sense.

Vaill (1989) aptly describes the nonlinear context for management as "permanent white water." White water is the frothy, turbulent water found in waterfalls, breakers, and rapids. This metaphor was suggested to Vaill by a manager who observed:

> Most managers are taught to think of themselves as paddling their canoes on calm, still lakes. They are led to believe that they should be pretty much able to go where they want, when they want, using means that are under their control. . . . But it has been my experience that you never get out of the rapids! . . . There are lots of changes going on at once. The feeling is one of continuous upset and chaos. (2)

Vaill points out that in management "things are only partially under control, yet the effective navigator of the rapids is not behaving randomly or aimlessly" (2). In summary, it is the dynamic nature of unfolding events resembling "permanent white water" that differentiates linear from nonlinear situations. Successful practice in the latter requires the kind of reflection that enables principals and teachers to constantly test what they know against what is happening.

Tight and Loose Structure

Weick (1976) has argued compellingly for viewing schools as loosely coupled organizations. Loose coupling does not mean that decisions, actions, and programs in effect are unrelated, but that they are only loosely related to each other (March and Simon, 1958:176).

The issue of school goals and purposes provides a good example. It is generally assumed that there is a tight connection between stated goals and the policies, decisions, and actions that take place in an organization. Yet, the problem is that schools have multiple goals and are expected to achieve them. Sometimes the goals conflict with each other such that making progress toward one means losing progress toward another. Always thinking in terms of discrete goals or even discrete multiple goals with each attended to sequentially, therefore, does not fit the special character of schools' unique value systems. Under nonlinear and loosely structured conditions, schools don't achieve goals as much as they respond to certain values and tend to certain imperatives that ensure their survival over time (Parsons, 1951).

Perhaps the most noticeable example of looseness in schools is the connection of teachers to rules. Principal Jane became aware of this reality the hard way as she tried to implement the required teaching evaluation system. When she was in class observing lessons using the instrument, she saw what she was supposed to because the teachers did what they were supposed to. Yet, when she left the classroom, teachers taught in ways that made sense to them and to their colleagues. They were more tightly connected to values, beliefs, and norms than they were to the imposed management system. Jane learned that the best way to connect teachers to each other and to their work was by changing the culture (Sergiovanni, 2001). At the heart of this new culture would be ideas, and leading with ideas would be at the center of her practice (Sergiovanni, 2005).

Ordinary and Extraordinary Commitment and Performance

The management and leadership needed to bring about "a fair day's work for a fair day's pay" and for transcending this minimum contract to achieve inspired and extraordinary commitment and performance in schools are different (see, e.g., Bass, 1985; Burns, 1978; Herzberg, 1966; Kelly, 1988; Sergiovanni, 1990). Traditional management theory and practice can provide the former but not the latter. Principal Jane noted, for example, that by practicing traditional management she was able to get teachers to do what they were supposed to but could not get sustained and extraordinary results.

There are two reasons why traditional management theory and practice are limited to achieving minimums, not maximums. First, the theory is based on bureaucratic and personal authority. Relying on rules, mandates, procedures, regulations, and formal expectations to get someone to do something are examples of bureaucratic authority. When this form of authority is used teachers are expected to comply or else face negative consequences. When principals rely on their human relations skills to get people to comply, they are using personal authority. These skills enable principals to successfully trade meeting needs of teachers for compliance with their wishes. Both bureaucratic and personal authority are external.

Teachers are motivated to respond for outside reasons rather than be motivated from within.

External authority works, and most teachers and students respond to it. But external authority has the tendency to cause people to respond as subordinates. Good subordinates always do what they are supposed to but little else. Transcending ordinary competence for extraordinary commitment and performance requires that people be transformed from subordinates to followers, which requires a different kind of theory and practice. Subordinates respond to external authority, but followers respond to ideas, values, beliefs, and purposes. Traditional theory encompasses the former but not the latter.

Second, traditional management theory, with its bureaucratic roots, is heavily biased toward standardization and routinization. Though many aspects of schooling should be routinized, traditional theory seeks to routinize that which should be varied as well. For schools to excel, teachers and administrators need to be concerned with uniqueness and specialness in their interactions with each other and with students. The test of their effectiveness is their ability to ensure that every student is successful in achieving high academic, social, and personal goals—a task that cannot be accomplished by applying a standard recipe for organizing, presenting the curriculum, and engaging in teaching and learning. Standardization and routinization may be the formula for simple work that takes place in a stable environment where modest results are acceptable, but it is not the formula for extraordinary commitment and performance.

SOME REFLECTIONS

1. The mindscapes of Neats and Scruffies differ. Which of the mindscapes best describes your principal? Give examples. With which mindscape are you most comfortable?
2. What is your reaction to the change in Jane's leadership practice? How does Jane manage to keep her supervisors happy while at the same time engaging in the new management and leadership?
3. According to Gleick, "Nonlinearity means that the act of playing the game has a way of changing the rules." Is this statement true in teaching? What about playing basketball or soccer? Is nonlinearity an advantage or disadvantage for one who wants to lead?

REFERENCES

Bass, Bernard M. 1985. *Leadership and Performance beyond Expectations.* New York: Free Press.

Burns, James MacGregor. 1978. *Leadership.* New York: Harper & Row.

Cziko, Gary A. 1989. "Unpredictability and Indeterminism in Human Behavior: Arguments and Implications for Educational Research," *Educational Researcher* 18(3), 17–25.

Gleick, James. 1987. *Chaos Making a New Science.* New York: Viking Penguin.

Herzberg, Frederick. 1966. *Work and the Nature of Man.* New York: World.

Hosford, Philip L. 1984. "The Problem, Its Difficulties and Our Approaches," in Philip L. Hosford (Ed.), *Using What We Know about Teaching.* Alexandria, VA: Association for Supervision and Curriculum Development.

James, William. 1892. *Talks to Teachers on Psychology: And to Students on Some of Life's Ideals.* New York: Holt.

Kelly, Robert E. 1988, November–December. "In Praise of Followers," *Harvard Business Review.*

March, James G., and Herbert A. Simon. 1958. *Organizations.* New York: Wiley.

Newmann, Fred M., Anthony S. Bryk, and Jenny K. Nagaoka. 2001, January. "Authentic Intellectual Work and Standardized Tests: Conflict or Coexistence?" in *Improving Chicago Schools.* Chicago: Consortium on Chicago School Research.

Parsons, Talcott. 1951. *Toward a General Theory of Social Action.* Cambridge, MA: Harvard University Press.

Schön, Donald A. 1983. *The Reflective Practitioner: How Professionals Think in Action.* New York: Basic Books.

Schön, Donald A. 1984. "Leadership as Reflection in Action," in Thomas J. Sergiovanni and John E. Corbally (Eds.), *Leadership and Organizational Culture* (pp. 64–72). Urbana: University of Illinois Press.

Schön, Donald A. 1987. *Educating the Reflective Practitioner.* San Francisco: Jossey-Bass.

Sergiovanni, Thomas J. 1990. *Value-Added Leadership: How to Get Extraordinary Performance in Schools.* New York: Harcourt Brace Jovanovich.

Sergiovanni, Thomas J. 2001. *Leadership: What's in It for Schools?* London: Routledge/Falmer.

Sergiovanni, Thomas J. 2005. *Strengthening the Heartbeat: Leading and Learning Together in Schools.* San Francisco: Jossey-Bass.

Vaill, Peter B. 1989. *Managing as a Performing Art.* San Francisco: Jossey-Bass.

Weick, Karl E. 1976. "Educational Organizations as Loosely Coupled Systems," *Administrative Science Quarterly* 2, 1–19.

4

A NEW THEORY
FOR THE PRINCIPALSHIP

o overcome the limits of traditional management and leadership, a new theory for the principalship must be developed—a theory more responsive to nonlinear conditions and loose structuring and that can inspire extraordinary commitment and performance. This theory should not replace but subsume the old. The role of traditional management must change, for example, from being the *strategic model* for developing school policies and practices to being a valued, albeit limited, *tactical option* within a new, more broadly based and powerful management theory. In constructing this new theory, many time-honored principles of traditional management will need to be rethought, expanded, and sometimes even inverted whenever nonlinear and loosely structured conditions or extraordinary performance requirements are present.

TOWARD A NEW THEORY

The following subsections discuss examples of such principles. This discussion is brief because the purpose is to outline a set of basic ideas that contrast the two theories. Elaborations and further examples illustrating the principles are provided in subsequent chapters.

The Issue of How Schools Are Structured

The Traditional Rule.   Schools are managerially tight but culturally loose.

The Problem.   This traditional rule assumes that schools are structured and function much like the mechanical workings of a clock made of cogs and gears, wheels, drives, and pins all tightly connected in an orderly and predictable manner. The task of management is to gain control of and regulate the master wheel and pin. The principal, for example, might put into place a well-oiled instructional delivery system composed of the "right" teacher evaluation system or the "right" alignment system or some other "right" control mechanism that defines in detail what teachers teach, and when and how. Once the master wheel and pin are under control, all the other wheels and pins will move responsively, and the principal's intents will be accomplished.

Although many aspects of the school are indeed tightly connected in this clockworks fashion, other aspects are not. Furthermore, teachers and students are more tightly connected to values and beliefs than they are to management systems and rules (see, e.g., Deal and Kennedy, 1982; March, 1984; Sergiovanni, 2007; Shils, 1961; Weick, 1982). The more typical view of how schools operate is that of clockworks gone awry—cogs, gears, and pins all spinning independently of each other. Although practices based on managerial tightness and cultural looseness can often get people to do what they are supposed to, the rule casts them in roles as subordinates and thus cannot inspire sustained and extraordinary commitment and performance. Furthermore, it is unable to provide the connections needed among loosely connected parts to get the job done well.

The Alternative.   Schools are managerially loose but culturally tight.

Weick (1986) pointed out "that indeterminacy can be organized not just by rules, job descriptions, and a priori specifications, but also by such things as shared premises, culture, persistence, clan control, improvisation, memory and imitation." Weick continues:

> In a loosely coupled system you don't influence less, you influence differently. The administrator . . . has the difficult tasks of affecting perceptions, and monitoring and reinforcing the language people use to create and coordinate what they are doing. . . . Administrators model the kind of behavior they desire . . . identify key issues so they can centralize control over a few (not all) issues and help people see them similarly. Leaders in loosely coupled systems have to move around, meet people face-to-face, and to do their influencing by interaction rather than by rules and regulations. . . . Personnel selection is more crucial than in other systems, because the common premises that are selected into that system will guide how the dispersed activities are executed. (10)

When schools are managerially loose and culturally tight, it is best to view leadership as a process that helps teachers, students, and others to construct meanings from their experiences. This idea is powerful, for it can bring together leadership and learning as constructivist twins. But constructivist leadership (and constructivist learning) cannot happen successfully in a tightly connected system. Linda Lambert (2002), for example, defines leadership as "the reciprocal process that enables participants in an educational community to construct meanings that lead toward a shared purpose of schooling" (42). She continues, "Leadership, like energy, is not finite, not restricted by formal authority and power; it permeates a healthy culture and is undertaken by whoever sees a need or an opportunity" (43). For leadership to take these forms, there needs to be more room for people to interact, more opportunities for them to decide, and more discretion for them to practice successfully. The alternate rule, schools are managerially loose but culturally tight, provides the discretion needed for leadership to reach out and touch people in a loosely connected world.

The Issue of Strategic Planning

The Traditional Rule.   Clarity, control, and consensus are important to effective management and are achieved by detailed planning. Therefore:

1. State measurable outcomes (indicate specifically what is to be accomplished).
2. Provide behavioral expectations (decide and communicate who will do what and how it will be done).
3 Practice monitoring (compare expected behavior with observed and correct when necessary).
4. Measure outcomes (compare observed outcomes with stated and correct when necessary).

The Problem.   There are many paradoxes in management, and planning is one of them. By planning in a linear-stepwise way, one assumes that it is possible to control the future, but often one actually loses control. Detailed plans and surefire objectives take over from people, becoming scripts that on the one hand program future actions and self-fulfilling prophecies and that on the other determine our destiny even when we are no longer interested in either the journey or the destiny. For linear conditions with tight structures, planning as traditionally conceived is a useful management tactic that can achieve the anticipated results, but as a strategy, traditional planning locks us into a course of action that often does not make sense once events are underway.

Further planning has the tendency to result in the "escalation of commitment" to a course of action that sustains itself irrationally long after the original course of action should have been abandoned (Staw, 1984). Sinking huge sums of money into facilities for the high school's interscholastic sports program makes it difficult to de-emphasize sports even when doing so may be a good idea. Commitment to the teacher evaluation system that took so many hours of planning time to develop is likely to remain firm even in light of evidence that the teaching effectiveness research on which it is based is faulty and teacher morale is suffering as a result.

And, finally, the measurement aspects of traditional planning place severe limits on developing powerful strategies that encourage innovation and excellence. By establishing worth as the consistency that exists between stated and observed outcomes, too many worthwhile outcomes not stated or unanticipated don't count. New priorities and new courses of action are missed, and innovation is discouraged—hardly conditions for excellence. Citing a study of planning in 75 corporations that appeared in the *Economist*, Peters (1989a) notes that firms without central planners tended to produce better results. A better strategy, Peters suggests, is that of General Bill Creech of the Tactical Air Command: "Organize as we fight . . . organize in accordance with the human spirit" as a way to best use talents of people, to respond to the idiosyncratic nature of situations, and to build esprit and small-group cohesiveness deep into the enterprise. It appears that planning, the sacred cow of traditional management, needs to be understood differently.

The Alternative.   Clarity, control, and consensus are important to effective management and are achieved by planning strategically. Therefore:

1. Be clear about basic directions (set the tone and charter the mission).
2. Provide purpose and build a shared covenant (determine shared goals, values, and operating principles).
3. Practice tight and loose management (hold people accountable to shared values but provide them with empowerment and enablement to decide what to do when and how).
4. Evaluate processes and outcomes (be sure that decisions and events embody shared values).

The principles that support this alternative rule are examined in some detail in subsequent chapters. Suffice to say here that, in a nonlinear and loosely structured world, it makes managerial sense to allow people to make decisions in ways that make sense to them providing that the decisions they make embody shared values and commitments.

The Issue of Where to Fit People into the Improvement Planning Process

The Traditional Rule.   When it comes to fitting people in:

1. First emphasize ends (determine objectives first).
2. Then emphasize ways (figure out how you will reach your objectives).
3. Then emphasize means (identify, train, place, and supervise people).

The Problem. Deciding where to fit people into the planning process influences the outcome in important ways (Hayes, 1985). Should one start with people first or fit them in after work requirements are identified? The traditional ends, ways, and means rule is compatible with a "cannonball" theory of management suitable for stable environments where targets don't move. Unfortunately, as Harry Quadracci (Peters, 1989b) points out, we live in a "cruise missile" world. Cannons are excellent weapons for hitting fixed targets under stable conditions; one need only identify the target (ends), take careful aim calculating distance and wind (ways), and give the order to fire to a well-trained crew (means). A hit is virtually guaranteed. However, hitting moving targets is another matter. Moreover, changing one's mind to enable hitting a better target than the initial one after the cannon has been fired is impossible. Yet, in the world of schooling most of our targets are moving, and different and more desirable targets are frequently discovered during the course of our actions. Cannons won't do here. Cruise missiles, to continue Quadracci's admittedly surly metaphor, have built into them the capacity to chase shifting targets and indeed to change targets after they are launched.

The Alternative. When it comes to school improvement:

1. First emphasize means (concentrate on people first, build them up, increase their commitment, link them to purposes, help them to be self-managing).
2. Then emphasize ways (let them figure out what to do and how).
3. Then emphasize ends (they will decide on and achieve objectives that are consistent with shared purposes).

Hayes (1985), who proposed this alternative rule, believes that it provides the basis for developing strategies that are more responsive to today's complex world. The key to concentrating on means first is to build up the capacity for people to be self-managing and to connect them to shared values and commonly held purposes. Kelly (1988:144) believes that self-management is an essential ingredient in being a good follower. Followers, he maintains, share a number of essential qualities:

- They manage themselves well.
- They are committed to the organization and to a purpose, principle, or person outside themselves.
- They build up their competence and focus their efforts for maximum impact.
- They are courageous, honest, and credible.

Once followership is built up, the other steps in the alternative rule's chain unfold in a manner that inspires performance and brings about extraordinary results. The traditional rule, by contrast, is based on authority and determinism. The likely result is the establishment of subordination rather than followership in the school, with mediocre rather than extraordinary results.

The Issue of Getting and Maintaining Compliance

The Traditional Rule.   To manage compliance:

1. Identify and announce your goals (determine your major objectives).
2. Use goals to develop work requirements (decide how the work will be done).
3. Use work requirements to develop your compliance strategy (given the above, determine how you will get people to do what they are supposed to do).
4. Observe involvement and commitment consequences and correct as necessary (determine if people are properly motivated; if not, determine ways to motivate them).

The Problem.   The organizational theorist Etzioni (1961) noted that one universal requirement of management is the need to obtain and maintain compliance. By compliance he means how schools get teachers and students involved in their work in the first place and how this involvement is maintained over time. A key point in his theory is that the strategy a manager uses to obtain and maintain involvement has a powerful influence on forming the kind of identification and attachment people have for their work and for the school itself, on shaping the goals of the school, and on the kind and character of work that takes place within the school as goals are pursued. This is so, even when goals and work requirements are set first. Goals and work requirements are ultimately shaped to fit the means that schools use to get and keep teachers involved in their teaching and to get and keep students involved in their learning. These means then influence the kind and degree of involvement with work and school.

Given this influence, it is too chancy to let the involvement strategy evolve naturally as a result of stated goals and work requirements. Some involvement strategies can actually result in the emergence of dysfunctional school goals and work processes with negative effects. Consider, for example, a prison that has as its goal order among the inmates. To achieve this goal, it relies on the establishment of closely monitored daily routines and a system of compliance based on punishment for infractions. As a result, prisoners became alienated and would not choose freely to stay in prison. Alienated involvement reinforces the use of rules and punishment to maintain compliance. Changing the goal for this prison from order to rehabilitation will not likely be accomplished without changing what prisoners do and the means for ensuring compliance with the new system. Prisoners will have to come to see the value of rehabilitation, and the activities they engage in will have to be more meaningful to them.

Etzioni (1961) suggests that the strategies an organization or manager uses to get and keep people involved can be grouped into three broad categories:

1. Coercive (people, students, and teachers, for example, are forced by the threat of penalties).

2. Remunerative (people are attracted by the promise of rewards such as money, career advancement, good grades, better working conditions, political advantage, enhanced social standing, and having psychological needs met).
3. Normative (people are compelled because they believe what they are doing is right and good and/or because they find involvement intrinsically satisfying).

Each of the three compliance strategies results in a particular kind of involvement, which in turn shapes the nature and character of school work and school goals. These relationships are illustrated in Table 4.1. Because the choice of compliance strategy is so important in determining what happens, the traditional rule needs to be inverted so that the principal and school begin first by deciding on the compliance strategy they will use.

The Alternative. To manage compliance:

1. First establish your compliance strategy. (How do we want to involve people in work and keep them involved? Use the strategy that reflects desired involvement.)
2. Develop complementary work requirements. (What kind of connections will people need to make for them to be properly involved?)

t a b l e **4.1** **How Compliance Is Achieved**

	School A	School B	School C
The School's Dominant Compliance Strategy	*Coercive:* Force people by using bureaucratic controls and penalties for infractions	*Remunerative:* Provide people with rewards in exchange for involvement	*Normative:* Bond people to shared values, beliefs, and norms
Resulting Involvement of Teachers and Students	*Indifferent,* often alienated (they won't be involved unless they have to)	*Calculated* (they will be involved as long as they get something of value back in exchange)	*Moral* (they will be involved because they believe it is the right thing to do)
How the Work of Teaching and Learning Gets Done	*Routinely* (the hand works only)	*Instrumentally* (the mind drives the hand)	*Intrinsically* (mind, hand, and heart work together)
The Resultant Dominant Goal of Management	*Maintain order* by getting and keeping control	*Barter by making the best deal* and monitoring the deal, patching cracks that appear	*Develop and maintain a strong culture*

3. Decide on work strategy. (Given the connections desired, what kind of work designs and settings do we need?)
4. Evaluate. (What kind of commitment and involvement is observed? Make adjustments in compliance strategy if necessary.)

Moral involvement has the best chance of ensuring and maintaining inspired commitment and performance from students, teachers, and parents. Commitment to moral involvement does not preclude the occasional use of coercive and remunerative compliance, but it does suggest that the overarching framework for compliance must be normative.

The Issue of Developing a Motivational Strategy

The Traditional Rule.   What gets rewarded gets done.

The Problem.   This rule works—what gets rewarded does get done. But what happens when rewards are not available to principals, teachers, students, or parents? Unfortunately, the rule's flip side is true, too. What does not get rewarded does not get done.

Relying on rewards to obtain compliance leads to calculated involvement (Etzioni, 1961). Furthermore, this rule has a tendency to change other kinds of work involvement to calculated involvement. A student, for example, might be engaged in a learning activity because of its intrinsic interest. No gold stars, grades, or other external rewards are provided for her or his involvement. Once such rewards are introduced, the student's connection to the learning activity has a tendency to change from intrinsic to extrinsic. Take the rewards away and the student is not likely to engage further in the activity (Deci and Ryan, 1985; Greene and Lepper, 1974). By the same token, teachers who are engaged in certain kinds of activities for moral reasons—that is, because they feel a sense of obligation or believe that something is right or important to do—forsake moral involvement for calculated once rewards (or punishments) are introduced.

The Alternative.   What is rewarding gets done, gets done well, and gets done without close supervision or other controls. What we believe in and feel obligated to do because of moral commitments gets done, gets done well, and gets done without close supervision or other controls.

Calculated involvement may be able to get people to do what they are supposed to as long as rewards are forthcoming, but it is not a potent enough strategy to inspire motivation and inspire people to become self-managing, to work without direction or supervision, and to remain engaged in their work even when extrinsic rewards are not available. A new theory of management for the principalship needs to subsume such ideas as what-gets-rewarded-gets-done into a broader motivational strategy that recognizes the importance of morality, emotions, and social bonds (Etzioni, 1988:xii). Although often underplayed and sometimes overlooked in traditional motivation theories, what counts most to people are what they believe, how they feel, and the shared norms and cultural messages that emerge from the small groups and communities with which they identify. Some principals, for example, have refused promotion or transfer because they felt a sense of obligation to see projects they initiated through to conclusion. They gave up extrinsic gains such as higher salaries, career advancement, and more prestige because of the obligation and commitment they had to what they were doing. Parents and teachers routinely sacrifice their own self-interests, wants, and needs to advance those of the children they have responsibility for raising.

Following Etzioni (1988), a new theory of management must provide for the development of motivation strategies that are based on all three motivation rules: what is rewarded gets done, what is rewarding gets done, and what is good gets done. In a new management theory, major emphasis would be given to the latter two. The three rules are depicted here:

The Rules	Why People Behave	Motivational Type	Involvement
What gets rewarded gets done	Extrinsic gain	Instrumental	Calculated
What is rewarding gets done	Intrinsic gain	Expressive	Intrinsic
What is good gets done	Duty/ obligation	Moral	Moral

The Issue of How Schools Are Led

The Traditional Rule.   Leadership should be value free.

The Problem.   This traditional rule assumes that leadership must be an objective process that separates leader, leadership, and effectiveness. Leadership is viewed as a tool that helps get things done. Effective leaders are those who get others to follow them. Effective leaders are good at achieving goals. "Effectiveness," says Ronald Heifetz (1994:22), "means reaching viable decisions that implement the goals of the organization." Effective leaders get the systemsworld right. Every organization has a systemsworld. This systemsworld takes the form of management designs, scripts, protocols, pathways, procedures, efficiencies, and accountability assurances that help us achieve our goals. These factors are important, but alone they miss the point. They place process over substance. They are concerned with means rather than ends. How things are done becomes more important than what is done. Getting people to follow the leader becomes more important than getting people to commit to and follow ideas that make sense for their particular context. Let's face it, leaders who excel at working the systemsworld of their schools can develop effective pathways that lead to the wrong place. To put it another way, there are many principals who excel at getting teachers and others to follow them. But some of these principals haven't the foggiest notion of where to go. Often following these principals leads to less effective schooling.

Still, the systemsworld of school is an important part of any leadership equation. Without carefully thought out and implemented means, little can be accomplished. But things are not that simple. Schools and other organizations also possess a lifeworld (Habermas, 1987; Sergiovanni, 2001). The lifeworld side of school life is concerned with leaders and their purposes, followers and their needs, and the unique values, traditions, beliefs, customs, and norms that define a school's culture. Though both systemsworld and lifeworld are necessary for schools to work well, it makes a big difference whether it is the lifeworld that determines the systemsworld or the systemsworld that determines the lifeworld. Our goals and purposes, our values and dreams, our culture and meaning, for example, should determine the means we select to achieve them. But when the systemsworld dominates the lifeworld it is the other way around. Testing is a good example. When tests come from the inside and reflect what we want students to learn, the lifeworld dominates. But when tests come from the outside and determine what students must learn, the systemsworld dominates. The curriculum of schools should be decided by people as they reflect on what students need to learn and what society requires them to learn. The curriculum should not be decided by tests.

The Alternative.   Leadership should be value-added. To Heifetz (1994) leadership is a normative activity imbued with values and meaning. It is not a mere instrumentality—a mere tool to get from here to there. In his words, "We have to take sides. When we teach, write about, and model the exercise of leadership, we inevitably support or challenge people's conceptions of themselves, their roles, and most importantly their ideas about how social systems make progress on problems. Leadership is a normative concept because implicit in people's notions of leadership are images of a social contract. Imagine the differences in behavior when people operate with the idea that 'leadership means influencing the community to follow the leader's vision' versus 'leadership means influencing the community to face its problems.' In the first instance, influence is the mark of leadership; a leader gets people to accept his vision, and communities address problems by looking to him. If something goes wrong, the fault lies with the leader. In the second, progress on problems is the measure of leadership; leaders mobilize people to face problems and communities make progress on problems because leaders challenge and help them do so. If something goes wrong, the fault lies with both leaders and the community" (14–15).

Value-free leadership now has the upper hand over value-added leadership. As a tool leadership emphasizes solving problems and, in our culture, solving them as quickly as possible. In a value-added approach getting the job done is important too. But at the heart of the matter leadership is an investment in others. This investment decreases dependency, builds capacity, and helps people become self-managing. People need leaders less, and that is a sign leadership is working. The emphasis is on helping others to understand the problems they face and to figure out how they can cope with them. Sometimes coping leads to a solution. But coping can also lead to changing the nature of the problem and changing the context for the problem. As a result the problem does not go away but becomes less troublesome and becomes easier to live with (Sergiovanni, 2005).

CONTROLLING EVENTS OR PROBABILITIES?

Both traditional and new management and leadership theories are concerned with control. Control is needed to increase reliability and predictability. Without control there can be no instructional coherence. Without control there can be no organizational coherence. The traditional theory seeks reliability and predictability by increasing control over events and over people. This is a *power over* approach to leadership and management. The new theory, by contrast, seeks reliability and predictability by controlling probabilities—the probability that shared goals and purposes are embodied and reached. This is a *power to* approach to management and leadership. Increasing the probability that shared goals and purposes will be realized typically means giving up control over events and people.

Think of six basic control strategies that schools can use: direct supervision, standardizing the work processes, standardizing outcomes, emphasizing professional socialization, emphasizing purposes, and structuring for collegiality and natural interdependence.* Although all six of the strategies might appropriately be used at one time or another, it makes a difference which of the six or which combination is the school's basic strategy for achieving control.

In this discussion I will rely on the work of Henry Mintzberg and in particular his six basic managerial strategies. Imagine, for example, a principal who decides to bring about more instructional coherence in his school by monitoring teachers in an effort to learn what they are doing and to find out whether the teaching and learning decisions they make match up with the conceptions of teaching favored by the school. Here are the principal's choices:

1. *Directly supervise* teachers to ensure that they will do what they said was good teaching. Use a one-to-one approach.
2. Increase efforts to *standardize the work process* by requiring teachers to use the same books and materials and the same schedule to teach the required curriculum.

---

*This discussion of managerial strategies is based largely on the typology proposed by Mintzberg (1979). His typology reflects the conclusions of March and Simon (1958) and Simon (1957). Important to the discussion as presented here is the work of Peters and Waterman (1982) and Weick (1982). See also Sergiovanni (1987, 1990).

3. *Standardize the outcomes* teachers are expected to achieve and leave the means up to them, knowing that the likelihood that approved methods will be used is great. It becomes inevitable that the ends determine the means, and controlling the ends is one way to control the means.
4. Use *professional socialization* strategies and factors that emphasize professional obligations teachers have to meet their commitments to shared goals.
5. Rely on *purposing and shared values* that provide the glue teachers need to form learning communities and communities of practice that rely on group norms to get the job done.
6. Rely on *collegiality and interdependence* that teachers feel and that encourages them to become members of a collaborative culture that functions as a community of practice.

Although any of the six can make sense from time to time, it makes a difference which of the six becomes the principal's basic strategy for achieving and maintaining coherence and control. Key in choosing one of the six is whether it fits the kind and amount of complexity found in the work that teachers need to do.

A new theory of management for the principalship therefore must give primary attention to professional socialization, shared values, and collegiality and interdependence as control strategies, because they match the complexity of teaching and learning. Relying on the other control strategies, by contrast, does not match the complexity of good teaching and learning. The result is that teaching and learning become simplified as they are shaped by the control strategy. As Mintzberg (1979) notes, direct supervision is effective for simple work, but as work becomes more complex, the emphasis needs to shift from direct supervision to standardizing the work, to standardizing the outputs, and finally to emphasizing professional socialization, purposing, colleagueship, and natural interdependence. Relationships between choice of control strategy and the kind of teaching one is likely to receive is shown in Table 4.2.

When professional socialization, purposing and shared values, and collegiality are emphasized, they function as substitutes for leadership. This means that the principal does not have to provide as much direct leadership as would be the case if other control strategy choices were made. Leadership is much less intense and much more informal as issues of control and coordination take care of themselves naturally.

Direct supervision, standardizing work, and standardizing outputs are simple ideas that require complex management systems. For these ideas to work, structures must be in place and roles must be identified and delineated. Furthermore, expectations must be explicit and systems of monitoring must be in place to ensure that everything is functioning properly. As this management system becomes more complex, the discretion of teachers is narrowed. As a result, teaching becomes more simplified, routine, and standardized.

Exactly the opposite is the case with socialization, shared values, and collegiality. These are complex ideas that require very simple management systems to implement. Because of this simplicity, they allow teachers to function in complex table **4.2** **Control Strategies and Consequences**

	Direct Supervision	Standardized Work	Standardized Outputs
Strategy Concept	Simple	Simple	Simple
Characteristics of Management	Complex	Complex	Moderate
Teachers' Behavior	Simple	Simple	Moderate
Authority for Leadership	Bureaucratic rules; the leader's personality	Bureaucratic rules; the leader's personality; management systems	The leader's personality; management systems

	Professional Socialization	Purposing and Shared Values	Collegiality and Interdependence
Strategy Concept	Complex	Complex	Complex
Characteristics of Management	Simple	Simple	Simple
Teachers' Behavior	Complex	Complex	Complex
Authority for Leadership	Professional values and norms	Moral values and norms	Professional values and norms; moral values and norms

Source: Adapted from Sergiovanni (1992), p. 97.

ways, which enables them to make more responsive decisions that fit the unique circumstances that they face. In short, complex structures result in simple behaviors, and simple structures result in complex behaviors. Moreover, simple ideas require complex systems for implementation, and complex ideas require simple systems. In the first case, teaching becomes simplified; in the second place, teaching is more complex. Understanding these relationships is key to building a new and more effective practice of management for the principalship.

THE NEW THEORY AND SCHOOL ORGANIZATION

Good organization provides the administrative structures, arrangements, and co-ordinating mechanisms needed to facilitate teaching and learning. What are the implications of the new management theory for how we organize schools?

Some Basic Principles of Organizing

Whatever decisions are made about organizing, the new theory suggests that they should reflect the following basic principles:

1. The principle of *cooperation:* Cooperative teaching arrangements facilitate teaching and enhance learning. Furthermore, they help overcome the debilitating effects of the isolation that currently characterizes teaching. In successful schools, organizational structures enhance cooperation among teachers.
2. The principle of *empowerment:* Feelings of empowerment among teachers contribute to ownership and increase commitment and motivation to work. When teachers feel like pawns rather than originators of their own behavior, they respond with reduced commitment, mechanical behavior, indifference, and, in extreme cases, dissatisfaction and alienation. In successful schools, organizational structures enhance empowerment among teachers.
3. The principle of *responsibility:* Most teachers and other school professionals want responsibility. Responsibility upgrades the importance and significance of their work and provides a basis for recognition of their success. In successful schools, organizational structures encourage teacher responsibility.
4. The principle of *accountability:* Accountability is related to empowerment and responsibility. It provides the healthy measure of excitement, challenge, and importance that raises the stakes just enough so that achievement means something. In successful schools, organizational structures allow teachers to participate in setting local standards and norms and then to be accountable for their decisions and achievements.
5. The principle of *meaningfulness:* When teachers find their jobs to be meaningful, jobs not only take on a special significance but also provide teachers with feelings of intrinsic satisfaction. In successful schools, organizational structures provide for meaningful work.
6. The principle of *ability–authority:* The noted organizational theorist Victor Thompson (1961) stated that the major problem facing modern organizations is the growing gap that exists between those who have authority to act but not the ability needed for their activism to be most effective, and those who have the ability to act effectively but not the authority to do so. This principle seeks to place those who have the ability to act in the forefront of decision making. In successful schools, organizational structures promote authority based on ability. In schools and school districts where it is necessary for authority to be formally linked to one's position in the organizational hierarchy, day-by-day practice is characterized by formal and informal delegation of this authority to those with ability.

As these principles are manifested in the ways in which schools are organized, schools increase their capacity to respond to their problems, principals are able to lead more effectively, teaching is enhanced, and learning increases.

CHANGING OUR METAPHORS

Because traditional management theory does not work well in nonlinear and loosely structured situations or under conditions that require extraordinary commitment and performance, a great deal is at stake in developing a new and better-fitting theory. For this to happen, our metaphors for management, leadership, and schooling must change. Subsuming "instructional delivery system" as a tactical option under the more encompassing and strategic "learning community" is an important beginning. What would schools be like if community was indeed the metaphor of choice? That is the topic of the next chapter.

SOME REFLECTIONS

1. There are two views of where people fit into the planning process.

    (A) First emphasize ends by determining objectives first. Then emphasize ways by figuring out how objectives will be reached. And finally, emphasize means by identifying, training, placing, and supervising people.

    (B) First emphasize means by concentrating on people first, building them up, linking them to purposes, and helping them to be self-managing. Then emphasize ways by letting them figure out what to do and how to do it. And finally, emphasize ends by having them help decide on objectives that are consistent with purposes.

    Ask 10 people to carefully consider each of the two ways and then to distribute 10 points across the two to indicate which of the two approaches makes the most sense. If the views are considered to be equally sensible, have them assign each 5 points. If one view is thought to be always more sensible and the other never, have them assign 10 points to one and zero to the other. How would you distribute your 10 points?

REFERENCES

Deal, Terrence E., and Allan A. Kennedy. 1982. *Corporate Cultures.* Reading, MA: Addison-Wesley.

Deci, Edward L., and Richard M. Ryan. 1985. *Intrinsic Motivation and Self-Determinism in Human Behavior.* New York: Plenum Press.

Etzioni, Amitai. 1961. *A Comparative Analysis of Complex Organizations.* New York: Free Press.

Etzioni, Amitai. 1988. *The Moral Dimension: Toward a New Economics.* New York: Free Press.

Greene, David, and Mark R. Lepper. 1974. "How to Turn Play into Work," *Psychology Today* 8(4).

Habermas, Jurgen. 1987. *The Theory of Communicative Action. Vol. 2: Lifeworld and System: A Critique of Functionalist Reason.* Trans. T. McCarthy. Boston: Beacon Press.

Hayes, Robert H. 1985, November–December. "Strategic Planning—Forward in Reverse?" *Harvard Business Review.*

Heifetz, Ronald A. 1994. *Leadership without Easy Answers*. Cambridge, MA: Harvard University Press.

Kelly, Robert E. 1988, November–December. "In Praise of Followers," *Harvard Business Review*.

Lambert, Linda. 2002. "Toward a Deepened Theory of Constructivist Leadership," in Linda Lambert, Deborah Walker, Diane P. Zimmerman, Joanne E. Cooper, Morgan Dale Lambert, Mary E. Gardner, and Margaret Szabo, *The Constructivist Leader* (2nd ed.). New York: Teachers College Press.

March, James G. 1984. "How We Talk and How We Act: Administrative Theory and Administrative Life," in T. J. Sergiovanni and J. E. Corbally (Eds.), *Leadership and Organizational Culture* (pp. 18–36). Urbana: University of Illinois Press.

March, James G., and Herbert A. Simon. 1958. *Organizations*. New York: Wiley.

Mintzberg, Henry. 1979. *The Structuring of Organizations*. Englewood Cliffs, NJ: Prentice-Hall.

Peters, Tom. 1989a, July 25. "Structure vs. Spirit Battle Lines Are Drawn," *San Antonio Light*.

Peters, Tom. 1989b, January 24. "Business Can Learn from Military Strategy," *San Antonio Light*.

Peters, Thomas J., and Robert H. Waterman. 1982. *In Search of Excellence*. New York: Harper & Row.

Sergiovanni, Thomas J. 1987. *The Principalship: A Reflective Practice Perspective*. Boston: Allyn and Bacon.

Sergiovanni, Thomas J. 1990. *Value-Added Leadership: How to Get Extraordinary Performance in Schools*. New York: Harcourt Brace Jovanovich.

Sergiovanni, Thomas J. 1992. *Moral Leadership*. San Francisco: Jossey-Bass.

Sergiovanni, Thomas J. 2001. *Leadership: What's in It for Schools?* London: Routledge/Falmer.

Sergiovanni, Thomas J. 2005. *Strengthening the Heartbeat: Leading and Learning Together in Schools*. San Francisco: Jossey-Bass.

Sergiovanni, Thomas J. 2007. *Rethinking Leadership: A Collection of Articles* (2nd ed.). Thousand Oaks, CA: NSDC/Corwin Press.

Shils, Edward A. 1961. "Centre and Periphery," in *The Logic of Personal Knowledge: Essays Presented to Michael Polanyi*. London: Routledge and Kegan Paul.

Simon, Herbert A. 1957. *Administrative Behavior* (2nd ed.). New York: Free Press.

Staw, Barry. 1984. "Leadership and Persistence," in T. J. Sergiovanni and J. E. Corbally (Eds.), *Leadership and Organizational Culture*. Urbana: University of Illinois Press.

Thompson, Victor A. 1961. *Modern Organizations*. New York: Knopf.

Weick, Karl E. 1982. "Administering Education in Loosely Coupled Schools," *Phi Delta Kappan* 27(2), 673–676.

Weick, Karl E. 1986, December. "The Concept of Loose Coupling: An Assessment," *Organizational Theory Dialogue*.

5

THE SCHOOL
AS A MORAL COMMUNITY

*L*eadership is about many things. At the top of the list is protecting the character of schools. What most citizens want is for schools to reflect the values and beliefs that are meaningful in their lives. At the center of a school's character are ideas and commitments that function as a source of authority for what people do. This authority establishes the form and content of values and purposes that determines initiatives aimed at achieving the school's own destiny.

Community strikes at the heart of a school's character. It provides the substance for finding and making meaning and the framework for culture building. Think of community as a powerful antioxidant that can protect the school and help it achieve its goals. Communities are collections of people who come together because they share common commitments, ideas, and values. Schools can be understood as

- Learning communities where students and other members of the school community are committed to thinking, growing, and inquiring, and where learning is an attitude as well as an activity, a way of life as well as a process
- Collaborative communities where members are connected to each other for mutual benefit and to pursue common goals by establishing a sense of felt interdependence and mutual obligation
- Caring communities where members make a total commitment to each other and where the characteristics that define their relationships are moral in character
- Inclusive communities where economic, religious, cultural, and other differences are brought together into a mutually respective whole

- Inquiring communities where principals and teachers commit themselves to a spirit of collective inquiry as they reflect on their practice and search for solutions to the problems that they face
- Communities of responsibility where principal, teachers, and students feel morally obliged to embody shared commitments and agreed-upon ways of doing things as part of their roles in the school
- Communities of practice within which the individual practices of teachers are informally connected to each other in such a way that a single shared practice of teaching begins to emerge

The learning theme is deeply embedded in definitions of community in schools, creating several learning intersections where learning is particularly rapid and deep. One of these learning intersections for teachers is where collaborative cultures crafted and sponsored from above meet informal communities of practice that voluntarily bubble up from below. Without this bubbling up, collaboration runs the risk of being contrived (Hargreaves, 1989).

Another learning intersection that plays a key role in effective teaching and learning is where learning communities and caring communities come together to create the right blend of emphasis on personalization and caring that ensures students will be academically engaged in learning and that their learning efforts will be successful.

$\mathscr{T}$HE STORY OF COMMUNITY

To understand community, one has to understand its story. What is the story of community? How does this story differ from other stories about schools? What narratives does the story of community encompass? What stories compete with community for our attention? The story of community includes unique ways of thinking about connections. In most schools, connections are understood using the narrative of social contracts.* In schools that are striving to become communities, connections are understood using the narrative of social covenants (see Sergiovanni, 2000:59–68).

The major storyline in the narrative of social contracts involves a deal. Each of the parties to the contract gives up something to the other party in order to get something else back that is valued. In this narrative, teachers, parents, and others invest their talents and energy in the school and its children in exchange for certain benefits. Similarly, children endure the rituals of schooling in order to get the gold stars and praise they covet from teachers, the attention they want from their par-

*This discussion of social contracts and social covenants is drawn from T. J. Sergiovanni, "The Elementary School as a Community in a Diverse Society," William Charles McMillan III Lecture, Grosse Pointe Academy, Grosse Pointe Farms, MI, March 10, 1999. © T. J. Sergiovanni. See also Sergiovanni (2000).

ents, and the grades they need to be admitted to college. This social contract with the school is maintained as long as each of the parties gets what it wants. When teachers no longer receive their contracted benefits, they are less willing to invest in the school. And when students no longer get the benefits they seek, they are less willing to endure the rituals of schooling. This narrative is about calculations involving trades that offer incentives in exchange for compliance. Self-interest is presumed to be paramount, and "let's make a deal" is the order of the day.

The narrative of social contracts guides the practice of the principal of the Locke Elementary School. He promised the student body that if 2,000 books were read during the month of October, on Halloween night he would dress up like a witch and kiss a pig on the roof of the school building. This goal was achieved, and to the apparent delight of the students, the deed was done. The Locke principal believes that contracts are important motivational devices. He reasons that unless teachers, parents, and students get something tangible for their efforts, they will not be motivated. You can't expect managers to manage well, workers to be diligent, or football players to play hard unless there is something in it for them. So, the principal asks, how can we expect teachers to teach well, parents to parent well, students to learn well, and schools to improve themselves without incentives? How can we expect, for example, teachers and students to display proper behaviors without providing exhaustive lists of rules and regulations or outcome requirements that are linked to clear consequences for noncompliance?

SOCIAL COVENANTS

The major storyline in the narrative of social covenants is much less conditional. In this narrative, connections are more moral than calculated. Marriages, extended families, civic associations, faith communities, caring groups, and friendship networks are examples of affiliations characterized by covenantal relationships. In the narrative of social covenants, connections among people are created when they are connected to shared ideas and values. Once achieved, this binding of people to ideas and this bonding of people together forms a fabric of reciprocal roles, duties, and obligations that are internalized by members of the group. This is a fabric that cannot easily be torn apart when a person no longer likes the deal. This is a fabric that perseveres even when the fun is gone, when needs are not being met, and when self-interest must be sacrificed.

The narrative of social covenants guides the practice of the principal of the Rousseau Elementary School. She encourages teachers and students to develop together a framework of values and norms that informs how everyone in the school should lead their lives together. Connected to a larger vision of school purposes, critical values, and pedagogical beliefs, this covenant provides the basis for an ongoing discussion about how teachers, administrators, parents, and students can meet their commitments to each other and to the school. Students at Rousseau, for example, expect teachers to work hard, to be caring, and to teach well. Since relationships are reciprocal, teachers expect students to respond similarly. Students are given considerable latitude in deciding important things at Rousseau. They help decide how learning goals will be achieved and help make decisions about how they will spend their time. But decisions must be responsible ones that embody and enhance the school's covenant. Both teachers and students work hard to make reading fun and useful while also increasing mastery.

The Rousseau principal believes that when given the opportunity to make important decisions about school goals, purposes, values, and other important school matters, teachers and students will respond by being morally obliged to embody these decisions in their actions. Further, this binding together of school members to shared ideas and ideals provides a normative environment that encourages moral responsiveness. Social contracts, she reasons, have important roles to play in the real world—but so do social covenants. The school is the place, she argues, to learn about social covenants, to practice developing them, and to use them in a practical way to govern affairs.

In comparing the two narratives, Sacks (1997) argues that a social contract is maintained by the promise of gain or the threat of external force. A social covenant is maintained by loyalty, fidelity, kinship, sense of identity, obligation, duty, responsibility, and reciprocity. A social contract, he points out, is instrumental, serving important political and corporate ends that ideally are in the national interest. A social covenant, by contrast, is concerned with quite different institutions—families, communities, friendship groups, and voluntary associations are examples. Social covenants provide the basis for our civil society. A healthy civil society also serves the national interest by being the moral foundation, bedrock, and wellspring that provides cultural purposes, unity, and strength. Social contracts are at the core of what connects people in the world of formal organizations, and social covenants are at the core of what connects people in the world of social organizations. The former are rules based; the latter are norms based.

A THEORY OF COMMUNITY

Communities are organized around relationships and the felt interdependencies that nurture them (Blau and Scott, 1962). They create social structures that unify people and that bind them to a set of shared values and ideas. They are defined by their centers of values, sentiments, and beliefs that provide the needed conditions for creating a sense of "we" from "I."

In communities, members live their lives with others who have similar intentions. In ordinary organizations, relationships are constructed by others and become codified into a system of hierarchies, roles, and role expectations. Both ordinary organizations and communities must deal with issues of control, but instead of relying soley on external control measures, communities rely more on norms, purposes, values, professional socialization, collegiality, and natural interdependence. As the ties of community become established in schools, they become substitutes for formal systems of supervision and evaluation that are designed to make sure teachers are doing what they are supposed to. They become substitutes as well for the management and organizational schemes that seek to "coordinate" what teachers do and how they work together. Finally, they become substitutes for leadership itself.

The ties of community also redefine how empowerment and collegiality are understood. In ordinary organizations, empowerment is understood as having something to do with shared decision making, site-based management, and similar schemes. Within communities, empowerment focuses less on rights, discretion, and freedom, and more on commitments, obligations, and duties that people feel toward each other and toward the school. Collegiality in ordinary organizations results from administrative arrangements, such as variations of team teaching that force people to work together and team-building skills of principals. In communities, collegiality is something that comes from within. Community members are connected to each other because of felt interdependencies, mutual obligations, and other emotional and normative ties.

Community often means different things in different disciplines. Sociologists speak of the African American community, political scientists of the rural community, theologians of the spiritual community, and psychologists of the emotional community. To capture the spirit of these various uses, I define *community* as follows: Communities are collections of individuals who are bonded together because they find this relationship to be intrinsically meaningful and significant and who are together bound to a set of shared ideas and ideals. This binding and bonding is tight enough to transform the individuals from a collection of "I's" into a collective "we." As a we, members are part of a tightly knit web of meaningful relationships. This we usually shares a common place and over time comes to share common sentiments and traditions that are sustaining.

The theory of gemeinschaft and gesellschaft can help us to understand this definition and the forms it might take as schools become communities. *Gemeinschaft* translates to community, and *gesellschaft* to society. Writing in 1887, Ferdinand Tonnies (1957) used the terms to describe the shifting values and orientations that were taking place in society as we moved first from a hunting-and-gathering society, to an agricultural society, and then on to an industrial society. Each of the societal transformations he described resulted in a shift away from gemeinschaft toward gesellschaft—that is, away from a vision of life as a sacred community toward a more secular society. Although gemeinschaft and gesellschaft do not exist in pure form in the real world, both are metaphors that bring to mind two "ideal types," two different ways of thinking and living, two different types of cultures, and two alternative visions of life.

Tonnies's basic argument was that as society moves toward the gesellschaft end of the continuum, community values are replaced by contractual ones. Among any collection of people, social relationships do not just happen. Individuals decide to associate with each other, and the reasons are important. In gemeinschaft, individuals decide to relate to each other because doing so has its own intrinsic meaning and significance. There is no selfish goal or benefit in mind for any of the parties to the relationship. In gesellschaft, rational will is the motivating force. Individuals decide to relate to each other to reach some goal, to gain some benefit. Without this benefit, the relationship ends. In the first instance, the ties among people are thick and laden with symbolic meaning; they are moral ties. In the second instance, the ties among people are thin and instrumental; they are calculated ties.

The modern formal organization is an example of gesellschaft. Within the organization, relationships are formal and distant, having been prescribed by rules and expectations. Circumstances are evaluated by universal criteria as embodied in policies, rules, and protocols. Acceptance is conditional. The more a person cooperates with the organization and achieves for the organization, the more likely she or he will be accepted. Relationships are competitive. Those who achieve more are valued more by the organization. Not all concerns of members are legitimate; legitimate concerns are bound by rules rather than needs. Subjectivity is frowned upon and rationality is prized. Self-interest prevails.

These same characteristics often undergird our present policies with respect to how schools are organized, how teaching and learning take place, how students are evaluated, how supervision is practiced, how principals and students are motivated and rewarded, and what leadership is and how it works. Most will agree that gesellschaft values make sense in getting such formal organizations as a corporation, bank, army, research university, and hospital to work effectively. But applying the same values to the family, rural church, neighborhood, social club, and school, however, raises important epistemological questions. Are gesellschaft values appropriate? If they are not and we use them anyway, do we run the risk of creating standards of practice and norms of behavior that do not fit schools?

Gemeinschaft

Gemeinschaft, according to Tonnies (1957), exists in three forms: community of relationships, of place, and of mind. Community of *relationships* characterizes the special kinds of connections among people that create a unity that is similar to that found in families and other closely knit collections of people. Community of *place* characterizes sharing a common habitat or locale. This type of sharing with others for sustained periods of time creates a special identity and a shared sense of belonging that connects people together in special ways. Community of *mind* emerges from the binding of people to common goals, shared values, and shared conceptions of being and doing. Together, the three forms represent webs of meaning that tie people together by creating a special sense of belonging and a strong common identity.

As schools struggle to become communities, they need to address questions such as the following: What can be done to increase the sense of connections, neighborliness, and collegiality among the faculty of a school? How can the faculty become more of a professional community where everyone cares about each other and helps each other to grow, to learn together, and to lead together? What kinds of relationships need to be cultivated with parents that will enable them to be included in this emerging community? How can the web of relationships that exist among teachers and between teachers and students be defined so that they embody community? How can teaching and learning settings be arranged so that they are more like a family? How can the school, as a collection of families, be more like a neighborhood? What are the shared values and commitments that enable the school to become a community of mind? How will these values and commitments become practical standards that can guide the lives community members want to lead, what community members learn and how, and how community members treat each other? What are the patterns of mutual obligations and duties that emerge in the school as community is achieved?

Although not cast in stone, community understandings have enduring qualities. These understandings are taught to new members, celebrated in customs and rituals, and embodied as standards that govern life in the community. Furthermore, they are resilient enough to survive the passage of members through the community over time. As suggested by Bellah and colleagues (1985), enduring understandings create a fourth form of community—community of *memory*. In time, communities of relationships, of place, and of mind become communities of memory by providing members with memories of common images and common learnings. Being a part of a community of memory sustains us when times are tough, connects us when we are not physically present, and provides us with a history for creating sense and meaning.

*T*HE IMPORTANCE OF RELATIONSHIPS

The web of relationships that stand out in communities are different in kind than those found in corporations, banks, and other formal organizations. They are more special, meaningful, and personalized. They result in a quality of connectedness that has moral overtones. In addition, because of these overtones, members feel a special sense of obligation to look out for each other.

It is generally acknowledged that quality of relationships is an important ingredient in the makeup of a good school. A report issued by the Institute for Education and Transformation (1992) at the Claremont Graduate School, for example, points to quality of relationships and other relationship themes as the critical leverage point for school improvement. The quality of relationships determines the quality of the school. Or, in the words of Claremont president John Maguire, "If the relationships are wrong between teachers and students, for whatever reason, you can restructure until the cows come home, but transformation won't take place" (Rothman, 1992:1).

The Claremont researchers spent 18 months studying four culturally diverse schools—two elementary, one middle, and one high school. They interviewed students, teachers, custodians, secretaries, cafeteria workers, parents, and others inside the schools. More than 24,000 pages of data were collected and analyzed. "Our data strongly suggest that the heretofore identified *problems* of schooling (lowered achievement, higher dropout rates, and problems in the teaching profession) are rather *consequences* of much deeper and more fundamental problems" (Institute, 1992:11). These deeper, more fundamental problems pointed to seven major issues that surfaced repeatedly throughout the study. Relationship themes are embedded in each of these issues, with relationships themselves being considered most important. The seven issues, as summarized from the institute's report, are presented here:

1. *Relationships.* Participants feel the crisis inside schools is directly linked to human relationships. Most often mentioned were relationships between teachers and students. Where positive things about the schools are noted, they usually involve reports of individuals who care, listen, understand, respect others and are honest, open and sensitive. Teachers report their best experiences in school are those where they connect with students and are able to help them in some way. They also report, however, there is precious little time during the day to seek out individual students. . . . Students of color, especially older students, often report that their teachers, school staff and other students neither like nor understand them. Many teachers also report they do not always understand students ethnically different than themselves. When relationships in schools are poor, fear, name calling, threats of or incidents of violence, as well as a sense of depression and hopelessness exist. This theme was prominently stated by participants and so deeply connected to all other themes in the data that it is believed this may be one of the two most central issues in solving the crisis inside schools.

2. *Race, Culture and Class.* A theme which ran through every other issue, like that of relationships, was that of race, culture and class. This is a theme with much debate and very little consensus. Many students of color and some Euro-American students perceive schools to be racist and prejudiced, from the staff to the curriculum. Some students doubt the very substance of what is being taught. . . . Teachers are tremendously divided on such issues. Some are convinced that students are right about racism, others are not. . . . Students have an intense interest in knowing about one another's culture but receive very little of that knowledge from home or school.

3. *Values.* There are frequently related conversations in the U.S. that suggest people of color and/or people living in economically depressed areas hold different basic values than others, and that it is these differences which create conflicts in schools and society. While cultural differences clearly do exist in the expression or prioritization of values, our data hold no evidence that people inside schools have significantly different fundamental values. Our data suggest that parents, teachers, students, staff and administrators of all ethnicities and classes value and desire education, honesty, integrity, beauty, care, justice, truth, courage and meaningful hard work. Participants' writings and transcripts of discussions are filled with references to basic values. However, very little time is spent in classrooms discussing these issues, and a number of restrictions exist against doing

so. In the beginning of our research many participants initially assumed other participants held different values. The more we talked, the more this assumption was challenged. Students desire a network of adults (parents and teachers) with whom they can "really talk about important things," and want to have these conversations about values with one another.

4. *Teaching and Learning*. Students, especially those past fifth grade, frequently report that they are bored in school and see little relevance of what is taught to their lives and their futures. Teachers feel pressure to teach what is mandated and sometimes doubt its appropriateness for their students. Teachers also are often bored by the curriculum they feel they must teach. . . . Students from all groups, remedial and advanced, high school to elementary, desire both rigor and fun in their schoolwork. They express enthusiasm about learning experiences that are complex but understandable, full of rich meanings and discussions of values, require their own action, and those about which they feel they have some choice.

5. *Safety*. Related to disconnected relationships and not knowing about one another's differences is the issue of safety. Very few participants on campus or parents feel schools are safe places. This is particularly true in our middle school and high school. Teachers, students and staff fear physical violence. The influence of drugs, gangs and random violence is felt by students. Students feel physically safest inside classrooms and least safe in large gatherings between classes or traveling to or from school.

6. *Physical Environment*. Students want schools that reflect order, beauty, space and contain rich materials and media. The desire for clean, aesthetically pleasing and physically comfortable spaces is expressed by all. The food served to students is a persistent complaint. Many would like foods more typical of their homes and home cultures. The lack of any significant personal space such as lockers is problematic to students and also leads to feelings of being devalued. The depressed physical environment of many schools, especially those in lower socioeconomic areas, is believed by participants to reflect society's lack of priority for these children and their education.

7. *Despair, Hope, and the Process of Change*. Many participants feel a hopelessness about schools that is reflected in the larger society and in the music and art of our youth. Paradoxically, hope seemed to emerge following honest dialogues about our collective despair. Participants are anxious for change and willing to participate in change they perceive as relevant. We have strong indications that change inside schools might best be stimulated through participatory processes. In these self-driven research processes, participants came to openly discuss their hopes and dreams. Through this process, we understood there were shared common values around which we could begin to imagine a more ideal school. (12–16)

The problematic relationships described in the report are the kinds of relationships that seem inevitably to evolve whenever schools are viewed as formal organizations. Furthermore, it is not likely that relationships will improve in schools unless this view is abandoned in favor of community.

THE PATTERN VARIABLES

Sociologist Talcott Parsons (1951) used Tonnies's (1957) concepts of gemeinschaft and gesellschaft to describe different types of social relationships. He argued that any relationship can be described as a pattern that comprises five pairs of variables that represent choices between alternative value orientations. The parties to this relationship, for example, have to make decisions as to how they will orient themselves to each other. When taken together, these decisions represent a pattern giving rise to Parsons's now famous "pattern variables."

> affective–affective-neutrality
> particularism–universalism
> diffuseness–specificity
> ascription–achievement
> collective orientation–self-orientation

In schools, for example, principals, teachers, and students have to make decisions about how they will perform their respective roles in relationship to others. Teachers have to decide: Will relationships with students be similar to a professional expert who treats students as if they were clients (affective-neutrality)? Or, will relationships be similar to a parent, with students treated as if they were family members (affective)? Will students be given equal treatment in accordance with uniform standards, rules, and regulations (universalism)? Or, will students be treated more preferentially and individually (particularism)? Will role relationships and job descriptions narrowly define specific topics for attention and discussion (specificity)? Or, will relationships be considered unbounded by roles and thus more inclusive and holistic (diffuseness)? Will students have to earn the right to be regarded as "good" and to maintain their standing in the school (achievement)? Or, will students be accepted completely, simply because they have enrolled in the school (ascription)? Do we decide that a certain distance needs to be maintained for professional interests and concerns to remain uncompromised (self-orientation)? Or, do we view ourselves as part of a teacher–student "we" that compels us to work intimately with students in identifying common interests, concerns, and standards for decision making (collective orientation)?

In addition to Parsons's five variables, two other "polar opposites" are worth considering: substantive and instrumental, and altruistic love and egocentric love. Substantive and instrumental speak to the issue of means and ends. In organizations a clear distinction is made between means and ends communicating an instrumental view of human nature and society. In communities these distinctions are blurred; ends remain ends, but means are also considered ends.

Altruistic love and egocentric love address the issue of motivation. Like Tonnies, Rousseau (1991) believes that it is the motives that bring people together that are key in determining whether community will be authentically achieved. To Rousseau, it is altruistic love that is the deciding factor. Altruistic love is an expression of selfless concern for others that stems from devotion or obligation. It is more cultural than psychological. Egocentric love, more characteristic of organizations, is self-gratifying. Relationships are implicit contracts for the mutual exchange of psychological satisfactions.

Taken together, the seven pairs of variables portray different ties for connecting people to each other and for connecting them to their work. In school as community,

- Relationships are both close and informal.
- Individual circumstances count.
- Acceptance is unconditional.
- Relationships are cooperative.
- Concerns of members are unbounded and therefore considered legitimate as long as they reflect needs.
- Subjectivity is okay.
- Emotions are legitimate.
- Sacrificing one's self-interest for the sake of other community members is common.
- Members associate with each other because doing so is valuable as an end in itself.
- Knowledge is valued and learned for its own sake, not just as a means to get something or go somewhere.
- Children are accepted and loved because that's the way one treats community members.
- The bonding of relationship ties helps the school become a community of relationships and a community of place.
- The binding of idea ties helps the school become a community of mind.

In time, these collective sentiments bring people together as a community of memory and sustain them even when they become separated from each other.

ƒINDING THE RIGHT BALANCE

It would be a mistake to take an either-or stance when selecting a framework for understanding schools. Yet, we need to decide which theory should dominate which spheres of our lives. Most everyone will agree that the family, the extended family, and the neighborhood should be dominated by gemeinschaft values. The corporation, the research laboratory, and the court system, however, might well lean more toward gesellschaft values. In modern times, the school has been solidly ensconced in the gesellschaft camp with unhappy results. It's time that the school was moved from the gesellschaft side of the ledger to the gemeinschaft.

$\mathcal{B}$ONDING AND BRIDGING

Community theory is not without its problems. Although designed to bring people together, its dimensions may comprise the same ingredients that create systems of "blood" that divide people (see, e.g., Sergiovanni, 1992). The hard reality is that community can be helpful or harmful. By its very nature, community is both inclusive and exclusive. It can bring some people together with good results while at the same time leaving others out. Further, community can exaggerate differences with others, causing fragmentation, disengagement, and conflict.* These problems are less likely to develop when both bonding community and bridging community are working together in a school.

Bonding and bridging (Putnam, 2000) are ways in which schools provide the community connections that students and their teachers need. Bonding connections look inward and are tilted toward exclusion, while bridging connections look outward and are tilted toward inclusion. It is possible for schools that are becoming bonding communities to be so concerned with developing common frameworks that commonness becomes synonymous with sameness. Should this happen, then the strong norms of community may well coerce everyone to think alike and be alike as the price of admission. Community as the antidote to connections problems in society, then, becomes the poison (Sergiovanni, 1992:141). This possibility is not likely to occur, however, when community is authentic. Community has many meanings. But at root it is the Latin *communis* and the Latin *communitas*, which provide the themes for defining authentic community. *Communis* means common, and *communitas* means fellowship. Thus, say Carey and Frohnen (1998):

> a true community, one that lives up to its name, is one in which members share something in common—something important enough to give rise to fellowship or friendship and to sustain it. There may be many kinds of communities with varying ends or goals. But each must form around characteristics, experiences, practices, and beliefs that are important enough to bind the members to one another, such that they are willing to sacrifice for one another as "fellows" or sharers of a common fate. (1–2)

Communis and *communitas* make the membership of a community as a whole more than the sum of its individual members.

When individuals (students, teachers, parents) are bound to shared ideas, values, beliefs, and frameworks, bonds of fellowship emerge that provide a moral climate that empowers the membership as a whole. In schools this fellowship has two dimensions: a sense of collegiality among faculty that resembles a community of practice and an Aristotelian view of leadership that involves a moral commitment to care for and nurture one's colleagues. For students, the image is a learning community characterized by high levels of caring and civility and of cooperative learning.

*This section is drawn from T. J. Sergiovanni, *Leadership: What's in It for Schools?* (London: Routledge/Falmer, 2001), pp. 66–67.

Aristotle (1962) argues that the motives for fellowship can be pleasantness, usefulness, or goodness. Community members enjoy each other, find association with each other to be mutually beneficial, and feel morally obliged to accept and look after each other. Though all three motives may be present in *communitas*, fellowship cannot exist in an authentic sense without the moral motive. Durkheim (1960) cites Rousseau to make this point: A community is

> a moral entity having specific qualities distinct from those of the individual beings which compose it, somewhat as chemical compounds have properties that they owe to none of their elements. If the aggregation resulting from these vague relationships really formed a social body, there would be a kind of common sensorium that would outlive the correspondence of all the parts. Public good and evil would not be merely the sum of individual good and evil, as in a simple aggregation, but would lie in the relationship that unites them. It would be greater than that sum, and public well-being would not be the result of the happiness of individuals, but rather its source. (82)

The last phrase of Rousseau's quote, that public well-being is the source of happiness and not the result, makes another point. Communities embody civic virtue—the willingness of individuals to sacrifice their self-interest on behalf of the common good. And this virtue, once established, is the reason why communities are so powerful in uniting parents, teachers, and students in common purpose. This common purpose provides the focus that contributes to school effectiveness (see, e.g., Bryk and Driscoll, 1988; Hill, Foster, and Gendler, 1990; Hill and Celio, 1998; Sergiovanni, 1994, 2000).

WHY IS COMMUNITY IMPORTANT?

Community provides the theory and the framework for schools to use to strengthen their commitment and efforts toward improving connections, coherence, capacity, commitment, and collaboration. Each of these five is a powerful contributor to improving student learning and student development. They are summarized here.

Connections

In leading a successful school, connections are everything. If students are not connected to the school and its goals, very little learning will take place. Connections are important to teachers as well. Teachers who are not connected will not be able to provide the commitment and know-how needed for students to be successful.

Personalization is an important way to get students connected. Sebring and Bryk (1996), for example, found that personalization combined with academic press were related to improving student learning. They measured personalization by asking students special questions about their relationship with teachers ranging from "whether students believed their teachers knew them and noticed that they were absent, to questions about whether students felt that teachers cared about them and listened to their concerns. Other questions dealt with whether their teachers noticed if students were having trouble learning and whether teachers were willing to help students with personal problems" (7). Of particular interest was whether teachers know their students, have confidence in their ability, help students catch up after an absence, and avoid "putting students down" in class. Sebring and Bryk defined academic press as schools expecting students "to work on intellectually challenging tasks, to come to class prepared, and to complete all homework assignments" (9). Students report that teachers expect them to do well, provide extra work and help when needed, and praise them when they do well.

From their research, Nel Noddings (1992) and more recently Angela Valenzuela (1999) have concluded that a prerequisite for students to care about schooling and the learning that goes with it was for them to be cared for by at least one adult in their school. Noddings believes that caring is more likely to occur in school when continuity is present. In her words,

> To meet the challenge to care in schools, we must plan for continuity:
>
> 1. *Continuity in purpose.* It should be clear that schools are centers of care—that the first purpose is caring for each other. This includes helping all students to address essential issues of human caring and, also, to develop their particular capacities in specialized areas of care.
> 2. *Continuity of school residence.* Students should stay in one school building long enough to acquire a sense of belonging. Although I would prefer smaller schools, it may be possible to create a feeling of community in larger schools if community is made a priority. Children should be in residence more than three, and preferably for six, years.
> 3. *Continuity of teachers and students.* Teachers, whether singly or in teams, should stay with students (by mutual consent) for three or more years.
> 4. *Continuity in curriculum.* The idea is to show our care and respect for the full range of human capacities by offering a variety of equally prestigious programs of specialization, each embedded in a universal curriculum organized around essential themes of caring. (1992: 72–73)*

The National Association of Secondary School Principals report *Breaking Ranks II: Strategies for Leading High School Reform,* summarized in Exhibit 2.1 (pp. 36–38), includes a number of recommendations themed to personalization and its twin connections including the following:

- Creating smaller units within large high schools as a way to banish anonymity

*Reprinted by permission of the publisher. From Nel Noddings, *The Challenge to Care in Schools: An Alternative Approach to Education,* 2nd ed. (New York: Teachers College Press, 2005), pp. 72–73. © 2005 by Teachers College, Columbia University. All rights reserved.

- Having teachers be responsible for no more than 90 students during a term, thus allowing them to give greater attention to student needs
- Providing each student with a personal plan for progress that is frequently reviewed to ensure that students' academic and social needs are being met and that allows students to take part in planning and monitoring their own learning
- Assigning a personal adult advocate to each school to help personalize the educational experience
- Ensuring that teachers convey a sense of caring
- Developing scheduling and student grouping patterns that help students succeed
- Engaging student families as partners

Coherence

Connections emphasize the bringing together of students, teachers, and others in a common commitment to school purposes so that they are meaningfully engaged in the work of the school. Coherence, a cousin of connections, emphasizes the bringing together of a set of interrelated programs that are guided by a common framework for curriculum, instruction, and assessment and that are pursued over a sustained period (Newmann et al., 2001).

Both instructional coherence and organizational coherence are important. The first has to do with bringing together in some meaningful way the various components of teaching and learning, and organizational coherence has to do with providing the necessary structures and programs that support teaching and learning. Newmann, Smith, Allensworth, and Bryk (2001) define instructional coherence as a set of interrelated programs guided by a common framework. This framework includes core beliefs about, expectations for, and key examples for guiding curriculum, instruction, assessment, and learning climate. Below are examples of survey items that Newmann and his colleagues (2001:303) use to measure instructional coherence:

- You can see real continuity from one program to another in this school.
- Once we start a new program, we follow up to make sure that it's working.
- Curriculum, instruction, and learning materials are well coordinated across the different grade levels at this school.
- There is consistency in curriculum, instruction, and learning materials among teachers in the same grade level at this school.
- Most changes introduced at this school help promote the school's goals for learning.

When instructional coherence is present, teachers expect one another to implement the framework, decide on professional development topics that support the framework, plan assessments that match the framework, and prepare and share lessons that teach the framework. This strong and disciplined focus is an important contributor to instructional coherence. Instructional coherence is related to student achievement as measured by test score gains over time and other indicators.

Leadership from the principal plays an important role in strengthening instructional coherence. Newmann and his colleagues point out that in their research "stronger instructional program coherence was rooted in a principal's decision to adopt or develop a schoolwide instructional program framework and to make it a priority" (2001:306). Their recommendation is that "school principals should focus their improvement plans, professional development, and acquisition of instructional materials on a few core educational goals pursued through a common instructional framework" (315).

The instructional coherence question does not end here. We have to worry about the impact such coherence has on the principal's ability to lead and the teachers' ability to teach. Both leadership and teaching require a fair amount of discretion. In a large sense, when there is no discretion there can be no leadership. And where there is no discretion there can be no responsive teaching.

But we do not have to choose sides. There are vast differences between standardizing strategies that seek instructional and other kinds of coherence and hyper-rationality. State-mandated teacher evaluation systems that rely on lengthy lists of teaching behaviors that must be demonstrated by the teacher under observation are an example. By and large teachers willingly demonstrate required behaviors when they are being observed. But what happens when the evaluators are not there? As you can imagine, when no one is looking teachers typically teach in ways that make sense to them. Newmann et al. (2001) point out, "Strong school-level leadership is central to the development of stronger instructional program coherence, but coherence achieved by administrative fiat is of questionable value when it suppresses the development of equally essential supports for learning, such as teachers' professional community and shared ownership of an instructional program" (311).

Perhaps the answer is finding the right balance between a bureaucratic version of coherence that relies on *control* and a more professional version of coherence that relies on *commitment* (Rowan, 1990). But this balance cannot be an arbitrary cut of a deck of cards. A school's coherence strategy needs to have a clear identity and must be implemented with spirit if it is to work. Control strategies help ensure that the routines of learning get deliberate and systematic attention, while commitment strategies help ensure that authentic learning content and processes are mastered.

In sum, communities cannot exist without a meaningful sense of coherence. Finding the right balance between individual discretion and community coherence is important for successful leadership.

Capacity

In successful schools community and capacity go together. Learning communities rise or fall based on the extent to which they remain adaptive. And remaining adaptive requires a continuous commitment to learning. Investing time, resources, and energy in teacher learning, for example, ensures that future capacity will be assured. There is no doubt that school-level variables are important in promoting student learning. As a result of his research and the research of others Marzano (2000) identifies eight school-level factors that contribute to student achievement.* The factors, in order of their influence on student achievement, are these: opportunities for students to learn, the amount of time students spend learning, monitoring of student progress, providing a reasonable amount of pressure for students to achieve, parental involvement, a supportive school climate, leadership, and cooperation. But things may not be as they seem. Leadership plays by different rules. It has, for example, many lives. One of its lives is to stand alone as a factor that contributes directly to student achievement. In its other lives, however, leadership serves to fuel and enhance school-level and teacher-level variables in ways that help these variables influence student achievement.

Marzano (2000) notes, for example, that as a group the school-level variables account for about 7 percent of the variance influencing student achievement. Teacher-level variables such as instructional strategies, curriculum design, and classroom management accounted for about 13 percent of the variance. Student-level variables—home atmosphere, prior knowledge, motivation, aptitude, and interest—account for 80 percent of the variance, with home atmosphere having the most powerful effect on student achievement.

Compared to student-level variables the effects of school-level and teacher-level variables seem not to count very much. But they do. Marzano notes, for example, that "the finding that schools account for only 10 percent of the difference in student achievement translates into a percentile gain of about 23 points. That is, the average student who attends a 'good' school will have a score that is 23 percentile points higher than a student who attends a poor school. From this perspective schools definitely can make a difference in student achievement" (cited in Association for Supervision and Curriculum Development, 2003:1). When we take the indirect effects leadership has on teachers, students, and school-level variables into account, then we get a different picture. Leadership emerges as a powerful force that provides the conditions and support schools' need to succeed and teachers' need to be effective. With the right kind of leadership, teacher effects on student achievement are likely to be higher.

In summary, Marzano's work and that of others strongly suggest that leadership is often less visible in practice and thus less likely to show its impact statistically. Nonetheless, leadership is an important precursor to success (Marzano, 2003), and that is good news for principals. Virtually every variable that

---

*This discussion of capacity is drawn from Chapter 5 of T. J. Sergiovanni, *Strengthening the Heartbeat: Leading and Learning Together in Schools* (San Francisco: Jossey-Bass, 2005). Used by permission of John Wiley & Sons, Inc.

affects student achievement in school is itself affected by leadership either from the principal or from others. As leadership grows in quality and quantity, school effects and teacher effects become better able to influence student learning and school achievement in positive ways. Clearly every success that teachers have depends on increasing their learning. Thus building the capacity of teachers becomes one of the most powerful levers that principals have in improving learning for students. Any effort designed to improve student quality as a means to increase student learning must also include leadership in its equation. Kent Peterson (2002) concludes, "For schools to be effective centers of learning strong principals are critical for shaping the culture and the climate" (6).

Commitment

Commitment is both a cause and an effect. In a moral community commitment is strong because of the bonds that develop among people and the binding that they share. The greater is their commitment to shared purposes and frameworks, the more obligated do members feel to embody them in their practice. The result is even more commitment. As this commitment grows connections to the school and its purposes become more covenantal than contractual. As pointed out earlier in this chapter, covenants are more than agreements, they are promises. Promises play an important role in the functioning of moral communities. They imply certain mutually held actions and commitments that are considered obligatory. Unlike legal documents and other formal agreements that spell out all of the technical details, covenants are planted within the hearts of people, bind them together morally, and obligate them morally to the conditions of the covenant. Cultural connections and covenantal relationships are the foundational pillars of collaborative cultures that function as communities of responsibility.

Collaboration

One characteristic of successful schools is their ability to organize around and to effectively use collaborative cultures. These cultures are the backbone of dynamic learning communities that bring leadership and learning together. This joining of the two is the strategy not only for the day by day work of schools but for launching change initiatives and for continuous improvement. Despite the importance of collaboration, in most schools teaching is regarded as an individual practice. Thus, thirty teachers working in the same school are thought of as a collection of thirty individual practices. This reality is in strong contrast to what is found in most other professions. We should be concerned because "competence in any organization can rarely be traced to a single individual. Organizational competence typically resides in the relationships, norms, memories, habits, and collective skills of a network of people" (Wilkins, 1989:41). Organizational competence is the sum of everything everybody knows and uses that leads to increased learning (see, e.g., Stewart, 1997). This competence is measured not only by what we know, but by how much of it we know, how widely it is distributed, how broad is its source, how much of it is applied collectively, and how much of it is generated by cooperation with others.*

Too often competence is divided among different people. The consequence of this fragmentation is to dilute what each individual knows and to ignore the collective intelligence that schools might otherwise have. There may be lots of smart people in schools, but we will not have smart schools unless their knowledge is aggregated.

When collaborative cultures work, everyone in the school is part of a role that defines his or her obligations and everyone is part of a reciprocal role relationship that spells out mutual obligations. Reciprocal role relations exist within role sets that are the seeds for the bubbling up of informal communities of practice in a school and the trickling down of collaborative cultures. When informal communities of practice become part of collaborative cultures we find the balance we need between individual autonomy and collaborative work.

Communities of practice bubble up as a result of felt needs of teachers to cooperate. Collaborative cultures are more deliberate, having been initiated and supported by leaders from above. They differ from communities of practice in that they become institutionalized as part of the formal norm system of the school and as part of its organizational structure. When communities are working right, the two come together as one, creating a strong bond of people committed to working together toward goals and purposes that they share. When the two come together the foundation of schools becoming authentic communities with moral overtones is being laid.

In a way communities of practice serve individual needs and intents. Institutionalized collaborative cultures, by contrast, build on the personal strength of individuals and transfer this improved individual capacity into aggregated organizational competence that serves the school's goals. Richard Elmore (2002) refers to benefits that serve individual interests and that build their capacity on their own terms as a private good. By contrast, aggregated organizational competence that serves school purposes is a public good. Together they create a powerful force of capacity and commitment that helps develop more effective pathways to student learning.

PATHWAYS TO STUDENT LEARNING

Experts agree that high student engagement in the life and world of the school is related to high student achievement as measured by grades, standardized test scores, and other more powerful indicators of learning such as learning exhibitions and projects. The rule here is that the right educational context antecedents equals high engagement, and high engagement equals high levels of student learning.

But what are the educational context antecedents? What aspects of the school and what aspects of the classroom promote student engagement? In their review

---

*This discussion of collaborative cultures is drawn from T. J. Sergiovanni, "Collaborative Cultures and Communities of Practice," *Principal Leadership* 5(1). © 2004 T. J. Sergiovanni.

of the literature Fredricks, Blumenfeld, and Paris (2004) group student engagement antecedents into two main categories as follows:

1. *School-level antecedents,* which include choice, a focus on clear and consistent goals, small size that enables students to be deeply involved in the life of the school, opportunities for developmentally appropriate involvement of students in school policy and management, opportunities for teachers, for students, and for teachers and students to collaborate with each other, structures and arrangements that encourage shared responsibility and commitment to shared goals, opportunities to care for others and to be cared for by others, and serious academic work that results in the development of artifacts and products for learning. "Using the National Educational Longitudinal Study, Lee and Smith (1993, 1995) found that students in schools with more elements of communal organization showed higher engagement and greater gains in engagement over time" (Fredricks, Blumenfeld, and Paris, 2004:73).

2. *Classroom-level antecedents* include high levels of both academic and interpersonal support. This finding matches the research of Sebring and Bryk (1996:7–10), who found that "academic press" and "personalization" together were related to improved student learning. Neither alone was able to do the job. One hallmark of intellectual quality in classrooms is serious and deep engagement in learning. Newmann points out that this engagement is more likely "in classrooms where the tasks (a) are authentic; (b) provide opportunities for students to assume ownership of their conception, execution, and evaluation; (c) provide opportunities for collaboration; (d) permit diverse forms of talents; and (e) provide opportunities for fun" (Newmann, 1991; Newmann, Wehlage, and Lamborn, 1992).

Disengagement, lack of connections, and other manifestations of alienation stand in the way of creating the kinds of schools we want and the learning environments students need to achieve at high levels. That is the problem. But research and informed practice in schools suggest that this problem can be overcome. Every one of the antecedents to high student engagement discussed here is encouraged by the presence of community. This presence, in turn, strengthens the antecedents. *As community grows the antecedents grow, and as the antecedents grow community grows.* Cardinal rule for anyone who is serious about school reform is to embrace the concept of community as the metaphor for schooling.

$\mathcal{S}$OME REFLECTIONS

1. Give examples of a learning intersection being created by the bringing together of collaborative community and communities of practice.

How true are the following statements in your department, grade level, team, or school?

1. *The Principle of Maximization.* We learn as much from our failures as we do our successes.

Never		Sometimes		Always
1	2	3	4	5

Give examples: _____

2. *The Principle of Continuous Learning.* We don't wait for a time to learn but are continuously learning. For us learning is an ongoing process and not an event.

Never		Sometimes		Always
1	2	3	4	5

Give examples: _____

3. *The Principle of Dispersion.* We share what we learn with others. We see to it that knowledge finds its way to the teachers or units that need it the most.

Never		Sometimes		Always
1	2	3	4	5

Give examples: _____

4. *The Principle of Craft Knowledge.* Designated leaders assume that those of us who are closest to the classroom and its work are often in the best position to know about teaching and learning. Competence is an important entitlement to leadership regardless of one's position in the school. And craft knowledge plays a key role in building competence.

Never		Sometimes		Always
1	2	3	4	5

Give examples: _____

5. *The Principle of Expansion.* We are on the watch for what we can learn and use from those outside of our unit or school. We pay particular attention to all we can learn from other schools and from outside experts.

Never		Sometimes		Always
1	2	3	4	5

Give examples: _____

6. *The Principle of Collaboration.* We take every opportunity to collaborate with each other.

Never		Sometimes		Always
1	2	3	4	5

Give examples: _____

7. *The Principle of Professionalism.* We believe that continuous learning is a professional virtue. We believe that we are obligated to embody this virtue in our practice.

Never		Sometimes		Always
1	2	3	4	5

Give examples: _____

f i g u r e **5.1**   **Hallmarks of a Learning Community Inventory**

Source: The Hallmarks of Learning Community Inventory is drawn from *Strengthening the Heartbeat: Leading and Learning Together in Schools* (pp. 132–133) by T. J. Sergiovanni, 2005, San Francisco: Jossey-Bass. This material is used by permission of John Wiley & Sons, Inc. For a similar list see Henry Mintzberg, Bruce Ahlstrand, and Joseph Lampel, *Strategy Safari: A Guided Tour Through the Wilds of Strategic Management* (New York: Free Press, 1998), pp. 214–215.

2. Check out the phrase "contrived collegiality" in Andrew Hargreaves's work. Would you say that collegiality is contrived in your school all of the time, most of the time, some of the time, never? Give examples.

3. In the discussion of gemeinschaft, it was noted that as schools strive to become communities they need to address several questions including "What can be done to increase the sense of connections, neighborliness, and collegiality among the faculty of a school?" Alone, or with a colleague or two, respond to these questions and share your thoughts with others in your class or school.

4. At the point where communities of practice bubble up and collaborative cultures trickle down, learning communities emerge. Learning communities are good at maximizing their learning. They learn from both successes and failures. They are good at continuous learning and at dispersing what they know, especially to places where it is most needed. Learning communities have faith in the craft knowledge and wisdom of those closest to the classroom. They are on constant lookout for new learning opportunities as ways to expand what they know and can do. They believe in collaboration and view learning as a professional obligation. How does your school measure up to these hallmarks? Use the Hallmarks of a Learning Community Inventory in Figure 5.1 to find out. Be sure to provide examples and to share your perceptions with a colleague.

*R*EFERENCES

Aristotle. 1962. *Nicomachean Ethics.* Trans. M. Ostwald. Indianapolis: Bobbs-Merrill.

Association for Supervision and Curriculum Development. 2003, Winter. "An 'Insider's' View of ASCD: What's behind ASCD's What Works in Schools Program." *Associate News.*

Bellah, Robert N., Richard Madsen, William M. Sullivan, Ann Swidler, and Steven M. Tipton. (1985). *Habits of the Heart: Individualism and Commitment in American Life.* New York: Harper & Row.

Blau, Peter M., and W. Richard Scott. 1962. *Formal Organizations: A Comparative Approach.* San Francisco: Chandler.

Bryk, Anthony S., and M. E. Driscoll. 1988. *The School as Community: Theoretical Foundations, Contextual Influences and Consequences for Teachers and Students.* Madison, WI: National Center for Effective Secondary Schools.

Carey, George W., and Bruce Frohnen (Eds.). 1998. *Community and Tradition: Conservative Perspectives on the American Experience.* Lanham, MD: Rowman & Littlefield.

Durkheim, Emile. 1960. "Rousseau's Social Contract," in *Montesquieu and Rosseau: Forerunners of Sociology* (pp. 65–138). Trans. R. Manheim. Ann Arbor: University of Michigan Press.

Elmore, Richard. 2002. *Bridging the Gap between Standards and Achievement: The Imperative for Professional Development in Education.* Washington, DC: Albert Shanker Institute.

Fredricks, Jennifer A., Phyllis C. Blumenfeld, and Alison H. Paris. 2004, Spring. "School Engagement: Potential of the Concept, State of the Evidence," *Review of Educational Research* 74(1), 59–109.

Hargreaves, Andrew. 1989. Contrived collegiality and the culture of teaching. Presentation at the annual meeting of the Canadian Society for the Study of Education, Quebec City, Canada.

Hill, Paul T., and Mary Beth Celio. 1998. *Fixing Urban Schools.* Washington, DC: Brookings Institution Press.

Hill, Paul T., Gail E. Foster, and Tamar Gendler. 1990. *High Schools with Character.* Santa Monica, CA: RAND Corporation.

Institute for Education and Transformation. 1992. "Voices from the Inside. A Report on Schooling from inside the Classroom, Part I: Naming the Problem," Claremont, CA: Claremont Graduate School.

Lee, Valerie E., and J. B. Smith. 1993. "Effects of School Restructuring on the Achievement and Engagement of Middle School Students," *Sociology of Education* 66, 164–187.

Lee, Valerie E., and J. B. Smith. 1995. "Effects of High School Restructuring and Size on Early Gains in Achievement and Engagement," *Sociology of Education* 68, 241–270.

Marzano, Robert J. 2000. *A New Era of School Reform: Going Where the Research Takes Us.* Aurora, CO: Mid-Continent Research for Educational Learning.

Marzano, Robert J. 2003. *What Works in Schools: Translating Research into Action.* Alexandria, VA: Association for Supervision and Curriculum Development.

National Association of Secondary School Principals. 2004. *Breaking Ranks II: Strategies for Leading High School Reform.* Reston, VA: Author.

Newmann, Fred. 1991. "Student Engagement in Academic Work: Expanding the Perspective on Secondary School Effectiveness," in J. R. Bliss and W. A. Firestone (Eds.), *Rethinking Effective Schools: Research and Practice* (pp. 58–76). Englewood Cliffs, NJ: Prentice Hall.

Newmann, Fred M., BetsAnn Smith, Elaine Allensworth, and Anthony S. Bryk. 2001, Winter. "Instructional Program Coherence: What It Is and Why It Should Guide School Improvement Policy." *Educational Evaluation and Policy Analysis* 23(4), 297–321.

Newmann, Fred, G. G. Wehlage, and S. D. Lamborn. 1992. "The Significance and Sources of Student Engagement," in Fred Newmann (Ed.), *Student Engagement and Achievement in American Secondary Schools* (pp. 11–39). New York: Teachers College Press.

Noddings, Nel. 2005. *The Challenge to Care in Schools: An Alternative Approach to Education* (2nd ed.). New York: Teachers College Press.

Parsons, Talcott. 1951. *The Social System.* Glencoe, IL: Free Press.

Peterson, Kent. 2002, Winter. "The Necessary Principal, The Importance of Instructional Leadership." *Curriculum Update.*

Putnam, Robert D. 2000. *Bowling Alone: The Collapse and Revival of American Community.* New York: Simon & Schuster.

Rothman, R. 1992, December 2. "Study 'From Inside' Finds a Deeper Set of Problems," *Education Week* 12(13).

Rousseau, Mary F. 1991. *Community: The Tie That Binds.* New York: University Press of America.

Rowan, B. 1990. "Commitment and Control: Alternative Strategies for the Organizational Design of Schools," *Review of Research in Education* 16, 353–389.

Sacks, Jonathan. 1997. "Rebuilding Civil Society: A Biblical Perspective," *Responsive Community* 7(1), 11–20.

Sebring, Penny, and Anthony Bryk. 1996. "Student-Centered Learning Climate," in Penny Sebring and Associates, *Charting Reform in Chicago: The Students Speak.* Chicago: Consortium on Chicago School Research.

Sergiovanni, Thomas J. 1992. *Moral Leadership: Getting to the Heart of School Improvement.* San Francisco: Jossey-Bass.

Sergiovanni, Thomas J. 1994. *Building Community in Schools.* San Francisco: Jossey-Bass.

Sergiovanni, Thomas J. 2000. *The Lifeworld of Leadership: Creating Culture, Community, and Personal Meaning in Our Schools.* San Francisco: Jossey-Bass.

Stewart, Thomas A. 1997. *Intellectual Capital: The New Wealth of Organizations.* New York: Doubleday.

Tonnies, Ferdinand. 1957. *Community and Society (Gemeinschaft und Gesellschaft).* Trans. and Ed. C. P. Loomis. New York: Harper & Row. (Originally published 1887.)

Valenzuela, Angela. 1999. *Subtractive Schooling: U.S.–Mexican Youth and the Politics of Caring.* Albany: State University of New York Press.

Wilkins, Alan L. 1989. *Developing Corporate Character: How to Successfully Change an Organization without Destroying It.* San Francisco: Jossey-Bass.

6

THE FORCES OF LEADERSHIP AND THE CULTURE OF SCHOOLS

*P*rincipals are important! Indeed, no other school position has greater potential for maintaining and improving quality schools. These assertions are bolstered by findings that emerge from research and from more informal observation of successful schools. It is clear that when schools are functioning especially well and school achievement is high, much of the credit belongs to the principal (Marzano, 2000; Marzano, Waters, McNulty, 2005). Not only is this the case today, but it has been the case for several decades. A 1972 governmental study, for example, reached the following conclusions (U.S. Senate, 1972):

> In many ways the school principal is the most important and influential individual in any school. . . . It is his leadership that sets the tone of the school, the climate for learning, the level of professionalism and morale of teachers and the degree of concern for what students may or may not become. . . . If a school is a vibrant, innovative, child-centered place; if it has a reputation for excellence in teaching; if students are performing to the best of their ability one can almost always point to the principal's leadership as the key to success. (305)

Although principals are important, their mere presence does not automatically result in the required leadership being provided. Often, circumstances prevent principals from becoming the leaders they want to be. Consider, for example, what one principal has to say about constraining circumstances:

I go almost every year to conventions for principals, and there's always a speech telling us we need to be educational leaders, not managers. It's a great idea. And yet the system doesn't allow you to be an educational leader. Everyone wants the power to run schools in one way or another—the central office, the union, the board, the parents, the special-interest groups. What's left for the principal to decide isn't always very much. There's so little we have to control or to change. The power, the authority, is somewhere else, though not necessarily the responsibility. (Boyer, 1983:219)

Still, as we discussed in Chapter 2, many principals are able to rise above these and other difficulties. Key to realizing the potential for leadership in the principalship is to recognize that schools provide opportunities for expressing a unique form of leadership. These opportunities spring from special characteristics that schools possess.

As a result of their research, Blumberg and Greenfield (1980) conclude that "principals who lead seem to be highly *goal oriented* and to have a keen sense of *goal clarity*" (246). They point out that successful principals are alert to opportunities or create opportunities favoring their ability to affect what is going on in the school. Although they rely heavily on operational goals of a long-term nature, they emphasize day-by-day actions as well. They have a good sense of themselves, feel secure as individuals and as principals at work, and are able to accept failure as failure of an idea rather than of them as persons. These principals have a high tolerance for ambiguity and are able to work in loosely structured environments. With respect to authority, they test the limits of the boundaries they face and do not make premature assumptions about what they can or cannot do. They are sensitive to the dynamics of power existing in the school district and school community, and they are accomplished in establishing alliances and in building coalitions that enable them to harness this power on behalf of the school. Approaching problems from an analytical perspective, they are able to remove themselves from the situation; that is, they do not become consumed by the problems and situations they face.

When it comes to the "bottom line," most successful principals will tell you that getting the culture right and paying attention to how parents, teachers, and students define and experience meaning are two widely accepted rules for creating effective schools. We still have to worry about standards, the curriculum, teacher development, tests, resources, getting students connected to learning, and the creation of appropriate management designs that help get things done. But these concerns will not matter much unless the right culture is in place and unless parents, teachers, and students interact with the school in meaningful ways.

In this chapter, the intent is to focus beneath these descriptions and to examine principal leadership as a set of forces available for improving and maintaining quality schooling. Suggestions are provided as to how principals can use these forces.

$\mathcal{T}$HE FORCES OF LEADERSHIP

Leadership can be viewed metaphorically as comprising a set of forces. Each of the "forces" can be used by the principal to push the school forward toward effectiveness or to prevent it from being pushed back. Different forces have different consequences for school effectiveness (Sergiovanni, 1984).

Five "forces of leadership"—technical, human, educational, symbolic, and cultural—are discussed in the following subsections. All five are important. Technical, human, and educational are foundational forces that must be provided to ensure that schools will work. Symbolic and cultural are stretcher forces that help schools rise to levels of extraordinary commitment and performance.

The Technical Force

The first force available to principals is the power of leadership derived from using sound management techniques. This force is concerned with the technical aspects of leadership. When expressing the technical force, principals can be thought of as assuming the role of "management engineers," who emphasize such concepts as planning and time management, contingency leadership theories, and organizational structures. As management engineers, principals provide planning, organizing, coordinating, and scheduling to the school and are skilled at manipulating strategies and situations to ensure optimum effectiveness. The technical leadership force is very important because its presence, competently articulated, ensures that the school will be managed properly.

Proper management is a basic requirement of all organizations if they are expected to function properly day by day and to maintain support from external constituents. School boards and other segments of the public will not tolerate inefficient and poorly managed schools. Furthermore, it is clear from the research that poorly managed enterprises can have debilitating effects on workers. Hackman (1969:158), for example, found that "poor organization of work" resulted in such negative feelings among workers as frustration and aggression, anxiety, personal inadequacy, and even social rejection. It is apparent that workplaces need to be characterized by a degree of order and reliability that provides security for people *and* that frees them to focus wholeheartedly on major purposes and central work activities. The technical force of leadership serves this important need.

The Human Force

The second force available to principals is the power of leadership derived from harnessing the school's social and interpersonal potential—its human resources. This force is concerned with human aspects of leadership. Principals expressing this force can be thought of as assuming the role of "human engineer," emphasizing human relations, interpersonal competence, and instrumental motivational techniques. As human engineers, principals provide support, encouragement, and growth opportunities for teachers and others.

It is hard to imagine a school functioning properly without the strong presence of this human force of leadership. Schools are, after all, human intensive, and the interpersonal needs of students and teachers are of sufficient importance that, should they be neglected, schooling problems are likely to follow. High student motivation to learn and high teacher motivation to teach are prerequisite for quality schooling and must be effectively addressed by principals. This force is so fundamental that the development of human resources appears as either the dominant or underlying theme of each of this book's chapters.

The Educational Force

The third force available to principals is the power of leadership derived from expert knowledge about matters of education and schooling. This force is concerned with educational aspects of leadership. At one time, educational aspects were dominant in the literature of educational administration and supervision. Principals were considered to be instructional leaders, and emphasis on schooling characterized university training programs. In the latter part of the 1950s and during the 1960s, advances of management and social science theory in educational administration and supervision brought to center stage technical and human aspects of leadership; indeed, educational aspects were often neglected. As a result, the principalship was often viewed as a school management position separate from teaching. During this period, the original meaning of principal as "principal teacher" became lost. John Goodlad (1978) has been a persistent critic of the displacement of educational aspects of leadership in favor of the technical and human. He states:

> But to put these matters [technical and human] at the center, often for understandable reasons of survival and expediency, is to commit a fundamental error which, ultimately, will have a negative impact on both education and one's own career. *Our work, for which we will be held accountable, is to maintain, justify, and articulate sound, comprehensive programs of instruction of children and youth.* (326)

Goodlad states further, "It is now time to put the right things at the center again. And the right things have to do with assuring comprehensive, quality educational programs in each and every school in our jurisdiction" (331).

Matters of education and schooling are again in the forefront. This renewed emphasis on the educational force of leadership is a happy result of recent school effectiveness and teaching effectiveness research and of other reports of research (Good and Brophy, 2003; Marzano, 2003; Marzano, Pickering, and Pollock, 2001; Newmann and Associates, 1996). Many national policy studies on the present status and future of education, such as NASSP's *Breaking Ranks II: Strategies for Leading High School Reform* (2004), Darling-Hammond (1997), and Resnick (2001/2002) have also contributed to enhancing this renewed emphasis on educational aspects of leadership. The following statement from Boyer's seminal book (1983) regarding the preparation of principals is representative of current thought:

> New preparation and selection programs are required. Principals cannot exercise leadership without classroom experience. Specifically, we recommend that the preparation pattern for principals follow that of teachers. Without a thorough grounding in the realities of the classroom, principals will continue to feel uncomfortable and inadequate in educational leadership roles. Moreover, they will continue to lack credibility in instructional matters with their teachers. (223)

More recently, the Interstate School Leaders Licensure Consortium (Council of Chief State School Officers, 1996) stated that "effective school leaders are strong educators, anchoring their work on central issues of learning and teaching and school improvement" (5). The first of seven principles used to guide the development of its licensure standards reads, "Standards should reflect the centrality of student learning" (7). The most recent standards are provided in Appendix 2.1 (pp. 61–67). A quick review of them will show that the educational force plays a key role. Clearly, the educational force is receiving increased attention today.

When expressing the educational force, the principal assumes the role of "principal teacher" who brings expert professional knowledge and bearing to teaching, educational program development, and supervision. As principal teacher, the principal is adept at diagnosing educational problems; counseling teachers; providing for supervision, evaluation, and staff development; and developing curriculum.

Sometimes the educational force takes the form of principal as strong instructional leader, and at other times as knowledgeable colleague or leader of leaders who engages with teachers on an equal basis on matters of teaching and learning. The first expression of this educational force might be appropriate for new teachers, teachers with less than fully developed competencies, or teachers with doubtful commitment. The second expression is appropriate for more mature, competent, and committed teachers. Although instructional leadership might be appropriate for a particular circumstance or for a limited period of time, the overall goal is for principals to become leaders of leaders. As leadership builds, the principal strives to help the school become a community of leaders.

Technical, human, and educational forces of leadership—brought together in an effort to promote and maintain quality schooling—provide the critical mass needed for basic school competence. A shortage in any of the three forces upsets this critical mass, and less effective schooling is likely to occur. Studies of excellence in organizations suggest that despite the link between technical, human, and educational aspects of leadership and basic competence, the presence of the three does not guarantee excellence. Excellent organizations, schools among them, are characterized by other leadership qualities represented by symbolic and cultural forces of leadership.

The Symbolic Force

The fourth force available to principals is the power of leadership derived from focusing attention of others on matters of importance to the school. This force is concerned with the symbolic aspects of leadership. When expressing this force, the principal assumes the role of "chief," emphasizing selective attention or the modeling of important goals and behaviors, and signaling to others what is important and valuable in the school. Touring the school; visiting classrooms; seeking out and visibly spending time with students; downplaying management concerns in favor of educational concerns; presiding over ceremonies, rituals, and other important occasions; and providing a unified vision of the school through proper use of words and actions are examples of principal activities associated with this force.

The providing of *purposing* to the school is a major aspect of symbolic leadership. Vaill (1984) defines purposing as "that continuous stream of actions by an organization's formal leadership which has the effect of inducing clarity, consensus, and commitment regarding the organization's basic purposes." Leaders of the high-performing organizations he studied had in common the ability to provide purposing.

The symbolic force of leadership derives much of its power from the needs of persons at work to have a sense of what is important and to have some signal of what is of value. Students and teachers alike want to know what is of value to the school and its leadership; they desire a sense of order and direction, and they enjoy sharing this sense with others. They respond to these conditions with increased work motivation and commitment.

To understand the symbolic force, we need to look beneath the surface of what the principal does to what this behavior means. In symbolic leadership, what the principal stands for and communicates to others by his or her actions and words is important. In addition, providing meaning to teachers, students, and parents and rallying them to a common cause are the earmarks of effectiveness. Pondy (1978) suggests:

> What kind of insights can we get if we say that the effectiveness of a leader lies in his ability to make activity meaningful for those in his role set—not to change behavior but to give others a sense of understanding what they are doing, and especially to articulate it so they can communicate about the meaning of their behaviors? (94)

The noted administrative theorist James G. March (1984) echoes Pondy's thoughts as follows:

> Administrators manage the way the sentiments, expectations, commitments and faiths of individuals concerned with the organization fit into a structure of social beliefs about organizational life. Administrative theory probably underestimates the significance of this belief structure for effective organizations. As a result, it probably underestimates the extent to which the management of symbols is a part of effective administration. If we want to identify one single way in which administrators can affect organizations, it is through their effect on the world views that

surround organizational life; and those effects are managed through attention of the ritual and symbolic characteristics of organizations and their administration. Whether we wish to sustain the system or change it, management is a way of making a symbolic statement. (32)

Technical aspects of leadership are managing structures and events; human aspects are managing psychological factors such as needs; and educational aspects are managing the substance of our work. By contrast, symbolic aspects are managing sentiments, expectations, commitments, and faith itself. Because symbolic leadership affects the faith that people have in the school, it provides the principal with a powerful force for influencing school events.

The Cultural Force

The fifth force available to principals is the power of leadership derived from building a unique school culture and refers to cultural aspects of leadership. It is clear from reviews of the successful school's literature that the building of a *culture* that promotes and sustains a given school's conception of success is key. When expressing this cultural force, the principal assumes the role of "high priest," seeking to define, strengthen, and articulate those enduring values, beliefs, and cultural strands that give the school its unique identity over time. As high priest, the principal is engaged in legacy building, and in creating, nurturing, and teaching an organizational saga (Clark, 1972) that defines the school as a distinct entity with an identifiable culture that builds institutional character.

Leadership activities associated with the cultural view include articulating school purposes and mission; socializing new members to the school; telling stories and maintaining or reinforcing myths, traditions, and beliefs; explaining "the way things operate around here"; developing and displaying a system of symbols (as exemplified in the fourth force) *over time;* and rewarding those who reflect this culture. The net effect of the cultural force of leadership is to bond students, teachers, and others together and to bind them to the work of the school as believers. The school and its purposes become revered, and in some respects they resemble an ideological system dedicated to a sacred mission. As persons become members of this strong and binding culture, they are provided with opportunities for enjoying a special sense of personal importance and significance. Their work and their lives take on a new importance, one characterized by richer meanings, an expanded sense of identity, and a feeling of belonging to something special—all of which are highly motivating conditions (Peters and Waterman, 1982).

Culture can be described as the collective programming of the mind that distinguishes the members of one school from another (Hofstede, 1980:13). Cultural life in schools is constructed reality, and school principals can play a key role in building this reality. School culture includes values, symbols, beliefs, and shared meanings of parents, students, teachers, and others conceived as a group or community. Culture governs what is of worth for this group and how members should think, feel, and behave. The "stuff" of culture includes a school's customs and traditions; historical accounts; stated and unstated understandings, habits, norms, and expectations; common meanings; and shared assumptions. The more understood, accepted, and cohesive the culture of a school, the better able it is to move in concert toward ideals it holds and objectives it wishes to pursue. Ultimately, the intent of cultural leadership is to transform the school from an organization inhabited by a collection of I's to a moral community (see Sergiovanni, 1992; Sergiovanni, 2000; and Sergiovanni, 2005). These themes are described in Chapter 5.

Practicing Symbolic and Cultural Leadership

Culture building and practicing the art of purposing in schools are the essentials of symbolic and cultural leadership forces. The expression of these forces requires vision and an understanding of the semantics of daily activities.

Expressing Symbolic Leadership.   When principals are expressing symbolic aspects of leadership, they are typically working beneath the surface of events and activities; they are seeking to tap deeper meanings, deeper values. As Starratt (1973) suggests, leaders seek to identify the roots of meaning and the flow and ebb of daily life in schools so that they can provide students, teachers, and members of the community with a sense of importance, vision, and purpose above the seemingly ordinary and mundane. Indeed, they work to bring to the school a sense of drama in human life that permits persons to rise above the daily routine that often characterizes their day-by-day activities. Symbolic leaders are able to see the significance of what a group is doing and indeed could be doing. They have a feel for the dramatic possibilities inherent in most situations and are able to urge people to go beyond the routine, to break out of the mold into something more lively and vibrant. Finally, symbolic leaders are able to communicate their sense of vision by words and examples. They use language symbols that are easily understood but that also communicate a sense of excitement, originality, and freshness. These efforts provide opportunities for others in the school to experience this vision and to gain a sense of purpose, feeling that they share in the ownership of the school enterprise.

As a result of their classic work on educational leadership, Lieberman and Miller (1984) found that principals often practice symbolic leadership as opportunists and under serendipitous circumstances. They note, for example,

> when complimenting a teacher for a well-constructed and well-taught lesson, an administrator is making a statement that excellence is recognized and rewarded. When meeting with a teacher whose classroom is in revolt, the principal is expressing concern about what happens behind the closed doors of the classroom and signals a change from previous administrators who gave high marks to a teacher needing improvement. When attending department meetings that focus on curricular issues, the principal is supporting dialogue and informed action. All of these events and actions may be defined as educational leadership—not rational, linear, and planned; but ad hoc, responsive and realistic. Educational leadership happens, when it happens at all, within the cracks and around the edges of the job as defined and presently constituted. (76)

Bennis (1984) finds that compelling vision is the key ingredient of leadership among heads of the highly successful organizations he studied. *Vision* refers to the capacity to create and communicate a view of a desired state of affairs that induces commitment among those working in the organization. Vision becomes the substance of what is communicated as symbolic aspects of leadership are emphasized. Principal Tom Davis speaks of vision as follows:

> I think the first thing I think I'd do real well is I have a vision about what the school should be and about what this school should be in particular. . . . And I think that's essential to a number of things. I think it's important to inspire staff, both emotionally and intellectually. I think it needs to serve that function. Explicitly, I function to bring back the broader vision, the broader view . . . to bear on all the little pieces. That's something I work at very hard . . . so, because I've got all these semi-autonomous, really capable human beings out there, one major function is to keep it all going in one direction.

He continues:

> So the vision . . . has to inform the board, the parents, and staff—all the relationships. It's a whole community, so it all has to be part of it. The vision has to include not only a vision of what you do with children, but what you do in the process of doing it with children. It has to be all of one fabric. (Prunty and Hively, 1982:66)

Lieberman and Miller (1984) speak of the power of the principal as the school's "moral authority," who by actions, statements, and deeds makes symbolic statements. In describing this power from case study notes involving student discrimination, they state:

> Principals can maintain neutrality and let things progress as they always have; even that is a moral statement. Or they may take an active stance, threatening the assumptions of staff members and moving a school in more progressive or more regressive directions. Principals condone or condemn certain behaviors and attitudes; they model moral precepts as they go about the job. When the administrators at Albion took the side of minority students in the lunchroom radio incident, they gave a clear message to faculty that discrimination by race was not to be tolerated. A powerful message was transmitted. Had there been administrative apathy, an equally powerful point would have been made. (76)

Principals are cast into powerful symbolic roles whether they intend it or not and whether they like it or not. Inaction, in certain circumstances, can be as powerful a symbolic statement as is action.

The Semantics of Cultural Leadership. To understand and practice symbolic and cultural leadership, the emphasis needs to be on the semantics of leadership, not the phonetics. What the leader does represents the phonetics. What the leader's actions and behaviors mean to others represents the semantics. Focusing on semantics helps in the understanding that very often it is the little things that count.

One does not have to mount a white horse and charge forward in a grand dramatic event in order to be a symbolic leader. Simple routines and humble actions properly orchestrated can communicate very important messages and high ideas.

Saphier and King (1985), for example, point out that the content of symbolic and cultural leadership need not be different from that of technical, human, and educational leadership. In their words, "Cultures are built through the everyday business of school life. It is the way business is handled that both forms and reflects the culture. . . . Culture building occurs . . . through the way people use educational, human and technical skills in handling daily events or establishing regular practices" (72). Dwyer reaches a similar conclusion. In describing his research (Dwyer et al., 1983), Dwyer notes:

> Another fundamental characteristic of these principals was the routine nature of their actions. Instead of leaders of large-scale or dramatic innovation, we found men and women who shared a meticulous attention to detail. We observed an attention to the physical and emotional elements of the school environment, school–community relations, the teaching staff, schoolwide student achievement, and individual student progress. Their most essential activities included forms of monitoring, information control and exchange, planning, direct interaction with students, hiring and staff development, and overseeing building maintenance. (1984:37)

It is through such routines that the principal focuses attention, demonstrates commitments, and otherwise "embarks on a slow but steady campaign to create a consensus of values and beliefs in a setting" (Dwyer, 1989:22). Appendix 6.1 shows how Frances Hedges, one of the principals studied by Dwyer and his colleagues, managed to practice symbolic and cultural leadership by tending to both routine and varied aspects of her work. The relationships between the five leadership forces and successful schooling are summarized in Table 6.1.

$\mathcal{T}$HE DYNAMIC ASPECTS OF SCHOOL CULTURE

Appendix 6.2, "A Primer on School Culture," provides an overview of school culture and its dimensions. Included are discussions of why culture is an integral and unavoidable part of school life, the levels of school culture, how culture can be developed, and the dark side of school culture.

All schools have cultures, but successful schools seem to have strong and functional cultures aligned with a vision of quality schooling. Culture serves as a compass setting to steer people in a common direction; it provides a set of norms defining what people should accomplish and how, and it is a source of meaning and significance for teachers, students, administrators, and others as they work. Strong and functional cultures are *domesticated* in the sense that they emerge deliberately— they are nurtured and built by the school leadership and membership.

Once shaped and established in a school, strong culture acts as a powerful socializer of thought and programmer of behavior. Yet, the shaping and establishment of such a culture don't just happen; they are, instead, a negotiated product of t a b l e **6.1** The Forces of Leadership and Excellence in Schooling

Force	Leadership Role Metaphor	Theoretical Constructs	Examples	Reactions	Link to Excellence
Technical	"Management engineer"	Planning and time management strategies Contingency leadership theories Organizational structure	Plan, organize, coordinate, and schedule Manipulate strategies and situations to ensure optimum effectiveness	People are managed as objects of a mechanical system. They react to efficient management with indifference but have a low tolerance for inefficient management.	Presence is important to achieve and maintain routine school competence but not sufficient to achieve excellence. Absence results in school ineffectiveness and poor morale.
Human	"Human engineer"	Human relation supervision Psychological theories of motivation Interpersonal competence Conflict management Group cohesiveness	Provide needed support Encourage growth and creativity Build and maintain morale Use participatory decision making	People achieve high satisfaction of their interpersonal needs. They like the leader and the school and respond with positive interpersonal behavior. A pleasant atmosphere exists that facilitates the work of the school.	
Educational	"Principal teacher"	Professional knowledge and bearing Teaching effectiveness Educational program design Clinical supervision	Diagnose educational problems Counsel teachers Provide supervision and evaluation Provide inservice Develop curriculum	People respond positively to the strong expert power of the leader and are motivated to work. They appreciate the assistance and concern provided.	Presence is essential to routine competence. Strongly linked to, but still not sufficient for, excellence in schooling. Absence results in ineffectiveness.

(continued)

table 6.1   Continued

Force	Leadership Role Metaphor	Theoretical Constructs	Examples	Reactions	Link to Excellence
Symbolic	"Chief"	Selective attention Purposing Modeling	Tour the school Visit classrooms Know students Preside over ceremonies and rituals Provide a unified vision	People learn what is of value to the leader and school, have a sense of order and direction, and enjoy sharing that sense with others. They respond with increased motivation and commitment.	Presence is essential to excellence in schooling though absence does not appear to negatively affect routine competence.
Cultural	"High priest"	Climate, clan, culture Tightly structured values—loosely structured system Ideology "Bonding" motivation theory	Articulate school purpose and mission Socialize new members Tell stories and maintain reinforcing myths Explain SOPs Define uniqueness Develop and display a reinforcing symbol system Reward those who reflect the culture	People become believers in the school as an ideological system. They are members of a strong culture that provides them with a sense of personal importance and significance and work meaningfulness, which is highly motivating.	

Source: Adapted from Sergiovanni (1984), p. 12. Used by permission.

the shared sentiments of school participants. When competing points of view and competing ideologies exist in the school, deciding which ones will count requires some struggling. Principals are in an advantageous position to strongly influence the outcome of this struggle. They are, for example, in control of the communications system of the school and thus can decide what information to share and with whom. Furthermore, they control the allocation of resources and are able to reward desirable (and sanction undesirable) behavior. Bates (1981) elaborates on the principal's influence in shaping school culture:

> The culture of the school is therefore the product of conflict and negotiation over definitions of situations. The administrative influence on school language, metaphor, myths and rituals is a major factor in the determination of the culture which is reproduced in the consciousness of teacher and pupils. Whether that culture is based on metaphors of capital accumulation, hierarchy and domination is at least partly attributable to the exercise of administrative authority during the negotiation of what is to count as culture in the school. (43)

Can a culture emerge in a school based on agreements to disagree, on the maintenance of ambiguity over certainty, and on norms of variety and playfulness rather than order? Key for the concept of culture is the importance of collective ideology, shared values and sentiments, and norms that define acceptable behavior. The actual substance of culture is, by contrast, less important (see, e.g., Sergiovanni, 1994). Thus, not all schools with strong cultures are characterized by "harmony." Indeed, agreeing to disagree may well be the core value of a given school culture. This is often the case with respect to colleges and universities and to school research and development enterprises.

School Culture Building

Culture building requires that school leaders give attention to the informal, subtle, and symbolic aspects of school life. Teachers, parents, and students need answers to questions such as these: What is this school about? What is important here? What do we believe in? Why do we function the way we do? How are we unique? How do I fit into the scheme of things? Answering these questions imposes an order on one's school life that is derived from a sense of purpose and enriched meanings. Purpose and meaning are essential in helping the school become a community of mind. As Greenfield (1973) states:

> What many people seem to want from schools is that schools reflect the values that are central and meaningful in their lives. If this view is correct, schools are cultural artifacts that people struggle to shape in their own image. Only in such forms do they have faith in them; only in such forms can they participate comfortably in them. (570)

What is the purpose of leadership conceived as a cultural force? "The task of leadership is to create the moral order that binds them [leaders] and the people around them," notes Greenfield (1984:159). Quinn (1981) states, "The role of the leader, then, is one of orchestrator and labeler: taking what can be gotten in the way of action and shaping it—generally after the fact—into lasting commitment to a new strategic direction. In short, he makes meanings" (59). Leadership as culture building is not a new idea but one that is solidly embedded in our history and well known to successful school and other leaders. In 1957, Philip Selznick wrote:

> The art of the creative leader is the art of institution building, the reworking of human and technological materials to fashion an organism that embodies new and enduring values. . . . To institutionalize is to infuse with value beyond the technical requirements of the task at hand. The prizing of social machinery beyond its technical role is largely a reflection of the unique way it fulfills personal or group needs. Whenever individuals become attached to an organization or a way of doing things as persons rather than as technicians, the result is a prizing of the device for its own sake. From the standpoint of the committed person, the organization is changed from an expendable tool into a valued source of personal satisfaction. . . . The institutional leader, then, is primarily an expert in the promotion and protection of values. (28)

In 1938, noted theorist Chester Barnard stated the following about executive functions: "The essential functions are, first to provide the system of communications; second, to promote the securing of essential efforts; and third, to formulate and define purpose." He continued: "It has already been made clear that, strictly speaking, purpose is defined more nearly by the aggregate of action taken than by any formulation in words" (vii).

Successful Schools and Central Zones

One of the findings revealed in the successful schools literature and in the community-building literature is that these schools have central zones comprising values and beliefs that take on sacred characteristics. Indeed, it might be useful to think of them as having an official "religion" that gives meaning and guides appropriate actions. As repositories of values, these central zones are sources of identity for teachers and students from which their school lives become meaningful. The focus of cultural leadership, then, is on developing and nurturing these central zone patterns so that they provide a normative basis for action within the school.

In some respects, the concept of central zone suggests that successful schools are tightly structured. This means that they are closely organized in a highly disciplined fashion around a set of core ideas spelling out the way of life in the school and governing the way in which people should behave. This is in contrast to recent developments in organizational theory that describe schools as being loosely structured entities (these developments were discussed in Part I). Cohen, March, and Olsen (1972), for example, speak of educational organizations as being "organized anarchies." Similarly, Weick (1982) uses the phrase "loose coupling" to describe the ways in which schools are organized. Indeed, Weick believes that one reason for ineffectiveness in schools is that they are managed with the wrong theory in mind.

Contemporary thought, Weick (1982) argues, assumes that schools are characterized by four properties: the existence of a self-correcting rational system among people who work in highly interdependent ways; consensus on goals and the means to obtain these goals; coordination by the dissemination of information; and predictability of problems and responses to these problems. He notes that, in fact, *none* of these properties is a true characteristic of schools and how they function. Principals in loosely coupled schools, he argues, need to make full use of symbol management to tie the system together. In his words, "People need to be part of sensible projects. Their action becomes richer, more confident, and more satisfying when it is linked with important underlying themes, values and movements" (1982:675). He further states: "Administrators must be attentive to the 'glue' that holds loosely coupled systems together because such forms are just barely systems" (675). Finally, Weick notes that

> the administrator who manages symbols does not just sit in his or her office mouthing clever slogans. Eloquence must be disseminated. And since channels are unpredictable, administrators must get out of the office and spend lots of time one on one—both to remind people of central visions and to assist them in applying these visions to their own activities. The administrator teaches people to interpret what they are doing in a common language. (676)

Some commentators on the successful schools literature point out that these schools are not loosely coupled or structured at all but instead are tightly coupled (Cohen, 1983). A more careful study of this literature leads one to believe that successful schools are *both* tightly coupled and loosely coupled, an observation noted as well by Peters and Waterman (1982) in their studies of America's best-run corporations. There exists in successful schools a strong culture and clear sense of purpose that defines the general thrust and nature of life for their inhabitants. At the same time, a great deal of freedom is given to teachers and others as to how these essential core values are to be honored and realized. This combination of tight structure—around clear and explicit themes representing the core of the school's culture—and of autonomy—so that people can pursue these themes in ways that make sense to them—may well be a key reason why these schools are so successful.

The combination of tight structure and loose structure matches very well three important human characteristics associated with motivation to work, commitment, enthusiasm, and loyalty to the school:

1. The need for teachers, students, and other school workers to find their work and personal lives meaningful, purposeful, sensible, and significant
2. The need for teachers, students, and other school workers to have some reasonable control over their work activities and affairs and to be able to exert reasonable influence over work events and circumstances

3. The need for teachers, students, and other school workers to experience success, to think of themselves as winners, and to receive recognition for their success

People are willing to make a significant investment of time, talent, and energy in exchange for enhancement and fulfillment of these three needs (Hackman and Oldham, 1980; Peters and Waterman, 1982). The concept of combined tight and loose coupling in schools is developed further in Part IV of this book as the importance of school goals and purposes is discussed. In the language of community, focusing on central zones of values, shared conceptions, covenants, and other idea structures are key to building a community of mind.

$\mathcal{S}$OME REFLECTIONS

1. Use the grid below to provide examples of principals and assistant principals using each of the five forces of leadership. Take your examples from an average work week.

	Technical	Human	Educational	Symbolic	Cultural
Your Principal					
Another Principal					
Your Assistant Principal					
Another Assistant Principal					

Which of the forces of leadership do your principal and your assistant principal emphasize? Which of the forces do other principals and other assistant principals emphasize? Record your examples in the appropriate boxes. Do any patterns emerge? Do principals and assistant principals differ in the forces they emphasize? Which forces get the least attention?

2. What examples of educational, symbolic, and cultural leadership can you find in the Frances Hedges's principalship practice? See Appendix 6.1 for the "Frances Hedges and Orchard Park Elementary School" story.

3. Should the loyal opposition be trusted? Or is the opposition just that, the opposition? Have there been occasions when you and your principal shared

similar goals but had important differences in how these goals were best achieved? Did your principal view you as a member of the opposition? Or as a member of the loyal opposition? What if you did not share either the goals or the means to achieve them, yet you trusted and respected each other? Is a good relationship enough for you to join the ranks of the loyal opposition? Or are you doomed to the ranks of the opposition? In what ways can the loyal opposition help you be a better principal?

REFERENCES

Barnard, Chester I. 1938. *The Functions of the Executive.* Cambridge, MA: Harvard University Press.

Bates, Richard. 1981. "Management and the Culture of the School," in Richard Bates and Course Team (Eds.), *Management of Resources in Schools: Study Guide I* (pp. 37–45). Geelong, Australia: Deakin University.

Bennis, Warren. 1984. "Transformation Power and Leadership," in Thomas J. Sergiovanni and John E. Corbally (Eds.), *Leadership and Organizational Culture.* Urbana: University of Illinois Press.

Blumberg, Arthur, and William Greenfield. 1980. *The Effective Principal: Perspectives on School Leadership.* Boston: Allyn and Bacon.

Boyer, Ernest. 1983. *High School: A Report on Secondary Education in America.* New York: Harper & Row.

Clark, Burton R. 1972. "The Organizational Saga in Higher Education," *Administrative Science Quarterly* 17(2), 178–184.

Cohen, Michael. 1983. "Instructional Management and Social Conditions in Effective Schools," in Allan Odden and L. Dean Webb (Eds.), *School Finance and School Improvement: Linkages in the 1980's.* Yearbook of the American Educational Finance Association.

Cohen, Michael D., James G. March, and Johan Olsen. 1972. "A Garbage Can Model of Organizational Choice," *Administrative Science Quarterly* 17(1), 1–25.

Council of Chief State School Officers. 1996. *Interstate School Leaders Licensure Consortium: Standards for School Leaders.* Washington, DC: Author.

Darling-Hammond, Linda. 1997. *The Right to Learn: A Blueprint for Creating Schools That Work.* San Francisco: Jossey-Bass.

Dwyer, David. 1984. "The Search for Instructional Leadership: Routines and Subtleties in the Principal's Role," *Educational Leadership* 41(5).

Dwyer, David. 1989. "School Climate Starts at the Curb," *School Climate—The Principal Difference* (pp. 1–26). Monograph Series #1. Hartford: Connecticut Principals' Academy.

Dwyer, David, Ginny Lee, Brian Rowan, and Steven Bossert. 1983. *Five Principles in Action: Perspectives on Instructional Management.* San Francisco: Far West Laboratory for Educational Research and Development.

Good, Thomas L., and Jere E. Brophy. 2003. *Looking in Classrooms.* Boston: Allyn and Bacon.

Goodlad, John L. 1978. "Educational Leadership: Toward the Third Era," *Educational Leadership* 35(4), 322–331.

Greenfield, Thomas B. 1973. "Organizations as Social Inventions: Rethinking Assumptions about Change," *Journal of Applied Behavioral Science* 9(5).

Greenfield, Thomas B. 1984. "Leaders and Schools: Willfulness and Non-Natural Order in Organization," in Thomas J. Sergiovanni and John E. Corbally (Eds.), *Leadership and Organizational Culture.* Urbana: University of Illinois Press.

Hackman, J. Richard, and Greg R. Oldham. 1980. *Work Redesign.* Reading, MA: Addison-Wesley.

Hackman, Ray C. 1969. *The Motivated Working Adult.* New York: American Management Association.

Hofstede, G. 1980. *Cultures Consequences.* Beverly Hills, CA: Sage.

Lieberman, A., and L. Miller. 1984. *Teachers, Their World, and Their Work.* Arlington, VA: Association for Supervision and Curriculum Development.

March, James G. 1984. "How We Talk and How We Act: Administrative Theory and Administrative Life," in Thomas J. Sergiovanni and John E. Corbally (Eds.), *Leadership and Organizational Culture* (pp. 18–35). Urbana: University of Illinois Press.

Marzano, Robert J. 2000. *A New Era of School Reform: Going Where the Research Takes Us.* Aurora, CO: Mid-continent Research for Educational Learning.

Marzano, Robert J. 2003. *What Works in Schools: Translating Research into Action.* Alexandria, VA: Association for Supervision and Curriculum Development.

Marzano, Robert J., Debra J. Pickering, and Jane E. Pollock. 2001. *Classroom Instruction That Works: Research-Based Strategies for Increasing Student Achievement.* Alexandria, VA: Association for Supervision and Curriculum Development.

Marzano, Robert J., Timothy Waters, and Brian A. McNulty. 2005. *School Leadership That Works: From Research to Results.* Alexandria, VA: Association for Supervision and Curriculum Development; Aurora, CO: Mid-continent Research for Educational Learning.

National Association of Secondary School Principals. 2004. *Breaking Ranks II: Strategies for Leading High School Reform.* Reston, VA: Author.

Newmann, Fred M., and Associates. 1996. *Authentic Achievement: Restructuring Schools for Intellectual Quality.* San Francisco: Jossey-Bass.

Peters, Thomas J., and Robert H. Waterman, Jr. 1982. *In Search of Excellence.* New York: Harper & Row.

Pondy, Louis. 1978. "Leadership Is a Language Game," in Morgan W. McCall, Jr., and Michael M. Lombardo (Eds.), *Leadership: Where Else Can We Go?* Durham, NC: Duke University Press.

Prunty, John J., and Wells Hively. 1982, November 30. "The Principal's Role in School Effectiveness: An Analysis of the Practices of Four Elementary School Leaders." National Institute of Education (G 8-01-10) and CEMRL, Inc.

Quinn, James B. 1981, Winter. "Formulating Strategy One Step at a Time," *Journal of Business Strategy.*

Resnick, Lauren. 2001/2002, Fall/Winter. "Learning Leadership on the Job," *Wallace-Readers Digest Funds Leaders Count Report* 1(2).

Saphier, John, and Matthew King. 1985. "Good Seeds Grow in Strong Cultures," *Educational Leadership* 42(6), 67–74.

Selznick, Philip. 1957. *Leadership and Administration: A Sociological Interpretation.* New York: Harper & Row.

Sergiovanni, Thomas J. 1984, February. "Leadership and Excellence in Schools," *Educational Leadership* 41(5), 4–13.

Sergiovanni, Thomas J. 1992. *Moral Leadership: Getting to the Heart of School Improvement.* San Francisco: Jossey-Bass.

Sergiovanni, Thomas J. 1994. *Building Community in Schools.* San Francisco: Jossey-Bass.

Sergiovanni, Thomas J. 2000. *The Lifeworld of Leadership: Creating Culture, Community, and Personal Meaning in Our Schools.* San Francisco: Jossey-Bass.

Sergiovanni, Thomas J. 2005. *Strengthening the Heartbeat: Leading and Learning Together in Schools.* San Francisco: Jossey-Bass.

Starratt, Robert J. 1973. "Contemporary Talk on Leadership: Too Many Kings in the Parade?" *Notre Dame Journal of Education* 4(1), 5–14.

United States Senate, Select Committee on Equal Educational Opportunity. 1972. "Revitalizing the Role of the School Principal," in *Toward Equal Educational Opportunity* (pp. 305–307). Senate Report No. 92-0000.

Vaill, Peter B. 1984. "The Purposing of High Performing Systems," in Thomas J. Sergiovanni and John E. Corbally (Eds.), *Leadership and Organizational Culture* (pp. 85–104). Urbana: University of Illinois Press.

Weick, Karl E. 1982. "Administering Education in Loosely Coupled Schools," *Phi Delta Kappan* 27(2), 673–676.

Frances Hedges and Orchard Park Elementary School

The year 1982 marked Orchard Park Elementary School's 35th year in the city of Hillsdale. Surrounding the school were rows of white, grey, pale green and pastel yellow houses, whose neatly trimmed yards were, by late summer, straw-colored from lack of water. The neighborhood itself was quiet, but the noises from a nearby freeway attested to its urban setting. The community's only distinctive landmark was an old church which occupied a large corner lot adjacent to the school. Its three onion-shaped spires had for years cast a sense of permanence over the entire community.

"Permanent," however, would be a somewhat misleading description of the area. Prior to 1960, white, middle-class families of Italian descent predominated in the neighborhood. Over the next few years increasing numbers of ethnic minorities moved out of the city's poorer neighborhoods to areas like Orchard Park's community, seeking better schools and better living conditions. As a result, Orchard Park's neighborhood lost its homogeneity, and some of its quiet, as a number of racial conflicts marred the community's tranquility. The school also was affected, and staff had to find a way to adapt the program to the needs of the newer students.

The new student body at Orchard Park Elementary School was characterized by a diversity of racial groups from various ethnic backgrounds. District records showed that as many as 10 different language groups were represented in the school's student population. Fifty-nine percent of the students were black; 13 percent reflected Spanish heritage; 16 percent were Asian (Chinese, Filipino, Samoan, Laotian, and Vietnamese); and 11 percent were white. Other ethnic groups composed the remaining one percent. The majority of the students' families were of low- or lower-middle income status. These students were energetic and active, frequently exhibiting aggressive behavior that stemmed more from overexuberance than from any other motivation. Groups at play were observed to be multiethnic and solicitous of affection and approval from teachers and the principal. Warm hugs exchanged between staff members and students were common occurrences on the playground.

Orchard Park employed 25 teachers, the majority of whom were very experienced. There were few signs of negativism, criticism or conflict among these teachers despite the fact that their instructional approaches differed markedly. Generally, they were supportive of the school and particularly of the principal. One teacher told us that there was only one reason for staff turnover at Orchard Park—retirement. Further evidence of their satisfaction with the status quo came at the end of the year of our study. The staff, together with the community, rallied to prevent the transfer of their principal and came together to hold a "Principal Appreciation" gathering to honor Hedges' leadership.

The center of attention at that ceremony, Frances Hedges, was a 60-year-old black woman who had served at Orchard Park for six and a half years. She conveyed to all who met her a sense of elegance through her well-matched clothes, golden earrings, oversized glasses and neatly fashioned white hair. Her appearance contrasted to the casual style adhered to by most of her staff; she was easily distinguished as the person in charge.

Long before coming to Orchard Park, Hedges had attended a teachers' college in her hometown, originally intending to become a child psychologist. But economic considerations prevented her from pursuing this goal. Instead, she spent 21 years as a classroom teacher, mostly in the district that includes Orchard Park. After receiving a Masters Degree in educational administration, she gradually climbed to her current position by working as a reading resource teacher, a district program coordinator, and a vice principal.

Hedges' manner with staff and students was personable. Whether discussing professional matters or just making small talk, she conveyed warmth and friendliness through smiles and laughter. She was generous with compliments to both students and teachers. She also communicated often and comfortably through touches, hugs and embraces. As a result, she frequently was referred to by both students and teachers as Orchard Park's "mother figure."

Hedges' way of acting was consistent with her philosophy. She strongly adhered to what she termed "humanistic" beliefs about education. She explained:

> My philosophy is that if we are warm and humane and nurturing, we maximize the learning of children. There is just no way to separate out those basic needs.

Believing that she was "acutely sensitive to . . . children's needs as well as adults' needs," Hedges strove to keep everyone in her learning community "reasonably happy" and worked to help everyone strengthen their self-concepts.

Attending to the basic needs of children logically led to Hedges' attention to safety and order in her school. She was a strict disciplinarian and never hesitated to reprimand children for misbehavior. Her harsh words, however, always would be followed by her efforts to help children understand their mistakes and become more responsible for their own behavior. She said:

> I believe that if we are really going to change the behavior of children, we can't just say "stop that," without going a step further and really having some kind of dialogue about what took place, why, and what are the options.

Her philosophy of education also included tenets about instruction. She strongly believed in the importance of academics, particularly reading. She pronounced:

> Reading is by far our number one priority. I believe that if children don't know how to read, they really cannot make it in this world.

Thus, Hedges' beliefs about education were related to her concerns for both the social and academic well-being of her students. It came as no surprise to find that her goals for the school reflected those convictions.

Hedges' primary goal at Orchard Park was to build a program conducive to the emotional and social growth of her students. She wanted her staff both to instill in each child a love for learning and to foster an awareness of social responsibility. She was adamant that her staff actively seek to strengthen students' self-concepts. These goals, she believed, were pre-eminent. They were a foundation upon which successful academic experiences could be built.

The principal's concern for the academic growth of her students was always stated from a "whole-child" perspective. Delineating her academic goals, she said:

> We work very hard to try to make sure that in the six or seven years that boys and girls are in elementary school, that they leave this school operating at grade level or above. . . . I'd like to see them at grade level for at least their last two years so that they can go into junior high school as much stronger and more confident children.

Hedges actively promoted both her social and academic goals to her faculty. During the year of our study with her, she utilized a district mandate to develop and implement an integrated, three-year instructional plan as a major vehicle to communicate her goals and develop her staff's commitment to them. Evidence that she had been very successful in this aspect of her work accumulated as we interviewed teachers about their beliefs and goals. In virtually all instances, their statements echoed Hedges' own.

How did Frances Hedges bring about the warm and productive climate at Orchard Park? Hedges demonstrated a propensity for direct, face-to-face interaction with participants in her setting. In total, 51 percent of her activities were verbal exchanges of varying length. The other glaring fact in the Orchard Park story is that her routine actions directly affected the climate at Orchard Park, making it conducive to teaching and learning.

Both the value she placed on students' emotional well-being and her goal to improve students' self-esteem contributed to a vision of school climate as an important end in itself. In addition, her beliefs about schools and schooling linked climate to instruction in several ways: she considered students' emotional well-being as an important precursor to their learning; she regarded an orderly, disciplined environment as a necessary condition for teaching and learning to take place; and she believed that the improvement of teachers' instructional practices was best achieved in a setting that built on the positive aspects of their skills. Thus, she strove to maintain an environment that contributed to the happiness, safety, and productivity of all participants.

We see in many of Hedges' routine actions the keys to the development and maintenance of Orchard Park's social milieu. Her actions, as she supervised students in the building and on the playgrounds, attended simultaneously to the need to maintain safety and order at the school and to build students' self-esteem. She monitored their conduct and corrected them when necessary, exchanging her views about responsible behavior and reinforcing school rules. She constantly reminded students to pick up trash, bus their trays in the cafeteria, play in the correct areas of the play yard, walk instead of run in the hallways, refrain from pushing and shoving, and be quiet in the corridors and auditorium. She utilized these same actions to carry out her more social goals: she frequently stopped to talk to students, expressing delight at seeing them or remarking about the clothes they were wearing. Children often approached her to describe important events in their lives. Many of these brief interactions were concluded with a hug exchanged between the principal and the youngster.

An additional strategy Hedges used in her supervision of students was to model appropriate behavior. She might, for example, pick up a piece of trash and deposit it in a container or take a food tray to the cafeteria kitchen as she reminded students of the rules, often mentioning that they should keep the school as tidy as they would their homes.

Hedges' desire to counsel students played a large part in her interactions with children, especially those who had committed some infraction of school rules. We witnessed many instances of her counselor-like approach as she dealt with students whom she had seen misbehaving or who had been sent to her for fighting, stealing, acting inappropriately in class, or failing to complete their school work. In all instances, she carefully took the time to listen to what the students had to say about their behavior. Hedges explained this strategy in terms of her humanistic philosophy:

> If you don't do something, [children] feel . . . that their problems are falling on deaf ears. I tell the staff all the time, "You really do have to take the time out, let a child explain what happened, and be willing to at least listen, whether it's what that particular child wants, or not . . . it's just that someone has listened."

Students were aware that Hedges would act vigorously and appropriately if they misbehaved as well as listen to their problems. When infractions were serious, Hedges would tell students that she was going to phone their parents to report incidents . . . she always followed through. As a result Orchard Park's students understood that their principal was serious about discipline and true to her word.

We mentioned earlier the importance that Hedges placed on building on the positive aspects of people in the school. This approach was most apparent in her dealings with problem students as she implemented special plans to communicate to them that, despite misbehavior, they were still worthy human beings and could act responsibly. We observed one instance in which Hedges appointed the worst offenders in the school as "Chair Captains" and allowed them to pick their own squads who would help set up and take down chairs in the auditorium. The youngsters saw this as an important and enjoyable responsibility that gave them status among their peers. In another instance, Hedges urged that a child who had a particularly negative attitude toward school be assigned to the traffic detail. His teacher remarked that this made a dramatic improvement in the boy's classroom behavior and attitude.

When infractions were serious, Hedges often assigned offenders work projects around the school that would contribute to the school's overall welfare. She tenaciously pursued alternatives to suspension. One teacher reported of the principal's efforts to deal with problem students:

> [Hedges] has a relationship with almost all of the children that regularly act out, the ones that are really on your blacklist . . . if it's your child that's constantly acting out, you would almost want her to say, "Doggone! Let's give up on that kid." But she never really does.

Hedges not only worked creatively with problem students but encouraged growth in responsibility among all students at Orchard Park. For example, she taught leadership to all members of the school's student council.

Orchard Park's teachers also were encouraged to promote positive social values in the school through classroom activities. In an unusual departure from Hedges' policy of permitting a good deal of staff autonomy concerning the selection of classroom materials, for example, she established a schoolwide focus on her social goals through the introduction of a set of self-esteem materials. At the first faculty meeting of the year, Hedges presented the materials and asked staff members to use them as a regular part of their programs. Although the use of these materials was not systematically monitored, her message was clear to her staff. Subsequently, teachers were observed using an array of esteem-building activities in their classrooms, including magic circle activities, life box materials, and art projects to stimulate discussions about feelings and attitudes.

Thus Hedges aggressively pursued a positive school climate at Orchard Park. By demonstrating her values in her daily interactions and conversations. Hedges encouraged an environment in which staff members shared her child-centered approach. Participants in the setting directly and indirectly exhibited their satisfaction: there was very little vandalism by students in the school, teachers felt lucky to be at the school and left only because of retirement, and the district held a waiting list of teachers anxious to join this faculty.

Hedges also directly or indirectly manipulated such important elements of the organization as class size and composition, scheduling, staff assignments, the scope and sequence of curriculum, the distribution of instructional materials, and even teaching styles. On the surface, a principal actively and successfully engaged in shaping the conditions for and of instruction in a school seems perfectly natural—principals are supposed to be instructional leaders, right? But we also know that teachers enjoy and expect autonomy in matters related to classroom instruction. It is not uncommon for teachers to actively or passively resist principals' instructional improvement campaigns.

Hedges was able to transcend this problem for two reasons. First, her own 21 years of experience as a classroom teacher and reading specialist legitimated her expertise in the eyes of her faculty. The second ingredient to Hedges' success at influencing her staff's classroom practices was her ability to establish a culture of instruction at the school, facilitated by the emphasis she placed on building on people's strengths and emphasizing the positive. Thus, experience coupled with style enabled her to provide information to teachers without alienating them. Her staff regarded her as competent and nonthreatening. They not only accepted her suggestions, but actively sought her advice and counsel.

While there were many strategies that Hedges used to influence instruction both directly and indirectly at the school, the most potent and pervasive was the informal classroom visit. Hedges monitored instruction by regularly dropping into teachers' classrooms. These visits provided opportunities to make suggestions that did not carry the onus that might accompany recommendations made as the result of formal classroom evaluations. On many of Hedges' informal visits, we observed her assisting teachers by working with students and making brief constructive and supportive comments to her staff.

These often-repeated behaviors were key features in her strategy to reduce teachers' anxieties about her visits. She mentioned that she spent time building positive rapport with teachers before providing suggestions for changes in their instructional patterns:

> I operate with the idea that we really are all a team. If I can just . . . give [the staff] enough strokes on those positives, then I can get [at] those areas that are not so well done.

When Hedges did feel a need to comment on teachers' deficiencies, she did so in a low-key, nonthreatening manner without embarrassing, confronting, or demeaning them.

Hedges also promoted a norm of teacher-to-teacher sharing because she did not see herself as the only source of instructional expertise in the school. She often advised teachers to talk with their colleagues for assistance or ideas. Frequently this required Hedges to organize opportunities for staff members to get together. For example, she commonly arranged for the school's reading specialist to help teachers create reading centers in a classroom or help classroom teachers evaluate those students who required remedial instruction. There were many instances of Hedges arranging meetings between teachers who were successful with new methods and teachers who were less successful. In this way, she served as a "linking agent" or "information broker." Because Hedges' classroom visits were regular, her recommendations were timely and the staff found them very helpful. Hedges also used classroom visits as opportunities to impress upon children the importance she attached to academic success. By publicly complementing students on their individual or group successes, she not only strengthened their self-esteem, but created an ethos about learning that children would want to share. . . .

Her philosophy is marked by simple tenets: all people are fundamentally good; everyone can learn and grow in a warm and nurturing environment; any successful enterprise is the result of teamwork and everyone can and must contribute to the whole. From experience, Hedges adds to these beliefs a strongly held value regarding the importance of reading as an essential skill that children must master to realize their highest potential. These humane attributes are wrapped in her tough-minded awareness about the importance of setting limits and making children and staff responsible for their own behavior.

Hedges leads her school by continually communicating her beliefs to parents, students, and staff members through her routine actions. By constant word and deed she demonstrates how the vision she holds of the "good" school must work. Mostly she proceeds through patient, subtle suggestions and reminders. Occasionally, she mandates changes or additions to organizational structures, procedures, and curricula. But the key to her success is the relentless pursuit of her goals and her talent in getting others to adopt those goals.

Over years at Orchard Park, staff have experimented with procedures and techniques Hedges has recommended. They have been continually bombarded with her rationale. As they experience success, the procedures and rationales become embedded in their own experiences and slowly alter their own beliefs. Slowly, a working consensus about the "right" way to teach and run a school emerges. As those beliefs fade into assumptions and become habituated, an organizational culture is born. Its progenitor, its patient nurseryman, was Frances Hedges.

Source: Excerpted from "School Climate Starts at the Curb," *School Climate—The Principal Difference* by David Dwyer, 1989, Hartford: The Connecticut Principals' Academy. Reprinted by permission.

A Primer on School Culture

In every school there are observable behavioral regularities defined by the rules of the game for getting along. These rules are norms that define for people what is right and correct to do, what is acceptable, and what is expected. Norms are expressions of certain values and beliefs held by members of the work group. When trying to understand how norms emerge and work, the metaphor of culture can be helpful. Some experts may debate whether schools really have cultures or not, but the issue is less the reality of culture and more what can be learned by thinking about schools as cultures. The metaphor *school culture* helps direct attention to the symbols, behavioral regularities, ceremonies, and even myths that communicate to people the underlying values and beliefs that are shared by members of the organization.

External Adoption
and Internal Integration

Schein believes that the term *culture* "should be reserved for the deeper level of *basic assumptions* and *beliefs* that are shared by members of an organization, that operate unconsciously, and that define in a basic 'taken-for-granted' fashion an organization's view of itself and its environment" (1985:6). The concept of culture is very important, for its dimensions are much more likely to govern what it is that people think and do than is the official management system. Teachers, as suggested earlier, are much more likely to teach in ways that reflect the shared assumptions and beliefs of the faculty as a whole than they are in ways that administrators want, supervisors say, or teacher evaluation instruments require.

Following Argyris (1964), Merton (1957), and Parsons (1951), Schein (1985) points out that schools and other organizations must solve two basic problems if they are to be effective: external adoption and survival and internal integration. The problems of *external adoption* and *survival* are themed to

- Mission and strategy (how to reach a shared understanding of the core mission of the school and its primary tasks).
- Goals (developing a consensus on goals that are linked to the core mission).
- Means (reaching consensus on the managerial and organizational means to be used to reach goals).
- Standards (reaching consensus on the criteria to be used to determine how well the group is doing in fulfilling its goals and whether it is meeting its commitments to agreed-upon processes).
- Correction (reaching consensus on what to do if goals are not being met).

The problems of *internal integration* are themed to

- Developing a common set of understandings that facilitates communication, organizes perceptions, and helps to categorize and make common meanings.
- Developing criteria for determining who is in and out and how one determines membership in the group.
- Working out the criteria and rules for determining who gets, maintains, and loses power.
- Working out the rules for peer relationships and the manner in which openness and intimacy are to be handled as organizational tasks are pursued.
- Knowing the group's "heroic and sinful behaviors . . . ; what gets rewarded with property, status and power; and what gets punished in the form of withdrawal of the rewards and, ultimately, excommunication" (Schein, 1985:66).
- Dealing with issues of ideology and sacredness: "Every organization, like every society, faces unexplainable and inexplicable events, which must be given meaning so that members can respond to them and avoid the anxiety of dealing with the unexplainable and uncontrollable" (Schein, 1985:66).

As issues of external adoption and internal integration are solved, schools and other organizations are better able to give full attention to the attainment of their goals and have the means for allowing people to derive sense and meaning from their work lives—to see their work as being significant. In summarizing his stance, Schein (1985) notes that culture is "a pattern of basic assumptions—invented, discovered or developed by a given group as it learns to cope with its problems of external adaptation and internal integration—that has worked well enough to be considered valid and, therefore, to be taught to new members as the correct way to perceive, think, and feel in relation to those problems" (9). Because the assumptions have resulted in decisions and behaviors that have worked repeatedly, they are likely to be taken for granted. This point is important because the artifacts of culture, such as symbols, rites, traditions, and behaviors, are different from the actual content and substance of culture; the basic assumptions that govern what is thought to be true, what is right, and for all intents and purposes, what is reality for the school. As mentioned in earlier discussions of culture, the central zone that Shils (1961) speaks of is composed of assumptions, values, and beliefs. The values and beliefs are often manifest, but the assumptions are typically tacit.

Levels of Culture

Because assumptions and basic beliefs are typically tacit, they are inferred from manifestations of cultures such as the school's climate (Dwyer, 1989) and the rites

appendix *6.2* **Continued**

and rituals of the school's organizational life (Deal, 1985). To account for both, it is useful to think about dimensions of school culture as existing at least four levels (Dyer, 1982; Schein, 1981, 1985). The most tangible and observable level is represented by the *artifacts* of culture as manifested in what people say, how people behave, and how things look. Verbal artifacts include the language systems that are used, stories that are told, and examples that are used to illustrate certain important points. Behavioral artifacts are manifested in the ceremonies and rituals and other symbolic practices of the school. The interpersonal life of the school as represented by the concept of school climate is an important artifact of culture.

Less discernible but still important is the level of *perspectives*. Perspectives refer to the shared rules and norms to which people respond, the commonness that exists among solutions to similar problems, how people define the situations they face, and the boundaries of acceptable and unacceptable behavior. Often, perspectives are included in statements of the school's purposes or its covenant when these include ways in which people are to work together as well as the values that they share.

The third level is that of *values*. Values provide the basis for people to judge or evaluate the situations they face, the worth of their actions and activities, their priorities, and the behaviors of people with whom they work. Values not only specify what is important but often the things that are not important. In schools the values are arranged in a fashion that represents the covenant that the principal, teachers, and others share. As discussed in Chapter 10, this covenant might be in the form of an educational or management platform, statements of school philosophy, mission statements, and so forth.

The fourth level is that of *assumptions*. Assumptions are "the tacit beliefs that members hold about themselves and others, their relationships to other persons, and the nature of the organization in which they live. Assumptions are the nonconscious underpinnings of the first three levels—that is, the implicit, abstract axioms that determine the more explicit system of meanings" (Lundberg, 1985:172).

Identifying the Culture of Your School

The four levels of culture provide a framework for analyzing the culture of a school. Because assumptions are difficult to identify firsthand, they often must be inferred from what is found at the artifacts, perspectives, and values levels. Much can be learned from examining the school's history. Deal (1985) points out, for example, that each school has its story of origin, the people or circumstances that launched it, and those who presided over its course thereafter. Through evolutionary development—crises and resolutions, internal innovations and external pressures, plans and chance occurrences—the original concept was shaped and reshaped into an organic collection of traditions and distinctive ways. Throughout a school's history, a parade of students, teachers, principals, and parents cast sustaining memories. Great accomplishments meld with dramatic failures to form a potentially cherishable lore. (615)

The following questions might be helpful in uncovering a school's history:

- How does the school's past live in the present?
- What traditions are still carried on?
- What stories are told and retold?
- What events in the school's history are overlooked or forgotten?
- Do heroes and heroines exist among teachers and students whose idiosyncrasies and exploits are still remembered?
- In what ways are the school's traditions and historical incidents modified through reinterpretation over the years? Can you recall, for example, a historical event that has evolved from fact to myth?

Believing that an organization's basic assumptions about itself can be revealed through its history, Schein (1985) suggests that the organization's history be analyzed by identifying all major crises, crucial transitions, and other times of high emotion. For each event identified, reconstruct how management dealt with the issue, how it identified its role, and what it did and why. Patterns and themes across the various events identified should then be analyzed and checked against current practices. The next step is to identify the assumptions that were behind the actions taken in the past and check whether those assumptions are still relevant for present actions.

To uncover beliefs, ask what are the assumptions and understandings that are shared by teachers and others, though they may not be explicitly stated. These may relate to how the school is structured, how teaching takes place, the roles of teachers and students, what is believed about discipline, and the relationship of parents to the school. Sometimes assumptions and understandings are written down somewhere in the form of a philosophy or other value statements. Whether that is the case or not, beliefs can best be understood by being inferred from examples of current practices.

According to Schein (1985), one important set of basic assumptions revolves around the theme of what is believed about human nature and how these beliefs then affect policies and decisions. To address this issue, he suggests that an attempt be made to identify organizational heroes and villains, successful people, and those who are less successful, and compare the stories that are told about them. He recommends as well that recruitment selection and promotion criteria be examined to see if indeed they are biased toward selecting a certain type of person into the organization and promoting that type. An analysis of who gets rewarded and who gets punished can also be revealing. Do patterns emerge from this sort of analysis? Are there common assumptions about people that begin to emerge?

Values can be identified by asking what things the school prizes. That is, when teachers and principals talk about the school, what are the major and recurring value themes underlying what they say? When problems emerge, what are the values that seem to surface as being relied on in developing solutions?

Norms and standards can be identified by asking what are the oughts, shoulds, dos, and don'ts that govern the behavior of teachers and principals, and examining what behaviors get rewarded and what behaviors get punished in the school. What are the accepted and recurring ways of doing things, the patterns of behavior, the habits and rituals that prevail?

Hansen (1986) suggests that teachers discuss the following questions when seeking to identify the culture of their school: Describe your work day both in and outside of the school. On what do you spend your time and energy? Given that most students forget what they learn, what do you hope your students will retain over time from your teaching? Think of students whom you are attracted to—those whom you admire, respect, or enjoy. What common characteristics do these students share? What does it take for a teacher to be successful in your school? What advice would you give to new teachers who want to be successful? What do you remember about past faculty members and students in your school? If you were to draw a picture or take a photo or make a collage that represented some aspect of your school, what would it look like? How are students rewarded?

The Dark Side of School Culture

The benefits of a strong school culture are clear. Culture represents an effective means of coordination and control in a loosely connected and nonlinear world. Its covenant or center of purposes and shared values represents a source of inspiration, meaning, and significance for those who live and work in the school. These qualities can lead to enhanced commitment and performance that are beyond expectations. As a result, the school is better able to achieve its goals.

Yet, there is a dark side to the concept of school culture, as well. Weick (1985) points out, for example, that a coherent statement of who we are makes it harder for us to become something else. Strong cultures are tenacious cultures. Because a tenacious culture can be a rigid culture that is slow to detect changes and opportunities and slow to change once opportunities are sensed, strong cultures can be backward, conservative instruments of adaptation. (385)

Furthermore, the presence of a strong norm system in a school can collectively program the minds of people in such a way that issues of reality come into question. If this is carried to the extreme, the school might come to see reality in one way but its environment in another. Finally, there is the question of rationality. As commitment to a course of action increases, people become less rational in their actions. Strong cultures are committed cultures, and in excess, commitment takes its toll on rational action.

Schein points out that, as organizations mature, the prevailing culture becomes so entrenched that it becomes a constraint on innovation. Culture preserves the glories of the past and hence becomes valued as a source of self-esteem and as a means of defense rather than for what it represents and the extent to which it serves purposes (Schein, 1985).

The Importance of a Loyal Opposition

If the purposes and covenants that constitute cultural centers are highly dynamic and fluid, school cultures are likely to be weak and ineffectual. By the same token, if they are cast in granite, they can squelch individuality and innovation. The alternative is to build a resilient culture—one that can bend to change here and there, but not break; that can stretch in a new direction and shrink from an old, but still maintain its integrity; a culture that is able to bounce back and recover its strength and spirit, always maintaining its identity. Key to resiliency is the cultivation of a small but energetic loyal opposition made of

> people with whom we enjoy an honest, high-trusting relationship but who have conflicting visions, goals or methods. . . . The task of the (loyal opposition) is to bring out the best in us. We need to be grateful for those who oppose us in a high-trust way, for they bring the picture of reality and practicality to our plans. (Block, 1987:135–136)

Block believes that it is important when working with the loyal opposition that the leader communicate the extent to which they are valued. Leaders can do this, in his view, by reaffirming the quality of the relationship and the fact that it's based on trust. They should be clear in stating their positions and the reasons why they hold them. They should also state in a neutral way what they think positions of the loyal opposition are. The leader reasons as follows:

> We disagree with respect to purpose, goals, and perhaps even visions. Our task is to understand their position. Our way of fulfilling that task is to be able to state to them their arguments in a positive way. They should feel understood and acknowledged by our statement of their disagreement with us. (Block, 1987:137)

With this kind of relationship in place, the leadership and the loyal opposition are in a position to negotiate differences in good faith.

References

Argyris, Chris. 1964. *Integrating the Individual and the Organization.* New York: Wiley.

Block, Peter. 1987. *The Empowered Manager.* San Francisco: Jossey-Bass.

Deal, Terrence E. 1985. "The Symbolism of Effective Schools," *The Elementary School Journal* D85(5).

Dwyer, David C. 1989. "School Climate Starts at the Curb," in *School Climate—The Principal Difference.* Hartford: Connecticut Principals' Academy.

Dyer, W. G., Jr. 1982. *Patterns and Assumptions: The Keys to Understanding Organizational Culture.* Office of Naval Research, Technical Report TR-O NR-7.

Hansen, Corwith. 1986. "Department Culture in a High-Performing Secondary School." Unpublished dissertation, Teachers College, Columbia University.

Lundberg, Craig C. 1985. "On the Feasibility of Cultural Intervention in Organizations," in Peter J. Frost, Larry F. Moore, Meryl Reis Louis, Craig C. Lundberg, and Joanne Martin (Eds.), *Organizational Culture.* Beverly Hills, CA: Sage.

Merton, Robert K. 1957. *Social Theory and Social Structure.* New York: Free Press.

Parsons, Talcott. 1951. *The Social System.* New York: Free Press.

Schein, Edgar H. 1981. "Does Japanese Management Style Have a Message for American Managers?" *Sloan Management Review* 24(1), 55–68.

Schein, Edgar H. 1985. *Organizational Culture and Leadership.* San Francisco: Jossey-Bass.

Shils, Edward A. 1961. "Centre and Periphery," in *The Logic of Personal Knowledge: Essays Presented to Michael Polanyi.* London: Routledge and Kegan Paul.

Weick, Karl E. 1985. "The Significance of Culture," in Peter J. Frost, Larry F. Moore, Meryl Reis Louis, Craig C. Lundberg, and Joanne Martin (Eds.), *Organizational Culture.* Beverly Hills, CA: Sage.

7

THE STAGES OF LEADERSHIP
A Developmental View

*T*wo themes are developed in this chapter. The first theme is the importance of taking a developmental view by understanding the stages of leadership. Different stages are appropriate for different circumstances. Successful principals are able to gauge the situations they are in to provide the kind of leadership that best fits those circumstances. As circumstances change so should the kind of leadership the principal offers change. The second theme examines three leadership archetypes: artists, craftsmen, and technocrats. Each of the three types brings certain strengths to leadership in a school. But not all three are equally important. Though recognizing that artists and technocrats have important roles to play, it is the leader as craftsman that emerges as the critical link between vision and making vision a reality.

Not every situation a principal faces requires the same leadership strategy. The principal of a highly competent and well-motivated faculty will have to proceed one way and the principal of a developing and uncommitted faculty will have to proceed another way. As is the case with most craftlike fields where one must create her or his practice in use depending on circumstances, no one best approach to leadership will work. Instead, principals must practice leadership in light of the context they face. In this chapter we are concerned with four leadership strategies and tactics that are available to principals, each being appropriate at different times* during the development of an effective school (Sergiovanni, 1990, 1994):

---

*In earlier editions of this book the four stages were bartering, building, bonding, and binding. I now understand that the bonding of people to each other is usually a result of their being bound to shared values and ideas. Thus, the four stages are reordered with binding preceding bonding.

1. *Bartering.* Principals and teachers strike a bargain within which the leader gives to those led something they want in exchange for what the leader wants. The emphasis in bartering is on trading wants and needs for cooperation and compliance. This approach works best when the principal and teachers do not share common goals and interests—when their stakes in the school are different.

2. *Building.* Principals provide the climate and interpersonal support that enhances teachers' opportunities for fulfillment of individual needs for achievement, responsibility, competence, and esteem. The emphasis in building is less on trading and more on providing the conditions that enable teachers to experience psychological fulfillment. Once a minimum level of common effort has been achieved, this approach is recommended to shift the emphasis from extrinsic to intrinsic rewards.

3. *Binding.* Principals and teachers develop together a set of shared values about the relationships they want to share and the ties they want to create so that together they can become a community of learners and leaders—a community of practice.

4. *Bonding.* Principal and teachers are connected together in community that changes their relationships and changes their commitments in such a way that school improvements are institutionalized into the everyday life of the school. The emphasis in bonding is on relationships characterized by mutual caring and the felt interdependence that comes from mutually held obligations and commitments. It is at the bonding stage that sustained leadership and sustained improvements are secured. People come together as a community of mind, heart, and practice. Moral authority is established.

Taken together the strategies can be thought of as developmental stages, each suited to different levels of school competence and excellence. The stages are elaborated in Table 7.2 later in this chapter. But first, let's turn our attention to the sources of authority for leadership—the assumptions and theories that principals use to legitimize their leadership practice.

*T*HE SOURCES OF AUTHORITY FOR LEADERSHIP

When leadership is viewed as developmental stages, the emphasis is not on which leadership strategy is best, but on which of the strategies makes most sense given the stage of school improvement in question. Leadership by bartering, for example, makes most sense in schools that are not working very well. Leadership by binding, by contrast, makes sense when basic competence is not the issue, when a healthy interpersonal climate has been established and as people become connected to a common framework for action. Each of the stages and leadership strategies can be understood by examining the sources of authority for leadership and by being linked to the transactional and transformational leadership types provided by Burns (1978).

The challenge for principals is to provide the leadership needed to achieve a basic level of competence and then to transcend this competence to get extraordinary commitment and performance not only when rewards are available but when they are not. Sustained commitment and performance require an approach to leadership that connects people to work for moral reasons. Moral reasons emerge from the purposes, values, and norms that form the cultural center of the school. This center binds people together in a common cause. For this reason, the leadership that is required is referred to as binding leadership. Binding leadership is key in cultivating self-management among teachers. This leadership is contrasted with the more common traditional and human resources approaches to leadership as follows:

1. *Traditional leadership* practices emphasize hierarchy, rules, and management protocols and rely on bureaucratic linkages to connect people to work by forcing them to respond as subordinates.
2. *Human resource leadership* practices emphasize leadership styles, supportive climates, and interpersonal skills and rely on psychological linkages to motivate people to work by getting them to respond ultimately as self-actualizers.
3. *Binding leadership* practices emphasize ideas, values, and beliefs and rely on moral linkages to compel people to work by getting them to respond as followers.

Traditional leadership practices rely on bureaucratic values as their source of authority. Teachers (and students, too, since this discussion of sources of authority and their implicit assumptions applies to the leadership that both principals and teachers use in relating to students) are expected to comply with the rules and to follow the provided scripts or face the consequences. In a sense, they trade compliance to avoid problems with the system. Bureaucratic authority has a place even in the most progressive of schools. Yet, when this source of authority is central, the following assumptions seem to be implicit:

Teachers are subordinates in a hierarchically arranged system.
Principals are trustworthy, but you cannot trust teachers.
The goals and interests of teachers and principals are not the same; therefore, principals must be watchful.
Hierarchy equals expertise; thus, principals know more than do teachers about everything.
External accountability works best. (Sergiovanni and Starratt, 1993:25)

The consequences of relying on a leadership based primarily on bureaucratic authority have been carefully documented. Without proper monitoring, principals wind up being loosely connected to bureaucratic systems complying only when they have to (Sergiovanni, 1990–1991; Weick, 1976). When this monitoring is effective, teachers respond as technicians who execute predetermined scripts and whose performance becomes narrowed. They become, to use the jargon, "deskilled" (McNeil, 1986; Rosenholtz, 1989; Wise, 1979). When teachers are not able to use their full talents and when they are caught in the drudgery of routine, they become separated from their work, viewing teaching as a job rather than a vocation and treating students as cases rather than persons.

Very few people mean to advocate a leadership practice based primarily on bureaucratic authority or mean to accept the implicit assumptions that are behind this practice. Not many principals, for example, believe that teachers as a group are not trustworthy and do not share the same goals and interests about schooling as they do. Even fewer would accept the idea that hierarchy equals expertise, and, thus, they know more about everything than do teachers. Even so, most principals are likely to feel that teachers are subordinates in a hierarchically arranged system and that external monitoring works best. For this reason, supervision based on external monitoring persists. Principals still rely heavily on "expect and inspect," on monitoring predetermined standards, on inservicing teachers, and on providing direct supervision aimed at control rather than capacity building.

Human resources leadership practices rely heavily on personal expertise and skill in motivating and manipulating people as their source of authority. Essentially the idea is to figure out which psychological buttons to push when motivating teachers, and if the right ones are chosen, then teachers willingly trade compliance with the principal's wishes for getting needs met. When principals place personal authority at the center of their leadership practice, the following assumptions seem to be implicit:

> The goals and interests of teachers and principals are not the same. As a result, each must barter with the other so that both get what they want by giving something that the other party wants.
> Teachers have needs and if these needs are met at work, their work gets done as required in exchange.
> Congenial relationships in pleasant interpersonal climates make teachers easier to work with and more apt to cooperate with the principal.
> Principals must be experts at reading the needs of teachers and otherwise handling them in order to barter successfully for their cooperation and commitment. (Sergiovanni and Starratt, 1993:27)

The typical reaction of teachers to personal authority is to respond when rewards are available, but not otherwise. Teachers become involved in their work for calculated reasons, and as such, their performance is difficult to sustain over time without continually renegotiating the bartering arrangement.

Binding leadership practices rely heavily on moral values as their source of authority. Moral authority is derived from obligations and duties that teachers feel toward each other and toward the school as a result of their connection to widely shared values, ideas, and ideals. When moral authority is in place, teachers respond to shared commitments and to the felt interdependence that comes from the sense of we that is created. As moral authority becomes the center of a principal's practice, the school is transformed into a moral community. Moral authority, for example, is the central tenant of the discussion on building community that appears in Chapter 5. The sources of authority and their relationship to leadership practice are summarized in Table 7.1.

THE STAGES OF LEADERSHIP

In 1978, James MacGregor Burns proposed a theory of leadership that has shaped the way leadership practice is now understood. According to Burns, leadership is exercised when persons with certain motives and purposes mobilize resources so as to arouse and satisfy the motives of followers. He identified two broad kinds of leadership: transactional and transformative. *Transactional leadership* focuses on basic and largely extrinsic motives and needs; *transformative leadership* focuses on higher-order, more intrinsic, and ultimately moral motives and needs. This latter point is important to understanding Burns's theory. Burns (1978) described transformational leadership, for example, as a process within which "leaders and followers raise one another to higher levels of morality and motivation" (20). Transformative leadership is in two stages, one concerned with higher-order psychological needs for esteem, autonomy, and self-actualization, and the other with moral questions of goodness, righteousness, duty, and obligation.

In his groundbreaking examination of the moral dimension in management and motivation, Etzioni (1988) provides a compelling case for moral authority as a source of motivation and basis for management. Etzioni acknowledges the importance of extrinsic and intrinsic motivation, but points out that ultimately what counts most to people is what they believe, how they feel, and the shared norms and cultural messages that emerge from the groups and communities with which they identify. Morality, emotion, and social bonds, he maintains, are far more powerful motivators than are the extrinsic concerns of transactional leadership and the intrinsic psychological concerns of the early stages of transformative leadership.

In transactional leadership, leaders and followers exchange needs and services in order to accomplish independent objectives. It is assumed that leaders and followers do not share a common stake in the enterprise, and thus some kind of bargain must be struck. This bargaining process was described earlier as a form of *leadership by bartering*. The wants and needs of followers and the wants and needs of the leader are traded, and a bargain is struck. Positive reinforcement is given for good work, merit pay for increased performance, promotion for increased persistence, a feeling of belonging for cooperation, and so forth.

In transformative leadership, by contrast, leaders and followers are united in pursuit of higher-level goals that are common to both. Both want to become the best. Both want to shape the school in a new direction. When transformative leadership is practiced successfully, purposes that might have started out being separate become fused.

t a b l e **7.1** **The Sources of Authority for Leadership and Practice**

Source	Assumptions When Use of This Source Is Prime	Leadership/ Supervisory Strategy	Anticipated Consequences
Bureaucratic Authority			
Hierarchy	Teachers are subordinates in a hierarchically arranged system.	"Expect and inspect" is the overarching rule.	With proper monitoring, teachers respond as technicians executing predetermined scripts. Their performance is narrowed.
Rules and regulations		Rely on predetermined standards to which teachers must measure up or face sanctions.	
Mandates	Supervisors are trustworthy, but you cannot trust subordinates very much.		
Role expectation		Directly supervise and closely monitor the work of teachers to ensure compliance.	
Teachers are expected to comply or face consequences.	Goals and interests of teachers and supervisors are not the same; thus, supervisors must be watchful.	Figure out how to motivate them and get them to change.	
	Hierarchy equals expertise; thus, supervisors know more than do teachers.		
	External accountability works best.		
Personal Authority			
Motivation technology	The goals and interests of teachers and supervisors are not the same but can be bartered so that each gets what each wants.	Develop a school climate characterized by congeniality among teachers and between teachers and supervisors.	Teachers respond as required when rewards are available but not otherwise. Their involvement is calculated and performance is narrowed.
Interpersonal skills		"Expect and reward."	
Human relations leadership	Teachers have needs, and if those needs are met at work, the work gets done as required in exchange.	"What gets rewarded gets done."	
Teachers will want to comply because of the congenial climate provided and to reap rewards offered in exchange.	Congenial relationships and harmonious interpersonal climates make teachers content, easier to work with, and more apt to cooperate.		

table **7.1** Continued

Source	Assumptions When Use of This Source Is Prime	Leadership/ Supervisory Strategy	Anticipated Consequences
Moral Authority			
Felt obligations and duties derived from widely shared community values, ideas, and ideals Teachers respond to shared commitments and felt inter-dependence	Schools are professional learning communities. Communities are defined by their center of shared values, beliefs, and commitments. In communities: What is considered right and good is as important as what works and what is effective. People are motivated as much by emotion and beliefs as by self-interest. Collegiality is a professional virtue.	Identify and make explicit the values and beliefs that define the center of the school as community. Translate the above into informal norms that govern behavior. Promote collegiality as internally felt and morally driven interdependence. Rely on ability of community members to respond to duties and obligations. Rely on the community's informal norm system to enforce professional and community values.	Teachers respond to community values for moral reasons. Their practice becomes collective, and their performance is expansive and sustained.

Source: Adapted from Sergiovanni (1992).

Initially, transformative leadership takes the form of *leadership by building*. Here the focus is on arousing human potential, satisfying higher-order needs, and raising expectations of both leader and follower in a manner that motivates both to higher levels of commitment and performance. Burns points out that ultimately transformative leadership becomes moral because it raises the level of human conduct and ethical aspiration of both leader and led. When this occurs, transformative leadership takes the form of *leadership by binding*. Here the leader focuses on arousing awareness and consciousness that elevate school goals and purposes to the level of a shared covenant that binds together leader and follower in a moral commitment. Leadership by binding responds to such intrinsic human needs as a desire for purpose, meaning, and significance in what one does. The key concepts associated with transformative leadership by binding are cultural and moral leadership.

Leadership by bartering, building, and binding, when viewed sequentially, make up the stages of leadership for school improvement referred to earlier.

Bartering provides the push needed to get things started; building provides the push needed to create the psychological support system necessary for people to respond to higher levels of need fulfillment; and binding provides the inspiration needed for performance and commitment that are beyond expectations.

Leadership by bonding is the fourth stage of school improvement. When people are connected to similar values and ideas their relationships change. They become more open with each other, more supportive of each other, and more helpful to each other. Bonds of trust emerge that make collaboration easy. The likelihood that communities of practice emerge in the school increases.

When practicing leadership by bonding, the principal ministers to the needs of the school and works to serve others so that they are better able to perform their responsibilities. In addition to manager, minister, and servant, the leader functions as a "high priest" by protecting the values of the school. The high priest function is an expression of the cultural force of leadership discussed in Chapter 6.

Each of the stages of leadership can be thought of as comprising distinct school improvement strategies. However, tactically speaking, bartering, building, binding, and bonding can be thought of as leadership styles to be used simultaneously for different purposes or people within any of the stages. A recalcitrant teacher, for example, may well require leadership by bartering regardless of one's overall strategy.

Leadership by bartering is an especially effective strategy when the issue is one of competence. However, once competence has been achieved, one needs to look to leadership by building and binding for the strategies and tactics that will help transcend competence to inspire commitment and extraordinary performance. The stages of leadership and their relationship to school improvement are summarized in Table 7.2.

$\mathcal{W}$HY LEADERSHIP BY BINDING AND BONDING WORKS

Binding and bonding leadership works because

- They are aligned with a realistic view of how schools actually work; thus, their practices are practical.
- They are based on a theory of human rationality that enhances both individual and organizational intelligence and performance.
- They respond to higher-order psychological and spiritual needs that lead to extraordinary commitment, performance, and satisfaction.

When a school leader chooses a theory from which to practice, a particular image of rationality is assumed whether or not it fits the real world. A better fit between theory and practice will occur by starting the other way around. First choose the image of rationality that fits the real world, and then find a theory that fits that image of rationality.

table **7.2**   **The Stages of Leadership and School Improvement**

Leadership Type	Leadership Styles	Stages of School Improvement
Transactional Leadership	Leadership as bartering	*Getting started* by exchanging human needs and interests that allow satisfaction of independent (leader and follower) but organizationally related objectives
Transformational Leadership	Leadership as building	*Muddling through* by arousing human potential, satisfying higher needs, raising expectations of both leader and followers that motivate to higher levels of commitment and performance
	Leadership as binding	*Seeking a transformative breakthrough* by arousing awareness and consciousness that elevate organizational goals and purposes to the level of a shared covenant and that bond together leader and followers in a moral commitment
	Leadership as bonding	*Promoting self-management* by ministering to the needs of the school, being of service, guarding the values while at the same time strengthening collegiality and encouraging the emergence of communities of practice

Shulman (1989) provides three images of human rationality. All three are true to a certain extent, but some are more true than others. It makes a difference which of the three or which combination of the three provides the strategic basis for one's leadership practice. The three are provided below. Using a total of 10 points, distribute points among the three to indicate the extent to which you believe each to be true.

1. Humans are rational; they think and act in a manner consistent with their goals, their self-interests, and what they have been rewarded for. If you wish them to behave in a given way, make the desired behavior clear to them and make it worth their while to engage in it.

2. Humans are limited in their rationality; they can make sense of only a small piece of the world at a time, and they strive to act reasonably with respect to their limited grasp of facts and alternatives. They must therefore construct conceptions or definitions of situations rather than passively accept what is presented to them. If you wish them to change, engage them in active problem solving and judgment—don't just tell them what to do.

3. Humans are rational only when acting together; since individual reason is so limited, men and women find opportunities to work jointly on important problems, achieving through joint effort what individual reason and capacity could

> never accomplish. If you want them to change, develop ways in which they can engage in the change process jointly with peers. (Shulman, 1989:171)

The first image of rationality fits traditional management theories and leadership by bartering practices very well. The second and third images, by contrast, are better accommodated by the Scruffies' view of management discussed in Chapter 3 and leadership by building and binding. Within the second and third images, rationality is achieved by helping people make sense of their world. As sense builds, some of the limits on rationality are overcome. The ability to make sense builds when people are able to construct their own definitions of situations and are involved with the leader in active problem solving. The limits, however, are typically too great for anyone to do it alone. Thus, a key strategy for sense building is the pooling of human resources and the fostering of collegial values in an effort that expands individual reason and capacity to function successfully.

Leadership as bartering responds to physical, security, social, and ego needs of people at work. In his well-known motivation-hygiene theory, Herzberg (1966) pointed out that these needs and the job factors that accommodated them had less to do with commitment and performance beyond expectations than with meeting ordinary basic job requirements. He pointed out that should the needs not be met, worker performance and commitment are likely to fall below a satisfactory level. But when the needs are met, all that results is that workers meet basic job requirements. However, when such job factors as opportunities for achievement, challenge, responsibility, recognition for one's accomplishment, and opportunities to demonstrate competence were present, then such higher-order needs as esteem, competence, autonomy, and self-actualization were likely to be met. These factors and needs are related to leadership by building. They are the bridges that leader and followers must cross together as they move from ordinary performance to performance that is beyond expectations.

The strength of leadership by binding and bonding is the ability to focus on arousing awareness and consciousness to elevate school goals and purposes to the level of a shared covenant that bonds leader and followers together and binds them to a set of ideas that comprise moral commitments. Leadership by binding and bonding responds to such higher-order needs as the desire for purpose, meaning, and significance in what one does. Both can provide the necessary cultural cement that holds people and organizations together.

*L*EADERSHIP STYLES COUNT TOO

Over a period of eight years Patricia Pitcher (1997) studied 15 executives in a global financial corporation. She was interested in the links between leadership, personality types, and organizational effectiveness. Pitcher's revelations about leadership are helpful because the archetypes she identified, while empirically grounded in the corporate world, are familiar to us (see, e.g., Blumberg, 1988). And further, her findings make intuitive sense when applied to our situation.

Pitcher's study revealed three archetypes: leaders as artists who are brilliant visionaries, people oriented, open minded, and intuitive; leaders as craftsmen who are empathetic and effective developers of people, who empower others, and who are skilled at bringing out the best in others; and leaders as technocrats who though often brilliant are prone to place hyperrationality over emotions and though meticulous and superb at managing things have difficulty managing people effectively. If properly matched to the right roles and responsibilities, each of the three types brings strengths to any organization. Mismatched placements, however, are a recipe for disaster. We often hear stories about principals who were successful in one school and unsuccessful in another. It is the context that matters. Some principals, for example, may not do well in a suburban school that serves privileged students and highly involved parents. They may have neither the patience nor the disposition to play the kind of "public relations" roles that schools of this type often demand. A transfer to a struggling school on the south side of town, however, brings out the best in them, and their performance is stellar.

Pitcher uses familiar language to describe the three archetypes. For example, most of us know that, though artist visionary leaders are important, they alone are rarely able to hold things together. Once they leave, the leadership vacuum that typically occurs takes its toll. Artists who surround themselves with craftsmen, however, are able to change the connections of people from them and their charisma to ideas, frameworks, and implementation routines.

CRAFTSMEN LEADERS ARE CRITICAL

Craftsmen know how to turn visions into reality, to take big ideas and make them understandable and useful, and to bring together the right mix of human resources to make schools work. To assume the craftsmen role effectively, leaders need to master the eight basic competencies that were discussed in Chapter 1. They are the management of attention, the management of meaning, the management of trust, the management of self, the management of paradox, the management of effectiveness, the management of follow-up, and the management of responsibility. Artists may sketch out the vision, but it is craftsmen, armed with these eight basic competencies, who will get the job done and who are able to sustain school improvements over the long haul.

In many schools we have too much vision and not enough people who can build strategies, develop programs, and marshal human resources to get the job done. For this to happen we need more craftsmen leaders. We could also probably do with fewer technocrats even though they have important, albeit limited, roles to play. Sitting on a mountain of rules and regulations, leaders from this archetype seek to lead by using a kind of management that is both scripted and impersonal. That technocrats are powerful is evidenced by the unprecedented standardization of teaching and learning and the ultrarational alignment of teaching and learning with standards and tests that now seem to characterize our everyday world of schooling. Pitcher worries about the proliferation of technocrats in top leadership roles. She argues that while technocrats may be useful lower in the organization or off to the side, they can do irreparable harm should they reach the principal's office or the superintendent's office.

*T*HE ARCHETYPES IN REVIEW

Artists view leadership as *vision* that transfers ideas into goals. Craftsmen view leadership as *design* that transfers ideas into things. And technocrats view leadership as a *script* that transfers ideas into rules, steps, and procedures. As visionaries, artists, says Pitcher (1997), are inclined to be emotional, imaginative, and entrepreneur-like. As realists, craftsmen are inclined to be stable, wise, and responsible. And as detail-oriented people, technocrats are inclined to be serious, meticulous, and methodical.

Leadership as vision, design, and script are all needed to make things work in schools. Thus the issue is not whether the three should be included or not but how and where they should be distributed in a school or a school district.

Artists have an important role to play by providing the initial spark, but it is craftsmen that create the designs, marshal the human resources, and in other ways move the school along. They even help technocrats get their acts together by linking their management skills with the designs for action needed to make the school work. If you have too many artists and too many technocrats, they wind up impeding progress by getting the school bogged down in theory as an end in itself or with management scripts that box people in, make decisions for them, and in other ways reduce their ability to work effectively.

Taking this message to heart suggests that the real heroes in schools may not be the visionaries at all but the people who are able to make those visions a reality. Sometimes they are the same person but often they are different persons. Craftsmen may not be flashy. They may not get as much attention as they should, and they may not be as exciting to be with. But you can count on them to make things work well for students every day.

*I*DEA-BASED LEADERSHIP

When values and beliefs become institutionalized into the everyday management life of the school, then management know-how, hierarchical authority, interpersonal skill, and personality are ultimately transcended as the leader becomes one who administers to the needs of the school and its members. The principal doesn't become less important, only differently important. On the one hand, she or he becomes the guardian of the values of the school's covenant, and on the other hand, she or he becomes a capable administrator who works hard to help others meet their commitments to the school. Once at this stage, leadership and followership become exceptionally close. As pointed out earlier, followers manage themselves well by thinking for themselves, exercising self-control, accepting responsibility and obligation, and believing in and caring about what they are doing (Kelly, 1988:144). Both followers and leaders are attracted to and compelled by the same things: ideas, values, and commitments. Thus, over time, leaders seek to restructure the chain of command so that followers are not connected to leaders in a hierarchical sense, but so that both leaders and followers respond to the same ideas, values, and commitments.

Traditional chain of command **(hierarchical authority)**	**New chain of command** **(moral authority)**
Leaders	Ideas, values, commitments
↓	↓
Followers	Leaders as followers and followers as leaders

When this happens, hierarchical authority and authority derived from one's personality give way to purpose and management. The leader is neither boss nor messiah but administrator.

The authority vested in the leader as boss is organizational and hierarchical; the authority vested in the leader as messiah is charismatic and interpersonal; and the authority vested in the leader as administrator is obligatory, stemming from the obligations that come from serving shared values and purposes (Sergiovanni, 1990:150).

School principals are responsible for "ministering" to the needs of the schools they serve, as defined by the shared values and purposes of the school's covenant. They minister by furnishing help and by being of service to parents, teachers, and students. They minister by providing leadership in a way that encourages others to be leaders in their own right. They minister by highlighting and protecting the values of the school. The principal as minister is one who is devoted to a cause, mission, or set of ideas and accepts the duty and obligation to serve this cause. Ultimately, her or his success is known by the quality of the followership that emerges in the school. The quality of followership is a barometer that indicates the extent to which moral authority has replaced bureaucratic. When moral authority drives leadership practice, the principal is at the same time a leader of leaders, follower of ideas, minister of values, and servant to the followership.

SOME REFLECTIONS

1. In 1978 James MacGregor Burns proposed a theory of leadership that remains the foundation for much of the literature on school leadership. He identified

two kinds of leadership: transactional and transformative. Transactional leadership focuses on basic extrinsic needs, and transformative focuses on higher order, more intrinsic and ultimately moral motives and needs. His book *Leadership* remains widely read. Refer to this book and become familiar with the transactional and transformative leadership themes. How applicable are his views to the school setting? As you review this book and other works in educational administration, to what extent have they been influenced by Burns's ideas?

2. Which of the three archetypes—artists, craftsmen, and technocrats—best describes your principal? Distribute 10 points across the three to indicate the extent to which each fits. Give examples.

3. Revisit the discussion of the eight basic competencies that appears in Chapter 1. How does your principal measure up to each of the competencies?

 # REFERENCES

Blumberg, Arthur. 1988. *School Administration as a Craft: Foundation of Practice*. Boston: Allyn and Bacon.

Burns, James MacGregor. 1978. *Leadership*. New York: Harper & Row.

Etzioni, Amitai. 1988. *The Moral Dimension: Toward a New Economics*. New York: Free Press.

Herzberg, Frederick. 1966. *Work and the Nature of Man*. Cleveland: World Publishing.

Kelly, Robert E. 1988, November–December. "In Praise of Followers," *Harvard Business Review*.

McNeil, Linda. 1986. *Contradictions of Control: School Structure and School Knowledge*. New York: Routledge and Kegan Paul.

Pitcher, Patricia. 1997. *The Drama of Leadership*. New York: Wiley.

Rosenholtz, Susan. 1989. *Teachers' Workplace: The Social Organization of Schools*. New York: Longman.

Sergiovanni, Thomas J. 1990. *Value-Added Leadership: How to Get Extraordinary Performance in Schools*. San Diego, CA: Harcourt Brace Jovanovich.

Sergiovanni, Thomas J. 1990–1991. "Biting the Bullet: Rescinding the Texas Teacher Appraisal System," *Teacher Education in Practice* 6(2), 89–93.

Sergiovanni, Thomas J. 1994. *Building Community in Schools*. San Francisco: Jossey-Bass.

Sergiovanni, Thomas J., and Robert J. Starratt. 1993. *Supervision: A Redefinition* (5th ed.). New York: McGraw-Hill.

Shulman, Lee. 1989. "Teaching Alone, Learning Together: Needed Agenda for New Reforms," in T. J. Sergiovanni and J. H. Moore (Eds.), *Schooling for Tomorrow: Directing Reforms to Issues That Count*. Boston: Allyn and Bacon.

Weick, Karl E. 1976. "Educational Organization as Loosely Coupled Systems," *Administrative Science Quarterly* 21.

Wise, Arthur E. 1979. *Legislated Learning: The Bureaucratization of the American Classroom*. Berkeley: University of California Press.

8

BECOMING A COMMUNITY
OF LEADERS

he idea of community has appeal to most principals, and many schools are
quick to label themselves as caring communities and learning communities. Yet, when the conversation shifts to a discussion of school as a community of leaders, many principals begin to feel uncomfortable. The literature, for
example, frequently encourages principals to provide strong and direct leadership in making schools effective. As a result, leadership is part of an interaction
influence system within which the leader, acting alone, interacts with others in an
effort to influence what they think and do.

As discussed in Chapter 7, we have come to understand this approach as leadership by bartering. The leader and the led strike bargains. The leader gives to the
led something they want in exchange for something the leader wants. Within this
view, leaders may have lofty visions and may want to do the right thing. But exercising leadership still means controlling events and people in a way that makes
events occur the way leaders think they should. Progressive leaders, however, are
not supposed to be dictatorial. Instead, they are encouraged to share some of their
responsibility for leadership with others and delegate some of their authority to
others. When they do this, so it is believed, the likelihood that others will respond
better and thus be more likely to do what the leader thinks is good for the school
is increased.

Despite its appeal, the concept of shared leadership may actually be part of the problem. Sharing leadership, for example, implies that leadership belongs to a designated leader. It is the leader's choice to share or not to share. Webster defines to share as "to grant or give a share" and sharing as ". . . the original holder grants to another the partial use, enjoyment, or possession of a thing." There is wide agreement that effective practice requires principals and other designated leaders to share leadership responsibilities they have by virtue of rank or position. But when leadership is "owned" by one person or group of persons at a given rank and then is shared with others who do not own it, too often others become dependent and their leadership responsibilities become diluted.

For leadership to be effective it needs to be fully resourced. This happens when one's responsibility and authority are matched. And this happens when others have the necessary discretion to lead. When there is not enough discretion, there will not be enough leadership to get the job done. This is a problem not just for teachers. Principals also are faced with underresourced leadership sharing from above. Increasingly the responsibilities they have far exceed the authority they have. No matter how hard they try to lead, when their discretion is compromised so is their leadership practice.

Struggling to make the school a community changes all of this. Leadership by bartering may be necessary in the beginning, but then the emphasis shifts to leadership by building, binding, and bonding. In creating community, what matters most is what the community shares together, what the community believes in together, and what the community wants to accomplish together. It is this shared idea structure, this community of mind, that becomes the primary source of authority for what people do. Together, principals and teachers become followers of the dream and are committed to making it real. Within this view, leadership is nothing more than a means to make things happen. Because not only the principal but all of the followers have an equal obligation to embody community values, principals and teachers must share equally together in the obligation to lead.

*P*RACTICAL ISSUES

The more that leadership is cultivated in a school, the more likely it is that everyone will get a chance to use their talents fully and the more committed everyone is likely to be. Furthermore, in a democracy such as ours, the more that leadership is shared and expressed, the better it is presumed to be. Exercising leadership for the good of everyone is considered to be one of the responsibilities of citizenship. An additional consideration is that, given today's complex world, shared leadership is necessary in order to figure out problems and in order to help schools work well. Sharing leadership is a way to aggregate what we know.

In their review of the literature on school improvement, Lieberman and Miller (1986) reached a similar conclusion. They found that any effort to improve schools must be grounded in the social realities of the classroom as revealed in the lives of teachers and their work. In their words:*

> What we have rediscovered are some tried and true notions that have become enriched and expanded over time. Among them:
>
>> Working with people rather than working on people.
>> Recognizing the complexity and craft nature of the teacher's work.
>> Understanding that there are unique cultural differences in each school and how these affect development efforts.
>> Providing time to learn.
>> Building collaboration and cooperation, involving the provisions for people to do things together, talking together, sharing concerns.
>> Starting where people are, not where you are.
>> Making private knowledge public, by being sensitive to the effects of teacher isolation and the power of trial and error.
>> Resisting simplistic solutions to complex problems; getting comfortable with reworking issues and finding enhanced understanding and enlightenment.
>> Appreciating that there are many variations of development efforts; there is no one best way.
>> Using knowledge as a way of helping people grow rather than pointing up their deficits.
>> Supporting development efforts by protecting ideas, announcing expectations, making provisions for necessary resources.
>> Sharing leadership functions as a team, so that people can provide complementary skills and get experience in role taking.
>> Organizing development efforts around a particular focus.
>> Understanding that content and process are both essential, that you cannot have one without the other.
>> Being aware of and sensitive to the differences in the worlds of teachers and other actors within or outside of the school setting. (Lieberman and Miller, 1986:108–109)

In a recent update of the social realities theme, Lieberman and Miller (1999) state:

> Perhaps the greatest lesson we have learned from our study of teachers and schools in the midst of change is that a new view of teaching and community is being crafted, one that takes place not only inside classrooms and schools but outside as well, one that respects diversity and confronts differences, that represents

---

*Reprinted by permission of the publisher from Ann Lieberman and Lynne Miller, *Rethinking School Improvement Research, Craft, and Concept* (New York: Teachers College Press, © 1986 by Teachers College, Columbia University. All rights reserved.) p. 108 (Lines 21–24); p. 109 (Lines 1–5).

a sensitivity to and engagement with the whole life of students as they live it. The creation of new learning communities that include rather than exclude, that create knowledge rather than merely apply it, and that offer both challenge and support provide the greatest hope for teachers who are in the process of transforming themselves, their world, and their work. (91)

This emphasis on creating new learning communities for teachers as a vehicle for change leads them to propose eight new understandings about the social realities of teaching and their link to teacher development and school improvement:

Creating a seamless web of values, practices and organizational structures.
Making professional development integral to school life.
Supporting teacher learning outside of school.
Leading and learning as a collective responsibility.
Maintaining balance [*among competing demands*].
Establishing conditions that support the new social realities of teaching.
Learning about and understanding the change process.
Protecting and nurturing hope, passion and commitment. (Lieberman and Miller, 1999:84–90)

Lieberman and Miller's lists suggest that successful school improvement efforts depend on reaching into the invisible aspects of school life and tapping the energy and commitment of teachers up close. Teachers have to take initiative, accept responsibility, and become active leaders. Together, principal and teachers must become a community of leaders.

*L*EADERSHIP AS A PRACTICE

The views of leadership described above lead to an important question: Must leadership always be linked with positions, or could we think of it as being a function too? One way to blur the distinction between position and function is to view the principalship as a practice whose responsibilities, functions, and actions are shared by principals and teachers. Teaching, too, could be thought of as a practice shared by teachers and principals. In each case sharing is a characteristic of the practice itself. It is not a separate decision controlled by a person. Principals, for example, are entitled to assume and are obligated to assume the role of principal teacher if they have the expertise and commitment to do so. And teachers, too, are entitled to and obligated to assume leadership roles as long as the roles they assume are matched with their levels of competency and commitment.

Thus, an alternative to the way we usually think about shared leadership is to view leadership as an entitlement that is linked to a practice. This leadership isn't indiscriminately distributed but distributed to those who have a legitimate entitlement to claim it. Entitlement is most often legitimized by expertise and commitment. Those who get to lead—indeed those who have a responsibility to lead—are those who have the will, expertness, temperament, and skills to help us achieve our goals in a particular area at a particular time. Others are entitled to step forward as leaders in other areas.

Entitlement is the solution to the ability–authority gap. As pointed out in Chapter 4, the principle of ability–authority was proposed by Victor Thompson in 1961. He argued that the major problem facing modern organizations is the growing gap that exists between those who have authority to act but not the ability to lead and those who have the ability to act but not the authority to lead. Entitlement seeks to place those who have the ability to act in the forefront of decision making. In successful schools, organizational structures promote authority based on ability. In schools and school districts where it is necessary for authority to be formally linked to one's position in the organizational hierarchy, day-by-day practice is characterized by formal and informal delegation of this authority to those with ability and commitment. But the long-term solution is to separate leadership from position by entitling anyone who qualifies to lead.

But will changing the conditions for deciding who will lead result in confusion? And will this confusion result in losing control over deciding what needs to be done, how, and by whom? The answer to these questions is, probably not. Separating leadership from position does not undermine a teacher's authority, a principal's authority, or a superintendent's authority. Position still counts, as does legal authority. It does mean, however, that in spite of position and legal authority, leadership remains an entitlement. If we do not have the necessary ability or if we are not sufficiently committed to lead then we do not have the entitlement to lead. Still, we remain in charge. It is still our responsibility, for example, to provide the necessary resources and management supports, to assess how well we are doing, and to otherwise look after the school. An important part of our job, as Bennis and Nanus (1985) remind us, is to provide the management support to ensure people do things right at the same time we focus leadership on doing right things for teaching and learning.

*N*EW LEADERSHIP VALUES FOR THE PRINCIPALSHIP

Becoming a community of leaders requires adopting new leadership values such as purposing, followership, empowerment, accomplishment, collegiality, intrinsic motivation, quality control, simplicity, reflection, and outrage. Together the values provide the substance for practicing leadership by binding and by bonding. They are considered in the following subsections in the form of leadership principles.

Purposing and Shared Values

Harvard Business School professor Abraham Zaleznik (1989) believes that the failure of management is the substitution of process for substance. The importance of management processes to school effectiveness should not be underestimated, but such processes are not substitutes for substance. It is important, for example, to know how to get from A to B, and sound management can help; however, the substance of administrative leadership is concerned with whether B is better than A and why. Furthermore, having determined the direction, substance is the means by which one brings together divergent human resources, inspires commitment, and achieves extraordinary performance.

Management processes alone turn workers into subordinates. Substances, by contrast, build followership. Subordinates comply with management rules and procedures and with the leader's directives; the job gets done. Followers, however, respond to ideas, ideals, values, and purposes; as a result, the job gets done well.

In his classic book *The Functions of the Executive*, Barnard (1938) stated: "The inculcation of belief in the real existence of a common purpose is an essential executive function"(87). The inculcation of belief comes from the embodiment of purposes as leaders act and behave, or, in the words of Vaill (1984), from purposing. He defines *purposing* as "that continuous stream of actions by an organization's formal leadership which has the effect of inducing clarity, consensus and commitment regarding the organization's basic purposes" (91). Vaill conducted extensive studies of high-performing systems (HPS) from a broad spectrum of U.S. society. He examined the characteristics held in common by these systems and the kind of leadership found within them. Key to success was the presence of purposing. "HPS's are clear on their broad purposes and on near-term objectives for fulfilling these purposes. They know why they exist and what they are trying to do. Members have pictures in their heads which are strikingly congruent" (86). He continues, "Commitment to these purposes is never perfunctory. . . . [M]otivation as usually conceived is always high" (86).

Purposing is a key characteristic found by others who have studied successful schools in the United States. This research establishes the importance of shared goals and expectations and approved modes of behavior that create a strong school culture. Important to this culture are the norms and values that provide a cohesion and identity and that create a unifying moral order from which teachers and students derive direction, meaning, and significance. One example is Joan Lipsitz's (1984) study of four successful middle schools. She found that the four schools achieved unusual clarity about the purposes of intermediate schooling and the students they teach, and made powerful statements, both in word and in practice, about their purposes. There was little disagreement about what they believed and little discrepancy between what they said they were doing and what they were actually doing.

It is through purposing and the building of shared values and agreements that a school culture emerges.

> The concept of culture refers to the total way of life in a society, the heritage of accumulated social learnings that is shared and transmitted by the members of that society. To put it another way a culture is a set of shared plans for living, developed out of necessities of previous generations, existing in the minds of the present generation, taught directly or indirectly to new generations. (White, 1952:15)

Purposing involves both the vision of the leader and a set of agreements that the group shares. Bennis (1984) describes vision as "the capacity to create and communicate a compelling vision of a desired state of affairs, a vision . . . that clarifies the current situation and induces commitment to the future" (66). Vision is an important dimension of purposing and without it the very point of leadership is missed, but the vision of the school must also reflect the hopes and dreams, the needs and interests, the values and beliefs of everyone who has a stake in the school—teachers, parents, and students. In the end, it is what the school stands for that counts. In successful schools, consensus runs deep. It is not enough to have worked out what people stand for and what is to be accomplished. A binding and solemn agreement needs to emerge that represents a value system for living together and that provides the basis for decisions and actions. This binding and solemn agreement represents the school's covenant.

When both vision and covenant are present, teachers and students respond with increased motivation and commitment and their performance is beyond expectations. The affirming of values that accompanies purposing is a motivational force far more powerful than the bureaucratic and psychological transactions that characterize leadership by bartering and building. They become the very basis upon which we construct our reality and from which we derive sense and meaning. As Gardner (1986) points out,

> A great civilization is a drama lived in the minds of people. It is a shared vision; it is shared norms, expectations and purposes. . . . If we look at ordinary human communities, we see the same reality: A community lives in the minds of its members—in shared assumptions, beliefs, customs, ideas that give meaning, ideas that motivate. (7)

Building Followership

In his classic book *Every Employee a Manager,* Meyers (1971) observes that the more managementlike jobs were, the more readily workers accepted responsibility and responded with increased motivation. By *managementlike,* he meant having the freedom to plan, organize, and control one's life, to make decisions, to accept responsibility, and to be held accountable for one's actions in light of this responsibility. Empowering every employee to be a manager is a goal of leadership because it contributes to leadership density. *Leadership density* refers to the extent to which leadership roles are shared and leadership itself is broadly based and exercised. To understand leadership density, one needs to understand how closely leadership and followership are linked and what the differences are between being a good follower and a good subordinate. Good followers manage themselves well. They think for themselves, exercise self-control, and are able to accept responsibility and obligation, believe in and care about what they are doing, and be self-motivated; therefore, they are able to do what is right for the school, do it well, do it with persistence, and, most importantly, do it without close supervision (Kelly, 1988). Followers are committed people—committed perhaps to a set of purposes, a cause, a vision of what the school is and can become, a set of beliefs about what teaching and learning should be, a set of values and standards to which they adhere, a conviction.

By contrast, good subordinates do what they are supposed to but little else. They want to know specifically what is expected of them, and with proper monitoring and supervision will perform accordingly. They are dependent on their leaders to provide them with goals and objectives and the proper ways and means to achieve them. They want to know what the rules of the game are and will play the game as required to avoid problems. For them and their leaders, life is comfortable and easy. For the school and the children they teach, excellence escapes and mediocrity becomes the norm.

Subordinates are not committed to causes, values, or ideas, but respond instead to authority in the form of rules, regulations, expectations of their supervisors, and other management requirements. This is a crucial distinction. Subordinates respond to authority; followers respond to ideas. The standard dictionary definition of a follower is one who is in the service of a cause or of another person who represents a cause; a follower is one who follows opinions and teachings—a disciple. Because followership is linked to ideas, it is difficult for principals to help others transcend subordinateness for followership in schools, without practicing leadership by purposing.

The concept of followership proposes a number of paradoxes. It turns out that effective following is really a form of leadership (Kelly, 1988). Commitment to a cause and the practice of self-management are hallmarks of good leadership and they are hallmarks of good followership as well. The successful leader, then, is one who builds up the leadership of others and who strives to become a leader of leaders. A successful leader is also a good follower—one who follows ideas, values, and beliefs. When followership is established, bureaucratic and psychological authority are transcended by moral authority. A new kind of hierarchy emerges in the school, one that places purposes, values, and commitments at the apex and teachers, principals, parents, and students below in service to these purposes.

Enabling Others to Function Autonomously on Behalf of Shared Purposes

There are three dimensions to enablement: (1) empowering principals, teachers, parents, and others by giving them the discretion they need to function autonomously on behalf of school goals and purposes; (2) providing them with the support and training they need to function autonomously; and (3) removing the bureaucratic obstacles that keep them from being autonomous.

Effective leaders practice the principle of power investment. They distribute power among others in an effort to get more power in return. They know that it is not power over people and events that counts, but power over the likelihood that accomplishments and shared goals and purposes will be realized. To gain control over the latter, they recognize that they need to delegate or surrender control over the former. In a nonlinear and loosely connected world, they are resigned to the reality that delegation and empowerment are unavoidable.

Empowerment without purposing is not what is intended by this value. The two must go hand in hand. When directed and enriched by purposing and fueled by empowerment, teachers and others respond not only with increased motivation and commitment but with surprising ability as well. They become smarter, use their talents more fully, and grow on the job. Thus, the first question that must be asked when thinking about empowerment is, *Empowered to do what?* The empowerment rule that they follow is *everyone is free to do the things that make sense to them, providing the decisions they make about what to do embody the values that are shared.* Furthermore, the best empowerment strategy is not to focus on teachers or to focus on any other particular role group, but to think about empowering the school site. It is principals, teachers, and parents, bonded together in a common cause, who are given the necessary discretion that they need to function effectively. Empowerment is the natural complement to accountability. One cannot hold teachers, parents, and schools accountable without giving them the necessary responsibility to make the decisions that they think are best. The mistake of equating empowerment with freedom must be avoided. Empowerment has to do with obligation and duty. One is not free to do what he or she pleases, but free to make sensible decisions in light of shared values.

Viewing Leadership as Power to Accomplish

Successful leaders know the difference between power over and power to. There is a link between leadership and power, and indeed leadership is a special form of power—power to influence. There are, however, two conceptions of power: power over and power to. Power over is controlling and is concerned with "How can I control people and events so that things turn out the way I want?" Power over is concerned with dominance, control, and hierarchy. One needs to be in a position of dominance, control, and hierarchy to exercise power over. One needs to have access to rewards and punishments, "carrots" and "bully sticks." In reality, however, most principals don't have many carrots or bully sticks. Furthermore, people don't like carrots or bully sticks and resist power-over leadership both formally and informally. Thus, this approach is rarely effective.

The concept of power over raises certain ethical questions relating to dominance and manipulation. Power to, however, is not instrumental but facilitative. It is power to do something, to accomplish something, and to help others accomplish something that they think is important. In power to, far less emphasis is given to what people are doing and far more emphasis is given to what they are accomplishing.

Putting Collegiality First

When combined with purposing, leadership density, and enablement, collegiality is an important strategy for bringing about the kinds of connections that make schools work and work well in a nonlinear and loosely structured world. Too often, however, collegiality is confused with congeniality (Barth, 1986). *Congeniality* refers to the friendly human relationships that exist among teachers and is characterized by the loyalty, trust, and easy conversation that result from the development of a closely knit social group. *Collegiality,* by contrast, refers to the existence of high levels of collaboration among teachers and between teachers and principal and is characterized by mutual respect, shared work values, cooperation, and specific conversations about teaching and learning. When congeniality is high, a strong, informal culture aligned with social norms emerges in the school; however, the norms may or may not be aligned with school purposes. Sometimes the norms contribute to and at other times interfere with increased commitment and extraordinary performance. By contrast, when collegiality is high, a strong, professional culture held together by shared work norms emerges in the school. The norms are aligned with school purposes, contributing consistently to increased commitment and extraordinary performance.

Research independently reported by Little (1981) and Rosenholtz (1989) provides compelling support for the importance of collegiality and building a professional culture of teaching on the one hand and in enhancing commitment and performance on the other. Both researchers found that the kind of leadership principals provided influences the collegial norm structure of the school. Rosenholtz found that teachers in highly collegial schools described their principals as being supportive and as considering problems to be schoolwide concerns that provided opportunities for collective problem solving and learning. Teachers and principals in less collegial schools, by contrast, reported being isolated and alienated. In her research, Little found that norms of collegiality were developed when principals clearly communicated expectations for teacher cooperation; provided a model for collegiality by working firsthand with teachers in improving the school; rewarded expressions of collegiality among teachers by providing recognition, release time, money, and other support resources; and protected teachers who were willing to go against expected norms of privatism and isolation by engaging in collegial behaviors. Although norms of collegiality can be enhanced within traditionally organized school structures, these structures often provide obstacles that prevent collegiality from developing fully. One advantage of the community image of schooling that was outlined in Chapter 5, which gave emphasis to smallness, shared goals, and moral connections, is that these characteristics can provide the opportunities for collegiality to be expressed within communities of practice.

Understanding Quality Control

Perhaps on no issue do ordinary and highly successful leaders differ more than in their beliefs about and concepts of quality control. To ordinary leaders, quality control is considered to be a management problem solvable by coming up with the right controls such as scheduling, prescribing, programming, testing, and checking. Although successful leaders recognize that such managerial conceptions of quality control have their place, they are likely to view the problem of quality control as being primarily cultural rather than managerial. Quality control, they have come to learn, is in the minds and hearts of people at work. It has to do with what teachers and other school employees believe, their commitment to quality, their sense of pride, the extent to which they identify with their work, the ownership they feel for what they are doing, and the intrinsic satisfaction they derive from the work itself. It is for this reason that quality control is not viewed so much as planning, organizing, scheduling, and controlling as it is viewed as purposing, enablement, leadership density, collegiality, and intrinsic motivation as a way to build identity and commitment.

Valuing Simplicity

Highly successful principals believe in lean, action-oriented, uncomplicated organizational structures. To them, "small is beautiful," and "simple is better." Smallness has the advantage of encouraging primary group relationships among teachers and students, providing more readily for empowerment, and increasing one's identity and feeling of belongingness. Simplicity is action oriented and to the point. It places emphasis on what needs to be accomplished and how best to do it without undue emphasis on protocols and procedural matters.

Smallness is a quality as well as a headcount. Though it may be a challenge for leadership, large schools too can adopt and live the quality of smallness and the quality of simplicity. Adlai Stevenson High School in Lincolnshire, Illinois, for example, houses 4,000 students in a caring environment and lives the benefits of smallness and simplicity in how it thinks and what it does. Stevenson's commitment to caring is legendary. Caring is institutionalized, for example, in the Pyramid of Interventions—a 12-stage program of support for students who are having difficulty making the transition to high school and are having problems with academic and social engagement. The Pyramid of Interventions begins with a summer session for students who are identified by both Stevenson and sending middle schools together, includes peer support, and ends with an enviable record of success in getting students connected to the school and engaged in learning.*

Reflection in Action

Leaders of highly successful schools view with suspicion quick fixes, sure-fire remedies, and one-best-way prescriptions for teaching and learning, supervising, and evaluating. Instead, they bring to their work a more complex view of schooling (see, e.g., Brandt, 1985; Glatthorn, 1984; Joyce and Weil, 1980). No single model of teaching is sufficient to address all the aims of schooling. The issue, for example, is not didactic and informal versus structured and direct, but costs and benefits of various approaches to teaching and learning. What is gained and what is lost by using a particular approach? Given one's present situation, are the gains worth the losses? Similarly, no single method of supervision and evaluation is sufficient for all teachers and all situations.

Successful principals resist accepting a direct link between research and practice. They recognize instead that the purpose of research is to increase one's understanding and not to prescribe practices (Tyler, 1984). Paying close attention to theory and research, they heed well the success stories emerging from practice, but they have a conceptual rather than an instrumental view of such knowledge (Kennedy, 1984). Knowledge viewed instrumentally is evidence for directly prescribing action. Knowledge viewed conceptually is information for informing thought and enhancing professional judgment—the prerequisites for action.

Leadership by Outrage

The standard prescription that emerges from traditional management is that leaders should be cool, calculated, and reserved in everything they say or do. Studies of successful leaders (e.g., Lipsitz, 1984; Peters and Waterman, 1982; Sergiovanni, 1990; Vaill, 1984) reveal quite a different image. Indeed, successful leaders typically bring to their practice a sense of passion and risk that communicates to others that if something is worth believing in then it's worth feeling strongly about. In his extensive studies of successful leaders, Vaill (1984) found that their leadership practice was characterized by *time, feeling,* and *focus.* Successful leaders put in extraordinary amounts of time, have strong feelings about the attainment of the system's purposes, and focus their attention and energies on key issues and variables. These characteristics are key contributors to building purposing in the enterprise. According to Vaill,

> Purposing occurs through the investment of large amounts of micro- and macro-Time, through the experience and expression of very strong Feeling about the attainment of purposes and importance of the system, and through the attainment of understanding of the key variables in the system success (Focus). All leaders of

*See Stevenson High School's website at www.district125.k12.il.us.

high-performance systems have integrated these three factors at a very high level of intensity and clarity. (1984:103)

Vaill noted that feeling was the important link between time and focus. His successful leaders cared deeply about the welfare of their particular enterprise, its purposes, structure, conduct, history, future security, and underlying values and commitments. They cared deeply enough to show passion, and when things were not going right, this passion often took the form of outrage.

Leadership by outrage is a symbolic act that communicates importance and meaning and that touches people in ways not possible when leadership is viewed only as something objective and calculated. Leaders use outrage to highlight issues of purpose defined by the school's shared covenant, and this outrage adds considerable value to their leadership practice.

The linking of outrage to purposes is very important. Binding leaders, for example, know the difference between real toughness and merely looking tough or acting tough. Real toughness is always principle-value based. Binding leaders expect adherence to common values but promote wide discretion in how these values are to be implemented (they practice enablement and emphasize followership). They are outraged when they see these values ignored or violated. The values of the common core represent nonnegotiables that comprise cultural strands that define a way of life in the school. No matter how free people may be to do and decide, they are expected to embody the values that are shared and make up the school's covenant. When this is not the case, outrage is expressed.

Kindling Outrage in Others

Outrage is not owned by the principal alone. When purposes are established, followership is understood, enabling is provided, collegiality is in place, and leadership by outrage is modeled by the designated leader; then, expressing outrage becomes an obligation of every person connected with the school. When the ideals and commitments that are shared are compromised, outrage is expressed. Binding leaders work hard at kindling outrage in others.

DISTRIBUTED LEADERSHIP

Viewing leadership as a group activity linked to a practice rather than just an individual activity linked to a person helps match the expertise that we have in a school with the problems and situations that we face. Of course both leadership as an individual activity and leadership as a group activity linked to a practice are necessary. But including group activity liberates leadership and provides the framework we need for widespread involvement in improving schools.

If leadership is a practice shared by many then it must be distributed among those who are in the right place at the right time (situation) and among those who have the unique competence to get the job done correctly (ability). The unique competence requirement determines who, among those with the necessary ability, should step forward to assume responsibility for leadership. This is an important point, for responsibility is the flip side of entitlement. A person who is entitled to lead should be responsible for leading. If that person refuses this entitlement without good reason, she or he refuses responsibility, raising moral questions of fairness, loyalty, and commitment.

Since the leadership functions needed vary with the situation, the abilities needed also vary. These complexities demonstrate just how untenable it is for us to continue to think about leadership as essentially an individual activity. As Spillane, Halverson, and Diamond (2001:24) see it, ". . . we develop a perspective on leading practice that attends to leaders' thinking and action *in situ*. Leadership involves the identification, acquisition, allocation, coordination, and use of the social, material, and cultural resources necessary to establish the conditions for the possibility of teaching and learning." They state further, "by taking leadership practice in the school as the unit of analysis, rather than an individual leader, our distributed theory of leadership focuses on how leadership practice is distributed among both positional and informal leaders" (24).

Since Spillane and his colleagues ground leadership in the activities that must be assumed if school goals and purposes are to be achieved, then it is the tasks around which leadership as a practice are planned, organized, and evaluated that must be identified and understood. Though visions and other big ideas are essential, they are no more essential than the insides of leadership—the practical goals that must be identified and the practical tasks that must be organized and completed for teaching and learning to take place. Practical goals and practical tasks are best addressed when roles and functions are brought together.

*R*ECIPROCITY IS KEY

Understanding roles and role expectations is important to leadership effectiveness. Roles are markers that help define what a person should do. But roles are definers for contracts too. This is especially true when role responsibilities are reciprocal and role relationships are interactive. My role is to fly the airplane, and your role is to navigate. We need each other to have a successful trip. And finally, roles are definers for covenants—the most sacred obligations and commitments we have toward each other, toward the school, and toward its purposes. Roles as definers of covenants obligate us to meet, even exceed, our responsibilities toward each other and toward the institutions and communities. Roles as markers work in schools when teachers, parents, and students are properly motivated. Roles as contracts work as long as parties to the contract get what they want in exchanges that resemble trades. Roles as covenants work when we feel morally obliged to meet our responsibilities even if we don't want to or whether we are getting something we want in exchange or not.

All these definitions of roles are played out in the everyday lives of schools, and all of these roles contribute to the development of relationships that make schools work. Thus the question is not which role definition is appropriate but is one of proper balance. Which definition of roles, for example, belongs at the center, and which definition of roles belongs at the periphery in our family lives, in our communal relationships, in schools, and in our social lives? When considering these kinds of organizations and groups, the answer for me is that roles defined as covenants should be at the center and roles defined as markers or as contracts should be at the periphery.

The Worth of the Leadership Values

None of the leadership values considered alone is powerful enough to make the difference in bringing about quality schooling. Indeed, a critical connectedness exists among them, and leadership is best understood as comprising interdependent parts. Practicing enabling leadership in the form of individual empowerment—for example, without practicing leadership that emphasizes purposing and the building of a covenant of shared values is more likely to result in laissez-faire management than in quality schooling. Furthermore, emphasizing management at the expense of leadership by providing controls and regulations, by emphasizing authority, by attempting to regulate the flow and work of schooling will not allow the practice of convincing and meaningful empowerment. A school that builds a covenant of shared values composed of technical statements of objectives, targets, and outcomes that fail to inspire; that are lacking in symbolic representations; and that do not allow principals, parents, teachers, and students to derive sense and meaning from their school lives will not likely be characterized by extraordinary commitment and performance.

CONSTRUCTIVIST LEADERSHIP

Lambert and colleagues (1995:33) define *leadership* as involving a reciprocal process that enables members of a school community to construct meaning that leads toward a common purpose. To these researchers, engaging in reciprocal relationships is the way we make sense of our worlds, continually define ourselves, and grow together. They refer to this kind of leadership as *constructivist* and view it as being less a role to be assumed by some and more a function to be assumed by all. Key to constructivist leadership is building capacity among people and in schools. Schools that are good at helping members construct meaning and craft common purposes are likely to be highly skilled at capacity building and in developing broad participation. This combination, Lambert (1998) points out, promotes learning and encourages acceptance of a collective responsibility for the success of the school. When the purpose of leadership becomes constructing meaning, facilitating learning, and developing collective responsibility, leadership is linked directly to the very heart of a school's culture.

A COMMUNITY OF LEADERS

In a major breakthrough, Rost (1991) offers a definition of *leadership* that can help connect its practice to community building: "Leadership is an influence relationship among leaders and followers who intend real changes that reflect their mutual purposes" (102). This definition contains four key elements—all of which, Rost argues, must be present for relationships between and among people to be called leadership. If any one of the four is missing, then these relationships might better be thought of as management or by some other expression—they may have merit, but they just aren't leadership. The four elements are as follows:

1. The relationship is based on influence.
2. Leaders and followers are the people in this relationship.
3. Leaders and followers intend real change.
4. Leaders and followers develop mutual purposes. (Rost, 1991:102–103)

Rost (1991) points out that conceiving of leadership as an influence relationship means that it is interactive and multidirectional. Leadership does not exist if influence is just top down. Furthermore, influence, in his definition, means the use of persuasion and not rewards and punishments or position and legal power. It is not leadership if a person orders, requires, seduces, or threatens another's compliance.

For something to be called leadership, according to Rost (1991), both followers and leaders must be doing the leadership. They need not be equal in the relationship nor must everyone be leading all the time, but in any given period of time or for any given episode, both share the burdens and obligations of leadership. Furthermore, for leader and followers to intend real changes, leadership acts must be purposeful; they must be motivated not by personal gain or by bureaucratic requirements, but by a desire to better serve purposes. Finally, the purposes themselves must be shared by both leaders and followers. In the ideal, they are developed together.

Rost's (1991) definition relies on the importance of compelling ideas and shared commitment to these ideas. Furthermore, the roles of followers and leaders are blurred. With shared ideas as the source of authority, everyone is a follower first, and when anyone takes the initiative to lead, followership becomes redefined as leadership. Leadership flourishes when leaders and followers view each other as being credible. The stronger this credibility, the more likely people will allow themselves to be influenced by leadership acts, no matter what their source.

To Rost and Smith (1992:199), credibility can be thought of as encompassing five Cs: *character*, defined as honesty, trust, and integrity; *courage*, defined as the willingness to change and to stand up for one's beliefs; *competence,* defined in both technical and interpersonal senses; *composure,* defined as being graceful under pressure and displaying emotion appropriately; and *caring,* defined as being concerned with the welfare of others.

The credibility of the five Cs suggests that certain relationship requirements must be met before leadership can be fully and widely expressed in a school—before the school, in other words, can become a community of leaders. Not surprising, the relationship requirements are gemeinschaft. How open are we to each other? Do we have the courage to speak, to express our true feelings, to ask for help, and to stand up for what we believe? Can we speak knowledgeably about teaching and learning? Are we sensitive to the views of others? Do we care about each other, our work, and the students we serve? How do we embody this caring? Becoming a community of leaders means that not only does everyone share in the obligations and responsibility of leadership in an effort to facilitate the work of the school, but everyone shares in the obligations and responsibilities of caring. Not only does leadership involve doing, but it involves being. Are we willing to care enough to accept responsibility together for the burdens of leadership?

$\mathcal{S}$OME REFLECTIONS

1. What are the differences between shared leadership and leadership by entitlement? Most principals are comfortable with the idea of shared leadership but may not be comfortable with the idea of leadership by entitlement. Why is this so? How comfortable are you with the idea of leadership by entitlement?
2. Zaleznik believes that the failure of management is the substitution of process for substance. What does he mean? Are you able to provide some examples where this is true in your own school or school district?
3. Give examples that illustrate the differences between power over and power to.

$\mathcal{R}$EFERENCES

Barnard, Chester. 1938. *The Functions of the Executive.* Cambridge, MA: Harvard University Press.

Barth, Roland. 1986. "The Principal and the Profession of Teaching," *Elementary School Journal* 86(4).

Bennis, Warren. 1984. "Transformative Power and Leadership," in Thomas J. Sergiovanni and John E. Corbally (Eds.), *Leadership and Organizational Culture* (pp. 64–71). Urbana: University of Illinois.

Bennis, Warren, and Burt Nanus. 1985. *Leaders: The Strategies for Taking Charge.* New York: Harper & Row.

Brandt, Ron. 1985. "Toward a Better Definition of Teaching," *Educational Leadership* 42(8).

Gardner, John. 1986, March. "The Tasks of Leadership." Leadership Papers No. 2. Washington, DC: Independent Sector.

Glatthorn, Alan. 1984. *Differentiated Supervision.* Alexandria, VA: Association for Supervision and Curriculum Development.

Joyce, Bruce, and Marsha Weil. 1980. *Models of Teaching* (2nd ed.). Englewood Cliffs, NJ: Prentice-Hall.

Kelly, Robert E. 1988, November–December. "In Praise of Followers," *Harvard Business Review.*

Kennedy, Mary. 1984. "How Evidence Alters Understanding and Decisions," *Educational Evaluations and Policy Analysis* 6(3), 207–226.

Lambert, Linda. 1998. "How to Build Leadership Capacity," *Educational Leadership* 55(7), 17–19.

Lambert, Linda, Deborah Walker, Diane P. Zimmerman, Joanne E. Cooper, Morgan Dale Lambert, Mary E. Gardner, and P. J. Ford Slack. 1995. *The Constructivist Leader.* New York: Teachers College Press.

Lieberman, Ann, and Lynne Miller. 1986. "School Improvement: Themes and Variations," in Ann Lieberman (Ed.), *Rethinking School Improvement: Research, Craft, and Concept.* New York: Teachers College Press.

Lieberman, Ann, and Lynne Miller. 1999. *Teachers—Transforming Their World and Their Work.* New York: Teachers College Press.

Lipsitz, Joan. 1984. *Successful Schools for Young Adolescents.* New Brunswick, NJ: Transaction Books.

Little, Judith. 1981. *School Success and Staff Development in Urban Desegregated Schools.* Boulder, CO: Center for Action Research.

Meyers, Scott. 1971. *Every Employee a Manager.* New York: McGraw-Hill.

Peters, Thomas J., and Robert H. Waterman. 1982. *In Search of Excellence.* New York: Harper & Row.

Rosenholtz, Susan. 1989. *Teacher's Workplace: A Social-Organizational Analysis.* New York: Longman.

Rost, Joseph. 1991. *Leadership for the Twenty-First Century.* New York: Praeger.

Rost, Joseph, and A. Smith. 1992. "Leadership: A Post-Industrial Approach," *European Management Journal* 10(2).

Sergiovanni, Thomas J. 1990. *Value-Added Leadership: How to Get Extraordinary Performance in Schools.* San Diego, CA: Harcourt Brace Jovanovich.

Spillane, James P., Richard Halverson, and John B. Diamond. 2001. "Investigating School Leadership Practice: A Distributed Perspective," *Educational Researcher* 30(3), 24.

Thompson, Victor A. 1961. *Modern Organizations.* New York: Knopf.

Tyler, Ralph. 1984. Quoted in Philip L. Hosford, "The Problem, Its Difficulties, and Our Approaches," in P. L. Hosford (Ed.), *Using What We Know about Teaching.* Alexandria, VA: Association for Supervision and Curriculum Development.

Vaill, Peter B. 1984. "The Purposing of High-Performance Systems," in T. J. Sergiovanni and J. E. Corbally (Eds.), *Leadership and Organizational Culture.* Urbana: University of Illinois Press.

White, Robert W. 1952. *Lives in Progress: A Study of the Natural Growth of Personality.* New York: Dryden Press.

Zaleznik, Abraham. 1989. *The Managerial Mystique: Restoring Leadership in Business.* New York: Harper & Row.

Part Four

INSTRUCTIONAL LEADERSHIP

9

CHARACTERISTICS OF SUCCESSFUL SCHOOLS

*S*ince the beginning of schooling in the United States, the relationship between quality of schools and quality of learning for students has been accepted as an article of faith. However, with the 1964 publication of Benjamin Bloom's *Stability and Change in Human Characteristics* and the 1966 publication of James Coleman and colleagues' *Equality of Educational Opportunity*, this faith was broken. Many teachers and principals joined the general public in a widespread acceptance of the belief that schools were not very important.

Coleman's study suggested that social inequality, poverty, and segregated schooling were key elements in determining inadequate levels of learning for many students and that improving learning would require the correction of these social factors. Regardless of one's race or region, it was the home environment (social class and income of parents, exposure to books, need for achievement, and modeling differentials) that was far more important in explaining differences in learning outcomes of students than were school facilities, teacher salaries, or even the curriculum itself.

Bloom's classic work on the development of educational capacity reinforced the primacy of nonschool over school factors in determining the amount and extent of student learning. He noted, for example,

> By about 4, 50% of the variation in intelligence at age 17 is accounted for . . . in terms of intelligence measured at age 17; from conception to age 4, the individual

195

develops 50% of his mature intelligence; from ages 4 to 8 he develops another 30%; and from ages 8 to 17, the remaining 20%. . . . We would expect the variations in the environments to have relatively little effect on the I.Q. after age 8, but would expect such a variation to have marked effect on the I.Q. before that age, with the greatest effect likely to take place between the ages of about 1 to 5. (Bloom, 1964:68)

As these ideas became accepted, principals and teachers came to believe that the home or basic educational capacity, not the school, accounted for major differences in student achievement. Some principals and teachers welcomed this news, seeing within it a legitimate excuse for their own results. After all, they reasoned, the research shows clearly that poor student performance is linked to conditions beyond control of the school.

The 1980s provided quite a different picture as to the relationship between schooling and quality of learning for students. The belief that schooling does make a difference became once more the accepted stand. Quality schooling indeed leads to quality learning, and an important key to quality schooling is the amount and kind of leadership that school principals provide directly and promote among teachers and supporting staff.

These assertions are supported by hundreds of studies on school effectiveness and success. For example, a classic study conducted in 1978 by Gilbert Austin compared 18 high-achieving and 12 low-achieving schools carefully selected from among all schools in Maryland, using that state's accountability data. Schools selected were considered "outliers" for scoring outside the average statistical band of test scores for all Maryland schools. This research indicated that one difference between high- and low-achieving schools was the impact of the principal. In higher-achieving schools, principals exerted strong leadership, participated directly and frequently in instructional matters, had higher expectations for success, and were oriented toward academic goals. It seems clear from this study, and many others like it, that quality of schooling is greatly influenced by leadership from the principal.

Many experts point out that the influence principals have on fostering school effectiveness is indirect (see, e.g., Hallinger and Murphy, 1985; Hallinger and Heck, 1996). The work of the Far West Lab, for example, concluded that principal behaviors have a direct effect on the school's overall climate and on its instructional organization (factors such as class size, school size, time available for learning, curriculum pacing and sequencing, staff development, and staff evaluation). These factors, in turn, seem related to student achievement and other effectiveness indicators (Bossert et al., 1982). Essentially, there is an interplay of *initiating variables*, defined as principal dispositions and behaviors, which influence *mediating variables*, defined as school climate and organizing for learning, which affects *school results variables* such as student achievement and other dimensions of goodness. These relationships are summarized in Appendix 14.1, "Studying the Climate of Your School" (see pp. 339–346).

Principal leadership is only part of the answer to establishing successful schools. Many experts and many supporting studies point out that equally significant—

perhaps even most significant—is the amount and quality of leadership density that exists in schools. As discussed in Chapter 8, *leadership density* refers to the total leadership available from teachers, support staff, parents, and others on behalf of the school's work. Of course, the principal plays a key role in building and maintaining leadership density. In this sense, principal leadership can be understood as an enabling process. Principals practice enabling leadership when they help teachers, students, and staff to function better on behalf of the school and its purposes, to engage more effectively in the work and play of the school, and to promote the achievement of the school's objectives. It is crucial to build up the leadership capacity of others, and in this sense the principal is a leader of leaders.

CHARACTERISTICS OF SUCCESSFUL SCHOOLS

It is still fashionable to talk about the correlates of effective schools. Many school districts and even states settle on a particular list of such correlates (e.g., strong instructional leadership from the principal, academic focus on the basic skills, safe and orderly environment, high expectations for students, close monitoring of instruction by supervision and testing) to apply uniformly to all schools. Recent research and reasoned thought, however, suggest that *correlates* may be too strong a designation, and uniform application of any particular list may be hazardous for the long-term health of the school. The research and thought, however, do provide us with a number of insights in the form of general characteristics that can help us decide what counts in our own unique situation.

Research Revelations

The seminal work of Brookover and Lezotte (1979), Brookover and colleagues (1979), and Edmonds (1979) consistently revealed that effective schools are characterized by high agreement among staff as to goals and purposes, a clear sense of mission, and the active presence of purposing. Studies by Bossert and colleagues (1982) and by Greenfield (1982) revealed that goal orientation and the articulation and modeling of school purposes by principals are also common characteristics.

Blumberg and Greenfield's (1980) research revealed that successful principals are proactive and direct behaviors at building and articulating a vision of what the school is and can become. This notion of vision is supported, as well, by the case study research of Prunty and Hively (1982) and of Newberg and Glatthorn (undated). Nearly all these studies, as well as that of Rutter and his colleagues (1979), identify the concept of ethos (shared goals and expectations and associated approved modes of behavior) or strong school culture as being an important characteristic. Important to this culture are norms and values that provide for cohesion and identity and that create a unifying moral order or ideology from which teachers and students derive direction, meaning, and significance.

Duttweiler's (1988, 1990) review of the more recent literature (Purkey and Smith, 1982; Roueche and Baker, 1986; Stedman, 1987; Wayson, 1988; Wimpelberg, Teddlie, and Stringfield, 1989) reveals a more comprehensive picture of what constitutes an effective school than that provided by earlier studies. Although Duttweiler continues to use the word *effective* to describe these schools, she has redefined the term. The following characteristics emerge from her synthesis (Duttweiler, 1990:72–74).

Effective Schools Are Student Centered.   Effective schools make an effort to serve all students, create support networks to assist students, involve students in school affairs, respect and celebrate the ethnic and linguistic differences among students, and have student welfare as a first priority. They use community volunteers, parents, teacher aides, and peer tutors to provide close, personal attention to students. They involve students in many of the activities of running a school. Student needs are given priority over other concerns. An atmosphere of cooperation and trust is created through a high level of interaction between students and teachers.

Effective Schools Offer Academically Rich Programs.   Student development and the provision of a well-rounded academic program are the primary goals. Effective schools address higher- as well as lower-order cognitive objectives, provide an enriched environment through a variety of options, have an active cocurricular program, provide in-depth coverage of content, and appropriately monitor student progress and provide feedback.

Effective Schools Provide Instruction That Promotes Student Learning.   Effective schools have a distinctive normative structure that supports instruction. They design their programs to ensure academic success and to head off academic problems. Teachers and administrators believe that all students can learn and feel responsible for seeing that they do. Teachers and administrators believe in their own ability to influence students' learning. Teachers communicate expectations to students, provide focused and organized instructional sessions, adapt instruction to student needs, anticipate and correct student misconceptions, and use a variety of teaching strategies. In general, effective schools set high standards, closely and regularly monitor performance, and recognize and reward effort and success.

Effective Schools Have a Positive School Climate.   Effective schools have a clear organizational personality, characterized by stated missions, goals, values, and standards of performance. They have a sense of order, purpose, and direction fostered by consistency among teachers; an atmosphere of encouragement in which students are praised and rewarded; a work-centered environment; and high optimism and expectations for student learning. Teachers and principals commit themselves to breaking down institutional and community barriers to equality. They create a learning environment that is open, friendly, and culturally inviting. Using community resources, they acknowledge the ethnic and racial identity of their students. They provide encouragement and take a positive approach to discipline. Administrators model the behaviors that they say are important.

Effective Schools Foster Collegial Interaction.   Effective schools strive to create professional environments for teachers that facilitate the accomplishment of their work. Teachers participate in decisions affecting their work, have reasonable control or autonomy to carry out work, share a sense of purpose and community, receive recognition for contributions to the organization, and are treated with respect and dignity by others in the workplace. Teachers work together as colleagues to carry out instruction, plan curriculum, and refine teaching practices.

Effective Schools Have Extensive Staff Development.   The teacher evaluation system is used to help teachers improve their skills. Inservice is practical, on-the-job training tailored to meet the specific needs of staff members. The emphasis is on the exchange of practical teaching techniques and on making training an integral part of a collaborative educational environment. Teachers and administrators conduct inservice programs and are provided with ample staff-development opportunities to help them develop further. Administrators and teachers are encouraged to reflect on their practices.

Effective Schools Practice Shared Leadership.   Instructional leadership does not depend solely on the principal. School administrators understand and use a leadership style appropriate for professionals; solve problems through collaboration, team, or group decision making; know their staff members and delegate authority; communicate and build cohesiveness; and use their positions to recognize and reward accomplishments of both staff and students. While no single leadership style dominates, common leadership features include setting and maintaining direction for the school and facilitating the work of teachers by adopting a wide range of supportive behaviors. Involvement in decision making is a critical element. Involvement begins with members of the school community developing the goals, mission, and values of the school. Decisions are made with input from those to be affected by the decision.

Effective Schools Foster Creative Problem Solving.   Staff members in effective schools are unwilling to accept defeat or settle for mediocrity. They turn their problems into challenges, design solutions, and implement them. They go about their tasks with commitment, creativity, persistence, and professionalism. Resources such as time, facilities, staff expertise, and volunteers are used to maximum advantage to facilitate the process of teaching and learning.

Effective Schools Involve Parents and the Community.   There is a partnership linkage between the school and the community. Effective schools establish a variety of methods for communicating as well as working with parents and the community. They involve parents and community members in the teaching and learning activities of the school, include them in the decision-making process, have them serve as resources to extend the efforts of the school, and depend on them to be advocates as well as to provide good public relations for the school. They make sure that parents are involved in all aspects of their children's learning. Effective schools are contributory partners to the community they serve. They teach young people that they have a responsible part to play in society and that their contributions are valued and needed.

To this list, Stedman (1987) adds ethnic and racial pluralism, student responsibility for school affairs, and shared governance with parents and teachers. Stedman's conclusions are interesting because they rely on studies of successful schools conducted in the 1960s and early 1970s, as well as more recent studies, and thus provide a more "longitudinal" view.

ACADEMIC PRESS AND COMMUNITY

Research points to academic press and community as important factors in promoting student achievement. The two contribute to the development and strengthening of a school's organizational character—its unique focus, purpose, and sense of well-being. As Sebring and Bryk (1996) explain, these schools where student achievement is high "are safe, orderly, and respectful; they demand that students do significant academic work; and the teachers and staff work hard to provide the students with moral and personal support" (5). The researchers relied on personalism as a measure of community. *Personalism* refers to the extent to which students feel personally known and cared for. *Academic press* refers to the extent to which expectations are strongly communicated that students will work on intellectually challenging tasks, come to class prepared, and complete all assignments. These themes are accomplished by widespread and intense concern on the one hand and by support on the part of teachers on the other. Extra help is provided when needed and students are praised when they try and do well.

Sebring and Bryk (1996) found that emphasizing both academic press and personalism had a significantly greater influence on students being academically engaged than did an emphasis on just one or the other factor alone. *Academic engagement*, considered a prerequisite for student achievement, is defined as the extent to which students are connected to their academic work, try hard, are persistent, and are committed to learning.

In their study of urban Catholic high schools that were effective with low-income minority children, Bryk, Lee, and Holland (1993) were able to link academic press (high expectations combined with clear and strongly held norms) and a strong sense of community with increases in academic achievement. Neither high-communality and low-academic-press nor high-academic-press and low-communality schools were very effective—a finding supported by Shouse (1996) in his national sample of high schools serving large numbers of low-income students.

It appears that personalism and academic press together are important in helping schools become caring and focused communities that are able to generate the necessary social capital that helps youngsters not only perform well but also behave well. But neither caring nor academic performance can be scripted. Both must emerge from a particular school's sense of what is important, a particular school's inventory of values and purposes, and a particular school's commitment to do well and to manifest other characteristics that provide it with uniqueness, focus, and ultimately character.

THE IMPORTANCE OF CHARACTER

Hill, Foster, and Gendler (1990) provide evidence of the link between school character and school effectiveness. These researchers studied 13 high schools in New York and Washington, DC. Some of these schools were Catholic, others were public comprehensive schools, and still others were public magnet schools. The researchers found that the more successful schools in this sample (the Catholic schools and the public magnet schools) had unique, clear, and simple purposes centered on improving student academic performance and attitudes and on providing the care, concern, and necessary arrangements to help the school achieve its unique goals. The Catholic and public schools with unique and clear missions were labeled as "focus schools," and their more undifferentiated and less effective public school counterparts were labeled as "zoned schools." In the words of Hill et al.:

> Focus schools [both Catholic and public] resemble one another and differ from zoned comprehensive public schools in two basic ways. First, focus schools have clear uncomplicated missions centered on the experiences the school intends to provide its students and on the ways it intends to influence its students' performance, attitudes and behavior. Second, focus schools are strong organizations with the capacity to initiate action in pursuit of their missions, to sustain themselves over time, to solve their own problems, and to manage their external relationships. . . . Students and staff in each focus school consider their school special, a unique creation that reflects their efforts and meets their needs. . . .
>
> Zoned public schools, in contrast, had diffuse missions defined by the demands of external funders and regulators. They are also profoundly compromised organizations, with little capacity to initiate their own solutions to problems, define their internal character, or manage their relationships with external audiences. Because zoned schools are essentially franchises reflecting a standard model established by central authorities, staff and students have less reason to consider the schools uniquely their own. (1990:vii)

The researchers found that not only did focus schools concentrate on student outcomes but they also had established social covenants that communicated reciprocal role responsibilities for parents, students, teachers, and administrators. Further, they had developed a strong commitment to caring and were able to rally everyone around a set of values and ideas aimed at increasing levels of caring and civility as well as academic performance. Perhaps most important, these schools had a great deal of discretion. They were able to develop unique ways of doing things by being relatively unencumbered by bureaucratic mandates and structures from the outside. Their success, the researchers argued, is built around themes of uniqueness and specialness. They have specific educational and ethical principles or central zones that are used to guide behavior. These central zones function as a moral center that is able to deeply involve students and teachers in the life of the school. Zoned schools, by contrast, were much more differentiated with a one-size-fits-all mentality that provided few authentic alternatives and much less discretion—resulting in the erosion of institutional character.

In a recent analysis of the research, Hill and Celio (1998) identify characteristics of effective schools that are widely accepted—even by reformers who disagree on the means to make schools effective. The characteristics are accepted, for example, by those who oppose market approaches to reform and those who support market approaches. *Effectiveness* was defined as high rates of student learning. The characteristics include small school size; personalization; high expectations for students; collaboration among teachers; a simple, focused, and coherent curriculum; aggressive leadership; consistent standards for student behavior; family support; and peer support. Hill and Celio point out that though all the characteristics are important, none alone is sufficient to improve student learning. They describe the characteristics as follows:

- Small schools allow faculty to know one another personally and to collaborate outside the big-school compartments of grade level and academic discipline. Small size also allows the principal to know every teacher and every student.
- Personalization, sometimes a consequence of small size, means that adults pay attention to the needs and development of every student and prevent emotional crises and learning plateaus from becoming serious problems.
- High expectations for all students lead faculty to regard a student's learning difficulties as a problem to be solved, not evidence of a permanent incapacity.
- Teacher collaboration implies that teachers coordinate their instruction so that students accumulate knowledge and understanding from course to course, and that teachers share responsibility for students' overall development.
- Aggressive school leadership focuses adult attention on the school's overall goals and fosters constant self-criticism, so that teachers do not assume that routines that worked for students in the past will also work today.
- Simple curricula focus the faculty's attention on a relatively small number of subjects, drawing all students toward learning a common core of challenging subjects.
- Consistent high standards for student behavior both inside and outside the school signal the school's commitment to learning and protect students from disruption by (and the temptation to disrupt) their peers. Such standards also eliminate corrosive doubts about the school's fairness toward students from different social classes and ethnic groups.
- Family support for the school ensures that parents will provide opportunities for homework and reinforce the school's demands on student time and attention.
- Supportive peer groups, which schools can foster at least in part by providing extracurricular opportunities and maintaining high standards for student behavior, weaken anti-school forces in the cool youth culture. (Hill and Celio, 1998:30–31)

Breaking Ranks

The 1996 NASSP report *Breaking Ranks: Changing an American Institution* and its sequel, *Breaking Ranks II: Strategies for Leading High School Reform* published by NASSP in 2004, provide a deep look at characteristics of successful schools. The characteristics are summarized in Chapter 2. The reports together, particularly *Breaking Ranks II,* can be used to help schools assess their own progress and for moving ahead.

Principal Leadership and Student Achievement

The link between principal leadership and student achievement is strong. In their seminal research on this theme, for example, Marzano, Waters, and McNulty (2005) used sophisticated meta-analysis research to examine sixty-nine studies. The researchers were looking for specific behaviors related to principal leadership and its effects on student achievement. They identified twenty-one categories, each strongly correlated with student academic achievement. The twenty-one categories with specific behaviors for each are shown in Table 9.1.

Average correlations are also provided. As you review the categories, specific behaviors, and average correlations, assume that each is recorded on a three-by-five index card. Now sort through the cards, grouping those that seem to share common characteristics. Principal behaviors 5, 8, 9, and 11, for example, deal with goals, purposes, and ideas. Principals promote shared belief and a sense of community, establish clear goals and purposes, communicate ideals and beliefs about schooling, and ensure that faculty and staff are aware of current theories and frameworks for achievement. All four are necessary and must be in place if principals are to lead with ideas rather than relying solely on bureaucratic operations or on their personality as the primary source of authority for what principals do.

*R*EFLECTIVE PRACTICE

Although lists of general characteristics are helpful, they should not be readily translated into specific prescriptions for management and leadership practice. What needs to be done to increase effectiveness and how one does it are situationally specific. What works for a failing school, for example, will not necessarily work for a competent school. What works for low socioeconomic status schools will not necessarily work for middle socioeconomic status schools. The early studies on school effectiveness, for example, pointed out the importance of strong instructional leadership by the principal. The principal's job, according to this view, is to establish procedures and criteria for evaluating teachers, observe classrooms regularly and meet with teachers to discuss and improve classroom practices, and reward teachers for excellence in teaching. Furthermore, every effort must table **9.1**   **Principal Behaviors Associated with Student Achievement**

The Extent to Which the Principal . . .	Average *r*
1. Recognizes and celebrates accomplishments and acknowledges failures	.19
2. Is willing to challenge and actively challenges the status quo	.25
3. Recognizes and rewards individual accomplishments	.24
4. Establishes strong lines of communication with and among teachers and students	.23
5. Fosters shared beliefs and a sense of community and cooperation	.25
6. Protects teachers from issues and influences that would detract from their teaching time or focus	.27
7. Adapts his or her leadership behavior to the needs of the current situation and is comfortable with dissent	.28
8. Establishes clear goals and keeps those goals in the forefront of the school's attention	.24
9. Communicates and operates from strong ideals and beliefs about schooling	.22
10. Involves teachers in the design and implementation of important decisions and policies	.25
11. Ensures faculty and staff are aware of the most current theories and practices and makes the discussion of these a regular aspect of the school's culture	.24
12. Is directly involved in the design and implementation of curriculum, instruction, and assessment practices	.20
13. Is knowledgeable about current curriculum, instruction, and assessment practices	.25
14. Monitors the effectiveness of school practices and their impact on student learning	.27
15. Inspires and leads new and challenging innovations	.20
16. Establishes a set of standard operating procedures and routines	.25
17. Is an advocate and spokesperson for the school to all stakeholders	.27
18. Demonstrates an awareness of the personal aspects of teachers and staff	.18
19. Provides teachers with materials and professional development necessary for the successful execution of their jobs	.25
20. Is aware of the details and undercurrents in the running of the school and uses this information to address current and potential problems	.33
21. Has quality contact and interactions with teachers and students	.20

Source: Robert J. Marzano, Timothy Waters, and Brian A. McNulty. 2005. *School Leadership That Works: From Research to Results.* Published jointly by the Association for Supervision and Curriculum Development and Mid-continent Research for Education and Learning. © Mid-continent Research for Education and Learning (McREL). Used with permission.

be made to ensure that what the teacher teaches is aligned with carefully delin-eated purposes, and both purposes and content are aligned with tests. Directing and monitoring the affairs of teaching and learning are essential to the principal's role.

Clearly, such principalship behaviors and expectations make sense in many situations but not in others. Being a strong instructional leader may be a good idea in schools where teachers are poorly trained or lacking in commitment, but it is not such a good idea in schools where competence and commitment are not issues. In some schools, for example, teachers know more than the principal about matters of teaching and learning. To persist in providing strong instructional lead-ership in such a situation locks in teachers as instructional followers or subordi-nates and puts a cap on the total amount of leadership available in the school to promote better teaching and learning.

A number of researchers (e.g., Gersten, Carnine, and Green, 1982; Pajak and Glickman, 1989) have found that the leadership provided by lead teachers, assis-tant principals, grade-level heads, central office supervisors, department chair-persons, and teams of teachers are often the most critical factors in improving teaching and learning. What seems crucial to school improvement is not so much who provides the leadership but how much leadership there is. To that end, the principal as the leader of leaders may well be a more appropriate role where competence and commitment are not issues than would the role of instructional leader.

In summary, indiscriminate application of school-effectiveness research find-ings and, in particular, the development of generic lists of correlates or indicators that are subsequently applied uniformily to schools pose serious questions about the proper use of research and can result in negative, unanticipated consequences for teaching and learning. Wimpelberg, Teddlie, and Stringfield (1989) put it more bluntly: "It is patently foolish to attempt 'effective schools' changes in schools that are wholly different from the settings in which 'effective schools' correlates were isolated" (103). List of effectiveness characteristics as proposed by knowledgable researchers remain useful if viewed as general indicators. They are not so much truths to be applied uniformly, but rather as understanding that can help prin-cipals and others make more informed decisions about what to do and how in improving schools.

Perhaps Cuban (1998) is right. Searching for a single answer to the question "What is a good school?" may be misguided. Good schools might be traditional or progressive; have principals who use direct leadership and thus empower staff less or who use indirect leadership and thus empower staff more; rely on literature-based reading programs or phonics-based reading programs; use inter-est groups or rely on direct teaching; have gerbils and rabbits walking around the classroom or don't. What really matters in defining goodness, Cuban maintains, are the following:

- "Are parents, staff, and students satisfied with what occurs in the school?"
- "Is the school achieving the explicit goals it has set for itself?"
- "Are democratic behaviors, values, and attitudes evident in the students [who graduate from this school]?" (48)

SOME REFLECTIONS

1. Revisit the discussion of *Breaking Ranks II* characteristics summarized in Chapter 2. How do they compare with the various summaries of characteristics of successful schools found in this chapter? Are they, for example, "research based"? Have the characteristics of successful schools changed over the years?
2. Assume that you and four others are responding to a request for a proposal (RFP) for a charter school that will be commissioned by your school district. Prepare an executive summary that describes the school you will propose using the characteristics discussed in Chapter 2 and in this chapter.

REFERENCES

Austin, Gilbert. 1978. "Process Evaluation: A Comprehensive Study of Outlines." Baltimore: Maryland State Department of Education. ERIC: ED 160 644.

Bloom, Benjamin S. 1964. *Stability and Change in Human Characteristics*. New York: Wiley.

Blumberg, Arthur, and William Greenfield. 1980. *The Effective Principal: Perspective on School Leadership*. Boston: Allyn and Bacon.

Bossert, Steven T., D. D. Dwyer, B. Rowan, and G. V. Lee. 1982. "The Instructional Management Role of the Principal," *Educational Administration Quarterly* 18(3), 34–64.

Brookover, Wilbur B., C. Brady, P. Flood, J. Schweigen, and J. Wisenbater. 1979. *School Systems and School Achievement: Schools Can Make a Difference*. New York: Praeger.

Brookover, Wilbur B., and Lawrence W. Lezotte. 1979. *Changes in School Characteristics Coincident with Changes in School Achievement*. East Lansing: Institute for Research on Teaching, Michigan State University.

Bryk, Anthony S., Valerie E. Lee, and Peter B. Holland. 1993. *Catholic Schools and the Common Good*. Cambridge, MA: Harvard University Press.

Coleman, James, Ernest Q. Campbell, Carol J. Hobson, James McParland, Alexander M. Mood, Frederick D. Weinfeld, and Robert L. York. 1966. *Equality of Educational Opportunity*. Vol. 2. Washington, DC: U.S. Government Printing Office, OE-38001.

Cuban, Larry. 1998, January 28. "A Tale of Two Schools: How Progressives and Traditionalists Undermine Our Understanding of What Is 'Good' in Schools," *Education Week*, 33, 48.

Duttweiler, Patricia Cloud. 1988. "New Insights from Research on Effective Schools," *Insights*, No. 4. Austin, TX: Southwest Educational Development Laboratory.

Duttweiler, Patricia Cloud. 1990. "A Broader Definition of Effective Schools: Implications from Research and Practice," in T. J. Sergiovanni and J. H. Moore (Eds.), *Target 2000: A Compact for Excellence in Texas's Schools*. Austin: Texas Association for Supervision and Curriculum Development.

Edmonds, Ronald. 1979. "Some Schools Work and More Can," *Social Policy* 9(2), 28–32.

Gersten, Russell, Douglas Carnine, and Susan Green. 1982, December. "The Principal as

Instructional Leader: A Second Look," *Educational Leadership* 40, 47–50.

Greenfield, William. 1982. A *Synopsis of Research on School Principals.* Washington, DC: National Institute for Education.

Hallinger, Philip, and Ronald H. Heck. 1996. "Reassessing the Principal's Role in School Effectiveness: A Review of the Empirical Research 1980–1995," *Educational Administration Quarterly* 32(1), 5–44.

Hallinger, Philip, and Joseph Murphy. 1985. "Assessing the Instructional Management Behavior of Principals," *The Elementary School Journal* 86(2), 217–247.

Hill, Paul T., and Mary Beth Celio. 1998. *Fixing Urban Schools.* Washington, DC: Brookings Institution Press.

Hill, Paul T., Gail E. Foster, and Tamar Gendler. 1990. *High Schools with Character.* Santa Monica, CA: RAND Corporation.

Marzano, Robert J., Timothy Waters, and Brian A. McNulty. 2005. *School Leadership That Works: From Research to Results.* Alexandria, VA: Association for Supervision and Curriculum Development; Aurora, CO: Mid-continent Research for Education and Learning.

National Association of Secondary School Principals. 1996. *Breaking Ranks: Changing an American Institution.* A Report of the Secondary School Principals Association on the High School for the 21st Century. Reston, VA: Author.

National Association of Secondary School Principals. 2004. *Breaking Ranks II: Strategies for Leading High School Reform.* Reston, VA: Author.

Newberg, Norman A., and Allan A. Glatthorn. Undated. "Instructional Leadership: Four Ethnographic Studies of Junior High School Principals." Washington, DC: National Institute for Education (G-81–008).

Pajak, Edward F., and Carl D. Glickman. 1989. "Dimension of School District Improvement," *Educational Leadership* 46(8), 61–64.

Prunty, John J., and Wells Hively. 1982. "The Principal's Role in School Effectiveness: An Analysis of the Practices of Four Elementary School Leaders." Washington, DC: National Institute for Education (G-8–01–10) and CEMRL, Inc.

Purkey, S. C., and M. S. Smith. 1982. "Synthesis of Research on Effective Schools," *Educational Leadership* (40)3, 64–69.

Roueche, J. E., and G. A. Baker. 1986. *Profiling Excellence in America's Schools.* Arlington, VA: American Association of School Administrators.

Rutter, M., B. Maughan, P. Mortimore, J. Ouston, and A. Smith. 1979. *Fifteen Thousand Hours: Secondary Schools and Their Effects on Children.* Cambridge, MA: Harvard University Press.

Sebring, Penny Bender, and Anthony S. Bryk. 1996. "Student Centered Learning Climate," in Penny Bender Sebring et al. (Eds.), *Charting Reform in Chicago: The Students Speak.* Report sponsored by the Consortium on Chicago School Research. Chicago: University of Chicago.

Shouse, Roger C. 1996. "Academic Press and a Sense of Community: Conflict, Congruence, and Implications for Student Achievement," *Social Psychology of Education* 1, 47–68.

Stedman, Lawrence C. 1987. "It's Time We Changed the Effective Schools Formula," *Phi Delta Kappan* 69(3), 215–227.

Wayson, W. W. 1988. *Up from Excellence: The Impact of the Excellence Movement on Schools.* Bloomington, IN: Phi Delta Kappan Foundation.

Wimpelberg, Robert K., Charles Teddlie, and Samuel Stringfield. 1989. "Sensitivity to Context: The Past and Future of Effective Schools Research," *Educational Administration Quarterly* 25(1), 82–108.

10

BECOMING A COMMUNITY
OF MIND

*n*o finding is more important to building a successful school than the link
that exists between the school being able to develop a climate of support
for learning and caring in the home, among peers at school, and in the
school itself. Social scientists refer to this climate of support as social capital. Successful schools provide social capital for all their students, and this capital affects
how the students are engaged in learning and their subsequent academic success (see, e.g., Putnam, 2000:296–306). This is the message underlying the theme
of Chapter 9, and this is a message reiterated in other chapters throughout this
book.

Social capital consists of norms, obligations, and trusts that are generated by
relationships among people in a school or school community (Coleman, 1988,
1990; Gamoran, 1996). When social capital is strong, students find the encouragement and support they need from their peers, from their parents, from their teachers, and from the school itself to succeed (Sergiovanni, 2005). Schools develop
social capital by being caring communities (see, e.g., Battistich et al., 1994; Bryk
and Driscoll, 1988; Sergiovanni, 1994). As social capital grows, so does human
capital (Coleman, 1987).

> Human capital is created by changes in persons that bring about skills and capa-
> bilities that make them able to act in new ways.
>
> Social capital, however, comes about through changes in the relations among
> persons that facilitate action. . . . Human capital facilitates productive activity,

social capital does as well. For example, a group within which there is extensive trustworthiness and extensive trust is able to accomplish much more than a comparable group without that trustworthiness and trust. (Coleman, 1988:S100–S101)

Building social capital in schools depends largely on the cultivation of a community of mind. In Chapter 5, *community* was defined as a collection of people who are together bound to a set of shared ideas and ideals. This mutual binding creates bonds among them that provide trust, direction, and support. This binding to ideas strengthens bonds so that they are tight enough to transform them from a collection of I's into a collective we. As a we, members are part of a tightly knit web of meaningful relationships. This we usually shares a common place and over time comes to share sentiments and traditions that are sustaining.

When this definition of community fits schools, they have become transformed from formal organizations to focused, caring, learning, and inquiring communities (see Chapter 5 for an elaboration of the theme that schools should be thought of as social organizations even though more often than not they are thought of as formal organizations). Key to this transformation is building new kinds of relationships among people. This requires restructuring living and learning environments in ways that enhance the identity of teachers and students with each other, with the work of the school, and with the school itself. The aim is to build new connections among people and between them and their work that are idea- and norm-based, and to sanctify and ritualize these connections in ways that make them traditions rich in meaning and significance. As connections build, schools become communities by relationship, of place, of mind, and of memory. Here is why community is so important:

> Unless students are committed to the school and its purposes and unless students are engaged in the life of the school they will not succeed. Alienation and disengagement are the real problems that too many schools face. If we solve these problems, we solve all the other problems that challenge us. This is why schools should be more like families and communities (social organizations) than department stores and banks (formal organizations). This is why we need a new leadership for the principalship—one based in community thinking and practice (see, e.g., Sergiovanni, 1994; Strike, 2004).

Among the four dimensions of community, none is more important than the struggle to create a community of mind that binds members to a shared ideology as it bonds them together in special ways. Schools, for example, cannot become caring communities unless caring is valued and unless a norm system develops that points the way toward caring, rewards caring behaviors, and frowns on non-caring behaviors. Nor can schools become focused, learning, or inquiring communities without valuing these respective images and without developing norm systems that guide their quest for embodying these images.

Community emerges from a network of shared ideologies. Ideologies are coherent sets of beliefs that tie people together and that explain their work to them in terms of cause and effect relationships (Trice and Beyer, 1984). Ideologies are the means by which we make sense of our lives, find a direction, and commit ourselves to courses of action. In communities, ideologies shape what principals and teachers believe and how they practice. They influence, as well, the norm structure and behavior of students.

THE IMPORTANCE OF GOALS

Goals are an important part of a school's community of mind. Nonetheless, disagreement exists among those who study schools as to how the term *goals* should be defined and understood, and even as to whether goals actually make a difference in the decisions that principals and teachers make about schooling. Many prominent organizational theorists doubt whether organizations actually have goals; for example, Perrow (1981) states, "The notion of goals may be a mystification, hiding an errant, vagrant, changeable world" (8). He continues:

> Do organizations have goals, then, in the rational sense of organizational theory? I do not think so. In fact, when an executive says, "This is our goal" chances are that he is looking at what the organization happens to be doing and saying, "Since we are all very rational here, and we are doing this, this must be our goal." Organizations in this sense, run backward; the deed is father to the thought, not the other way around. (8)

Other organizational theorists have commented that schools are loosely structured (Bidwell, 1965; Weick, 1976), suggesting that parts tend to operate independently of one another. Teachers, for example, work alone in classrooms; their work is not visible to others. Close supervision under these circumstances is difficult, and continuous evaluation of teaching is impossible. No mechanism exists to ensure that school mandates, such as stated goals, are reflected in actual teaching. Coordination of the work of several teachers is difficult to achieve.

Because direct supervision and tight coordination are difficult to implement successfully in loosely structured schools, principals need to rely on the management of symbols to rally teachers to a common cause. Although schools may be loosely structured in the way they are organized, effective schools combine this loosely structured characteristic with a tightly structured core of values and beliefs. This core represents the cultural cement that bonds people together, gives them a sense of identity, and provides them with guidelines for their work. In a loosely structured world it is accepted that bureaucratic means are not tight enough to connect students and teachers to their work and to sustain these connections over time. That is why cultural connections need to be emphasized. In effective schools, norms rule (Sergiovanni, 2005).

But are symbols the same as goals? At one level, symbols and goals share common characteristics and similar functions. Weick's view is that symbols are more like *charters* than goals. They tell people what they are doing and why they are doing it. They reveal to people the importance and significance of their work. Goals, however, provide direction and are devices for telling people when and how well they are doing things (Weick, 1982:676).

The more generally goals are stated, the closer they approximate symbols. As goals become more precise, they tend to lose symbolic value and to resemble instrumental objectives designed to program daily school activities. They serve less to provide a sense of purpose or to instill a feeling of significance and more to guide what teachers should be doing at a given moment. Goals as symbols sacrifice precision and detail to gain significance and meaning. They seek to capture the spirit of teachers at work. Objectives, however, sacrifice significance and meaning in an attempt to master the precision and detail that gives them the instrumental power over what teachers are doing at a given moment and to provide ready measures of how well they are performing these tasks.

Experts who describe schools as being loosely structured maintain that instrumental control is difficult to achieve. Behind closed classroom doors, they argue, teachers follow the beat of a different drummer—selecting learning materials and deciding on what and how to teach not in response to objectives, but in response to available materials, their own intuitions and abilities, their perceptions of student needs, time constraints, and other situational characteristics. Tight school structures, they maintain, simply cannot reach into the classroom and challenge this de facto autonomy of the teacher no matter how detailed such structures might be or how eloquently they might be described. Because the influence of direct control is blunted by de facto teacher autonomy, the significance of goal-symbols as a means of influence in schools is increased.

Goals as Patterns

Hills (1982) points out that, in the real world, principals rarely find themselves in a position where they can pursue goals one at a time. The problem they face is that schools have multiple goals. Furthermore, sometimes the goals conflict with each other. Making progress toward one goal may mean losing progress toward another. Always thinking in terms of discrete goals or even discrete multiple goals with each attended to sequentially by the principal, therefore, does not fit the special character of the school's unique value system. Under loosely structured conditions, schools don't achieve goals as much as they respond to certain values and tend to certain imperatives that ensure their survival over time.

Parsons (1951), for example, identified four imperatives that must be balanced against each other in such a way that each is maximized in order for the school or any other institution to survive. The neglect of any of these imperatives causes the other to decline, which means trouble for the school. The imperatives are goal attainment; internally maintaining day-to-day stability and functions; adopting to external demands, concerns, and circumstances; and, finally, tending to the cultural patterns and norms that hold the school together over time. External adoption, for example, often threatens internal stability and upsets cultural patterns. Maintaining cultural patterns often interferes with goal attainment, and so forth.

Rather than discrete goal attainment, Hills (1982) points out that principals bring to their practice what he calls "pattern rationality." They behave in response to "a conception of pattern development on a number of mutually limiting dimensions with respective gains in a given area having implications for others" (7). Successful principals become surfers, skilled at riding the wave of the pattern as it unfolds. They respond to value patterns when discrete goals are in conflict with each other. Important to the concept of pattern rationality is that principals be concerned with the costs and benefits of their actions.

Goals as Symbols

School boards, state departments of education, and other groups and institutions expect schools to have goals. Goal statements are therefore necessary to symbolically portray the school as being rational and thus legitimate to outsiders. Rational schools are supposed to have goals and purposes and are supposed to pursue them deliberately. Schools, for example, are expected to behave rationally by accrediting agencies, state governments, the local press, the local school board, and other groups. Thus, stated goals and purposes are necessary to obtain legitimacy from these and other groups.

Findings from the successful schools research parallel those of Peters and Waterman (1982) in their studies of excellent business corporations. In their words: "Every excellent company we studied is clear on what it stands for, and takes the process of value shaping seriously. In fact, we wonder whether it is possible to be an excellent company without clarity of values and without having the right sorts of values" (280). They continue:

> Virtually all of the better performing companies we looked at in the first study had a well-defined set of guiding beliefs. The less well-performing institutions, on the other hand, were marked by one of two characteristics. Many had no set of coherent beliefs. The others had distinctive and widely discussed objectives, but the only ones that they got animated about were the ones that could be quantified (the financial objectives, such as earnings per share and growth measures). (281)

This latter point is important, for we live in a "data-driven" world. Too often if we don't have the data we do nothing, and if we cannot measure something it does not count. Peters and Waterman (1982) are suggesting that perhaps "information-driven" makes more sense than does "data-driven." Information includes data and more. In an information culture there is lots of room for values, beliefs, assumptions, articles of faith, and other well-thought-out and coherent sets of ideas.

And perhaps most important, data are never privileged. Given a conflict between what the data say and our values, our values typically trump the data. Data should not tell us what to do but should inform the decisions that we make, along with other sources of information.

In describing his many years of experience at the helm of IBM, Thomas Watson, Jr., (1963) highlights the importance of goals and symbols as statements of beliefs as follows:

> I firmly believe that any organization, in order to survive and achieve success, must have a sound set of beliefs on which it premises all its policies and actions. Next, I believe that the most important single factor in corporate success is faithful adherence to these beliefs. And, finally, I believe that if an organization is to meet the challenge of a changing world, it must be prepared to change everything about itself except those beliefs as it moves through corporate life. In other words, the basic philosophy, spirit, and drive of an organization have far more to do with its relative achievements than do technological or economic resources, organizational structure, innovation, and timing. All these things weigh heavily in success. But they are, I think, transcended by how strongly the people in the organization believe in its basic precepts and how faithfully they carry them out. (4–6)

Corporations, of course, are different from schools. They are generally considered to be more quantitative, impersonal, and instrumental. Schools, by contrast, are much more human-intensive. Although values are important to both, they are presumed to be more central to the inner workings of schools. Thus, providing examples from the corporate world illustrating the importance of goals, values, and beliefs should serve as notice to principals and other educators that such statements are even more important to schools. Reflecting this reality, Mike Schmoker (1999, 2006) makes a compelling case for paying attention to goals in schools and for encouraging educators to be more information-driven than is now the case.

Using EDUCATIONAL PLATFORMS

Statements of belief provide the common cement, bonding people together as they work on behalf of the school. Operationally, such beliefs form an *educational platform* for the school and principal. Educational platforms should be thought of as encompassing the defining principles and beliefs that guide the actions of individuals and that provide a basis for evaluating these actions. Leaders of successful schools have well-defined educational platforms from which they operate. Indeed, successful schools contain fairly well-developed educational platforms serving as guides to teachers and others as they live and work in the school. Platforms are not objectives or specifications of what exactly is to be accomplished; instead, they contain guiding principles from which individuals decide what to do and how to do it. The more loosely structured the school, the more important is the concept of an educational platform in bringing about cohesion and concerted action. Platforms are the means by which mission statements and broad goals and purposes are articulated into practice.

When taken together, platforms, mission statements, and broad goals and purposes constitute a covenant of shared values that functions as the cultural center of the school—the repository of that which is held sacred by all. As pointed out in Chapter 4, at the heart of any culture is what the noted sociologist Edward A. Shils (1961) calls the "central zone." He believes that all societies and organizations within societies have central zones that provide a sense of order and stability and a source for the development of norms that gives meaning and significance to the lives of people. The school's central zone represents a repository for the emotions and values that become the basis for moral authority.

Centers evolve naturally in schools in response to human needs, but if left unattended they can take the form of "wild cultures." Wild cultures are driven by emotions and values that may or may not be compatible with school goals, may or may not be supportive of improved teaching and learning, may or may not be growth oriented, and may or may not be good for students. One of the jobs of the principal is to try to unravel and make manifest the wild culture so that it can be examined and understood. Doing so helps those involved come to grips with what is in relation to the values and beliefs that are desired. The idea is to "domesticate" this culture so that it emerges as a system of shared values and beliefs that define for all a way of life that is committed to quality teaching and learning. The goal of domestication is to create community.

When domesticated, the center that defines the school culture becomes the basis for collective decision making and the basis for moral action. The actions and behaviors of parents, teachers, students, and others are driven less by self-interest and more by what the school community considers to be right and good. In this chapter, *center* is referred to as the *covenant* of shared values that determines for the school what is right and good, points to the school's mission, defines obligations and duties, and spells out what must be done to meet commitments.

$\mathcal{P}$URPOSING IS THE LINCHPIN

Key to domesticating the culture of the school along the lines of community is the building of a covenant of shared values that replaces more implicit and informal norms. Zaleznik (1988) believes that "the failure of American management is the substitution of process for substance." He attributes this substitution to an exaggerated belief that schools can be improved by perfecting management systems, structures, and programs and by emphasizing human relationships in order to better control what people do. Too often, process and relationship means become ends in themselves, resulting in vacuous school improvement strategies (Sergiovanni and Duggan, 1990).

To Zaleznik (1988), "leadership is based on a compact that binds those who lead and those who follow into the same moral, intellectual and emotional commitment" (15). Purposing is what principals do to develop this compact. Purposing involves both the vision of the leader and the covenant that the group shares.

Vision in school leadership needs to be understood differently than the way it emerges from the corporate sector. Peters and Austin (1985), for example, point out that vision should start with a single person and suggest that one should be wary of "committee visions." There is some truth to this observation, but there are problems as well. Principals and superintendents have a responsibility and obligation to talk openly and frequently about their beliefs and commitments. They are responsible for encouraging a dialogue about what the school stands for and where it should be headed. Vision, however, should not be construed as a strategic plan that functions like a road map charting the turns needed to reach a specific reality that the leader has in mind. It should, instead, be viewed more as a compass that points the direction to be taken, that inspires enthusiasm, and that allows people to buy into and take part in the shaping of the way that will constitute the school's mission (Bricker, 1985). The fleshing out of this vision requires the building of a shared consensus about purposes and beliefs that creates a powerful force binding people together around common themes. This binding provides them with a sense of what is important and some signal of what is of value. With binding in place, the school is transformed from an organization to a community. When this happens relationships among community members change. Bonds among them get tighter.

Often overlooked is the importance of the personal visions of teachers. As Barth (1986) points out:

> All of us who entered teaching brought with us a conception of a desirable school. Each of us had a personal vision and was prepared to work, even fight, for it. Over time our personal visions became blurred by the visions, demands, and requirements of others. Many teachers' personal visions are now all but obliterated by external prescriptions. (478)

Vision is a noun that describes what principals and others bring to the school. *Purposing* is a verb that points to what principals do to bring about a shared consensus tight enough and coherent enough to bond people together in a common cause and to define them as a community, but loose enough to allow for individual self-expression.

Purposes in Action

Purposes let people know where the school is going, why, and how. Sometimes purpose statements contain bedrock beliefs that comprise value assumptions about the nature of people. The following four beliefs, for example, are based on Purkey and Novak's (1988) proposal for an approach to schooling they call *invitational education:*

1. Teachers, parents, students, and everyone else with whom the school works are able, valuable, and responsible and should be treated accordingly.
2. Education should be a collaborative, cooperative activity.
3. Teachers, parents, students, and everyone else with whom the school works possess untapped potential in all areas of human endeavor.
4. Human potential can best be realized by places, policies, and processes that are designed to invite development and by the actions and behaviors of people who are intentionally inviting.

When adopted, the four beliefs become a policy platform from which decisions are made about how to organize the school and its curriculum, how people are to work together, and the tone of teaching that is expected. The first belief, for example, frames policies about success and failure. If the principal and teachers believe that every parent is worthy of respect and can learn, then they will find ways for parents to improve their parenting skills, to learn about how to help their children at home with their lessons, and so forth. Excuses such as "they are barely literate themselves" and "they don't speak English" would not be acceptable. This formula applies as well to student success.

Similarly, the second belief frames policies in the direction of cooperation rather than competition. Good policies and practices in a school committed to those beliefs are those that do things with people rather than to people. They give parents, teachers, and students voices, and they listen to these voices. Similar guidelines for action can be derived from beliefs three and four.

Sometimes purposes take the form of a set of common principles that combine beliefs with understandings and expectations. "The Common Principles" of the Coalition of Essential Schools, a national effort to restructure secondary schools founded by Theodore Sizer, is an example of this approach. Sizer believes that no two good schools are quite alike. Instead, each should be a creation of its unique school-community. Thus, advocating common principles rather than proposing a model to be emulated makes sense. The principles of the coalition are as follows:

1. An Essential school should focus on helping adolescents learn to use their minds well. Schools should not attempt to be "comprehensive" if such a claim is made at the expense of the school's central intellectual purpose.
2. The school's goals should be simple: that each student master a limited number of essential skills and areas of knowledge. While these skills and areas will, to varying degrees, reflect the traditional academic disciplines, the program's design should be shaped by the intellectual and imaginative powers and competencies that students need, rather than by "subjects" as conventionally defined.

The aphorism "less is more" should dominate. Curricular decisions should be guided by the aim of thorough student mastery and achievement rather than by an effort merely to "cover content."

3. The school's goals should apply to all students, although the means to these goals will vary as those students themselves vary. School practice should be tailor-made to meet the needs of every group or class of adolescents.

4. Teaching and learning should be personalized to the maximum feasible extent. Efforts should be directed toward a goal that no teacher have direct responsibility for more than 80 students. To capitalize on personalization, decisions about the course of study, the use of students' and teachers' time, and the choice of teaching materials and specific pedagogics must be unreservedly placed in the hands of the principal and staff.

5. The governing practical metaphor of the school should be student-as-worker, rather than the more familiar metaphor of teacher-as-deliverer-of-instructional-services. A prominent pedagogy will be coaching, to provoke students to learn how to learn and thus to teach themselves.

6. Students entering secondary school studies should be those who can show competence in language and elementary mathematics. Students of traditional high school age but not yet at appropriate levels of competence to enter secondary school studies should be provided intensive remedial work to help them meet these standards. The diploma should be awarded upon a successful final demonstration of mastery for graduation—an "exhibition." This exhibition by the student of his or her grasp of the central skills and knowledge of the school's program may be jointly administered by the faculty and by higher authorities. The diploma is awarded when earned, so the school's program proceeds with no strict age grading and with no system of credits collected by time spent in class. The emphasis is on the students' demonstration that they can do important things.

   The tone of the school should stress values of unanxious expectation ("I won't threaten you but I expect much of you"); of trust (until abused); and of decency (the values of fairness, generosity, and tolerance). Incentives appropriate to the school's particular students and teachers should be emphasized, and parents should be treated as essential collaborators.

7. The principal and teachers should perceive themselves as generalists first (teacher and scholars in general education), and specialists second (experts in one particular discipline). Staff should expect multiple obligations (teacher-counselor-manager), and demonstrate a sense of commitment to the entire school.

8. Ultimate administrative and budget targets should include, in addition to total student loads per teacher of 80 or fewer pupils, substantial time for collective planning by teachers, competitive salaries for staff, and an ultimate per pupil cost not to exceed that at traditional schools by more than 10 percent. To accomplish this, administrative plans might include the phased reduction or elimination of some services now provided for students in many traditional comprehensive secondary schools. (Sizer, 1989:2–4)

See Peggy Silva and Robert Mackin's (2002) story on page 227 about how the principles of the Coalition of Essential Schools were used to create a new 1,000-student high school—Souhegan High School in Amherst, New Hampshire. Silva is a teacher at Souhegan and Mackin was the founding principal.

The principles of the coalition stand next to the recommendations for *Breaking Ranks* (NASSP), issued in 1996. *Breaking Ranks II* (NASSP, 2004) updates the progress being made in implementing the principles. The three documents provide a rich source of ideas that can be used to guide decision making. Principles stated, however, inevitably run up against the real world and call for compromises to sustain them. Principle 8—calling for 80 or fewer students as the total student load per teacher—and pleas to scale down the size of schools to make them more personal and coherent learning environments are examples. Moving in both directions overnight would shock both the minds and the pocketbooks of schools, school districts, and citizens. But such principles can be viewed as benchmarks to be met over a period of years. In *Breaking Ranks II*, for example, vignettes are provided that tell the stories of three schools who are on the way to implementing the various recommendations (see Chapter 2 for details).

"Expeditionary learning" (Outward Bound USA Convenor, 1992), one of several models of schools advocated by New American Schools, is another example of how school purposes can provide the kind of idea structure that gives direction and guides decisions that schools make. Those involved in this movement seek to transform schools into centers of expeditionary learning. They believe that learning is an expedition into the unknown that requires bringing together personal experience and intellectual growth to promote self-discovery and construct knowledge. Schools committed to the expeditionary learning approach are not provided with scripts to implement but with design principles and components. As is the case with the essential schools movement, the design principles and components serve to inform the decisions that schools make. The principles, along with a handful of key program components that provide a standard for how the principles should be implemented, appear in Table 10.1.

*T*HE PRINCIPLES OF LEARNING

Many schools adopt theories of action, usually in the form of assumptions presumed to be true, to back up leadership. Sometimes these assumptions are based on convictions, but sometimes they are research based too. Perhaps the most well-known research-based theory of action these days is the Principles of Learning developed by the Institute for Learning at the University of Pittsburgh. The principles are summarized in Table 10.2. When linked to standards the Principles of Learning not only inform what will be taught, they govern how students will be taught and how they will be assessed. Yet there are no scripts. Plenty of room table **10.1** Expeditionary Learning Outward Bound® Design Principles and Components

Principles

1. **The Primacy of Self-Discovery:** Learning happens best with emotion, challenge, and the requisite support. People discover their abilities, values, "grand passions," and responsibilities in situations that offer adventure and the unexpected. They must have tasks that require perseverance, fitness, craftsmanship, imagination, self-discipline, and significant achievement. A primary job of the educator is to help students overcome their fear and discover they have more in them than they think.

2. **The Having of Wonderful Ideas:** Teach so as to build on children's curiosity about the world by creating learning situations that provide matter to think about, time to experiment, and time to make sense of what is observed. Foster a community where students' and adults' ideas are respected.

3. **The Responsibility for Learning:** Learning is both a personal, individually specific process of discovery and a social activity. Each of us learns within and for ourselves and as a part of a group. Every aspect of a school must encourage children, young people, and adults to become increasingly responsible for directing their own personal and collective learning.

4. **Intimacy and Caring:** Learning is fostered best in small groups where there is trust, sustained caring, and mutual respect among all members of the learning community. Keep schools and learning groups small. Be sure there is a caring adult looking after the progress of each child. Arrange for the older students to mentor the younger ones.

5. **Success and Failure:** All students must be assured a fair measure of success in learning in order to nurture the confidence and capacity to take risks and rise to increasingly difficult challenges. But it is also important to experience failure, to overcome negative inclinations, to prevail against adversity, and to learn to turn disabilities into opportunities.

6. **Collaboration and Competition:** Teach so as to join individual and group development so that the value of friendship, trust, and group endeavor is made manifest. Encourage students to compete, not against each other, but with their own personal best and with rigorous standards of excellence.

7. **Diversity and Inclusivity:** Diversity and inclusivity in all groups dramatically increases richness of ideas, creative power, problem-solving ability, and acceptance of others. Encourage students to investigate, value, and draw on their own different histories, talents, and resources together with those of other communities and cultures. Keep the schools and learning groups heterogeneous.

8. **The Natural World:** A direct and respectful relationship with the natural world refreshes the human spirit and reveals the important lessons of recurring cycles and cause and effect. Students learn to become stewards of the earth and of the generations to come.

9. **Solitude and Reflection:** Solitude, reflection, and silence replenish our energies and open our minds. Be sure students have time alone to explore their own thoughts, make their own connections, and create their own ideas. Then give them opportunities to exchange their reflections with each other and with adults.

10. **Service and Compassion:** We are crew, not passengers, and are strengthened by acts of consequential service to others. One of a school's primary functions is to prepare its students with the attitudes and skills to learn from and be of service to others.

(continued)

table **10.1** **Continued**

Components

1. **Schedule, Structure, Teacher–Student Relationships:** Implementing Expeditionary Learning will require a complete reconsideration of the relationships among staff and students, as well as the schools' arrangements of time and space. Schools should be prepared to eliminate the 50-minute period as the basic scheduling unit and to replace it with a schedule organized to accommodate learning expeditions that may engage students full time for periods of days, weeks, or months.

   Interdisciplinary learning expeditions will replace subject-separated classes. Tracking will be eliminated; Teachers work with the same group of students for periods of several years.

2. **Curriculum:** Expeditionary Learning engages the learner in situations that provide not only context but consequence. The curriculum makes intellectual learning and character development of equal importance and encourages self-discovery.

3. **Assessment:** Expeditionary Learning uses real-world performance as the primary way to assess effectiveness in teaching and learning. The International Baccalaureate is used as a framework for establishing world-class standards.

4. **Staff Development:** Expeditionary Learning depends on and invests in the ongoing development and renewal of staff. An apprenticeship model, flexibility in hiring or reassignment, and a substantial investment in year-round staff growth is required.

5. **Linkages to Community and Health Service Organizations:** To provide necessary support to students and their families, expeditionary centers will develop working relations with the appropriate service agencies.

6. **Budget:** Expeditionary Learning achieves its goals through reorganization of existing resources and should not require significant additional funding after an initial period of transition.

Sources: Expeditionary Learning Outward Bound®. (1993). *The Expeditionary Learning Reader,* Expeditionary Learning: Cambridge, MA. Vol. 1. The above principles have been informed by Kurt Hahn's "Seven Laws of Salem," by Paul Ylvisaker's "The Missing Dimension," and by Eleanor Duckworth's *"The Having of Wonderful Ideas" and Other Essays on Teaching and Learning* (New York: Teachers College Press, Columbia University, 1987).

exists for teachers to use their ingenuity and to rely on pedagogical methods that they understand and enjoy.

Still, there are limits. A serious walk-through of classrooms should reveal that the Principles of Learning are reflected in the pedagogical decisions that teachers make. In Resnick and Glennan Jr.'s (2001) words: "These principles do not constitute a rigid specification of a design. Specifics of the organization and operations vary from one district to another, depending on a district's history, its size, the population it serves, and the particular characteristics of its staff. Not static, these principles evolve as the Institute and its member districts learn from their experiences" (10–11).

Still a fundamental assumption underlying the principles is that the details of teaching should not be left to teachers alone. Districts need to have an important say and in the name of instructional coherence should provide the same t a b l e **10.2**   **Principles of Learning**

1. Organize your school for effort-based learning by assuming that under the right conditions all students can learn. These effort-based conditions include persistence by students and the provision of support by the school for every learner. Organizing for effort requires setting standards that every student is expected to meet in each of the subject areas; teaching a curriculum that prepares them to meet the standards; providing additional instruction and learning as needed; and holding students responsible for completing their work.

2. Set clear expectations by not only delineating standards but making these standards known and discussing them with students. Further, providing benchmarks that enable students to know how well they are doing and what they must do to get better is important. Finally, help students use the standards and benchmarks to evaluate their own work.

3. Emphasize combining academic rigor in a thinking curriculum that provides opportunities for students to practice problem solving throughout the curriculum. "This curriculum must also reflect the well-established findings that learning takes root only when students actively manipulate and use the knowledge that is presented to them, in effect constructing key concepts for themselves . . ." (19).

4. Adopt accountable talk as the basis for effective classroom oral and written conversations and deliberations. "This talk must meet standards of reasoning, evidence, and factual accuracy" (19). And this talk must include careful listening to others. Accountable talk requires a shift from teaching equals talking and learning equals listening to teaching equals listening and learning equals talking.*

5. Acknowledge the importance of a set of endowed cognitive skills but give primary attention to the acquired propensities for applying these skills. "These beliefs and propensities can be socialized if children regularly spend time in learning environments that press them to invent procedures, explain concepts, justify their reasoning, and seek information" (20).

6. View learning as an apprenticeship that engages students in creating learning products and in evaluating and revising their work. Provide opportunities for students to participate "in authentic tasks that have truly interested audiences, working under the mentorship of people who have special expertise in the task at hand, correcting and redoing work until it meets quality standards . . ." (20).

7. Include teachers as learners, and view teachers and students together as learning communities. In an effort-based environment "professionals are defined as individuals who are continually learning rather than as people who already know. Their roles include both teacher and learner, master and apprentice, and these roles are continually shifting according to the context. For example, an individual may be a teacher of her students; a student of her classroom coach and other professional developers; an apprentice to master teachers in the district; and on occasion, a mentor to her peers. When a professional is defined as someone who is continually learning, and learning is seen as a function of effort more than aptitude, it is the willingness, initiative, persistence, and individual responsibility a person demonstrates toward the rigorous process of instructional improvement that defines his or her professional value" (Resnick and Hall, 1998:110).

---

*Attributed to Deborah Meier.

Source: Summarized from Lauren Resnick, Anthony Alvarado, and Richard Elmore, "Developing and Implementing High-Performance Learning Communities," a proposal from the Learning Research and Development Center, University of Pittsburgh, Solicitation Number RC-96-1370, August 12, 1996. For more recent iterations of the Principles of Learning see www.instituteforlearning.org. The principles also appear in T. J. Sergiovanni, *Strengthening the Heartbeat,* 2005.

professional development and the same system of supervision and assessment for all teachers so that they will be successful in implementing the principles.

The bottom line is that instructional coherence should enhance but not undermine the work of teachers. Newmann and colleagues (2001) clarify as follows:

> It is important to place strong instructional program coherence in perspective and to understand it not as the overriding task of school improvement or as a substitute for key supports for teaching and learning, but as a strategy for maximizing those supports. Strong instructional program coherence could, for instance, undermine the development of teachers' professional community if it insisted on such regimented instruction that teachers had no opportunity to exercise expertise or raise questions about selected methods or programs. . . . Similarly, teachers' professional development opportunities might be made so uniform as to prevent individuals from learning skills unique to their teaching situation or background. The pursuit of greater program coherence must respond to appropriate forms of differentiation and be receptive to new or altered programming for staff and for students when clearly necessary. (313)

Newmann and his colleagues continue,

> A school could become highly coherent (and could even increase student scores on standardized tests) by instituting instructional frameworks that are narrowly focused on the most rudimentary academic tasks. . . . Thus the ultimate value of strong program coherence will always depend on the perceived educational legitimacy of what students learn and how they learn it. (2001:313)

It is fair to conclude from these caveats that, despite the critical nature of instructional program coherence to the change process that addresses students learning, there are limits. Instructional coherence works best when teachers are able to teach to their strengths. But teaching whatever they would like whenever they would like to is not the answer to the problem. Think of coherence as a compass that carefully and deliberately points the way while allowing travelers enough discretion so that they may choose one path over another providing that instructional coherence is not endangered.

*L*EADING WITH IDEAS

Using ideas to back up leadership depends on communicating stories. Sometimes these stories are provided by the leader. But at other times stories percolate up from a variety of sources including teachers and students. In every case the effective use of ideas provides individuals and groups with a personal group identity. These stories communicate what is important and provide a way for teachers and others to gauge their fit with the school and its beliefs. Howard Gardner (1995) explains:

> A leader is likely to achieve success only if she can construct and convincingly communicate a clear and persuasive story; appreciate the nature of the audience(s), including its changeable features; invest her own (or channel others') energy in the building and maintenance of an organization; embody in her own life the principal contours of the story; either provide direct leadership or find a way to achieve influence through indirect means; and finally, find a way to understand and make use of, without being overwhelmed by, increasing technical expertise. (302)

In a way ideas and the stories they communicate serve to persuade, to manage, to bind, and to legitimize. Ideas serve to persuade others, to convince them to adopt a point of view, and to feel obligated to embody these ideas and the story they represent in their practice. They serve as well to manage what is going on by providing public benchmarks that everyone can use to gauge the extent to which their own commitments and behaviors embody the ideas and the extent to which the school itself embodies these ideas. Teachers, administrators, students, and others examine their own work in light of its impact on the school's vision and identify ways in which their school lives can better embody the school's vision. How well are we doing? Various constituent groups can answer this question by examining their behaviors in light of the commitments that they make. Having made a public commitment constituent groups feel obligated to embody these ideas in their practice, and thus the ideas themselves become accountability tools as well as guidelines for what one should or should not do.

Ideas serve also to bind people together. When ideas are shared, relationships among individuals who share these ideas change. They take on a moral character that provides tight and obligatory links among those who share the ideas. And finally, ideas serve to legitimize what it is that people do. Ideas, as pointed out above, comprise a source of authority for our actions. No doubt teachers, principals, students, and other members of the school engage in their responsibilities for a variety of reasons themed to getting rewards or avoiding punishments. But the effectiveness of these strategies pales when compared to engaging in one's responsibilities because it is the right thing to do or one feels obligated for other reasons. When push comes to shove it is cognitive leadership that counts the most, not personality-based leadership and not bureaucratic leadership.

There is no mystery as to how to lead with ideas. The Principles of Learning, for example, provide a formal list whose source of authority is embedded in research and/or the experiences of those involved in school reform. A less formal approach is for a school to decide to use its own promises and its own examples of commitments as part of its idea structure. These promises and commitments might be listed on posters that are scattered throughout the school—in classrooms, on corridor walls, in the cafeteria, the principal's office, the main foyer of the school, and in other public places. Different posters might address different themes as follows:

- Five promises that we make to students
- Five promises that we make to each other
- Five characteristics that you will see in our teaching
- Five examples of great student work
- Five examples of great assignments that teachers give
- Five things that we expect from students
- Five things that we expect from parents
- Five things that parents can expect from us
- Five reasons why this is a great place to be a teacher

Engaging in conversations to reach agreement about promises, characteristics, examples, and expectations has value in and of itself. But when this work is made public it provides both a set of guidelines for what it is that each of the role constituents ought to do and a set of ideas for holding each of the groups accountable. Of course some of these poster themes will be slow in changing. The five promises we make to students and the five promises we make to each other might be examples. The content of other poster themes, perhaps examples of great student work and examples of great assignments that teachers give, would be changed more frequently—perhaps once a month or once every two or three weeks. Providing lists of five is a compelling and easily understood way for a school to share and then evaluate its standards for what students ought to do and its standards for the kind of classroom environment that teachers ought to provide.

What about accountability? Think of the lists of five as public benchmarks that are widely shared. If teachers, administrators, parents, and students provide evidence that documents the extent to which they are "keeping their promises" then we have in the works a meaningful and continuous accountability system with both formative and summative features.

Characteristics of Purpose Statements

There is no recipe for developing a covenant of shared values. It is a "personal" statement that is developed and owned by a particular school-community. A good convenant, however, should communicate a school's key purposes. Here are some general characteristics of purposes that might be helpful to schools. Purposes should meet the following nine criteria:

1. Clear enough so that you know you are achieving them
2. Accessible enough so that they can be achieved with existing resources
3. Important enough to reflect the core values and beliefs that are shared by those with a stake in the school
4. Powerful enough that they can inspire and touch people in a world that is managerially loose and culturally tight
5. Focused and few in number so that it is clear as to what is important and what is not

6. Characterized by consonance (the purposes should "hang together" as a group); it should be clear that contradictory purposes can be managed
7. Difficult enough to evoke challenge and cause people to persevere, to persist
8. Resilient enough to stand the test of time and thus not be easily changed
9. Flexible enough to be changed after careful consideration

Taken together, a good set of purposes should encourage cooperation within the school, and not competition. Cooperative purposes encourage people to work together by allowing each member to share in what the group achieves or attains. Everyone benefits when anyone is successful. Competitive purposes, by contrast, pit one person against another. Each member receives rewards independent of the success of the group and contingent only on her or his own performance, regardless of how well the group does.

From Mind-Set to Mission to Norms and to Action

The argument so far in this chapter is that in today's world, strong and effective leadership depends on a strong and effective framework that puts substance at the center and pushes process off to the sides. If this recentering of leadership is successful, then the source of authority for our leadership and practice changes (see Table 7.1 for details). Instead of teachers following principals because they control the bureaucratic incentive system that rewards compliance and punishes deviance; and instead of teachers following principals because they are charming and have effective interpersonal skills, their followership is tied to shared values and beliefs, successful theories and practices, and other substantive attributes that might be referred to as "ideas."

When we allow bureaucratic things to make up the sources of authority for leadership, we make certain assumptions. Teachers, for example, are viewed as subordinates in a hierarchically arranged system. Principals are thought to be trustworthy even though many believe that you cannot trust teachers very much. Further, goals and interests of teachers and principals are thought to be different. This assumption in particular requires that principals be watchful. Moreover, it is assumed that hierarchy equals expertise. That is, the higher you are ranked in the school or district, the more you are thought to know about teaching and learning and other matters of schooling. This is why external accountability seems to work best. If you want to know how things are going, don't just ask teachers to share their practice with each other and with you. Instead formalize the procedures and put distance between people at various levels of the hierarchy so that bureaucratic objectivity and disinterest are thought to be preserved.

When personal authority is used as the basis for leadership practice the following assumptions are typically made. The goals and interests of teachers and supervisors are not the same but they can be bartered. Teachers have needs and if these needs are met at work, the work gets done as required in exchange. Congenial relationships and harmonious interpersonal climates are dominant and make teachers content, easier to work with, and more apt to cooperate. Leadership becomes established as a form of bartering in which the principal gives teachers what they want in return for teachers giving the principal what she or he wants.

When ideas are used as the source of authority for leadership and practice, then the following assumptions are made. Schools are considered to be professional learning communities that rally around a set of ideas which provides the school with focus and meaning and engenders their commitment (DuFour and Eaker, 1998; DuFour et al., 2006; NASSP, 1996, 2004; Silva and Mackin, 2002). These communities are defined by their centers of shared values, beliefs, and commitments. In these communities what is considered right and good is as important as what works and what is effective. People are motivated as much by emotion and belief as they are by self-interest. Indeed they willingly sacrifice their self-interest on behalf of the common good. And finally, it is assumed that collegiality is a professional virtue (Sergiovanni 2001, 2005).

Silva and Mackin (2002) suggest that critical friends groups function as professional learning communities when they learn to talk to each other in more authentic ways and when they learn to direct their energies by intensely focusing on improving teaching and learning. Critical friends groups seek to accomplish the following:

- Design learning goals for students, stated specifically enough that others can observe them in operation
- Design strategies that move students toward those goals
- Gather evidence on the effectiveness of those strategies
- Analyze and reflect upon that evidence
- Adapt teaching strategies and reformulate learning goals (Silva and Mackin, 2002:123)

Members of Professional Learning Communities (PLCs) that emerge from Critical Friends Group (CFG) practices work hard to share their teaching practice. They seek to take collegiality to the next level—the development of a network of communities of practice in their school. They are keenly interested in examining student work together as a way to further develop their own practice and to hone their beliefs, hoping that they will be able to transform these ideas into realities.

Toward a Moral Authority

What are the consequences of using different sources of authority? When bureaucratic authority is used, it takes the form of proper monitoring. Teachers respond as technicians executing predetermined scripts. Because of this tight alignment, their performance is narrowed. When personal authority is used as the basis for leadership, teachers respond when rewards are available but not otherwise. Their involvement is calculated and their performance is narrowed. And finally, when t a b l e **10.3**   **Leading with Ideas at Souhegan High School, Amherst, NH**

1. *From mind-set to mission.*
   Create a democratic culture committed to personalization as embodied in the common principles of the Coalition of Essential Schools and the common characteristics of *Breaking Ranks II.* Use the mind-set to develop the Souhegan High School mission statement as follows:

   "Souhegan High School aspires to be a community of learners born of respect, trust, and courage. We consciously commit ourselves:
   - To support and engage an individual's unique gifts, passions, and intentions.
   - To develop and empower the mind, body, and heart.
   - To challenge and expand the comfortable limits of thought, tolerance, and performance.
   - To inspire and honor the active stewardship of family, nation, and globe."

2. *From mission to norms.*
   Use the mission as a living document that provides norms and represents rules for living together as follows:

   "The Souhegan Six:
   1. Respect and encourage the right to teach and the right to learn at all times.
   2. Be actively engaged in the learning; ask questions, collaborate, and seek solutions.
   3. Be on time to fulfill your daily commitments.
   4. Be appropriate; demonstrate behavior that is considerate of the community, the campus, and yourself.
   5. Be truthful; communicate honestly.
   6. Be responsible and accountable for your choices."

3. *From norms and rules to action.*
   Assign responsibility to various constituent groups (i.e., parents, teachers, students, and administrators). Have them answer such questions as: What must you and others who share your role do in order to better embody our vision in our practice? What responsibilities must you accept if our vision is to be better manifested in our daily lives?

The progression from mind-set to mission to norms to action illustrates how leading with ideas works at Souhegan High School in Amherst, NH.

---

ideas are used as the source of authority for leadership, teachers respond to community values for moral reasons. Strong norms emerge. Their practice becomes more collective and sustained. Ideas become the basis for developing moral authority in the school. Table 10.3 depicts how Souhegan High School formed its mission and used it as a bank of ideas that function as a source of authority for what people do and why they do it.

Mind-set and mission are at the beginning. Effectively developed, they shape what we do and why we do it. Their purpose is to provide the framework that drives norms and actions. As Silva and Mackin (2002) explain, "Unlike most high schools, the role of the Souhegan 'mission' takes on an almost supernatural importance, as it drives every action of the school" (26). They state further, "It is worth thinking about this concept of mission for a moment. Historically, most institutions, including schools, have a statement of philosophy or mission—a public commitment to a set of beliefs or values that drive the institution. Unfortunately, in practical terms, these statements often have little significance. . . . Rarely does a mission statement serve as a true basis for designing school programs or affecting teacher practice" (2002:29). This is not the case for Souhegan. The mission statement was in fact a daily guide for action and the basis for defining human expectations. Silva and Mackin note that the mission statement was such a powerful force "that students at times felt annoyed by continually having it in their face."

Thick Visions Become Powerful Ideas

The concept of thick visions was introduced in Chapter 2. Recall that thick visions are more than mission statements. They are, in essence, contracts that detail our roles and responsibilities to the school and its vision. Principals have important responsibilities in creating thick visions and in transforming them into powerful ideas. It is their job to see that visions do become useful.

It is helpful if principals know how powerful ideas provide the primary source of authority for their leadership. Bureaucratic requirements and sound management frameworks help. So does effective interpersonal skill. But these sources of authority are not as powerful as ideas. When vision statements are not working documents they are not used to help make decisions or to assess the decisions that are made. One reason that many vision statements are lots of show and not much tell is that, alone, they fail to provide the direction and fail to spell out the commitments that are needed from various constituent groups to make these visions work. They do not tell us what we need to do and they do not tell us what our responsibilities are for implementing the vision.

DuFour argues that when all we have are lofty vision statements, role relationships are likely to be vague. The nature of their reciprocity is not spelled out and this limits their usefulness.* Value is added, however, when visions are accompanied by the promises and commitments each constituent group makes to help move the school closer to its vision. Effective visions obligate people who share them. This obligation ups the ante from visions as management tools to visions as moral statements. Stevenson's vision runs deep and is useful in helping its people make decisions and assess progress. Visions and commitments together obligate people to each other and to their work.

*References to DuFour and to the collective commitments of various Stevenson constituents are from Stevenson High School (2003), available online at http://district125.k12.il.us/about/district_vision.html. Stevenson High School is also well-known for its work in using professional learning communities effectively. See, for example, DuFour et al. (2006).

BOTH DISCIPLINE AND DISCRETION ARE KEY

Shared purposes, covenants, design principles, and other agreements should provide enough discipline to ensure that focus, clarity, and harmony characterize what teachers do. This discipline, however, must be achieved without taking away the discretion teachers need to make decisions in light of the unique circumstances that they face. A good idea structure, in other words, doesn't tell people what to do but informs the decisions they make about what to do. One way to achieve both discipline and discretion is by striking a balance among instructional, problem-solving, and expressive outcomes (Eisner, 1969, 1979) as curriculum experiences are planned. Instructional outcomes are set beforehand and in fairly specific ways. They are stated in terms of what the student is supposed to be able to do as a result of teaching. Curriculum and teaching decisions are made by designing down from the instructional outcomes. Problem-solving outcomes are shaped by the decisions made about problems that students must solve and exhibitions they must master and perform. Expressive outcomes are discovered during and after the teaching of trusted subject matter and the use of trusted teaching activities—*trusted* meaning that they are known for their ability to stimulate learning.

In a sense, instructional outcomes represent baseball strike zones. Teaching to them represents the pitching of learning into a particular strike zone. Balls and strikes must be called to keep track of how effective the teaching is in achieving the outcomes. For example, in teaching a lesson or unit on the jury system, we might state the following instructional outcomes: (1) The student will be able to differentiate between the roles and functions of various principles in a jury trial (e.g., prosecuting attorney, defense attorney, bailiff, types of witnesses) and (2) the student will be able to write two coherent paragraphs that describe the differences in rules of evidence for civil trials as opposed to criminal trials. If the student performs according to the specified behaviors, then we have a strike. If she or he does not, then it's a ball. When a ball is called, the teaching pitches do not count, even though what the student learns may be as important or more important than the instructional outcome that was stated. The student, for example, may not be able to differentiate the rules of evidence as required, but is able to detect flaws in arguments better than before. The student may not be able to differentiate the various roles very well, but she or he has a greater appreciation for the fairness and effectiveness of the judicial system. Sorry, it's still a ball. The learning doesn't count because it does not fit into the strike zone.

In the real world of teaching, good teachers often change their minds as they teach. Sometimes they chase a student's ideas and wind up at a place different than originally intended. The strike zone that counts for them moves to another position; however, the strike zone that counts officially stands still, converting perfectly sound and sensible strikes into balls.

When using only instructional outcomes, the curriculum intended, the curriculum taught, and the curriculum learned must always be aligned with each other. Thus, once outcomes are set (discipline), teachers have increasingly less say over the taught and learned curriculum (discretion). It often makes sense to insist that students be able to demonstrate exactly what they are supposed to demonstrate. Thus, instructional outcomes have an important role to play, but so, too, do problem-solving and expressive outcomes. Balance is needed among the three if both discipline and discretion are to be achieved.

Problem-solving outcomes are harder to nail down in a specific way beforehand, but they are hardly serendipitous. By carefully crafting a problem, we can increase the likelihood that certain kinds of outcomes will emerge. Eisner (1979) explains:

> The problem-solving objective differs in a significant way from the behavioral [instructional] objective. In the problem-solving objective, the students formulate or are given a problem to solve—say to find out how deterrents to smoking might be made more effective, or how to design a paper structure that will hold two bricks sixteen inches above a table, or how the variety and quality of food served in the school cafeteria could be increased within the existing budget. (101)

It's not enough just to state the problem; certain criteria need to be provided that set a standard for how the problem will be solved. The more specific the criteria, the more the range of outcomes becomes narrowed. The forms of the solution, however, remain infinite. With instructional outcomes, both questions and answers are set ahead of time. With problem-solving objectives, the question is set but the answer is not definite.

Problem-based learning provides a happy balance between discipline and discretion for both teachers and students. Teachers might agree, for example, on the problems that students will solve in a given unit, course, or grade level. However, because no single answer or no one solution exists for the typical problem, teachers have flexibility in making choices about what will be studied, what materials will be used, what teaching approaches to use, what learning settings to invent, and so forth. Furthermore, students have discretion; within the parameters of the problem, they decide how they will learn and what they will learn. As teachers monitor learning, they make decisions that shape what students are doing and that are shaped by what students are doing. Despite discretion, a certain coherence and focus is maintained by the parameters the problem provides.

Problem-solving outcomes play a major role in organizing the curriculum, arranging learning experiences, teaching, and evaluating in schools that are committed to the principles of both the Coalition of Essential Schools and expeditionary learning. These schools rely heavily on exhibitions of mastery as the construct for organizing the curriculum, for teaching and learning, and for evaluating.

Expressive outcomes, according to Eisner (1969), are what one ends up with, whether intended or not, after being engaged in a learning experience. "Expressive outcomes are the consequences of curriculum activities that are intentionally planned to provide a fertile opportunity for personal purposing and experiences" (26). The emphasis is on the activity itself, the learning experience that the student will be engaged in, and the content or the subject matter, not the specifics of what the student will learn as a result of this engagement.

Although expressive outcomes are not anticipated prior to the actual teaching, they represent valued learnings nonetheless. Good teachers, for example, know and trust the potential of certain ideas, activities, and experiences to promote learning. They know that when students engage in them, good things happen. Although the teacher cannot say exactly what students will get out of the experience, she or he has always found that they learned a great deal when engaging in the learning activity.

Instructional outcomes, problem-solving outcomes, and expressive outcomes all have important roles to play in curriculum planning. When brought together, they allow teachers to make decisions that reflect the discipline necessary for purposeful community building. Furthermore, this discipline is achieved without compromising the discretion needed to make informed decisions in light of the ambiguities found in the typical teaching and learning situation. Discretion increases the likelihood that effective teaching and learning decisions will be made and that effective caring decisions will be made. Discretion allows the building of an inquiring community as teachers puzzle together over what decisions make the most sense. In addition, discretion embodies professional community by allowing teachers to take control of their practice.

*P*ROVIDING THE NECESSARY LEADERSHIP

Shared goals and purposes, agreed-upon covenants, and other statements of what is believed are the nerve center of a successful school. They provide the necessary signals, symbols, substance, and direction needed for coordinated action on behalf of quality in schooling. The clarity and coherence they provide cannot be duplicated by close supervision, management controls, and other regulatory measures, for these latter practices require a much tighter connection among school parts, roles, and activities than is typically found in schools. Loosely structured schools achieve coordinated action by creating a powerful normative system that serves to socialize newcomers and to provide reinforcement to those already socialized. Furthermore, this normative system provides a source of meaning and direction to those who live and work in the school.

Principal leadership in tight value and loose decision-making schools is more complicated than first seems apparent. It requires the balancing of both flexible and resilient leadership styles. Effective principals display a great deal of resiliency when concerned with the school's goal structure, educational platform, and overall philosophy. At the same time, they display a great deal of flexibility when concerned with the everyday articulation of these values into teaching and learning practices and designs. Before continuing with this discussion, let's examine the Style Flexibility Index (SFI) and the Style Resilience Index (SRI) shown in Exhibits 10.1 and 10.2. The items in these indexes were suggested by W. J. Reddin's (1970) discussion of style flexibility and style resilience. Respond to each of the indexes and obtain flexibility and resilience scores. Keep in mind that both indexes suggest only how you might be perceived on these dimensions by others with whom you work.

Now let's examine the concepts of flexibility and resilience. Flexibility is perhaps best understood by understanding its relationship to drifting. As leadership concepts, both flexibility and drifting comprise the same behaviors. Yet, expressions of these behaviors might result in effectiveness in one situation and ineffectiveness in another. When the behavior expressed matches the situation, the

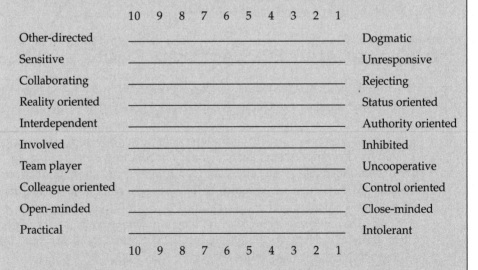

exhibit **10.1**

Style Flexibility Index

Think of occasions, situations, and incidents when you, as a school principal, were interacting directly with teachers about day-to-day and week-to-week decisions involving instructional materials, subject-matter content, classroom organization, and the provision of teaching and learning. As a result of this interaction, indicate how teachers would describe you, using the 10 paired statements provided below.

	10 9 8 7 6 5 4 3 2 1	
Other-directed		Dogmatic
Sensitive		Unresponsive
Collaborating		Rejecting
Reality oriented		Status oriented
Interdependent		Authority oriented
Involved		Inhibited
Team player		Uncooperative
Colleague oriented		Control oriented
Open-minded		Close-minded
Practical		Intolerant
	10 9 8 7 6 5 4 3 2 1	

Scoring: Sum the scores given to each of the 10 scales of the Style Flexibility Index. Scores will range from a low of 10 to a high of 100. The higher the score, the more flexible one is perceived to be. An improved indication of style flexibility would be obtained by having teachers actually describe their principal.

Style Resilience Index

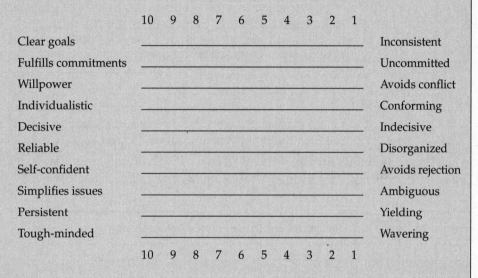

Think of occasions, situations, and incidents when you, as a principal, were interacting directly with teachers about general goals and purposes, educational platform, and overall philosophy of the school. As a result of this interaction, indicate how teachers would describe you, using the 10 paired statements provided below.

	10 9 8 7 6 5 4 3 2 1	
Clear goals	_____	Inconsistent
Fulfills commitments	_____	Uncommitted
Willpower	_____	Avoids conflict
Individualistic	_____	Conforming
Decisive	_____	Indecisive
Reliable	_____	Disorganized
Self-confident	_____	Avoids rejection
Simplifies issues	_____	Ambiguous
Persistent	_____	Yielding
Tough-minded	_____	Wavering
	10 9 8 7 6 5 4 3 2 1	

Scoring: Sum the scores given to each of the 10 scales of the Style Resilience Index. Scores will range from a low of 10 to a high of 100. The higher the score, the more resilient one is perceived to be. An improved indication of style resilience would be obtained by having teachers actually describe their principal.

principal will be viewed as being highly flexible. When the exact same behavior is expressed in inappropriate situations, the principal is viewed as drifting.

Reddin (1970) points out that style flexibility in leadership is characterized by high ambiguity tolerance, power sensitivity, an open belief system, and other-directedness. Highly flexible principals are comfortable in unstructured situations, are not control oriented, bring to the work context very few fixed ideas, and display a great deal of interest in the ideas of others. These characteristics are very desirable when articulated within the loosely structured discretionary space of schools, but in matters of the school's goal structure and educational platform, flexibility by the principal is often viewed negatively by teachers and others. When this is the case, the principal's style can be described as drifting rather than flexible. Drifting suggests a lack of direction and an absence of commitment to a purpose or cause.

Rigidity is the concept that Reddin suggests to understand counterproductive expressions of resilience. The resilient leadership style is characterized by will-power, tough-mindedness, self-confidence, and self-discipline. Principals of effective schools display these qualities when dealing with aspects of the school's value core. Expressing these same qualities, when dealing with the day-to-day decisions that teachers make in classrooms as they work with students, would result in the principal's being perceived as rigid. The two dimensions of resilience and flexibility are illustrated in Figure 10.1 in the form of a leadership grid. Note that, at the base of the grid, resiliency ranges from a low score of 0 to a high of 100. Plot your score from the Style Resilience Index on this dimension of the grid. To the left is the flexibility dimension, ranging from 0 to 100. Plot your score from the Style Flexibility Index on this dimension.

High resiliency scores combined with low flexibility scores would place one in the lower right corner of the grid and represent the Rigid style. A flexibility score of 80 combined with a resiliency score of 30, however, would place one in the upper left quadrant of the grid, representing the Drifting leadership style. High scores on both flexibility and resilience would place one in the upper right

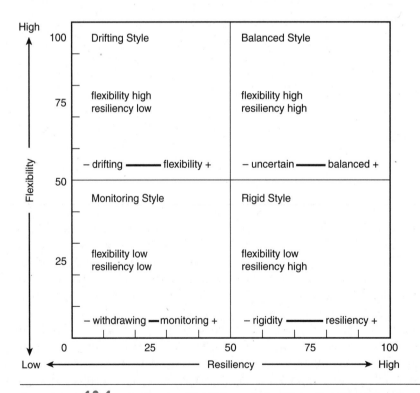

figure **10.1** **Styles for Flexible and Resilient Principal Leadership**

quadrant—the Balanced leadership style. Low scores on both dimensions would place one in the lower left quadrant—the Monitoring style. Let's examine each of the four styles with reference to principals as they manage issues of tight and loose coupling in schools.

The Drifting style can work when important values are not at stake and might be appropriate for issues common to the school's loosely structured, high discretionary area. However, when principals are flexible in dealing with their school's core of values, they appear to teachers to be drifting and are not viewed as able to provide necessary purposing and direction.

The Rigid style can work for issues relating to the school's core of values. Using this style with teachers on issues of providing for daily teaching and learning, however, is likely to be viewed negatively. Instead of appearing resilient, principals will be seen as autocratic and their style as rigid.

The Monitoring style can work in instances in which jobs can be programmed in such detail that the emphasis is less on persons and goals and more on monitoring the work flow, thus ensuring reliability. Teacher-proof designs for schooling support the Monitoring style. The enforcement of school rules and providing drill-practice work in teaching and learning might be examples appropriate for the Monitoring style. When principals use this style excessively or in the wrong instances, they are viewed as having withdrawn their concern for people as individuals and for goals and purposes.

The Balanced style provides flexible leadership in the articulation of the school's values, goals, and platform as teachers work day by day. At the same time, this style provides resilient leadership with respect to the promotion and maintenance of important values. This approach characterizes principal leadership found in successful schools. The concept of balanced leadership characteristic of successful schools should be the cornerstone of one's management platform and is an important dimension of reflective practice in the principalship.

Appendix 10.1 provides an inventory of assumptions that school faculties can use to begin a conversation about what they believe and what they don't believe about teaching and learning and about the nature of school knowledge. The assumptions they settle on can become values used to "design out" how they relate with students, how teaching and learning are planned and practiced, and how curriculum and evaluation decisions are made. Further, Appendix 10.1 can be used to assess the extent to which assumptions, values, and beliefs that are held are actually being implemented in your school. If, for example, you are lukewarm to most of the assumptions, then that reluctance should be embodied in the actual practices you observe in your school. To help in your assessment, "reality check" questions are provided for the first 13 items themed to assumptions about Motivation, Conditions for Learning, and Social Learning. These questions can serve as prompts for you to assess what your reality check response would be to the remaining assumptions.

$\mathcal{S}$OME REFLECTIONS

1. Under the section "The Importance of Goals," Perrow argues that organizations run backwards and that "the deed is father to the thought, not the other way around." What does he mean by this statement? Is it true for some of the schools you know? Give an example.
2. Assume that your school has decided to use the "lists of five" approach to sharing what it believes and is committed to. What five promises would you like the teachers, parents, and students in your school to make to each other? Ask the teachers in your grade level, team, or department to bring examples of student work they think represents the standards they hold for students.

$\mathcal{R}$EFERENCES

Barth, Roland. 1986. "The Principal and the Profession of Teaching," *Elementary School Journal* 86(4).

Battistich, V., D. Solomon, M. Watson, and E. Schaps. 1994. *Students and Teachers in Caring Communities and School Communities.* Paper presented at the annual meeting of the American Educational Research Association, April 4–8, New Orleans.

Bidwell, Charles E. 1965. "The School as a Formal Organization," in James G. March (Ed.), *Handbook of Organization* (pp. 972–1022). Chicago: Rand McNally.

Bricker, H. 1985, November–December. As quoted in Robert H. Hayes, "Strategic Planning Forward in Reverse?" *Harvard Business Review.*

Bryk, A. S., and M. E. Driscoll. 1988. *The School as Community: Theoretical Foundations, Contextual Influences and Consequences for Students and Teachers.* Madison: National Center on Effective Schools, University of Wisconsin.

Coleman, J. 1987. "Families in Schools," *Educational Research* 16(6), 32–38.

Coleman, J. 1988. "Social Capital in the Creation of Human Capital." *American Journal of Sociology* 94(Supplement), S95–S120.

Coleman, J. 1990. *Foundations of Social Theory.* Cambridge, MA: Harvard University Press.

DuFour, Richard, and Robert Eaker. 1998. *Professional Learning Communities at Work: Best Practices for Enhancing Student Achievement.* Bloomington, IN: Solution Tree.

DuFour, Richard, Rebecca DuFour, Robert Eaker, and Thomas Many. 2006. *Learning by Doing: A Handbook for Professional Learning Communities at Work.* Bloomington, IN: Solution Tree.

Eisner, Elliot. 1969. "Instructional and Expressive Educational Objectives: Their Formulation and Use In Curriculum," in W. James Popham (Ed.), *Curriculum Evaluation: Instructional Objectives.* AERA Monograph Series. Chicago: Rand-McNally.

Eisner, Elliot. 1979. *The Educational Imagination: On the Design and Evaluation of School Programs.* New York: Macmillan.

Gamoran, A. 1996. "Student Achievement in Public Magnet, Public Comprehensive and Private City High Schools," *Educational Evaluation and Policy Analysis* 18(1), 1–18.

Gardner, Howard. 1995. *Leading Minds: An Anatomy of Leadership.* New York: Basic Books.

Hills, Jean. 1982. "The Preparation of Educational Leaders: What's Needed and What's Next?" UCEA occasional paper no. 8303. Columbus, OH: University Council for Educational Administration.

National Association of Secondary School Principals. 1996. *Breaking Ranks: Changing an American Institution.* A Report of the Secondary School Principals Association on the High School for the 21st Century. Reston, VA: Author.

National Association of Secondary School Principals. 2004. *Breaking Ranks II: Strategies for Leading High School Reform.* Reston, VA: Author.

Newmann, Fred M., BetsAnn Smith, Elaine Allensworth, and Anthony S. Bryk. 2001. "Instructional Program Coherence: What It Is and Why It Should Guide School Improvement Policy," *Educational Evaluation and Policy Analysis* 23(4), 297–321.

Outward Bound USA Convenor. 1992. "Expeditionary Learning: A Design for New American Schools." A proposal to the New American Schools Development Corporation. Greenwich, CT: Author.

Parsons, Talcott. 1951. *Toward a General Theory of Social Action.* Cambridge, MA: Harvard University Press.

Perrow, Charles. 1981. "Disintegrating Social Sciences," *New York University Education Quarterly* 10(2), 2–9.

Peters, Thomas J., and Robert H. Waterman, Jr. 1982. *In Search of Excellence: Lessons from America's Best-Run Companies.* New York: Harper & Row.

Peters, Tom, and Nancy Austin. 1985. *A Passion for Excellence.* New York: Random House.

Purkey, William W., and J. M. Novak. 1988. *Education: By Invitation Only.* Bloomington, IN: Phi Delta Kappan Foundation.

Putnam, Robert D. 2000. *Bowling Alone.* New York: Simon & Schuster.

Reddin, W. J. 1970. *Managerial Effectiveness.* New York: McGraw-Hill.

Resnick, Lauren, and Megan W. Hall. 1998. "Learning Organization for Sustainable Education Reform," *Daedalus* 127(4), 89–118.

Resnick, Lauren B., and Thomas K. Glennan, Jr. 2001. "Leadership for Learning: A Theory of Action for Urban School Districts." Pittsburgh: Institute for Learning. Online at www.instituteforlearning.org/media/docs/TheoryofActionResnickGlenna.pdf, accessed January 22, 2004.

Schmoker, Mike. 1999. *Results: The Key to Continuous School Improvement* (2nd ed.). Alexandria, VA: Association for Supervision and Curriculum Development.

Schmoker, Mike. 2006. *Results Now: How We Can Achieve Unprecedented Improvements in Teaching and Learning.* Alexandria, VA: Association for Supervision and Curriculum Development.

Sergiovanni, T. J. 1994. *Building Community in Schools.* San Francisco: Jossey-Bass.

Sergiovanni, Thomas J. 2001. *Leadership: What's In It For Schools?* London: Routledge/Falmer.

Sergiovanni, Thomas J. 2005. *Strengthening the Heartbeat: Leading and Learning Together in Schools.* San Francisco: Jossey-Bass.

Sergiovanni, Thomas J., and Brad Duggan. 1990. "Moral Authority: A Blueprint for Managing Tomorrow's Schools," in T. J. Sergiovanni and J. H. Moore (Eds.), *Target 2000: A Compact for Excellence in Texas's Schools.* The 1990 Yearbook of the Texas Association for Supervision and Curriculum Development. San Antonio, TX: Watercress Press.

Shils, Edward A. 1961. "Centre and Periphery," in *The Logic of Personal Knowledge: Essays Presented to Michael Polanyi.* London: Routledge and Kegan Paul.

Silva, Peggy, and Robert A. Mackin. 2002. *Standards of Mind and Heart: Creating the Good High School.* New York: Teachers College Press.

Sizer, Theodore R. 1989. "Diverse Practice, Shared Ideas: The Essential School," in H. J. Walberg and J. J. Lane (Eds.), *Organizing for Learning: Toward the 21st Century.* Reston, VA: National Association of Secondary School Principals.

Strike, Kenneth A. 2004. "Community, the Missing Element of School Reform: Why Schools Should Be More Like Congregations than Banks," *American Journal of Education* 110(3), 215–232.

Trice, Harrison M., and Janice M. Beyer. 1984. "Studying Organizational Cultures through Rites and Ceremonials," *Academy of Management Review* 9(4), 653–669.

Watson, Thomas J., Jr. 1963. *A Business and Its Beliefs: The Ideas That Helped Build IBM.* New York: McGraw-Hill.

Weick, Karl. 1976. "Educational Organizations as Loosely Coupled Systems," *Administrative Science Quarterly* 21(2), 1–19.

Weick, Karl. 1982. "Administering Education in Loosely Coupled Systems," *Phi Delta Kappan* 27(2), 673–676.

Zaleznik, Abraham. 1988, September 3. Quoted in Doran P. Levin, "G.M. Bid to Rejuvenate Leadership." *New York Times.*

Assumptions about Learning and Knowledge

Instructions: Somewhere along each line, make a mark that best represents your own feelings about each statement.

Example: School serves the wishes and needs of adults better than it does the wishes and needs of children.

strongly agree	agree	no strong feeling	disagree	strongly disagree

Reality Check. In my school, most decisions made by the teachers and administrators serve the wishes and needs of adults better than the wishes and needs of children.

strongly agree	agree	no strong feeling	disagree	strongly disagree

Assumptions about Children's Learning

Motivation

Assumption 1. Children are innately curious and will explore their environment without adult intervention.

strongly agree	agree	no strong feeling	disagree	strongly disagree

Reality Check 1. In my school, we provide many opportunities for students to explore their environment.

strongly agree	agree	no strong feeling	disagree	strongly disagree

Assumption 2. Exploratory behavior is self-perpetuating.

strongly agree	agree	no strong feeling	disagree	strongly disagree

Reality Check 2. In my school, we make decisions that assume students are capable of being self-managing learners.

strongly agree	agree	no strong feeling	disagree	strongly disagree

Conditions for Learning

Assumption 3. Children will display natural exploratory behavior if they are not threatened.

strongly agree	agree	no strong feeling	disagree	strongly disagree

Reality Check 3. We work hard to eliminate threats and fear.

strongly agree	agree	no strong feeling	disagree	strongly disagree

Assumption 4. Confidence in self is highly related to capacity for learning and for making important choices affecting one's learning.

strongly agree	agree	no strong feeling	disagree	strongly disagree

Reality Check 4. We make decisions that build self-confidence among learners.

strongly agree	agree	no strong feeling	disagree	strongly disagree

Assumption 5. Active exploration in a rich environment, offering a wide array of manipulative materials, will facilitate children's learning.

strongly agree	agree	no strong feeling	disagree	strongly disagree

Reality Check 5. We encourage active exploration and offer a wide variety of manipulative materials for learning.

strongly agree	agree	no strong feeling	disagree	strongly disagree

Assumption 6. Play is not distinguished from work as the predominant mode of learning in early childhood.

strongly agree	agree	no strong feeling	disagree	strongly disagree

Reality Check 6. Opportunities for play are a natural part of the pedagogy in the early grades of my school.

strongly agree	agree	no strong feeling	disagree	strongly disagree

Assumption 7. Children have both the competence and the right to make significant decisions concerning their own learning.

strongly agree	agree	no strong feeling	disagree	strongly disagree

Reality Check 7. We involve students in significant decisions concerning their own learning.

strongly agree	agree	no strong feeling	disagree	strongly disagree

Assumption 8. Children will be likely to learn if they are given considerable choice in the selection of the materials they wish to work with and in the choice of questions they wish to pursue with respect to those materials.

strongly agree	agree	no strong feeling	disagree	strongly disagree

Reality Check 8. We give students considerable choice in the selection of learning materials and the choice of learning questions.

strongly agree	agree	no strong feeling	disagree	strongly disagree

Assumption 9. Given the opportunity, children will choose to engage in activities that will be of high interest to them.

strongly agree	agree	no strong feeling	disagree	strongly disagree

Reality Check 9. Our decisions reflect the belief that students will choose to engage in learning that interests them.

strongly agree	agree	no strong feeling	disagree	strongly disagree

Assumption 10. If a child is fully involved in and is having fun with an activity, learning is taking place.

strongly agree	agree	no strong feeling	disagree	strongly disagree

Reality Check 10. Our decisions reflect the belief that involvement and enjoyment are good indicators that learning is taking place.

strongly agree	agree	no strong feeling	disagree	strongly disagree

Social Learning

Assumption 11. When two or more children are interested in exploring the same problem or the same materials, they will often choose to collaborate in some way.

strongly agree	agree	no strong feeling	disagree	strongly disagree

Reality Check 11. We encourage students to collaborate with each other whenever possible.

strongly agree	agree	no strong feeling	disagree	strongly disagree

Assumption 12. When children learn something that is important to them, they will wish to share it with others.

strongly agree	agree	no strong feeling	disagree	strongly disagree

Reality Check 12. We encourage students to share what they learn with others.

| strongly agree | agree | no strong feeling | disagree | strongly disagree |

Intellectual Development

Assumption 13. Concept formation proceeds very slowly.

| strongly agree | agree | no strong feeling | disagree | strongly disagree |

Assumption 14. Children learn and develop intellectually not only at their own rates but in their own styles.

| strongly agree | agree | no strong feeling | disagree | strongly disagree |

Assumption 15. Children pass through similar stages of intellectual development, each in their own way and at their own rates and in their own time.

| strongly agree | agree | no strong feeling | disagree | strongly disagree |

Assumption 16. Intellectual growth and development take place through a sequence of concrete experiences followed by abstractions.

| strongly agree | agree | no strong feeling | disagree | strongly disagree |

Assumption 17. Verbal abstractions should follow direct experience with objects and ideas, not precede them or substitute for them.

| strongly agree | agree | no strong feeling | disagree | strongly disagree |

Evaluation

Assumption 18. The preferred source of verification for a child's solution to a problem comes through the materials with which he or she is working.

strongly agree	agree	no strong feeling	disagree	strongly disagree

Assumption 19. Errors are necessarily a part of the learning process; they are to be expected and even desired, for they contain information essential for further learning.

strongly agree	agree	no strong feeling	disagree	strongly disagree

Assumption 20. Those qualities of a person's learning that can be carefully measured are not necessarily the most important.

strongly agree	agree	no strong feeling	disagree	strongly disagree

Assumption 21. Objective measures of performance may have a negative effect on learning.

strongly agree	agree	no strong feeling	disagree	strongly disagree

Assumption 22. Learning is best assessed intuitively, by direct observation.

strongly agree	agree	no strong feeling	disagree	strongly disagree

Assumption 23. The best way of evaluating the effect of the school experience on the child is to observe him or her over a long period of time.

strongly agree	agree	no strong feeling	disagree	strongly disagree

Assumption 24. The best measure of a child's work is his or her work.

strongly agree	agree	no strong feeling	disagree	strongly disagree

Knowledge

Assumption 25. The quality of being is more important than the quality of knowing; knowledge is a means of education, not its end. The final test of an education is what a person *is*, not what he or she *knows*.

strongly agree	agree	no strong feeling	disagree	strongly disagree

Assumption 26. Knowledge is a function of one's personal integration of experience and therefore does not fall into neatly separate categories or "disciplines."

strongly agree	agree	no strong feeling	disagree	strongly disagree

Assumption 27. The structure of knowledge is personal and idiosyncratic; it is a function of the synthesis of each individual's experience with the world.

strongly agree	agree	no strong feeling	disagree	strongly disagree

Assumption 28. Little or no knowledge exists that is essential for everyone to acquire.

strongly agree	agree	no strong feeling	disagree	strongly disagree

Assumption 29. It is possible, even likely, that an individual may learn and possess knowledge of a phenomenon and yet be unable to display it publicly. Knowledge resides with the knower, not in its public expression.

strongly agree	agree	no strong feeling	disagree	strongly disagree

Source: Adapted from "So You Want to Change to an Open Classroom" by Roland S. Barth, 1971, *Phi Delta Kappan* 53(2), 98–99. The "reality checks" have been added.

11

TEACHING, LEARNING, AND COMMUNITY

*J*ust a few years ago, it seemed that the issue of defining effective teaching and understanding how students learn was settled. We had in hand a body of knowledge based on "effective teaching" research and on behaviorist learning principles that provided a crystal clear picture of how students learn and of what teachers needed to do to maximize this learning. Included in this picture were beliefs that learning was an individual matter involving the accumulation of bits and pieces of knowledge and skills. This learning could be facilitated by providing lots of direct teaching and guided practice, and could be motivated by providing the right rewards.

Things are different today. Whereas the effective teaching findings of the 1970s and early 1980s cannot be ignored, more recent research provides a richer picture of how students learn and of what good teaching is. This research is based on constructivist cognitive psychology and on cultural views of human being and learning.

COMPARING THE THEORIES

In this chapter, the two views of teaching and learning are compared. If one believes that teaching is a deliberate act that is situationally responsive, then it is important that both views of teaching be understood and used. Direct instruction, or active teaching, as it is sometimes called, might make sense for some children in some contexts and for some purposes but not for other children in other contexts or for other purposes. The same is true for constructivist views of teaching and learning. It does makes a difference, however, which of the views is primary and which of the views is secondary; which view provides the overall framework for making decisions about curriculum, teaching, learning, and assessment and which view is a supplement; which view defines the overall pedagogical strategies a teacher or school uses and which view is a tactic that is used to serve a more narrow purpose or limited function.

Deciding which of the two views of teaching and learning should be the overall framework for curriculum building, supervision, staff development, and leadership practice is important, because theories create the realities that we have to deal with. As theories change, so do the realities. In the image of teaching based on the early effective teaching research described on the previous page, the emphasis in curriculum building is on explicitness and on strict alignment of what will be learned with preset objectives, with approaches to teaching, and with assessment strategies. Supervision becomes a process of monitoring the various parts of this alignment and making the needed corrections. Staff development becomes training, and leadership becomes a process of planning, organizing, motivating, and evaluating the work of others. Within the constructivist cognitive view of teaching and learning, the emphasis is on emergent curriculum, collegial supervision, teacher development as inquiry and reflection, and leadership as community building. In both cases it is the theory of teaching and learning that determines what good practice is. If we want to change existing practice, we will first have to change what we believe is true about teaching and learning.

Exhibit 11.1 lists seven pairs of beliefs about teaching and learning. As you read the pairs, distribute 10 points to reflect the extent to which you think each is true. If, for example, you think belief 1a and belief 1b are equally true, give them each 5 points. If you think belief 1a is absolutely true and 1b is absolutely false, assign 10 points to a and none to b, and so forth.

By totaling the points you assigned to the *a* statements and to the *b* statements, you can get an idea of the extent to which you agree with each of the two theories of teaching and learning.

The choices we make about the beliefs we hold determine, for example, what is considered effective supervisory practice. The rating, inspecting, and inservicing practices that often account for what principals are expected to do are based on beliefs about teaching and learning implied by the *a* statements of each pair. This supervision takes the form of tightly linking teachers to detailed objectives, to curriculum content outlines, to teaching schedules, and to corresponding evaluation schemes that rely on checking to be sure that teachers are following the approved script. Effective teaching is expressed as research-validated generic behaviors. These behaviors often comprise lists that principals use in observing teachers.

The beliefs implied by the *b* statements are based on constructivist cognitive psychological principles that suggest different teaching and supervisory practices. Tyson (1990) describes some of these differences:

exhibit

11.1

Beliefs about Teaching and Learning

1. (a) Learning is a process of accumulating isolated
   bits of information and skills.   (a) _____
   (b) Learning involves active construction of meaning and
   understanding.   (b) _____ = 10

2. (a) Students are empty vessels who receive and store
   information that is taught.   (a) _____
   (b) Students' prior understandings influence what they
   learn during instruction.   (b) _____ = 10

3. (a) Learning is defined as a change in student behavior. (a) _____
   (b) Learning is defined as a change in a student's cognitive
   structure and world view.   (b) _____ = 10

4. (a) Teaching and learning involves interactions between
   teachers and students.   (a) _____
   (b) Teaching and learning involves active construction of
   meaning by students.   (b) _____ = 10

5. (a) Students are individual learners, and motivation should
   be competitively based.   (a) _____
   (b) Learning in cooperation with others is important in
   motivating students and in enhancing outcomes.   (b) _____ = 10

6. (a) Teachers must work hard at delivering instruction to
   students to be successful.   (a) _____
   (b) Teachers must arrange for students to do the work
   of learning.   (b) _____ = 10

7. (a) Thinking and learning skills are generic across content
   areas and context.   (a) _____
   (b) Thinking and learning skills are content- and
   context-specific.   (b) _____ = 10
                                                                  _____
                                                            = 70

Source: From *Supervision: A Redefinition,* 6th ed. (p. 107) by Thomas J. Sergiovanni and Robert J. Star-ratt, 1999, New York: McGraw-Hill. Reproduced with permission of The McGraw-Hill Companies. Adapted from James Nolan and Pam Francis, "Changing Perspectives in Curriculum and Instruction" in Carl Glickman (Ed.), *Supervision in Transition,* 1992 Yearbook of the Association for Supervision and Curriculum Development (pp. 11–15). Alexandria, VA: ASCD.

School structures and routines should be shaped more by students' needs than by the characteristics of the disciplines, and less by teachers' and administrators' need for control and convenience. Young children learn best when they become active workers rather than passive learners. They make more progress, and are much more interested in schoolwork, when they are permitted to work together in groups to solve complex tasks, allowed to engage in class discussions and taught to argue convincingly for their approach in the midst of conflicting ideas and strategies. Even young children can do these things well with a little encouragement . . . many children, particularly those with little home support, learn best in a more familial school atmosphere. (22)

Believing that teaching is not the same as telling, Tyson (1990) concludes that

Generic pedagogy, which has spawned generic in-service training programs and generic teacher evaluation systems, overlooks the intimate and necessary connection between a discipline and teaching methods. Powerful, subject-specific and topic-specific pedagogy, most of it in mathematics and science, is becoming available. These new techniques make the battles over relative importance of content knowledge and pedagogical knowledge seem futile. Effective teaching requires both kinds of knowledge, developed to a high degree, and applied flexibly and artistically to particular topics and students. (24)

Much of the new research on teaching leads to the conclusion that script-following may have its place but that, overall, teaching is much more than script-following and supervision is much more than making sure that those scripts are followed (Brandt, 1993; Good and Brophy, 2003; Marzano, 1992; Marzano, Pickering, and Pollock, 2001; Newmann and Associates, 1996; Resnick and Klopfer, 1989). Several issues of *Educational Leadership* (April 1992; April 1993; November 1994; March 1997; November 1998) provide readable and compelling summaries of this research.

*I*MPLICATIONS FOR SUPERVISION

The *b* beliefs from Exhibit 11.1 about teaching and learning provide a different image of how supervision should be thought about and practiced. According to Nolan and Francis (1992):

1. Teachers will be viewed as active constructors of their own knowledge about teaching and learning;
2. Supervisors will be viewed as collaborators in creating knowledge about teaching and learning;
3. The emphasis in data collection during supervision will change from almost total reliance on paper and pencil observation instruments [designed] to capture the events of a single period of instruction to the use of a wide variety of data sources to capture a lesson as it unfolds over several periods of instruction;
4. There will be greater emphasis on context specific knowledge and skills in the supervisory process; and
5. Supervision will become more group oriented rather than individually oriented. (58)

To this list we can add a sixth image:

6. The emphasis will be less on changing behaviors, per se, and more on changing theories, beliefs, and assumptions.

This image suggests new roles and responsibilities for teachers. They will, for example, become more active as participants in knowledge and collaborators in creating new knowledge about teaching and learning. They must assume roles not only as cosupervisors with principals and other administrators, but also as cosupervisors with other teachers. They must join together with their principals to help the school become a learning and inquiring community. These themes will be further developed in Chapters 12 and 13. The following sections briefly review the research on effective teaching and then compare this research with the new insights that have emerged from constructivist cognitive psychology.

*R*ESEARCH ON "EFFECTIVE TEACHING"

Without question, the early research on effective teaching contributed to our understanding, provided a base upon which to build new insights into effective teaching, and still provides some useful ideas for certain teaching and learning situations. The findings are apt to sound familiar to experienced teachers and might even be considered applications of common sense. This research showed that certain teacher behaviors were related to student gains on both criterion- and norm-referenced tests. Examples of the behaviors most frequently cited by this research are the following:

- Provide classroom rules that allow pupils to take care of personal and procedural needs without having to check with the teacher
- Communicate high expectations to students
- Begin each class by reviewing homework and by reviewing material covered in the previous few classes
- Make objectives of teaching clear to students
- Teach directly the content or skills that will be measured on the tests
- After teaching, assess student comprehension by asking questions and by providing practice
- Provide opportunities for successful practice and monitor this practice by moving around the classroom
- Be sure that students are directly engaged in academic tasks
- Assign homework
- Hold review sessions weekly and monthly

How applicable are these teaching behaviors? Are they likely to be as effective in teaching complex subject matter that requires interpretation and teaching higher-order thinking skills as they are for teaching simple subject matter and basic skills? Are they equally effective for teaching music, physics, reading, arithmetic, or more advanced mathematics? Most effective teaching researchers would answer no. The research findings were never intended to be applicable to all situations. Many consultants, workshop providers, and policy makers, however, are often quick to answer yes. In their enthusiasm to find simple answers to complex questions, they tend to consider the findings as generic and thus applicable to all situations.

How teaching effectiveness is defined creates another problem. Definitions of effectiveness create realities. With different definitions we get different effective teaching practices. Some teacher evaluation instruments, for example, define effective teaching as the display of behavior associated with the research on direct instruction or active teaching. Other instruments define effectiveness as the embodiment of constructivist teaching and learning principles. "Effectiveness," in each case, is a function of how effectiveness is defined originally.

Most of the studies that led to the effective teaching findings were concentrating on the teaching of basic skills in reading and arithmetic in the early grades of elementary schools. Whether these teaching behaviors are appropriate for higher-level learning in reading and mathematics or for learning in other areas such as history or music is an open question. The indicators of teaching effectiveness are neither objective nor independent, but are directly linked to how researchers define effectiveness.

*T*EACHING AND BASIC SKILLS SCORE GAINS

Good and Brophy go one step further by summarizing the most frequently quoted research that compares teacher characteristics with score gains on achievement tests. Overall the most effective teachers are active. They set the goals, make the decisions, decide on the pace, select the content, assign work, correct work, give tests, and determine grades. Active teachers drive the bus. By comparison students are passive and go along for the ride.

Active teachers instruct by "demonstrating skills, explaining concepts and assignments, conducting participatory activities, and reviewing when necessary. They teach their students rather than expecting them to learn mostly from curriculum materials. However, they do not stress just facts or skills; they also emphasize concepts and understanding" (Good and Brophy, 2003:368). The following characteristics are important:*

- *Teacher Expectation/Role Definition/Sense of Efficacy.* These teachers accept responsibility for teaching their students. They believe that the students are

*From Good, Thomas L., and Jere E. Brophy, *Looking in Classrooms* (9th ed.). Published by Allyn and Bacon, Boston, MA. Copyright © 2003 by Pearson Education. Reprinted by permission of the publisher.

capable of learning and that they (the teachers) are capable of teaching them successfully. If students do not learn something the first time, they teach it again, and if the regular curriculum materials do not do the job, they find or make other ones.

- *Student Opportunity to Learn.* These teachers allocate most of their available time to instruction rather than to nonacademic activities or pastimes. Their students spend many more hours each year on academic tasks than do students of teachers who are less focused on instructional goals. Furthermore, the mix of academic tasks allows their students not just to memorize but to understand key ideas, appreciate their connections, and explore their applications.
- *Classroom Management and Organization.* These teachers organize their classrooms as effective learning communities and use group management approaches that maximize the time that students spend engaged in lessons and activities.
- *Curriculum Pacing.* These teachers move through the curriculum rapidly but in small steps that minimize student frustration and allow continuous progress.
- *Teaching to Mastery.* Following active instruction on new content, these teachers provide opportunities for students to practice and apply it. They monitor each student's progress and provide feedback and remedial instruction as needed, making sure that the students achieve mastery.
- *A Supportive Learning Environment.* Despite their strong academic focus, these teachers maintain pleasant, friendly classrooms and are perceived as enthusiastic, supportive instructors (Good and Brophy, 2003:368).

*R*ECENT RESEARCH

What does the new research tell us? This research points out that learning requires knowledge, which comes in many forms. Some knowledge is limited, and other knowledge is generative. Limited knowledge does not lead anywhere; it is simply accumulated, stored, and recalled. Generative knowledge, however, leads to more learning, new learning, more expansive learning, and the transfer of learning. Generative knowledge is used to create new knowledge. It is knowledge that can be used to understand new situations, to solve unfamiliar problems, to think and reason, and to continue to learn. Constructivist cognitive research reveals that before knowledge becomes generative in the minds of students, they must elaborate and question what they learn, be able to examine new information in relationship to other information, and build new structures of knowledge.

A further distinction is made between declarative knowledge and procedural knowledge. *Declarative knowledge* refers to subject-matter content, and *procedural knowledge* refers to processes such as how to think, and how we solve problems, and how we synthesize. Knowing what a virus is, how democracy works, what

Federalist Paper No. 10 is about, what the Civil Rights Act includes, and who wrote *The Great Gatsby* are examples of declarative knowledge. Using coordinates to fix a position on a map, finding words in a dictionary, proofreading an essay, synthesizing existing information into new wholes, differentiating fact from fiction, and using a problem-solving strategy are examples of procedural knowledge.

Whether declarative knowledge turns out to be limited or generative depends on how content and thinking skills are taught. Are they taught separately or at the same time? A combination of the two is needed to create a curriculum that emphasizes thinking. Subject matter becomes the primary site for developing problem solving and reasoning. Resnick and Klopfer (1989) explain:

> In this vision of the Thinking Curriculum, thinking suffuses the curriculum. It is everywhere. Thinking skills and subject-matter content are joined early in education and pervade instruction. There is no choice to be made between a content emphasis and a thinking-skills emphasis. No depth in either is possible without the other. (6)

*T*EACHING FOR UNDERSTANDING

In the new research, the emphasis is on teaching subject matter for understanding and on generative use of knowledge. In order for knowledge to be understood and used, students must be involved in its active construction. This means not just telling and explaining, but providing students with opportunities to answer questions, to discuss and debate meanings and implications, and to engage in authentic problem solving in real contexts. According to Brophy (1992):

> Early in the process, the teacher assumes most of the responsibility for structuring and managing learning activities and provides students with a great deal of information, explanation, modelling and cuing. As students develop expertise, however, they can begin regulating their own learning by asking questions and by working on increasingly complex applications with increasing degrees of autonomy. The teacher still provides task simplification, coaching, and other "scaffolding" needed to assist students with challenges that they are not ready to handle on their own. Gradually, this assistance is reduced in response to gradual increases in student readiness to engage in self-regulated learning. (6)*

*Source: From "Probing the Subtleties of Subject-Matter Teaching" (p. 6), by Jere Brophy. In *Educational Leadership* 49(7), April, 1992. Used with permission. The Association for Supervision and Curriculum Development is a worldwide community of educators advocating sound policies and sharing best practices to achieve the success of each learner. To learn more, visit ASCD at www.ascd.org.

Relying on the research of Anderson (1989) and Prawat (1989), as well as his own work, Brophy (1992) identifies the following principles of good subject-matter teaching:

1. The curriculum is designed to equip students with knowledge, skills, values, and dispositions useful both inside and outside of school.
2. Instructional goals underscore developing student expertise within an application context and with emphasis on conceptual understanding and self-regulated use of skills.
3. The curriculum balances breadth with depth by addressing limited content but developing this content sufficiently to foster understanding.
4. The content is organized around a limited set of powerful ideas (key understandings and principles).
5. The teacher's role is not just to present information but also to scaffold and respond to students' learning.
6. The students' role is not just to absorb or copy but to actively make sense and construct meaning.
7. Activities and assignments feature authentic tasks that call for problem solving or critical thinking, not just memory or reproduction.
8. Higher-order thinking skills are not taught as a separate skills curriculum. Instead, they are developed in the process of teaching subject-matter knowledge within application contexts that call for students to relate what they are learning to their lives outside of school by thinking critically or creatively about it or by using it to solve problems or make decisions.
9. The teacher creates a social environment in the classroom that could be described as a learning community where dialogue promotes understanding. (6)

Good and Brophy (2003) elaborate: "We will call this orientation *teaching for understanding* for short, but bear in mind that it implies appreciation and life application as well. *Understanding* means that students learn both the individual elements in a network of related content and the connections among them, so that they can explain the content in their own words. True understanding goes beyond the ability to define concepts or supply facts. It involves making connections between new learning and prior knowledge, subsuming the new learning within larger networks of knowledge, and recognizing at least some of its potential applications (Case, 1997; Perkins, 1992; Resnick, 1987). *Appreciation* means that students value what they are learning because they understand that there are good reasons for learning it. *Life application* goals are accomplished to the extent that students retain their learning in a form that makes it readily retrievable and usable when needed in other contexts" (406). They continue: "While deepening our understanding of the role of the teacher in stimulating student learning, recent research has also emphasized the role of the student. This reflects the influence of developmental and cognitive psychologists who hold *constructivist* views of learning and teaching. Constructivists believe that students learn through a process of active construction that involves making connections between new information and existing networks of prior knowledge. Constructivists emphasize the importance of relating new content to the knowledge that students already possess, as well as providing opportunities for students to process and apply the new learning. They believe that before knowledge becomes truly *generative*—usable for interpreting new situations, solving problems, thinking and reasoning, and learning generally—students must elaborate and question what they are told, examine the new content in relation to more familiar content, and build new knowledge structures. Otherwise, the knowledge may remain *inert*—recallable when cued by questions or test items similar to those used in practice exercises, but not applicable when it might be useful in everyday life" (2003:407–408).

Further, Good and Brophy (2003) point out that "Constructivist theory and research has focused primarily on learning rather than teaching, but it suggests principles for how teachers can support their students' learning. In this section, we consider four basic principles: (1) learners construct their own unique representations of knowledge; (2) this knowledge is represented as networks structured around powerful ideas; (3) learners make sense of new information by relating it to their prior knowledge; and (4) sometimes new learning results in a restructuring of existing knowledge or a change in the learner's understanding of a key concept" (408).

Checklist for Teaching for Understanding

Exhibit 11.2 is a checklist to help teachers assess whether and to what extent they are teaching for understanding. Use the checklist to visit with a teacher or two about what teaching for understanding looks like in practice. In each case try to find examples to support your responses.

A New Standard

Zemelman, Daniels, and Hyde (1998, 2005) note that a strong consensus exists regarding how teachers should be teaching and regarding how students should be learning. They identify six practices common to teachers who are successful in teaching to this new standard. These practices are ways of structuring teaching that flow from both teaching for understanding and understanding by design:

1. *Integrative Units.* These involve multiweek chunks of curriculum around large themes or topics, which enable teachers to deal with many curriculum areas, such as math, biology, history, art, ecology, and health. This allows students to learn discrete things within a larger framework that provides meaning and connections. While this practice is easier in elementary grades where teachers tend to be involved in all learning areas, there is evidence that high school teachers can schedule themselves in back-to-back classes or work with block scheduling several days a week to involve students in more integrative learning units.

exhibit

11.2

Checklist for Teaching for Understanding

YOU KNOW YOU ARE TEACHING FOR UNDERSTANDING WHEN . . .

The learning is generative:

☐ Instruction is focused around a few central topics.

☐ The topics are personally significant for you and your students.

☐ Students are actively engaged in their work.

☐ An atmosphere of genuine inquiry pervades the classroom.

The understanding goals are clear and explicit:

☐ Overarching goals or throughlines are explicitly stated and posted in the classroom.

☐ Goals for particular units are closely related to overarching goals.

☐ You and your students regularly discuss and reflect on unit-long and overarching goals to help students make the connection between what they are doing and why they are doing it.

Students are working on performances of understanding almost constantly:

☐ Students work actively in varied formats: pursuing projects and reflecting alone, collaborating and conferencing in small groups, and interacting in whole groups.

☐ Students are thinking and making that thinking visible in the contexts of performances of understanding that challenge their misconceptions, stereotypes, and rigid thinking.

☐ Students can explain why they are doing what they are doing.

☐ You spend your time coaching, conferencing, leading, participating in discussions, and sometimes lecturing.

☐ The room is filled with student work, both finished and in progress.

☐ Responsibility and authority for the work is shared between you and your students.

The assessment is ongoing:

☐ Students engage in cycles of drafting, reflecting, critiquing, responding to, and revising their own and others' work.

☐ You and your students share responsibility for assessment.

☐ Everyone assesses work according to stated criteria and standards for quality, which are closely related to the understanding goals.

☐ Assessment is often casual, conversational, and spontaneous; periodically it is more formal, recorded, and planned.

☐ Self-reflection occurs frequently, in a variety of forms.

Source: From Tina Blythe and Associates, *The Teaching for Understanding Guide* (p. 105), San Francisco: Jossey-Bass, 1998.

2. *Small Group Activities.* Teachers involve students in collaborative learning in pairs, threes, ad hoc groups, and long-term teams. Some of this work involves jigsaw-type processes of teaching one another; some involves critiquing one another's work; some involves study teams competing against other study teams; and some involves students cycling through learning centers within the classroom for 20 to 40 minutes each day.

3. *Representing to Learn.* Originally built around the "writing to learn" design, the activity has expanded to using a variety of representations to focus attention, raise questions, clarify insights, and visualize what one is trying to learn. These representations include drawing pictures, using Venn diagrams, jotting down speculations or hypotheses, brainstorming possible solutions, rephrasing central questions, diagramming relationships, and mapping potential causes and effects or intervening influences. These representations open up spaces for teachers and students to talk one-on-one to clarify questions, to get focused or refocused, and/or to clear away unnecessary distractions in a student's thinking. Successful teachers get students to keep learning logs, sketchbooks, or idea maps so that they can review them frequently to see where students are moving in the learning process.

4. *Classroom Workshops.* This represents a chunk of time (30 minutes to an hour) when students can *do* the subject: read a story, study a historical source document, complete an art project, write a creative piece. An essential quality to the classroom workshop is that students get to choose what they will do during that time. If a student finishes a project before the allotted time is up, she or he is expected to begin another project during the remaining time. During the workshop, the teacher moves around and conducts brief, one-on-one conversations with individual students. These workshops require original tone setting with the group and establishing ground rules that all agree to live by.

5. *Authentic Experiences.* This practice involves teacher–student dialogue about their interests and about topics connected to their lives and the real world. This includes activities that require students to connect with current events in the news. In some instances, it means connecting learning with the multiple intelligences students bring to the work, or connecting the work with family or local community people. Authentic experiences require student self-assessment of their learning, as well as assessment by members of the community. Some teachers use video cameras as tools to pursue learning projects or to express the results of learning projects.

6. *Reflective Assessment.* This is the practice of having students keep records of what they are doing and learning, such as portfolios of their best work. These records enable students to confer with their teacher and discuss the work; they also enable teachers to combine instruction with assessment. The ongoing self-assessment continues the activity of learning so that students can check frequent mistakes and take steps to correct them, or so that students may see how their work has been one-dimensional and now must move into a more complex and challenging set of performances.

THE CLASSROOM AS LEARNING COMMUNITY

Recall Good and Brophy's work described earlier. Note that two characteristics of Brophy's principles stand out. One is the importance of helping the classroom become a social community, and the other is the power of learning through engagement in real work. Much of the earlier literature on effective teaching makes the assumption that teaching and learning are rather solo affairs and focuses primarily on the individual learner. Constructivist cognitive psychology points out the importance of social relationships and the need for classrooms to become learning communities and communities of inquiry. Much of the new research, for example, points to the value of cooperative living and learning within the classroom as a learning community.

In a learning community, knowledge exists as something that is both individually owned and community owned at the same time. The two feed off each other. A particular student's own individual growth and accumulated knowledge contributes to the shared growth and accumulated knowledge that exists in a classroom as a whole. As this accumulated knowledge expands, so does individual knowledge. This view of shared knowledge is based on several assumptions.

> First, learning is an active process of knowledge construction and sense-making by the student. Second, knowledge is a cultural artifact of human beings: we produce it, share it, and transform it as individuals and as groups. Third, knowledge is distributed among members of a group, and this distributed knowledge is greater than the knowledge possessed by any single member. (Leinhardt, 1992:23)

AUTHENTIC LEARNING

Perhaps the most basic lessons that the constructivist cognitive research teaches are the importance of relating new learning to prior knowledge and the importance of immersing teaching in the world of real or "authentic" learning. Generative learning—learning that is understood and can be used to create new learning—doesn't take place in a vacuum. It is always contextual. What is learned depends on one's prior knowledge; learning takes place best when bridges or scaffolds are developed that link the new with the old.

Sometimes prior knowledge interferes with learning or encourages one to learn the wrong thing. Students, for example, often bring misconceptions or naive theories and notions to their studies. Linking new ideas to prior knowledge that is wrong may result in the further accumulation of faulty learning. This problem highlights the importance of personalized learning, intimate settings for learning, and acknowledging the social nature of learning. Teachers have to get "up close" to understand where kids are coming from. This doesn't happen when the old tell-teach-practice-reteach practices are used.

The importance of authentic learning and the provision of "cognitive apprenticeships" to promote it cannot be underestimated. Students learn best by doing, and doing is best when it is lifelike—when it involves engagement with real or near real problem solving. Effective learning settings allow for learners to use shared knowledge to solve problems, allow students to practice their skills in real-life settings, and allow for the integration of abstract and practical learning activities. These are the conditions that increase the likelihood that teaching will be for understanding and that students will indeed be learning.

Standards for Authentic Learning

Newmann, Secada, and Wehlage (1995) define *authentic learning* as resulting in students being actively engaged with the materials of the curriculum. Authentic learning calls for student work to reflect the construction of knowledge—through disciplined inquiry—to produce discourse, products, and performances that have meaning to students beyond being successful in school. The authors propose four standards that need to be met to verify the presence of authentic learning:

1. Higher-order thinking (construction of knowledge): instruction involves students in manipulating information and ideas by synthesizing, generalizing, explaining, hypothesizing, or arriving at conclusions that produce new meaning and understandings for them. (29)
2. Deep knowledge (disciplined inquiry): instruction addresses central ideas of a topic or discipline with enough thoroughness to explore connections and relationships and to produce relatively complex understanding. (31)
3. Substantive conversation (disciplined inquiry): students engage in extended conversational exchanges with the teacher and/or their peers about subject matter in a way that builds an improved and shared understanding of ideas and topics. (35)
4. Connections to the world beyond the classroom (value beyond school): students make connections between substantive knowledge and either public problems or personal experiences. (40)

But learning cannot be separated from teaching, and neither learning nor teaching can be separated from the tasks, assignments, and other definers of the curriculum. Together, the three are referred to as *authentic pedagogy*. Newmann and colleagues (1995) propose a three-pronged strategy for assessing authentic pedagogy: assessing tasks that teachers give students to complete, assessing the dynamics of teaching and learning, and assessing the work students actually do. They then provide research-based standards and scoring criteria for assessing tasks, teaching and learning, and student work. The protocols for assessing tasks are provided in Appendix 11.1. Teacher-learning and student work protocols are available from the Wisconsin Center for Education Research (see, e.g., Newmann et al., 1995). Use the standards provided in Appendix 11.1 to examine the extent to which the tasks you assign to your students require the level of cognitive work described in each standard. Work together with two other teachers. As a group, how are you measuring up? How can the assessment protocols be used as a staff development vehicle in your school?

*A*N INTEGRATED VIEW

Taking the new research on teaching and learning seriously means making some changes in the way we have thought about organizing the classroom, planning for teaching, and arranging the curriculum. The key will be changing from a coverage mentality to a mastery mentality. Gardner explains:

> The greatest enemy of understanding is coverage. As long as you are determined to cover everything, you actually ensure that most kids are not going to understand. You've got to take enough time to get kids deeply involved in something so they can think about it in lots of different ways and apply it—not just at school but at home and on the street and so on. (quoted in Brandt, 1993:7)

Furthermore, we will have to rely far less on textbooks that provide the broad stroke and more on other materials that provide in-depth coverage of fewer topics. The curriculum will have to be revisited and serious inquiries made to identify essential and nonessential material, the fundamental structures of the disciplines that are generative by their very nature, and the aspects of the curriculum that comprise more limited or dead-end knowledge. Learning will have to emphasize solving problems. The curriculum will need to be more emergent as teachers and students, representing a community of learners, make decisions about what to do and when and how as they are involved in the process of thinking and learning.

Robert Marzano (1992:154–155) offers a "dimensions of learning" framework that is composed of five sets of questions he believes teachers need to answer as they plan for teaching and learning. Exhibit 11.3 lists the dimensions and questions.

Answers to the questions in Dimension 1 lay the groundwork for developing the kind of social relationships that provide students with shared meaning, shared funds of knowledge, and a shared basis for creating new knowledge. The remaining dimensions focus on teaching strategies and skills and decisions about knowledge.

Marzano (1992) recommends two broad strategies for teaching: presentation strategies and workshop strategies. Presentation strategies help students acquire and integrate new knowledge whether it be declarative or procedural, and thus help with the second dimension of learning. They also help extend and refine knowledge that helps with the third dimension of learning.

Presentation strategies incorporate many of the features of the original teaching effectiveness research. Examples are the importance of stimulating interest in the topic to be learned, relating the new information to existing information, providing clear goals and directions to students, modeling important activities, and

Dimensions of Learning

Dimension 1

1. What will be done to help students develop positive attitudes and perceptions about the learning climate?
   a. What will be done to help students feel accepted by the teacher and their peers?
   b. What will be done to help students perceive the classroom as a comfortable and orderly place?
2. What will be done to help students develop positive attitudes and perceptions about classroom tasks?
   a. What will be done to help students perceive classroom tasks as valuable?
   b. What will be done to help students believe they can perform classroom tasks?
   c. What will be done to help students understand and be clear about classroom tasks?

Dimension 2

Declarative Knowledge

1. What are the general topics?
2. What are the specifics?
3. How will students experience the information?
4. How will students be aided in constructing meaning?
5. How will students be aided in organizing the information?

6. How will students be aided in storing the information?

Procedural Knowledge

1. What skills and processes do students really need to master?
2. How will students be aided in constructing models?
3. How will students be aided in shaping the skill or process?
4. How will students be aided in internalizing the skill or process?

Dimension 3

1. What information will be extended and refined?
2. What activities will be used to help students extend and refine knowledge?

Dimension 4

1. What are the big issues?
2. How many issues will be considered?
3. Who will structure the tasks?
4. What types of products will students create?
5. To what extent will students work in cooperative groups?

Dimension 5

1. Which mental habits will be emphasized?
2. Which mental habits will be introduced?
3. How will the mental habits be reinforced?

Source: From *A Different Kind of Classroom: Teaching with Dimensions of Learning* by Robert J. Marzano (Figure 7.1, pp. 154–155), Alexandria, VA: ASCD, 1992. Used with permission. The Association for Supervision and Curriculum Development is a worldwide community of educators advocating sound policies and sharing best practices to achieve the success of each learner. To learn more, visit ASCD at www.ascd.org.

providing closure. Yet, instead of viewing these functions in a linear stepwise fashion with one following the other, and instead of insisting that each of the functions be a part of every presentation type of teaching, the five are understood differently. Marzano points out that not all need to be part of every presentation nor do they need to be performed in any set order. The five functions might be depicted, then, not as a linear list, but as follows:

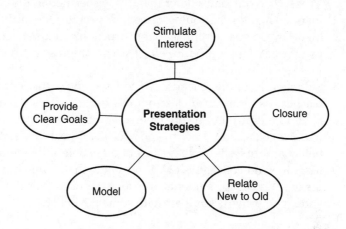

Students and teachers, for example, might begin a new unit with the end, with modeling what is to be learned, or with an activity that stimulates interest, and then move to one or another of the functions in any way that makes sense.

Marzano recommends workshop strategies for the questions included in Dimension 4 of his learning framework. The metaphor of workshop suggests teaching is more student directed and activity oriented. A "workshop lesson" would generally begin with a mini-lesson designed to provide guidance and give assistance to students as they begin to work on projects. Mini-lessons provide students with essential information, resources, and so forth. The major block of teaching would be the *activity.* Here, students work individually, in pairs, or in small groups on projects. Finally, there would be a *sharing period* that allows students to discuss a variety of topics and issues. "The hallmark of a sharing period is that the students and teacher freely discuss their learning as students work on their projects" (Marzano, 1992:162).

$\mathcal{P}$ URPOSES AND OBJECTIVES

Stating purposes and stating objectives are important to both active teaching and constructivist teaching for understanding. The purposes end of the continuum is more general, allowing for more teacher discretion and encouraging the creation of one's teaching practice in use. Teachers plan to teach as they teach in order to be responsive to changing conditions. Stating objectives is more targeted, allowing for less discretion. Three generalizations from the research on goal setting can be helpful as we seek to find the proper place on the continuum between stating purposes and stating objectives. These generalizations are drawn from Marzano, Pickering, and Pollock (2001:94–95):

1. Instructional goals narrow what students focus on. One of the more interesting findings in the research is the negative effect that setting goals or objectives has on outcomes other than those specified in the objectives.

2. Instructional goals should not be too specific. One fairly stable finding in the literature on goal setting is that instructional goals stated in behavioral objective format do not produce effect sizes as high as instructional goals stated in more general formats.

3. Students should be encouraged to personalize the teacher's goals. Once the teacher has established classroom learning goals, students should be encouraged to adapt them to their personal needs and desires. This is one of the reasons goals should not be too specific. If goals are stated as highly specific behavioral objectives, they are not amenable to being adapted by students. Marzano and colleagues (2001) conclude that, while it is important for teachers to set goals for students, it is also important for these goals to be general enough to provide students with some flexibility.

SOME REFLECTIONS

1. Early studies of constructivist teaching and learning depict learning as a solitary activity. More recently the emphasis has shifted to the importance of social interaction in learning. Learning together is important for students. Learning together is important for teachers. And learning together is important for both principals and teachers when they are working together. Combining learning together with the active construction of meaning leads to "social constructivism" (Vygotsky, 1962, 1978). Thus, we have two broad views of teaching and learning. One view emphasizes the transmission of information and the other view emphasizes the social construction of knowledge. The differences between the two are summarized in Table 11.1.

   Following the scoring procedure used for Exhibit 11.1, distribute 10 points across the matched pairs to reflect the extent to which you think each is true. If you think statement 1 and statement 1a are equally true, give them each 5 points. If you think statement 1 is always true and statement 1a is rarely true, assign 10 points to 1 and none to 1a. Now remove or cover the headings "Transmission View" and "Social Construction View" and the title of the table, leaving the items 1–8 and 1a–8a only. Share this list of pairs with teachers in your department, team, or grade level and ask them to distribute points as described above. In the ideal a good mix makes the most sense. Much of knowledge is, after all, a fixed body of information that is best transmitted from teacher to student. But much knowledge is not. Deep and long-term learning requires that we acknowledge that developing interpretations and constructing meanings through discussion are also important. The questions for principals to ask in a given situation are What kind of knowledge are we t a b l e **11.1** **Comparing Transmission of Information and Social Construction of Knowledge Views**

Transmission View	Social Construction View	Total
1. __ Knowledge as fixed body of information transmitted from teacher or text to students	1a. __ Knowledge as developing interpretations constructed through discussion	10
2. __ Texts, teacher as authoritative sources of expert knowledge to which students defer	2a. __ Authority for constructed knowledge resides in the arguments and evidence cited in its support by students as well as by texts or teacher; everyone has expertise to contribute	10
3. __ Teacher is responsible for managing students' learning by providing information and leading students through activities and assignments	3a. __ Teacher and students share responsibility for initiating and guiding learning efforts	10
4. __ Teacher explains, checks for understanding, and judges correctness of students' responses	4a. __ Teacher acts as discussion leader who poses questions, seeks clarifications, promotes dialogue, helps group recognize areas of consensus and of continuing disagreement	10
5. __ Students memorize or replicate what has been explained or modeled	5a. __ Students strive to make sense of new input by relating it to their prior knowledge and by collaborating in dialogue with others to coconstruct shared understandings	10
6. __ Discourse emphasizes drill and recitation in response to convergent questions; focus is on eliciting correct answers	6a. __ Discourse emphasizes reflective discussion of networks of connected knowledge; questions are more divergent but designed to develop understanding of the powerful ideas that anchor these networks; focus is on eliciting students' thinking	10
7. __ Activities emphasize replication of models or applications that require following step-by-step algorithms	7a. __ Activities emphasize applications to authentic issues and problems that require higher-order thinking	10
8. __ Students work mostly alone, practicing what has been transmitted to them in order to prepare themselves to compete for rewards by reproducing it on demand	8a. __ Students collaborate by acting as a learning community that constructs shared understandings through sustained dialogue	10
____ TOTAL	____ TOTAL	80

Source: This instrument draws on the transmission of information versus social construction items that appear in Good and Brophy, 2003, *Looking in Classrooms,* p. 413.

dealing with? What purposes does the teacher have in mind? How rich is the prior knowledge that students are bringing to the learning task? Is this the information that is at the heart of learning to use one's mind well? Or is this the information that drives the definitions, nomenclatures, and clarity that are needed to prepare students to use knowledge in more advanced ways?

The message here is that teaching and learning are complex, and reaching a conclusion about just what is good teaching and good learning for a specific situation requires deep knowledge on the part of the principal. If principals want to be successful instructional leaders, they have no choice but to immerse themselves in what research and best practice tells us is most effective for advancing teaching and learning in their school.

2. Appendix 11.1 lists and discusses standards and scoring criteria for assessing the degree of authenticity in the assignments that teachers give their students. Three general standards and seven operational standards are provided along with scoring rubrics. Ask two of your colleagues to join you in gathering a dozen samples of assignments the three of you have given in recent weeks. Now familiarize yourself with the standards and protocols for using them to assess the tasks teachers give students. What do the standards mean in your context? Are you pleased with the work of your students? If not, what kinds of assignments could you give that might get a more authentic response?

Many principals are concerned that by focusing on "more authentic" learning their students will not be prepared to score well on standardized tests that emphasize "basic skills." But the evidence is compelling that the more authentic are the assignments teachers give the higher students score on standardized tests. This is true even though these tests did not receive the usual "drill and kill" approach that many believe is the only way to raise the score (see, e.g., Newmann, Bryk, and Nagaoka, 2001).

3. After carefully reviewing the findings about good teaching and effective learning in this chapter, write 10 principles of learning you would like to see reflected in the classrooms in your school after you become a principal. Be prepared to share them with a colleague.

REFERENCES

Anderson, L. 1989. "Implementing Instructional Programs to Promote Meaningful, Self-Regulated Learning," in J. Brophy (Ed.), *Advances in Research on Teaching, Vol. 1* (pp. 311–343). Greenwich, CT: JAI Press.

Brandt, Ron. 1993. "On Teaching for Understanding: A Conversation with Howard Gardner," *Educational Leadership* 50(7), 4–7.

Brophy, Jere. 1992. "Probing the Subtleties of Subject-Matter Teaching," *Educational Leadership* 49(7), 4–8.

Case, R. 1997. "Beyond Inert Facts and Concepts: Teaching for Understanding," in R. Case and P. Clark (Eds.), *The Canadian Anthology of Social Studies: Issues and Strategies for Teachers.* Vancouver, BC: Simon Fraser University.

Educational Leadership 49(2). 1992, April.

Educational Leadership 50(7). 1993, April.

Educational Leadership 52(3). 1994, November.

Educational Leadership 54(6). 1997, March.

Educational Leadership 56(3). 1998, November.

Good, Thomas L., and Jere E. Brophy. 2003. *Looking in Classrooms* (9th ed.). Boston: Allyn and Bacon.

Leinhardt, Gaea. 1992. "What Research on Learning Tells Us about Teaching," *Educational Leadership* 49(7), 20–25.

Marzano, Robert J. 1992. *A Different Kind of Classroom: Teaching with Dimensions of Learning*. Alexandria, VA: Association for Supervision and Curriculum Development.

Marzano, Robert J., Debra J. Pickering, and Jane E. Pollock. 2001. *Classroom Instruction That Works: Research-Based Strategy for Increasing Student Achievement*. Alexandria, VA: Association for Supervision and Curriculum Development.

Newmann, Fred M., Anthony S. Bryk, and Jenny K. Nagaoka. 2001. *Authentic Intellectual Work and Standardized Tests: Conflict or Coexistence?* Chicago: Consortium on Chicago School Research.

Newmann, Fred M., and Associates. 1996. *Authentic Achievement: Restructuring Schools for Intellectual Quality*. San Francisco: Jossey-Bass.

Newmann, Fred M., Walter G. Secada, and Gary G. Wehlage. 1995. *A Guide to Authentic Instruction and Assessment: Vision, Standards and Scoring*. Madison: Wisconsin Center for Education Research.

Nolan, James, and Pam Francis. 1992. "Changing Perspectives in Curriculum and Instruction," in Carl Glickman (Ed.), *Supervision in Transition*, Yearbook of the Association for Supervision and Curriculum Development (pp. 44–59). Alexandria, VA: Association for Supervision and Curriculum Development.

Perkins, D. 1992. *Smart Schools: From Training Memories to Educating Minds*. New York: Free Press.

Prawat, R. 1989. "Promoting Access to Knowledge, Strategy, and Disposition in Students: A Research Synthesis," *Review of Educational Research* 59, 1–41.

Resnick, Lauren. 1987. *Education and Learning to Think*. Washington, DC: National Academy Press.

Resnick, Lauren B., and Leopold E. Klopfer. 1989. *Toward the Thinking Curriculum: Current Cognitive Research*, Yearbook of the Association for Supervision and Curriculum Development. Alexandria, VA: Association for Supervision and Curriculum Development.

Tyson, Harriet. 1990, March. "Reforming Science Education/Restructuring the Public Schools: Roles for the Scientific Community" (pp. 22, 24). Prepared as a background paper for the New York Academy of Sciences and the Institute for Educational Leadership Forum on Restructuring K–12 Education. New York: Academy of Sciences.

Vygotsky, L. 1962. *Thought and Language*. Cambridge, MA: MIT Press.

Vygotsky, L. 1978. *Mind in Society: The Development of Higher Psychological Processes*. Ed. M. Cole, V. John-Steiner, S. Scribner, and E. Souberman. Cambridge: Harvard University Press.

Zemelman, Steven, Harvey Daniels, and Arthur Hyde. 1998. *Best Practice: New Standards for Teaching and Learning in America's Schools* (2nd ed.). Portsmouth, NH: Heinemann.

Zemelman, Steven, Harvey Daniels, and Arthur Hyde. 2005. *Best Practice: Today's Standards for Teaching and Learning in America's Schools* (3rd ed.). Portsmouth, NH: Heinemann.

Standards and Scoring Criteria for Assessment of Assignments (Tasks) Teachers Give

Overview and General Rules

The main point here is to estimate, for a given task, the extent to which the teacher communicates to students expectations consistent with the standards. To what extent does successful completion of the task require the kind of cognitive work indicated by each standard?

The seven standards reflect three more general standards for authentic achievement as follows:

Construction of knowledge:	Organization of information
	Consideration of alternatives
Disciplined inquiry:	Disciplinary content
	Disciplinary process
	Elaborated written communication
Value beyond school:	Problem connected to the world beyond the classroom
	Audience beyond the school

A. If a task has different parts that imply different expectations (e.g., worksheet/ short-answer questions and a question asking for explanation of some conclusions), the score should reflect the teacher's apparent dominant or overall expectations. Overall expectations are indicated by the proportion of time or effort spent on different parts of the task and by criteria for evaluation stated by the teacher.

B. Scores should take into account what students can reasonably be expected to do at the grade level.

Standard 1: Organization of Information

The task asks students to organize, synthesize, interpret, explain, or evaluate complex information in addressing a concept, problem, or issue.

Consider the extent to which the task asks the student to organize, interpret, evaluate, or synthesize complex information, rather than to retrieve or to reproduce isolated fragments of knowledge or to repeatedly apply previously learned algorithms and procedures. To score high, the task should call for interpretation of nuances of a topic that go deeper than surface exposure or familiarity.

3 = high
2 = moderate
1 = low

When students are asked to gather information for reports that indicates some selectivity and organizing beyond mechanical copying, but are not asked for interpretation, evaluation, or synthesis, give a score of 2.

Standard 2: Consideration of Alternatives

The task asks students to consider alternative solutions, strategies, perspectives, or points of view as they address a concept, problem, or issue.

To what extent does success in the task require consideration of alternative solutions, strategies, perspectives and points of view? To score high, the task should clearly involve students in considering alternatives, either through explicit presentation of the alternatives or through an activity that cannot be successfully completed without examination of alternatives implicit in the work. It is not necessary that students' final conclusions include listing or weighing of alternatives, but this could be an impressive indicator that it was an expectation of the task.

> 3 = high
> 2 = moderate
> 1 = low

Standard 3: Disciplinary Content

The task asks students to show understanding and/or use of ideas, theories, or perspectives considered central to an academic or professional discipline.

To what extent does the task promote students' understanding of and thinking about ideas, theories or perspectives considered seminal or critical within an academic or professional discipline, or in interdisplinary fields recognized in authoritative scholarship? Examples in mathematics could include proportion, equality, central tendency, and geometric space. Examples in social studies could include democracy, social class, market economy, or theories of revolution. Reference to isolated factual claims, definitions, algorithms—though necessary to inquiry within a discipline—will not be considered indicators of significant disciplinary content unless the task requires students to apply powerful disciplinary ideas that organize and interpret the information.

> 3 = Success in the task clearly requires understanding of concepts, ideas, or theories central in a discipline.
> 2 = Success in the task seems to require understanding of concepts, ideas, or theories central in a discipline, but the task does not make these very explicit.

    1 = Success in the task can be achieved with a very superficial (or even without any) understanding of concepts, ideas, or theories central to any specific discipline.

Standard 4: Disciplinary Process

The task asks students to use methods of inquiry, research, or communication characteristic of an academic or professional discipline.

    To what extent does the task lead students to use methods of inquiry, research, communication, and discourse characteristic of an academic or professional discipline? Some powerful processes of inquiry may not be linked uniquely to any specific discipline (e.g., interpreting graphs), but they will be valued here if the task calls for their use in ways similar to important uses within the discipline.

    3 = Success in the task requires the use of methods of inquiry or discourse important to the conduct of a discipline. Examples of methods of disciplinary inquiry would include looking for mathematical patterns or interpreting primary sources.

    2 = Success in the task requires use of methods of inquiry or discourse not central to the conduct of a discipline.

    1 = Success in the task can be achieved without use of any specific methods of inquiry or discourse.

Standard 5: Elaborated Written Communication

The task asks students to elaborate on their understanding, explanations, or conclusions through extended writing.

    This standard is intended to measure the extent to which a task requires students to elaborate on their ideas and conclusions through extended writing in a discipline. Expectations for elaborated communication can vary between disciplines. We indicate criteria for mathematics and social studies.

    4 = Analysis/Persuasion/Theory

      Mathematics: The task requires the student to show his/her solution path and to justify that solution path, that is, to give a logical argument, explain his/her thinking, or to justify results.

      Social studies: The task requires explanations of generalizations, classifications, and relationships relevant to a situation, problem, or theme. Examples include attempts to argue, convince, or persuade and to develop or test hypotheses.

3 = Report/Summary

Mathematics: The task requires some organization of material. The student is asked to give clear evidence of his/her solution path but is not required to give any mathematical argument, to justify his/her solution path, or to explain his/her thinking.

Social studies: The task calls for an account of particular events or series of events ("This is what happened"), a generalized narrative, or a description of a recurrent pattern of events or steps in a procedure ("This is what happens"; "This is the way it is done").

2 = Short-answer exercises

Mathematics: The task requires little more than giving a result. Students may be asked to show some work, but this is not emphasized and does not request much detail.

Social studies: Only one or two brief sentences per question are expected.

1 = Multiple-choice exercises; fill-in-the-blank exercises (answered with less than a sentence)

Standard 6: Problem Connected to the World beyond the Classroom

The task asks students to address a concept, problem, or issue that is similar to one that they have encountered, or are likely to encounter, in life beyond the classroom.

To what extent does the task present students with a question, issue, or problem that they have actually encountered, or are likely to encounter, in their lives beyond school? In mathematics, estimating personal budgets would qualify as a real-world problem, but completing a geometric proof generally would not. In social studies, defending one's position on compulsory community service for students could qualify as a real-world problem, but describing the origins of World War II generally would not.

Certain kinds of school knowledge may be considered valuable as cultural capital or cultural literacy needed in social, civic, or vocational situations beyond the classroom (e.g., knowing how a bill becomes a law, or how to compute interest on an investment). However, task demands for culturally valued, "basic" knowledge will not be counted here unless the task requires applying such knowledge to a specific problem likely to be encountered beyond the classroom.

When students are allowed to choose topics of interest to them, this might also indicate likely application of knowledge beyond the instructional setting. But tasks that allow student choice do not necessarily connect to issues beyond the classroom. To score high on this standard, it must be clear that the question, issue, or problem which students confront resembles one that students have encountered, or are likely to encounter, in life beyond school.

> 3 = The question, issue, or problem clearly resembles one that students have encountered, or are likely to encounter, in life beyond school. The resemblance is so clear that teacher explanation is not necessary for most students to grasp it.
>
> 2 = The question, issue, or problem bears some resemblance to real-world experiences of the students, but the connections are not immediately apparent. The connections would be reasonably clear if explained by the teacher, but the task need not include such explanations to be rated 2.
>
> 1 = The problem has virtually no resemblance to questions, issues, or problems that students have encountered, or are likely to encounter, beyond school. Even if the teacher tried to show the connections, it would be difficult to make a personal argument.

Standard 7: Audience beyond the School

The task asks students to communicate their knowledge, present a product or performance, or take some action to an audience beyond the teacher, classroom, and school building.

Authenticity increases when students complete the task with the intention of communicating their knowledge to an audience beyond the teacher and when they actually communicate with that audience. Such communication can include informing others, trying to persuade others, performing, and taking other actions beyond the classroom. This refers not to the process of working on the task, but to the nature of the student's final product.

> 4 = Final product is presented to an audience beyond the school.
>
> 3 = Final product is presented to an audience beyond the classroom, but within the school.
>
> 2 = Final product is presented to peers within the classroom.
>
> 1 = Final product is presented only to the teacher.

Source: From *A Guide to Authentic Instruction and Assessment: Vision, Standards and Scoring* (pp. 80–85) by Fred M. Newmann, Walter G. Secada, and Gary G. Wehlage, 1995, Madison: Wisconsin Center for Education Research. Reprinted by permission.

12

INSTRUCTIONAL LEADERSHIP, SUPERVISION, AND TEACHER DEVELOPMENT

A strong consensus is emerging that, whatever else they do, principals must be instructional leaders who are directly involved in the teaching and learning life of the school. And, while many people must assume supervisory roles and other helpful roles, the overall responsibility for supervision rests with the principal. And finally, high on any list of priorities for principals is to build the capacities of teachers by emphasizing teacher learning, and by increasing the collective intelligence that will become available as a result. Principals are responsible for helping their schools get smarter. Smarter schools mean more student learning.

No doubt many courses and books on the principalship separate the details of teacher supervision and teacher learning from the theme of instructional leadership. They focus on the importance of instructional leadership as a concept and may even define it. But the details are reserved for specialized courses and books. These courses and books will no doubt help. But missing from this approach is a bridge from instructional leadership as a concept to supervisory and teacher learning strategies; a bridge that assumes instructional leadership must be deeply embedded in the work of the principal; a bridge that assumes school leadership, teaching and learning cannot be easily separated; a bridge that lays a foundation of purpose, theory, and practice to courses and books that are devoted to the hows and whys of supervision; and a bridge that leads to improved student achievement of both authentic tasks and standardized tests. Chapters 12 and 13 provide these bridges.

Teacher learning is a key ingredient, for example, in any attempt to improve schools. David and Shields (1999), for example, found that the following are important contributors to improvement: (1) a strong and sustained district focus on teacher learning and quality instruction; (2) new conceptions of staff development that looked more like part of the everyday jobs of teachers; and (3) teacher learning strategies that emphasize learning new content and knowledge and new teaching approaches in one's own classroom by learning from colleagues, on-site staff developers, and one's own principal. David and Shields studied seven urban school districts involved in systemic standards-based reform. Reform was difficult to achieve, but where improvements were noted, the learning principles listed above were important.

In a study of twenty-four urban schools that were academically successful, Louis and Marks found that the most successful schools had teachers with a strong sense of community and a shared mission. Teachers had time to plan and talk together, to observe each other's teaching, and to reflect together on their practice. In other words, they had strong professional communities for support, and these communities were linked to higher levels of student achievement (Viadero, 1999:27). After closely examining teachers' practice in three schools, Peterson, McCarthey, and Elmore (1996) suggest that teacher learning occurs mainly as a function of specific problems that teachers face in their classrooms; that changing one's practice is largely a problem of learning rather than of organization; that, although school structures can provide opportunities for teacher learning, they do not cause the learning to occur; and that changes in school structure follow from good practice. Structures are important but do not lend themselves to forward mapping of changes in teaching practice. Instead, deciding on what is important in teaching and what kind of practice makes sense should come first, allowing the backward mapping to new structures. And this alternative involves learning. Teacher learning, it appears, is the springboard to school reform—not the other way around, as current policy now assumes.

How should principals help teachers learn more about themselves and their work? What should principals do to help teachers improve their teaching practice? Answers to these questions depend on the views that principals have about good teaching, how learning environments should be developed, what curriculum decisions make sense, how the schools should be organized for effective learning, and the extent to which schools are learning and inquiring communities not just for students but for teachers and other adults, as well. If a principal's view corresponds only to the active teaching research discussed in Chapter 11, one answer would make the most sense. If, however, a principal's view includes the newer cognitive research on teaching and places this research at the center, then a different set of decisions would make sense. There is a link between how principals want teachers to teach and how principals help them to teach in that way.

Let's review, for example, some of the principles of teaching and learning that are based on cognitive psychology:

- Learning is a process of making sense with the construction of personal meanings.
- Meanings are constructed by comparing existing understandings and developing connections among ideas, concepts, and blocks of information.
- Meanings are norm referenced and thus are constructed in social contexts and are influenced by the views of others.
- The student's prior knowledge is an important bridge to new learning.
- Motivation to learn is in part related to an individual's goals and aspirations, and in part influenced by an individual's connections to others and the resulting group norms that emerge.
- Learners differ in the time needed to learn the same thing and in the cognitive processes needed to learn.
- Learners differ in the kind of aptitudes and intelligences they bring to learning and are predisposed to learn when strengths are emphasized.
- Knowledge and skills are best learned in situations and under circumstances that resemble how they will actually be used.
- Learning is facilitated by emphasizing the mastery of generative knowledge, which helps learners to acquire new knowledge on their own.
- Active teaching has an important supporting role to play.

In this image of teaching and learning, learners are not consumers of knowledge but constructors, and the personal meanings they bring to learning are critical determinates of what will be learned and how well it will be learned. Helping teachers to learn to teach or to improve their teaching along these lines requires a shift in our understanding of teacher development. This view of teaching cannot be mastered by unduly emphasizing consumption, memorization, and replication. Training alone just won't do. Instead, principals will need to emphasize professional development and renewal improvement strategies. Training, professional development, and renewal strategies are described and contrasted in Table 12.1.

The term *emphasize* is key. All three strategies have important roles to play, but not all three strategies are equal. If we value teaching for understanding, the development of thinking, and the mastery of generative knowledge, then we will need to give less attention to training models and more attention to professional development and renewal models.

*T*RAINING MODELS

Training models of teacher development have important roles to play. They resemble traditional inservice programs that are well known to teachers and t a b l e **12.1**   **Models of Teacher Development**

	Training	Professional	Renewal
Assumptions	Knowledge stands above the teacher.	The teacher stands above knowledge.	Knowledge is in the teacher.
	Knowledge is therefore instrumental. It tells the teacher what to do.	Knowledge is therefore conceptual. It informs the teacher's decisions.	Knowledge is therefore personal. It connects teachers to themselves and others.
	Teaching is a job, and teachers are technicians.	Teaching is a profession, and teachers are experts.	Teaching is a calling, and teachers are servants.
	Mastery of skills is important.	Development of expertise is important.	Development of personal and professional self is important.
Roles	Teacher is consumer of knowledge.	Teacher is constructor of knowledge.	Teacher is internalizer of knowledge.
	Principal is expert.	Principal is colleague.	Principal is friend.
Practices	Emphasize technical competence.	Emphasize clinical competence.	Emphasize personal and critical competencies.
	Build individual teacher's skills:	Build professional community:	Build caring community:
	⏐ Through training and practice	⏐ Through problem solving and inquiry	⏐ Through reflection and reevaluation
	⏐ By planning and delivering training	⏐ By emphasizing inquiry, problem solving, and action research	⏐ By encouraging reflection, conversation, and discourse

principals and need little elaboration. They are best suited for when a problem can be defined as a deficit in knowledge of some kind—for example, when teachers don't know about something or need to improve their skills in some area. Outside or inside experts do the training. Training is linked to clear objectives and relies on conventional well-executed instruction. Teachers, for example, might be introduced to various ways in which interest centers can be set up, methods for evaluating student portfolios, new techniques for using simulation for teaching world history, tips on how to monitor student progress, or some basic teaching skills that help keep students "on task." Teachers generally assume passive roles. Techniques most often used are oral presentations, illustrated presentations, demonstrations, and observations of good practice. Effective training programs provide opportunities for teachers to practice what it is that they learn. Ideally, they receive coaching as they actually begin to use what they learned in their classrooms.

*P*ROFESSIONAL DEVELOPMENT MODELS

Although training has its place, most observers believe that it should no longer be the primary model for teacher development. Implementing lists of dos and don'ts, standard skill repertoires, and other scripts is not the way to help teachers to teach for understanding, to develop student thinking, and to promote generative knowledge. Instead, teachers need to learn how to think on their feet, inventing their practice as they go.

The relationship between teachers and the knowledge base for teaching is understood differently in professional development than in training. Professional development assumes that teachers are superordinate to the research on teaching. Unlike technicians who are trained to apply research findings, professionals view research as knowledge that informs the decisions that they make. Professionals create their practice in use.

Professional development approaches emphasize providing teachers with a rich environment loaded with teaching materials, media, books, and devices. With encouragement and support, teachers interact with this environment and with each other through exploration and discovery. Thelan (1971) suggests that the most useful teacher development programs are characterized by "intensity of personal involvement, immediate consequences for classroom practice, stimulation and ego support by meaningful associates in the situation, and initiating by teacher rather than outside" (72–73). Judith Warren Little (1993), a thoughtful commentator on teacher development, proposes six principles that she believes should guide the design of professional development experiences for teachers:

1. Professional development offers meaningful intellectual, social and emotional engagement with ideas, with materials, and with colleagues both in and out of teaching.
2. Professional development takes explicit account of the context of teaching and the experience of teachers. Focused study groups, teacher collaboratives, long-term partnerships, and similar models of professional development afford teachers a means of locating new ideas in relation to their individual and institutional histories, practices, and circumstances.
3. Professional development offers support for informed dissent. In the pursuit of good schools, consensus may prove to be an over-stated virtue.... Dissent places a premium on the evaluation of alternatives and the close scrutiny of underlying assumptions.
4. Professional development places classroom practice in the larger context of school practice and the educational careers of children. It is grounded in a big-picture perspective on the purposes and practices of schooling, providing teachers with a means of seeing and acting upon the connections among students' experience, teachers' classroom practice, and school-wide structures and cultures.

5. Professional development prepares teachers (as well as students and their parents) to employ the techniques and perspectives of inquiry. . . . It acknowledges that the existing knowledge is relatively slim and that our strength may derive less from teachers' willingness to consume research knowledge than from their capacity to generate knowledge and to assess the knowledge claimed by others.

6. The governance of professional development ensures bureaucratic restraint and a balance between the interests of individuals and the interests of institutions. (138–139)

Little offers the principles as alternatives to training models that when used excessively provide teachers with shallow and fragmented content and subject them to passive roles as they participate in scripted workshops. The principles are anecdotes to the "one-size-fits-all" problem that training too often presents. Furthermore, she argues that the principles challenge the view that teaching is a narrowly defined technical activity. Little believes that today's emphasis on teacher inservice is dominated by "a district-subsidized marketplace of formal programs over which teachers exert little influence or in which they play few leadership roles" (1993:139). In professional development models, the teacher's capacities, needs, and interests are paramount. They are actively involved in contributing data and information, solving problems, analyzing, and so forth. Principals are involved as colleagues. Together, principals and teachers work to develop a common purpose themed to the improvement of teaching and learning. Together, principals and teachers work to build a learning and inquiring community.

RENEWAL MODELS

Both training and professional development models share the purpose of helping teachers improve their practice. Bolin and Falk (1987) point out that, although improvement may be a legitimate goal, it is not powerful enough to tap the potential for teachers to grow personally and professionally. Bolin (1987), for example, writes:

> What would happen if we set aside the question of how to improve the teacher and looked instead at what we can do to encourage the teacher? . . . Asking how to encourage the teacher places the work of improvement in the hands of the teacher. It presupposes that the teacher desires to grow, to be self-defining, and to engage in teaching as a vital part of life, rather than as unrelated employment. This leads to looking at teaching as a commitment or calling, a vocation . . . that is not adequately contained in the term profession as it has come to be used. (11)

Bolin believes that when the emphasis shifts from improving teachers to encouraging them, both training and professional development give way to renewal. In her view, renewal is not driven so much by professional problems as by a teacher's commitment to teaching as a vocation. Renewal implies doing over again, revising, making new, restoring, reestablishing, and revaluing as teachers individually and collectively reflect on not only their practice but also themselves and the practice of teaching that they share in the school.

In training, the emphasis is on building each individual's teaching skills by planning and delivering instruction. In development, the emphasis is on building a professional community by helping teachers become inquirers, problem solvers, and researchers of their own practice. In renewal, the emphasis is on building a caring community by encouraging teachers to reflect and to engage in conversation and discourse.

TEACHER DEVELOPMENT AND TYPES OF TEACHER COMPETENCE

Zimpher and Howey (1987) describe four major types of teaching competence that can help sort out when each of the approaches—training, development, and renewal—might make the most sense. The four types of competence depicted and discussed in Table 12.2 are technical, clinical, personal, and critical. Teaching as an expression of technical competence is probably the most popular of the four. It remains the area that receives the most attention in teacher education programs and in school district and state-mandated teacher evaluation instruments. An example of an emphasis on technical competence is focusing on lists of teaching behaviors that are presumed to be standards. These lists are assessed by the use of rubrics that spell out levels of competence. Technical competence is important to successful teaching and learning, but once technical competence is ensured, primary attention should be given to developing the clinical, personal, and critical competencies of teachers.

When addressing clinical competence, the emphasis is on helping teachers become better problem solvers who are able to frame problems and issues and come to grips with solutions. The purpose of teacher development in this case is to enhance inquiry, encourage reflection, build problem-solving skills, and help teachers make more informed decisions about their practice.

When the emphasis is on personal competence, the intent is to help teachers understand and interpret their own teaching in a manner that provides them meaning and significance. Personal competence is enhanced as teachers increase their awareness and understand more fully their teaching practice.

Critical competence is concerned with issues of value and with the hidden meanings underlying teaching practice. Critical competence is developed as teachers are able to differentiate between effective and good practice, take ethical stands, and be concerned with worth and purpose.

t a b l e **12.2**   **Zimpher and Howey: Framework for Examining Four Types of Teaching Competence**

	Technical Competence	Clinical Competence	Personal Competence	Critical Competence
Conception of the Teacher	Determines in advance what is to be learned, how it is to be learned, and criteria by which success is to be measured	Instructional problem solver; clinician frames and solves practical problems; takes reflective action; inquirer	Understanding of self, self-actualized person who uses self as effective and humane instrument	Rational, morally autonomous, socially conscious change agent
Focus of Supervision	Mastery of methods of instruction: specific skills (how to ask good questions); how to apply teaching strategies; how to select and organize curriculum content; how to structure the classroom for learning what techniques to use to maintain control	Reflective decision making and action to solve practical problems (what should be done about disruptive behavior) as well as reconsideration of intents and practices to take action to solve practical problems	Increase self-awareness, identity formation, and interpretive capacities, e.g., self-confrontation; values clarification; interpersonal involvement; small-group processes; develop personal style in teaching role	Reflective decision making and action to form more rational and just schools, critique of stereotypes/ ideology, hidden curriculum, authoritarian/ permissive relationships, equality of access, responsibilities, and forms of repressive social control
Conception of the Supervisor	Technical expert/ master provides for skill development and efficient/effective use of resources in classroom; translator of research theory into technical rules for application in classrooms	Fosters inquiry regarding the relationship of theory and practice; fosters reflection about the relationship of intents and practice and reconsideration/ modification of intent/practice in light of evaluation of their conscience	Expert in interpersonal competence and theories of human development; nondirective participant; warm and supportive learning environment; responsiveness to teacher-defined needs and concerns; wisdom in guiding free exploration of teaching episodes, diagnosing theories-in-use	Collaborator in self-reflective communities of practitioner-theorists committed to examining critically their own/institutional practices and improving them in interests of nationality and social justice; provides challenges and support as do other participants in dialogue

t a b l e **12.2**   **Continued**

	Technical Competence	Clinical Competence	Personal Competence	Critical Competence
Type of Theoretical Knowledge	Technical guidelines from explanatory theory; analytic craft knowledge about what constitutes "good" practice	Synthesis of normative, interpretive, and explanatory knowledge to form intellectually and morally defensible practical judgments about what to do in a particular situation	Analytic and interpretive theory to understand and make explicit reasons underlying symbolic interaction essentially those which occur in the class	Critical theory of education; unite philosophical analysis and criticism and causal and interpretive science
Mode of Inquiry	Applied science, functional and task analysis, linear problem solving to determine how to accomplish given ends	Practical action research to articulate concerns, plan action, monitor action, and reflect on processes and consequences to improve our teaching practices; rationale building	Phenomenological, ethnographic, hermeneutic analysis and interpretation; analyze elements of teaching episodes	Collaborative action and reflection to transform the organization and practice of education; group inquiry regarding conditions of communicative interaction and social control
Level of Reflectivity	Specific techniques needed to reach stated objectives involve instrumental reasoning; means-end (if, then) relative to efficiency/ effectiveness	Practical reasoning and judgment relative to what should be done (best course of action under the circumstances)	Interpretation of intended meaning of verbal and nonverbal symbols and acts; introspection relative to self-awareness/identity	Critical self-reflection/reflexivity and social critique to uncover contradictions/ inadequacies and different conceptions of educational practice as values with society

Source: From "Adapting Supervisory Practices to Different Orientations of Teaching" (pp. 104–105), by Nancy Zimpher & Kenneth Howey. In *Journal of Curriculum and Supervision* 2(2), Winter 1987. Used with permission. The Association for Supervision and Curriculum Development is a worldwide community of educators advocating sound policies and sharing best practices to achieve the success of each learner. To learn more, visit ASCD at www.ascd.org.

Note: The authors wish to acknowledge the major contribution of Sharon Strom in the development of this framework.

Although training can help enhance the teacher's technical competence, it seems not to be powerful enough to enhance the other three types. Clinical competence seems best addressed by professional development models. Professional development can also help build personal competence, with renewal models being most appropriate for enhancing personal and critical competence.

$\mathcal{T}$HE NATURE OF PROFESSIONAL EXPERTISE

Wilson and Peterson (1997) point out that teachers are intellectuals who think about students and subject matter and construct bridges between the two. In their words:

> Good teachers must think hard about what they want their students to learn, contemplating myriad questions. A teacher must consider questions like: What is interesting about this subject for my students? What ideas and concepts are particularly difficult? Why? What are the different means I can use to help students grapple with these ideas? What do my students already know that might help? What do they believe that might get in the way? What time of the day is it? the year? What resources do I have access to? How do students construct their understandings? What teaching moves can I make to help that process of meaning construction? (8–9)

Futhermore, Wilson and Peterson point out that teachers are listeners and inquirers who research their practice by investigating students' thinking and searching for ways to teach for understanding.

Principals who view professional expertise as deliberative action take still another stance. They emphasize teachers learning how to think like teachers who model high levels of intellectual artisanship. Deliberative action recognizes that teaching practice is situated in a context that involves different resources, students, needs, time constraints, and curriculum frameworks. Indeed, deliberate teachers bring to this context different purposes and the interaction between purposes and contexts shapes what they do. Teachers analyze different situations and monitor how situations change as practice unfolds. They craft strategies that combine action with thinking. One idea leads to another until a pattern begins to emerge (Mintzberg, 1987:68). Once a pattern emerges, teachers are able to use both knowledge of general principles and their experiences to make good decisions. Since this analysis occurs within the context of one's unique teaching practice, it resembles the generation of knowledge in use (Schön, 1983). Professionals generate knowledge in use as they engage in the particulars of practice, spontaneously forming intuitions and discovering new paths that they were not able to anticipate beforehand.

Professional expertise in teaching, in other words, requires that teachers do more than master and apply a set of generalizations and regularities expressed as lists of skills that are context free and thus thought to apply to all students, on all occasions, everywhere (Sergiovanni, 2000).

$\mathcal{R}$EFLECTING ON SUPERVISION

Teacher development and supervision go hand in hand. Principals have a responsibility to help teachers improve their practice and to hold them accountable for meeting their commitments to teaching and learning. These responsibilities are usually referred to as *supervision*. Done well, supervision enhances teacher development.

A first step in building a practical and meaningful supervisory program is willingness by the principal and by teachers to face up to, struggle with, and accept a more complex view of supervision and evaluation. Required next is dealing with the negative stereotypes of supervision emerging from its history of hierarchy, dominance, and control.

From the start it should be clear that no one-best-way strategy, model, or set of procedures for supervision makes sense. Instead, a differentiated system of supervision more in tune with growth levels, personality characteristics, needs and interests, and professional commitments of teachers is needed.

$\mathcal{S}$UPERVISION AND EVALUATION

When the focus of supervision is on teaching and learning, evaluation is an unavoidable aspect of the process. The literature is filled with reports and scenarios highlighting the disdain with which teachers regard evaluation (see, e.g., Blumberg, 1980). One reason for such attitudes is that evaluation has been too narrowly defined in both purpose and method. Evaluation is, and will remain, a part of supervision, and this reality cannot be ignored. Attempts to mask evaluation aspects of supervision by avoiding use of the term, by denying that evaluation occurs, or by declaring that evaluation is reserved only for the annual administrative review of one's teaching performance will not be helpful. Such claims are viewed suspiciously by teachers and for good reason—evaluation cannot be avoided. We are constantly evaluating everything that we experience, and our experiences with teachers and their teaching is no different.

Evaluation can be less of a problem if we expand its meaning within supervision. Evaluation, for example, is often defined narrowly as a process for calculating the extent to which teachers measure up to preexisting standards. Standards might be a program goal or teaching intent, or perhaps a list of "desirable" teaching competencies or performance criteria. Broader conceptions of evaluation include describing what is going on in a particular classroom, discovering learning outcomes actually achieved, and assessing their worth. In broader conceptions, the focus of evaluation is less on measuring and more on describing and illuminating teaching and learning events, as well as on identifying the array of meanings that these events have for different people. Evaluation broadly conceived involves judgment more than measurement. Judgments of teaching and learning are less fixed, more personal, and embedded in a particular context or situation (Dewey, 1958). Of interest in judgmental evaluation are particular teachers and students; specific teaching situations and events, and the actual teaching and learning issues, understandings, and meanings emerging from teaching. Although measuring against preexisting standards has its place in the process of supervision and evaluation, the present onerous view of evaluation will be greatly lessened if principals emphasize judgmental aspects.

Using the word *evaluation* in its ordinary, rather than technical, sense will also help dissipate its negative effects among teachers. Commonplace in our ordinary lives, evaluation is an inescapable aspect of most of what we do. Whether we are buying a pair of shoes, selecting a recipe for a dinner party, rearranging the living room furniture, or enjoying a movie, baseball game, or art show, evaluation is part of the process. In its ordinary sense, evaluation means to discern, understand, and appreciate, on the one hand, and to value, judge, and decide on the other. These very same natural and ordinary processes are at play in evaluating teaching. As in ordinary life, these processes serve to heighten our understanding and appreciation of teaching and to inform our intuition as we make decisions about teaching. Heightened sensitivity and informed intuition are the trademarks of accomplished practice in all the major professions. It is by increasing and informing their sensitivities and intuitions that attorneys, architects, and physicians make better practice decisions and improve their performance. Professional practice in teaching, supervision, and the principalship improve similarly.

Supervision and evaluation of teaching should look for answers to the following questions:

- What is actually going on in this classroom?
- What is the teacher and what are students actually doing?
- What are the actual learning outcomes?
- What ought to be going on in this classroom, given our overall goals, educational platform, knowledge of how children learn, and understandings of the structure of the subject matter to be taught?
- What do these events and activities of teaching and learning mean to teachers, students, and others?
- What are the personal meanings that students accumulate regardless of teacher intents?
- How do teacher and principal interpretations of teaching reality differ?
- What actions should be taken to bring about even greater understanding of teaching and learning and better congruence between our actions and beliefs?

These questions provide a broader and more complex conception of the supervisory process than that implied just in rating teachers or in measuring outcomes for comparison with stated intents. Indeed, for supervision to work the way it should, teachers must share responsibility for its success. This means teachers have to assume roles as supervisors too—working with each other to improve their teaching and even to help maintain quality control. Unless teachers accept this responsibility, supervision will remain what it too often is today—principals going into classes with checklists and making quick evaluations that have doubtful validity and little or no meaning to most teachers.

Principals too have a responsibility to view themselves as coaches and principal teachers who work side by side with teachers in planning lessons together, teaching together, and trying to understand what is going on in the class together. Principals who supervise by practicing coaching by walking around can make a significant impact in helping, in building trust, and in learning with their teachers.

Purposes

The multifaceted nature of teacher supervision and evaluation can be illustrated by providing a framework for describing and bringing together key dimensions of the process. Included in this framework are general purposes of supervision and evaluation, specific perspectives that stem from these purposes, key competency areas that serve as benchmarks for evaluation, and critical knowledge areas that help define and describe teaching competence. This framework is designed to help principals analyze supervisory problems and plan supervisory strategies.

What is supervision for? Who is to be served? Why evaluate? How one answers such questions determines how one approaches the tasks of supervision and evaluation and influences the relationships emerging among teachers and between teachers and the principal. Supervision and evaluation have many purposes. These range from ensuring that minimum standards are being met and that teachers are being faithful to the school's overall purposes and educational platform, to helping teachers grow and develop as persons and professionals. Purposes can be grouped into three major categories:

1. *Quality Control.* The principal is responsible for monitoring teaching and learning in her or his school and does so by regularly visiting classrooms, touring the school, talking with people, and visiting with students.
2. *Professional Development.* The principal is responsible for helping teachers to grow and to develop in their understanding of teaching and classroom life, in improving basic teaching skills, and in expanding their knowledge and use of teaching repertoires.
3. *Teacher Motivation.* The principal is responsible for building and nurturing motivation and commitment to teaching, to the school's overall purposes, and to the school's defining educational platform.

One hallmark of a good supervisory system is that it reflects these multiple purposes. No supervisory system based on a single purpose can succeed over time. A system that focuses only on quality control invites difficulties with teachers and lacks needed expansive qualities. By the same token, a supervisory system concerned solely with providing support and help to teachers (and thus, by omission, neglects teaching deficiencies and instances where overriding purposes and defining platforms are ignored) is not sufficiently comprehensive. Quality control and teacher improvement are therefore basic purposes that should drive any system of supervision and evaluation. A third purpose, often neglected but important in the long run, is that of teacher motivation. Overwhelming evidence exists suggesting that "knowledge of results" is an important ingredient in increasing a person's motivation to work and in building commitment and loyalty to one's job (Hackman and Oldham, 1976; Hackman et al., 1975). Further, perhaps the strongest motivation is success. Teachers who are more successful are more committed, more willing to share their practice, and more likely to improve.

Different Purposes, Different Standards

Different teacher-evaluation purposes require different teacher-evaluation standards and criteria. When the purpose is quality control to ensure that teachers measure up, standards, criteria, expectations, and procedures take one form. When the purpose is professional improvement to help increase teachers' understanding and enhance teaching practice, standards, criteria, expectations, and procedures take on a different form. In evaluation for quality control, the process is formal and documented; criteria are explicit and standards are uniform for all teachers; criteria are legally defensible as being central to basic teaching competence; the emphasis is on teachers meeting requirements of minimum acceptability; and responsibility for evaluation is in the hands of administrators and other designated officials. When the purpose of teacher evaluation is professional improvement, the process is informal; criteria are tailored to the needs and capabilities of individual teachers; criteria are considered to be appropriate and useful to teachers before they are included in the evaluation; the emphasis is on helping teachers reach agreed-upon professional development goals; and teachers assume major responsibility for the process by engaging in self-evaluation and collegial evaluation and by obtaining evaluation information from students.

The outcome of evaluation for quality control is the protection of students and the public from incompetent teaching. Unquestionably, this is an important outcome and a highly significant responsibility for principals and other supervisors. The outcome of evaluation for professional improvement is quite different. Rather than ensuring minimum acceptability in teaching, professional improvement guarantees quality teaching and schooling for the students and the public.

The *80/20 quality rule* spells out what the balance of emphasis should be as schools engage in teacher evaluation. *When more than 20 percent of the principal's time and money is expended in evaluation for quality control or when less than 80 percent of the principal's time and money is spent in professional improvement, quality schooling suffers.* The 80/20 quality rule provides a framework for those responsible for evaluation of teachers to evaluate whether their efforts are indeed directed toward quality schooling. In making this assessment, one should give less attention to the rhetoric that one hears (i.e., to what those responsible for teacher evaluation say their purposes are) and more to the standards and procedures that they use. The standards and procedures associated with each of the two purposes of evaluation are outlined in Exhibit 12.1. If the standards at the left side of the exhibit are emphasized, quality control is the purpose of the evaluation regardless of what is claimed.

Teaching Competency Areas

The typical evaluation program puts the emphasis on the wrong thing. It relies almost exclusively on classroom observations of teaching behaviors and recording the presence or absence of these behaviors on instruments and forms. This results in placing the emphasis on whether the teacher can do the job as required while being observed. Even if it were possible to identify the correct list of teaching behaviors, the approach is still narrow. A good evaluation is not only concerned with "can do," but with other teaching competency areas, as well.

What are the major competency areas for which teachers should be accountable? Teachers should *know how* to do their jobs and to keep this knowledge current. The areas of knowledge for professional teaching include purposes, students, subject matter to be taught, and teaching techniques. However, knowing and understanding are not enough; teachers should be able to put this knowledge to work—to demonstrate that they *can do* the job of teaching. Demonstrating knowledge, however, is a fairly low-level competency. Most teachers are competent enough and adept enough to come up with the right teaching performance when they are required to do so. More important is whether they *will do* the job well consistently and on a sustained basis. Finally, all professionals are expected to engage in a lifelong commitment to self-improvement. Self-improvement is the *will-grow* competency area. Self-employed professionals, such as physicians and attorneys, are forced by competition and by more visible performance outputs to give major attention to the will-grow dimension. Teachers are "organizational" professionals whose "products" are difficult to measure and who have not felt as much external pressure for continued professional development. Increasingly, however, school districts are making the will-grow dimension a significant part of their supervision and evaluation program. As teachers strive for further professionalism, they too recognize the importance of this dimension.

Thus, a comprehensive system of supervision and evaluation is concerned with all four professional development competency areas: knowledge about

exhibit
12.1

Purposes and Standards for Evaluation

Purpose

Quality control (ensuring that teachers meet acceptable levels of performance).

Professional improvement (increasing understanding of teaching and enhancing practice).

Standards

The process is formal and documented.

The process is informal.

Criteria are explicit, standard, and uniform for all teachers.

Criteria are tailored to needs and capabilities of individual teachers.

Criteria are legally defensible as being central to basic teaching competence.

Criteria are considered appropriate and useful to teachers.

Emphasis is on meeting minimum requirements of acceptability.

Emphasis is on helping teachers reach agreed-upon professional development goals.

Evaluation by administrators and other designated officials counts the most.

Self-evaluation, collegial evaluation, and evaluation information for students count the most.

Outcome

Protects students and the public from incompetent teaching.

Fosters quality teaching and schooling for students and the public.

The 80/20 Quality Rule: When more than 20 percent of supervisory time and money is expended in evaluation for quality control *or* less than 80 percent of supervisory time and money is expended in professional improvement, quality schooling suffers.

Source: From *Supervision: A Redefinition,* 8th ed. (p. 236) by Thomas J. Sergiovanni and Robert J. Starratt, 2007, New York: McGraw-Hill. Reproduced with permission of The McGraw-Hill Companies.

teaching, ability to demonstrate this knowledge by actual teaching under observation, willingness to sustain this ability continuously, and demonstration of a commitment to continuous professional growth. Although each of the competency areas represents a discrete category that suggests different evaluation strategies, the four remain largely interdependent in practice. When observing classrooms, principals naturally are interested in the knowledge base exhibited by teachers. Most observations, in turn, lead to issues and ideas that form the basis for informing continuing growth plans and more formal staff development programs.

When one takes into account different evaluation purposes and perspectives and different teaching competence and substance areas, it becomes clear that limiting one's supervision and evaluation strategy to only classroom observation, rating scales, paper-and-pencil tests, target setting, clinical supervision, portfolio development, or any other single strategy does not account for the complexities involved in providing a comprehensive, meaningful, and useful system of evaluation. In summary, principals are responsible for the school's supervisory program. At the very minimum, this responsibility includes ensuring that a helpful, useful, and comprehensive system of supervision is operating. Teachers should report that they find the system helpful and satisfying. The following are questions that can reasonably be asked in evaluating a school's supervisory program:

- Are teachers involved in shaping, implementing, and evaluating the supervisory program?
- Are multiple purposes provided for? Does the program, for example, address issues of quality control, professional development, and teacher motivation and commitment? Are formative, summative, and diagnostic perspectives all included in the program?
- Is the program sufficiently comprehensive to include know how, can do, will do, and will grow as basic teaching performance expectations?
- Does the program focus on improving knowledge and skill in such basic teaching essentials as purpose, student needs and characteristics, subject matter, and teaching techniques?

These questions highlight the importance of including teacher development programs as part of the school's overall design for supervision. The major emphasis in supervision should be on teacher growth and development. Both supervision and teacher development should be planned and provided as interdependent parts of a school's overall commitment to striving for quality.

$\mathcal{L}$INKING TEACHER DEVELOPMENT TO SCHOOL EFFECTIVENESS

This chapter began by acknowledging the link between teacher learning and school improvement and it is on this theme that the chapter ends. It is now widely accepted that for schools to be effectively responsive to new demands to teach all students at a high level, teacher development must become a top priority. Writing in *The Education of Teachers: Ninety-Eighth Yearbook of the National Society for the Study of Education* (1999), Darling-Hammond points out:

> A growing body of research finds that teacher expertise is one of the more important school factors influencing student achievement, followed by the smaller but generally positive influences of small schools and small class sizes. That is, teachers who know much about teaching and learning and who work in environments that allow them to know students well are critical elements of successful learning.

Studies of student achievement in Texas [Ferguson, 1991], Alabama [Ferguson and Ladd, 1996], and New York [Armour-Thomas et al., 1989], for example, have concluded that teachers' qualifications (based on measures of knowledge, education, and experience) account for a larger share of the variance in students' achievement than any other single factor. (228)

Little (1997) sums up the importance of teacher development to school success as follows:

Schools that exhibit a high level of success with students, sometimes against considerable odds, supply consistent portraits of work environments conducive to teacher learning. In these portraits, teacher learning arises out of close involvement with students and their work; shared responsibility for student progress; sensibly organized time; access to the expertise of colleagues inside and outside the school; focused and timely feedback on individual performance and on aspects of classroom or school practice; and then overall ethos in which teacher learning is valued and professional community cultivated. (Chapter 12:1)

Little found that schools are likely to be successful to the extent that they emphasize teachers' individual and collective responsibility for student learning; organize teachers' work in ways that provide enhanced opportunities for teacher learning; use staff development resources to increase the school's ability to obtain feedback on its own performance and use this feedback in making better decisions; and redirect its staff development and other assessment efforts in a manner which is consistent with teacher learning.

HELPING TEACHERS ACHIEVE GOALS

The key to developing a supervisory approach that supports student learning is a very simple but deceptive axiom. Teachers have professional goals that are important to them. Given the opportunity, they will work diligently to achieve these goals. In many respects, supervision is little more than a system of help for teachers as they achieve goals that they consider important. Principals are needed to provide help as this process unfolds.

House (1971) proposed a "path-goal" theory of leadership that summarizes much of our discussion and provides a handle on key aspects of effective helping. He believes that leaders are responsible for "increasing the number and kinds of personal payoffs to the subordinates for the work-goal attainment and making paths to these payoffs easiest to travel by clarifying the paths, reducing roadblocks and pitfalls, and increasing the opportunities for personal satisfaction en route" (323).

Translated to teacher supervision, principals assume responsibility for "clarifying and clearing the path" toward goals that teachers consider important.

Clarifying the path requires that goals be set and reasonably defined and understood. Ambiguous and unstructured situations and unclear expectations can be a source of frustration and dissatisfaction for teachers. Thus, it becomes important to provide the necessary task emphasis to help clarify goals. Clearing the path requires that principals provide the necessary assistance, education, support, and reinforcement to help achieve goals. Key to a path-goal approach is understanding that the richer sources of satisfaction for teachers come not from an emphasis on human relationships and social interaction separate from the accomplishment of work but from having accomplished worthwhile and challenging tasks within a pleasant atmosphere.

SOME REFLECTIONS

1. How would you differentiate between supervision and evaluation?
2. The text notes that the 80/20 quality rule spells out what the balance of emphasis should be as schools engage in teacher evaluation. When more than 20 percent of the principal's time and money is expended in evaluation for quality control or when less than 80 percent of the principal's time and money is spent in professional improvement, quality schooling suffers. How is teacher evaluation/supervision time used in your school? Does the 80/20 rule fit? As you size up your principal and other principals that you know, what percent of their time are they spending on evaluation for quality control and what percent of their time are they spending in building the capacities of teachers so that they are more effective in the classroom?

REFERENCES

Armour-Thomas, Eleanor, et al. 1989. *An Outline Study of Elementary and Middle Schools in New York City: Final Report.* New York: New York City Board of Education.

Blumberg, Art. 1980. *Supervisors and Teachers: A Private Cold War* (2nd ed.). Berkeley, CA: McCutchan.

Bolin, Frances S. 1987. "Reassessment and Renewal in Teaching," in F. S. Bolin and J. McConnel Falk (Eds.), *Teacher Renewal: Professional Issues, Personal Choices.* New York: Teachers College Press.

Bolin, Frances S., and Judith McConnell Falk (Eds.). 1987. *Teacher Renewal: Professional Issues, Personal Choices.* New York: Teachers College Press.

Darling-Hammond, Linda. 1999. "Educating Teachers for the Next Century: Rethinking Practice and Policy," in Gary A. Griffin (Ed.), *The Education of Teachers: Ninety-Eighth Yearbook of the National Society for the Study of Education* (pp. 221–256). Chicago: University of Chicago Press.

David, Jane L., and Patrick M. Shields. 1999, April 14. "Standards Are Not Magic," *Education Week,* 40, 42.

Dewey, John. 1958. *Art as Experience.* New York: Putnam.

Ferguson, R. F. 1991, Summer. "Paying for Public Education: New Evidence on How and Why Money Matters," *Harvard Journal on Legislation* 28(2), 465–498.

Ferguson, R. F., and H. F. Ladd. 1996. "How and Why Money Matters: An Analysis of Alabama Schools," in Helen Ladd (Ed.), *Holding Schools Accountable* (pp. 265–298). Washington, DC: Brookings Institution.

Hackman, J. R., and Greg Oldham. 1976. "Motivation through the Design of Work: Test of a Theory," *Organizational Behavior and Human Performance* 16(2), 250–279.

Hackman, J. R., G. Oldham, R. Johnson, and K. Purdy. 1975. "A New Strategy for Job Enrichment," *California Management Review* 17(4).

House, Robert J. 1971. "A Path Goal Theory of Leader Effectiveness," *Administrative Science Quarterly* 16(3), 321–338.

Little, Judith Warren. 1993. "Teachers' Professional Development in a Climate of Educational Reform," *Educational Evaluation and Policy Analysis* 15(2), 129–151.

Little, Judith Warren. 1997, March. "Excellence in Professional Development and Professional Community," Working Paper, Benchmarks for Schools. Washington, DC: Office of Educational Research and Improvement, U.S. Department of Education.

Mintzberg, Henry. 1987, July–August. "Crafting Strategy," *Harvard Business Review* 65(4), 66–75.

Peterson, Penelope L., Sarah J. McCarthey, and Richard F. Elmore. 1996. "Learning from School Restructuring," *American Educational Research Journal* 33(1), 119–153.

Schön, Donald. 1983. *The Reflective Practitioner: How Professionals Think in Action.* New York: Basic Books.

Sergiovanni, Thomas J. 2000. *The Lifeworld of Leadership: Creating Culture, Community and Personal Meaning in Our Schools.* San Francisco: Jossey-Bass.

Thelan, Herbert. 1971. "A Cultural Approach to In-Service Education," in Louis Rubin (Ed.), *Improving In-Service Education* (pp. 72–73). Boston: Allyn and Bacon.

Viadero, Debra. 1999, February 10. "A Key to High Achievement," *Education Week,* 27.

Wilson, Suzanne M., and Penelope L. Peterson. 1997. "Theories of Learning and Teaching: What Do They Mean for Educators?" Working Paper, Benchmarks for Schools. Washington, DC: Office of Educational Research and Improvement, U.S. Department of Education.

Zimpher, Nancy L., and Kenneth R. Howey. 1987. "Adapting Supervisory Practice to Different Orientations of Teaching," *Journal of Curriculum and Supervision* 2(2), 101–127.

13

CLINICAL SUPERVISION, COACHING, PEER INQUIRY, AND OTHER SUPERVISORY PRACTICES

*P*rincipals can no longer get away with just talking about the importance of teacher quality to advancing teaching and learning and the importance of building up the collective intelligence of their schools. They must take the lead by visibly and directly assuming supervisory responsibilities. They can do this by modeling what they say they believe. And they can do this by helping teachers to accept their share of responsibility for building a culture of supervision in the school that encourages teachers to learn together and to work together.

This chapter provides a number of practices that principals and teachers can use as they share responsibility for leadership and supervision. Think of this chapter as a field guide that outlines suggestions for a faculty to consider. There are no hard, fixed rules as to how these ideas might be implemented. Thus, experimenting with them and creating variations that make sense for your context and needs is encouraged.

A good supervisory system has both common and differentiated features. Common features are necessary to ensure instructional coherence. Newmann and colleagues (2001) define instructional coherence as "a set of interrelated programs for students and staff that are guided by a common framework for curriculum, instruction, assessment, and learning climate and that are pursued over a sustained period" (297). They state further, "Reform that strengthens instructional program coherence contrasts with efforts to improve schools through the adoption of a wide variety of programs that are often uncoordinated or limited in scope or duration" (297). With instructional coherence in place the school is better able to communicate what it considers to be important, to tell its storyline, and to emphasize the expectations that it holds for everyone. These conditions make it easier for the school to implement its values and to achieve its purposes. Further, common aspects provide a framework of ideas that principals can use as a source of authority for their leadership. When a common system of supervision is combined with a differentiated system of supervision an even more powerful force is created. A differentiated system provides options and responds to the individual interests and needs of teachers. These interests and needs are linked, nonetheless, to a common framework that helps define what the school's purposes are and what needs to be done to achieve them. (See also the discussion of coherence that appears in Chapter 5.)

Teacher learning passes the accountability test when teachers are able to show how what they learn changes their practice and helps students to be more connected to learning and to achieve at higher levels. Communities of practice are strengthened by this learning. Members of communities of practice are committed to learning, sharing, and caring together. Trusting relationships are key. Why do we need communities of practice? Because they build up the critical collegiality that leads to a shared practice of teaching.

The rationale for a differentiated approach to supervision is simple: Teachers are different. They have different needs and temperaments, and these needs should be recognized. When they are, teachers are likely to respond more positively to supervision than when a one-best-way approach is used. To change the system, the roles of principals and teachers also have to change. Teachers will have to assume the responsibility for developing approaches to supervision that are responsive to the issues they face in their practice. They will also have to play key roles in deciding which options for supervision make most sense to them. Most importantly, they will have to accept responsibility for making the options work. They will, in other words, have to become supervisors, too—not supervisors in the old factory sense of monitoring, inspecting, and evaluating, but in the sense of colleagues working together to help each other understand their own teaching and to improve their practices.

In any professional field, supervision that is responsive to the needs of practice must be responsive as well to the learning requirements of professional practitioners. A good place to start is with what is known about how adults, particularly professionals, learn. They learn best when they have opportunities to become self-reliant, depending less on their institution and its programs and less on formal supervision. They learn best when what is being learned emerges from the problems they face in their everyday practice and when learning is situated in a real context. They learn best when they function as members of a community of practice who are connected together by reciprocal commitments and obligations to each other and to shared goals. They learn best when they have an opportunity to discover for themselves and to experiment with ideas and practices in their own contexts. They learn best when they have the time and encouragement to reflect on their practice and that of their colleagues.

In such a design, principals would not be excluded. They have important roles to play. They need to give leadership to the supervisory program, marshall resources to make sure the program works, help provide the administrative structures and other arrangements that will enable teachers to work effectively together, and participate as supervisors—engaging in dialogue and helping in the improvement of teaching wherever they can.

CLINICAL SUPERVISION AS AN EXAMPLE

It is important that supervision reach deeply into the culture of schools. This happens best when supervision is

- Sometimes direct and other times indirect
- Sometimes centered in the classroom and at other times centered out of class
- Sometimes focused on issues important to teachers and at other times focused on issues important to others
- Sometimes aimed at helping teachers understand and improve their practice and other times aimed to gauging their effectiveness
- Sometimes collaborative and, at other times, individual

When supervision is direct, centered in the classroom, focused on teachers' issues, aimed primarily at helping teachers understand and improve their teaching, and collaborative, the term *clinical supervision* is often used to describe it. Experts agree that clinical supervision in a variety of forms has potential to accelerate the rates of learning for teachers and to significantly improve teaching and learning in our schools. Still we have a long way to go in realizing this potential. Clinical supervision is time-consuming and takes a lot of effort to do well under our current bureaucratic patterns of schooling. But supervisors and teachers who are serious about improving schools will find clinical supervision to be a powerful and appealing strategy worth the extra effort. Much will depend on whether principals and other designated supervisors will invest in helping teachers assume more responsibility for supervising themselves than is now the case. Teacher leadership is essential if principals are to be the instructional leaders most aspire to be. Wise principals know they cannot do it alone. Morris Cogan (1973) defines *clinical supervision* as follows:

> The rationale and practice is designed to improve the teacher's classroom performance. It takes its principal data from the events of the classroom. The analysis of

these data and the relationships between teacher and supervisor form the basis of the program, procedures, and strategies designed to improve the students' learning by improving the teacher's classroom behavior. (54)

In a similar vein, Robert Goldhammer (1969) refers to clinical supervision as follows:

First of all, I mean to convey an image of face-to-face relationships between supervisors and teachers. History provides the principal reason for this emphasis, namely, that in many situations presently and during various periods in its development, supervision has been conducted as supervision from a distance, as, for example, supervision of curriculum development or of instructional policies framed by committees of teachers. "Clinical" supervision is meant to imply supervision up close. (54)

The purposes of clinical supervision are to help teachers to understand their practice better and to examine existing patterns of teaching in ways that make sense to them. Evaluation is therefore responsive to the needs and desires of the teacher. It is the teacher who decides the course of a clinical supervisory cycle, the issues to be discussed, and for what purpose. Obviously, principals and teacher colleagues who serve as clinical supervisors will bring to this interaction a considerable amount of influence; however, ideally, this influence should stem from their being in a position to provide the help and clarification needed by teachers. The supervisor's job is to help the teacher select goals to be improved and teaching issues to be illuminated, and to understand better her or his practice. This emphasis on understanding provides the avenue by which more technical assistance can be given to the teacher; thus, clinical supervision involves, as well, the systematic analysis of classroom events. Clinical supervision, then, is a framework for helping teachers research their practice. The role of supervisor can be assumed by a teacher, principal, or other colleague.

The Cycle of Clinical Supervision

Most authorities (e.g., Goldhammer, 1969) suggest that a sequence of clinical supervision contain five general steps or stages, as follows:

1. Preobservation conference
2. Observation of teaching and collection of other material that might be helpful
3. Analysis and strategy
4. Postobservation conference
5. Postconference analysis

Preobservation Conference.   No stage is more important than the preobservation conference. It is here that the framework for observations is developed and an agreement is reached between the person who is "supervising" and the person who is teaching. Sometimes this person is the principal, and at other times this person is a teacher colleague. After a brief warm-up period, the supervisor needs to become familiar with the class and with the teacher's way of thinking about teaching. How does the teacher view this class? What are the qualities and characteristics of this class? What frames of reference regarding purposes, models of teaching, classroom management, and so forth does the teacher bring to teaching? Getting into the teacher's "corner" and understanding the class from her or his perspective should help the supervisor understand what the teacher has in mind for the particular teaching sequence that will be observed. How the particular lesson in question fits into the teacher's broader framework of purposes and view of teaching is also essential to provide the supervisor with a perspective beyond the particular lesson at hand.

The supervisor is now ready to engage the teacher in a mental or conceptual *rehearsal* of the lesson. The teacher provides an overview of her or his intents, outcomes not formally anticipated but likely or possible, and problems likely to be encountered. An overview of how teaching will unfold, what the teacher and students will be doing, and anticipated responses from students should also be provided. The supervisor might wish to raise questions for clarification and, depending on the relationship existing between supervisor and teacher, to make suggestions for improving the lesson before it unfolds.

Typically, this conceptual rehearsal by the teacher identifies an array of teaching issues of interest. Clinical supervision is selective in the sense that an intense and detailed study is made of only a handful of issues at a time. Thus, supervisor and teacher must decide what aspects of teaching will be considered, with the teacher assuming major responsibility for setting the supervisory agenda. What would the teacher like to know about this class and the teaching that will take place? On what aspects of teaching would she or he like feedback? Teachers inexperienced with clinical supervision may have initial difficulty in suggesting agenda items, but careful prodding and guiding by the supervisor usually help to elicit meaningful issues that become the basis for a particular cycle of supervision. This phase of the conference concludes with the teacher and supervisor reaching a fairly explicit agreement or "contract" about the reasons for supervision, along with the teaching and learning agendas to be studied. The contract might contain, as well, some indication of the information to be collected, how this information will be collected, what the supervisor will be doing, and what the supervisor should not do. Clinical supervision advocates feel that the teacher should have as complete as possible a picture of events to occur as the process of supervision unfolds.

Observation of Teaching.   The second stage in a clinical supervision cycle—and basic to it—is the actual and systematic observation of teaching. Attention is given to the teacher *in action* and to the classroom story unfolding as a result of this action. Clinical supervision purists would argue that "canned" or standardized devices, or scales for ratings of general teaching characteristics, may well be useful but in themselves are not sufficient; and when used, they should stem from, and be related to, the actual observation of teaching and learning at issue. It is what the teacher actually says and does, how students react, and what actually occurs during a specific teaching episode under study that remains the center of evaluation to advocates of clinical supervision. Student interviews, collections of classroom artifacts, development of evaluation portfolios, bulletin board and classroom arrangements, photo essays, inventories of lessons accomplished by children or books read, and other evaluative data collection strategies should supplement and illuminate this actual teaching.

The teacher will know what to expect because of the preobservation conference. He or she should understand that the supervisor wishes to make an unobtrusive entrance and to remain as unobtrusive as possible. During the observation, the clinical supervisor may take copious notes attempting to record all classroom events. Notes should be descriptive—that is, free from inferences; for example, the supervisor would avoid writing "during the questioning of students on the use of microscopes by criminologists, the students were bored" in favor of something such as "John and Mary both did not hear the question when it was asked" and "two students were looking out the window; a third was playing with materials in his desk during the microscope questioning time." Sometimes the information collected is focused on a particular issue, such as cognitive level of questions, attention spans of children, time on task, or cooperative relationships among students. Then, instead of attempting to record everything that takes place during the lesson, the supervisor might record and rate each question asked on the Bloom Taxonomy of Educational Objectives or collect similar, more detailed information. Many clinical supervision purists insist on a written transcript or the collection of firsthand data by the supervisor, and many supervisors using clinical methods have been successful by using television and videotaping equipment or by using audiotaping equipment to record actual teaching. At the conclusion of the observation, the supervisor leaves the classroom as unobtrusively as possible.

Analysis and Strategy.   The third step in the cycle of clinical supervision is the analysis of teaching and the building of a supervisory strategy. The analysis stage requires that the supervisor convert the raw data, or information collected from the observation, into a manageable, meaningful, and sensible form. Clinical supervision advocates recommend that the analysis yield significant teaching patterns and that critical incidents be identified for use in the supervisory conference. Of paramount importance is the contract initially struck with the teacher. What was the purpose of the observation? How did the information collected illuminate this purpose? Can the supervisor arrange this information in a fashion that communicates clearly to the teacher the feedback she or he seeks but at the same time does not prejudge the teaching? This process identifies teaching patterns: recurring teacher verbal and nonverbal behaviors discovered in the course of teaching. Critical incidents are those occurrences that have a particularly noticeable positive or negative effect on the teaching and learning.

Having organized the information, the supervisor now gives attention to building a strategy for working with the teacher. The supervisor takes into account the nature of the contract originally struck, the evaluation issues uncovered during the observation and analysis, the quality of interpersonal relationships existing between teacher and supervisor, the authority base from which she or he is operating, and the competency or experience level of the teacher in deciding on this strategy.

Postobservation Conference. The fourth stage in the cycle of clinical supervision is the supervisory conference. The supervisor uses the specific information gathered to help the teacher analyze the lesson. Typically, this postobservation conference focuses on a handful of issues previously agreed on by the teacher and supervisor. It is appropriate as well for the supervisor to introduce new issues as circumstances warrant, but these issues should be few and cautiously introduced. The emphasis remains on providing information to the teacher for fulfilling the contract that was the basis for the observation cycle. Furthermore, the emphasis is not on providing evaluative information but on providing *descriptive* information. The process of making sense of this information is a joint one shared by teacher and supervisor.

Let's assume that the most important issue identified and agreed to in the preconference is "level of cognitive questioning" used by the teacher and cognitive level of assignments given to the students. The teacher uses objectives that span all six levels of the Bloom Taxonomy of Educational Objectives but wishes to emphasize the higher-level objectives of analysis and synthesis. Perhaps this teacher is not confident that actual teaching emphasizes these levels; or perhaps the supervisor, suspecting that teaching is not matching teacher intents, suggests that the level of cognitive questionings be examined. In either event, teacher and supervisor agree to use an inventory that enables the sorting of questions asked into the Bloom categories: remembering, understanding, solving, analyzing, creating, and judging. During the observation of teaching, each question asked by the teacher is classified into an appropriate level. A transcript of actual questions asked could be prepared. During the analysis and strategy stage of the supervisory cycle, the supervisor tallies questions and computes percentages.

The supervisor then decides on a strategy whereby the teacher is asked to restate her or his purposes for the lesson as well as for the unit of which the lesson is a part. The cognitive level of questioning information is then presented and compared with the teacher's intents. The supervisor is careful to avoid drawing conclusions or to elaborate on possible discrepancies, considering these conclusions to be the responsibility of the teacher. The teacher and supervisor might decide that it would be helpful to collect homework assignments given for other lessons in this

Some Suggestions for Providing Helpful Feedback to Teachers

exhibit

13.1

1. *When giving feedback to teachers, be descriptive rather than judgmental.* Clinical supervision is designed to help teachers improve ongoing teaching and should not be used as a device for summative evaluation designed to determine the value of a person or program. For example, instead of saying to a biology teacher, "You are spending too much time in lecture and not enough time with students engaged in field work and laboratory," try, "Your time log shows that you spent 85 percent of class time these past two weeks in lecture. Let's look at your objectives and plans for this unit and see if this is what you intended."

2. *When giving feedback to teachers, be specific rather than general.* General statements tend to be misunderstood more than specific statements. Instead of saying to a teacher, "You interrupt students and tend not to listen to what they are saying," try, "When you asked John a question, you interrupted his response and seemed uninterested in what he had to say." A cassette transcript of the question, response attempt, and interruptions would be helpful.

3. *When giving feedback to teachers, concentrate on things that can be changed.* A teacher may have little control over a nervous twitch or voice quality, but much can be done about arranging seats, grouping students, improving balance between knowledge level and other objectives, and disciplining students.

4. *When giving feedback to teachers, consider your own motives.* Often, feedback is given to impress teachers with one's knowledge or for some other reason that builds the supervisor's status. Feedback is intended for only one purpose—to help the teacher know and understand her or his actual behavior as a teacher and consequences of this behavior on teaching and learning.

5. *Give the teacher feedback at a time as close to the actual behavior as possible.* Details of events are likely to be forgotten easily. Furthermore, fairly prompt attention is likely to upgrade and personalize the importance of clinical supervision.

6. *When giving feedback to teachers, rely as much as possible on information whose accuracy can be reasonably documented.* Photographs of bulletin boards, audio- and videotapes of teachers and students at work, a portfolio of classroom tests, a record of books borrowed from the class library, the number of students who return to shop during free periods or after school, and a tally of questions asked by the teacher sorted into the hierarchy of educational objectives are examples of documented feedback. It will not always be possible or desirable to provide this type of highly descriptive feedback, but it is important, nevertheless, as a technique, for clinical supervision cannot be overemphasized.

particular teaching unit as well as to examine questions on tests that have been used. These assignments and test questions could also be categorized into the cognitive level of questioning format. Throughout the process, the supervisor's role is not to condemn, cajole, or admonish, but to provide information useful to the teacher and in a supportive atmosphere. Some suggestions for providing helpful feedback to teachers are provided in Exhibit 13.1.

Postconference Analysis. The fifth and final stage in a cycle of clinical supervision is the postconference analysis. The postconference phase is a natural springboard to staff development for both teacher and supervisor. The supervisor evaluates what happened in the supervisory conference and throughout the supervisory cycle for purposes of improving her or his own efforts. Was the integrity of the teacher protected? Did the teacher participate in the process as a cosupervisor? Was feedback given in response to the teacher's needs and desires? Was the emphasis more on teaching and the improvement of teaching than on teacher and evaluating the teacher? What can the supervisor do to improve her or his skills in clinical supervision? A typical outcome of the first four phases of clinical supervision is agreement on the kinds of issues to be pursued next as further cycles are undertaken. The postconference analysis is, therefore, both the end of one cycle and the beginning of another.

A SHORTCUT STRATEGY
FOR CLINICAL SUPERVISION

More often than not logistical issues, schedules, and other real-world demands will make it difficult to follow all of the steps as outlined above. If you are pressed, try the shortcut strategy outlined in Exhibit 13.2.

Sometimes clinical supervision works best when teachers join together in teams of three. This configuration allows teacher A to be helped by teachers B and C and then to rotate so that B is helped by A and C and finally C is helped by A and B. The clinical supervision checklist found in Exhibit 13.3 will be helpful in guiding this enlarged version of clinical supervision. Notice it is important that

 exhibit **Clinical Supervision Shortcut Strategy**

13.2

1. *Preconference*
   Identify the issue to be investigated. Develop a strategy for collecting data and other sources of information.
2. *Collecting the Information*
   Observe teaching, and collect other sources of information that may be important. Put this information into a form that the teacher will easily understand.
3. *Postconference*
   Share your findings. Help the teacher to make sense of them.

exhibit
13.3
Team Evaluation Checklist for Clinical Supervision

Issue Oriented

a) Did you identify a single issue or theme as a focus for your inquiry?

Collaboration

b) Did you *together* develop a strategy for how this strategy or theme might be researched?

Strategy

c) Was this strategy specific enough to detail both the kind of information (or data) that would be collected and the data collection means?

Critical Friend

d) Did you present the information as primarily "brute" data with a minimum of evaluative comments?

Self-Evaluation

e) Did you help the teacher make sense of this data (go from brute to sense data) and draw conclusions relating to the original issue or theme that was the focus of the inquiry in the first place?

Communities of Practice

f) Before you began this process of clinical supervision did you share your plans with other members of your team?

g) After the three investigations were conducted did you share your findings with each other?

the teacher being helped be involved in identifying the issue and in helping develop the strategy for supervision. This person also plays the key role in trying to make sense of the data and other information that is collected.

Is Clinical Supervision for Everyone?

Clinical supervision, as just outlined, is demanding in the time it requires from both supervisor and teachers. Principals who have difficulty finding the time to use this approach with all teachers might reserve it for working with two or three teachers at a time. If it is desirable for more teachers to be involved, then using collegial or peer clinical supervision may be the answer. Here, teachers take turns assuming the role of clinical supervisor as they help each other. Collegial clinical supervision, however, often results in teachers being burdened with additional time demands. Furthermore, participation requires much more training in conferencing, information collecting, interpreting, and other supervisory techniques than is typically necessary for other forms of supervision. If teachers are to be clinical supervisors, they will need to receive the proper training; this, too, can present problems because training takes time and is expensive.

A further issue is that formal clinical supervision may be too much supervision for some teachers. Although all teachers would profit from clinical supervision from time to time, it does not appear that this strategy should be used all the time for all teachers. Going through this process every second, third, or fourth year may be less burdensome and tiresome for some. Unfortunately, this supervisory process can become too routinized and ritualized if overused. Finally, teacher needs and dispositions as well as work and learning styles vary. Formal clinical supervision may be suitable for some teachers but not for others when these concerns are taken into consideration.

THE LESSON STUDY

The lesson study is a promising way to engage teachers in ongoing learning that is immersed in their practice and immersed in the practice of their colleagues. The lesson study has a research bent to it, encourages reflection, helps teachers engage in "shop floor" curriculum development, involves collegial study of a lesson or lessons while at the same time being practical for addressing issues teachers identify with and have to face in their daily practice. Not only are new lessons invented in the lesson study but they are field tested, revised, and improved as well. Old lessons get refitted. Indeed, even packaged lessons such as those one might find in a teachers' manual or in a professional journal can be improved by the lesson study. Further, norms of collegiality are transcended as teachers come together as members of communities of practice.

In their international studies James W. Stigler and James Hiebert (1999) found that the Japanese invest heavily in teacher learning and professional development and that they invest differently than we do with great success. The researchers noted that in Japan great emphasis is given to classroom lessons, how they are planned, what happens in live classrooms when specific lessons are used, and how these lessons might be continuously improved. In their words:

> In Japan, classroom lessons hold a privileged place in the activities of the school. It would be exaggerating only a little to say they are sacred. They are treated much as we treat lectures in university courses or religious services in church. A great deal of attention is given to their development. They are planned as complete experiences—as stories with a beginning, a middle, and an end. Their meaning is found in the connections between the parts. If you stay for only the beginning, or leave before the end, you miss the point. If lessons like this are going to succeed, they must be coherent. The pieces must relate to one another in clear ways. And they must flow along, free from interruptions and unrelated activities. . . . So the lesson must be a tightly connected, coherent story; the teacher must build a visible

record of the pieces as they unfold so connections can be drawn between them; and the lesson cannot be sidetracked or broken by interruptions. (95–96)

Because so many differences in conceptions and practices have cultural anchors, we must be cautious about wholesale borrowing of ideas for use in our schools. But one idea, the lesson study, may be worth considering for adoption in our culture. At the very least, the lesson study can be used to help develop a set of guidelines and standards. These guidelines and standards then might be used to invent something similar in intent but unique for use in our own schools.

In lesson study, groups of teachers meet regularly over a period of several months to design a new, or redesign an existing, lesson. This lesson is then implemented in view of colleagues who offer "critical friend" feedback. This critique and the suggestions that accompany it are directed to the lesson itself rather than the teachers. Thus, if things do not go well, it is assumed that everyone must work harder to refine or perhaps redefine the lesson itself, not the person teaching the lesson: From this test, a revised lesson is crafted and tried out followed by another critique and still more changes.

Stigler and Hiebert (1999) identify the following steps in the lesson study process:*

Step 1: *Defining the Problem.* Lesson study is, fundamentally, a problem-solving process. The first step, therefore, is to define the problem that will motivate and direct the work of the lesson-study group. The problem can start out as a general one (for example, to awaken students' interest in mathematics), or it can be more specific (for example, to improve students' understanding of how to add fractions with unlike denominators). The group will then shape and focus the problem until it can be addressed by a specific classroom lesson.

Step 2: *Planning the Lesson.* Once a learning goal has been chosen, teachers begin meeting to plan the lesson. Although one teacher will ultimately teach the lesson as part of the process, the lesson itself is seen by all involved as a group product. Often the teachers will start their planning by looking at books and articles produced by other teachers who have studied a similar problem. According to one Japanese book on how to prepare a research lesson, the useful research lesson should be designed with a hypothesis in mind: some idea to be tested and worked out within the context of classroom practice (Orihara, 1993). The goal is not only to produce an effective lesson but also to understand why and how the lesson works to promote understanding among students. The initial plan that the group produces is often presented at a schoolwide faculty meeting in order to solicit criticism. Based on such feedback, a revision is produced, ready for implementation. This initial planning process can take as long as several months.

Step 3: *Teaching the Lesson.* A date is set to teach the lesson. One teacher will teach the lesson, but everyone in the group will participate fully in the preparation. The night before, the group might stay late at school, preparing materials and engaging in a dress rehearsal, complete with role-playing. On the day of the lesson, the other teachers in the group leave their classrooms to observe the lesson being taught. The teachers stand or sit in the back as the lesson begins, but when students are asked to work at their desks, the teacher-observers walk around, observing and taking careful notes on what students are doing as the lesson progresses. Sometimes the lesson is videotaped as well, for later analysis and discussion.

Step 4: *Evaluating the Lesson and Reflecting on Its Effect.* The group generally stays after school to meet on the day the lesson has been taught. Usually, the teacher who taught the lesson is allowed to speak first, outlining in his or her own view on how the lesson worked and what the major problems were. Then other members of the group speak, usually critically, about the parts of the lesson they saw as problematic. The focus is on the lesson, not on the teacher who taught the lesson; the lesson, after all, is a group product, and all members of the group feel responsible for the outcome of their plan. They are, in effect, critiquing themselves. This is important, because it shifts the focus from a personal evaluation to a self-improvement activity.

Step 5: *Revising the Lesson.* Based on their observations and reflections, teachers in the lesson-study group revise the lesson. They might change the materials, the activities, the problems posed, the questions asked, or all these things. They often will base their changes on specific misunderstandings evidenced by students as the lesson progressed.

Step 6: *Teaching the Revised Lesson.* Once the revised lesson is ready, the lesson is taught again to a different class. Sometimes it is taught by the same teacher who taught the lesson the first time, but often it is taught by another member of the group. One difference is that this time all members of the school faculty are invited to attend the research lesson. This is quite dramatic in a large school, where there may be more faculty crowded into the classroom than there are students in the class.

Step 7: *Evaluating and Reflecting, Again.* This time, it is common for all members of the school faculty to participate in a long meeting. Sometimes an outside expert will be invited to attend as well. As before, the teacher who taught the lesson is allowed to speak first, discussing what the group was trying to accomplish, her or his own assessment of how successful the lesson was, and what parts of the lesson still need rethinking. Observers then critique the lesson and suggest changes. Not only is the lesson discussed with respect to what these students learned and understood, but also with respect to more general issues raised by the hypotheses that guided the design of the research lesson. What about teaching and learning, more generally, was learned from the lesson and its implementation?

Step 8: *Sharing the Results.* All this work has focused on a single lesson. But because Japan is a country with national education goals and curricular guidelines, what this group of teachers has learned will have immediate relevance for other Japanese teachers trying to teach the same concepts at the same grade level. Indeed, the teachers in one lesson-study group see the sharing of their findings as a significant part of the lesson-study process. This sharing can be done in several ways. One is to write a report, and most lesson-study groups do produce a report that tells the story of their group's work. Often these reports are published in book form, even if only for the school's teacher resource room. (112–115)

How viable is the lesson study as an option for supervision in our schools? What adjustments might be necessary for this approach to fit our way of doing things? Try sharing the description of the lesson study provided with some teachers in your school. What are their reactions? Do they have suggestions as to how this approach might be adapted? What principles does the lesson study embody that we can use to develop workable approaches to supervision that are rich in teacher learning? Stigler and Hiebert answer this last question as follows. The lesson study

- is based on long-term continuous improvement;
- maintains a continuous focus on student learning;
- focuses on the improvement of teaching in context;
- is collaborative;
- and involves teachers in the development of knowledge about teaching. (Stigler and Hiebert, 1999:121–125)

To this list we might add that the lesson study

- is teacher directed;
- deals with concrete reality and real issues of teaching and learning that teachers are facing;
- and leads to deep and reflective conversations about practice.

Supervision would be taking an important step in the right direction if these principles were our standard for the practice of supervision (Stepanek et al., 2007; Wiburg and Brown, 2007). Dennis Sparks, who is executive director of the National Staff Development Council, believes that we can close the "staff development gap" that exists in many schools by focusing our efforts on providing a practical model for continuous improvement of teaching that places teachers at the center of the school improvement process. He argues:

As both North American and international studies make clear, linking teacher learning to student learning and focusing on the daily improvement of instructional practice makes a difference in student achievement. While that may not be rocket science, research and practical experience are teaching us that it is the core premise that drives powerful staff development efforts. (2000:50)

Many school districts across the country are trying lesson study with good results. School 2, a K–8 school in Paterson, New Jersey, is an example (Viadero, 2004). The Paterson, New Jersey, story can be found at www.edweek.org/ew/ewstory .cfm?slug=22Lesson.h23&keywords=paterson%20.

PEER SUPERVISION

An alternative to structured and formal approaches to clinical supervision is to rely on teachers working with teachers as colleagues who research each other's practice more informally. Sometimes specific steps and protocols are followed, but the teachers decide together which will be used and how they will be used. Sometimes the structure for supervision emerges from conversations about the issues being investigated and from other concerns unique to the teachers' context. For example, in some schools, teachers might be organized into teams of three. In forming such teams, teachers would have an opportunity to indicate with whom they might like to work. Often, one member of the team is selected by the principal, but there are no rigid rules for selecting teams. Once formed, the teams may choose to work together in a number of ways, ranging from formal clinical supervision to less intensive and more informal processes. They may, for example, simply agree to observe each other's classes, providing help according to the desires of the teacher being observed. The teachers then might confer, giving one another informal feedback and otherwise discussing issues of teaching that they consider to be important. An approach relying on specific teaching steps and elements of lesson design might be used on another occasion. In this case, the emphasis on teaching might be narrowly focused on specific issues identified by the teacher. On still another occasion, the emphasis might be quite unfocused in order to provide a general feel or rendition of teaching. All that is needed is for team members to meet beforehand to decide "the rules and issues" for the observation and for any subsequent conversations or conferences.

It is a good idea for peer supervision to extend beyond classroom observation. It should provide a setting in which teachers can informally discuss problems they are facing, share ideas, help one another in preparing lessons, exchange tips, and provide other support to one another. Some suggestions for principals seeking to implement peer supervision are provided in Exhibit 13.4.

LOOKING AT STUDENT WORK

Establishing schools as professional learning communities is key to teacher learning and to student success. Professional learning communities are schools, or networks

exhibit
13.4

Guidelines for Implementing Peer Supervision

1. Teachers should have a voice in deciding with whom they work.
2. Principals should retain final responsibility for putting together peer supervisory teams.
3. The structure for peer supervision should be formal enough for the teams to keep records of how and in what ways time has been used and to provide a general *nonevaluative* description of peer supervisory activities. This record should be submitted annually to the principal.
4. The principal should provide the necessary resources and administrative support enabling peer supervisory teams to function during the normal range of the school day. The principal might, for example, volunteer to cover classes as needed, to arrange for substitutes as needed, to provide for innovative schedule adjustments enabling team members to work together readily.
5. If information generated within the team about teaching and learning might be considered even mildly evaluative, it should stay with the team and not be shared with the principal.
6. The principal should not seek evaluation data from one teacher about another.
7. Each teacher should be expected to keep a professional growth log that demonstrates that she or he is reflecting on practice and growing professionally as a result of peer supervisory activities.
8. The principal should meet with the peer supervisory team at least once a year for purposes of general assessment and for sharing of impressions and information about the peer supervisory process.
9. The principal should meet individually at least once a year with each peer supervisory team member to discuss her or his professional growth log and to provide any encouragement and assistance that may be required.
10. Generally, new teams should be formed every second or third year.

of groups within schools, where teachers depend on each other for caring and support and where teachers learn and inquire together as members of a shared practice. Collaboration is a key characteristic. See, for example, the work of Richard DuFour and his colleagues on professional learning communities (PLCs) (DuFour, 2003; DuFour et al., 2006). These authors believe that "the best way to provide powerful feedback to teachers and to turn data into information *that can improve teaching and learning* is through team-developed and team-analyzed common formative assessments" (DuFour et al., 2006:148). They argue that if any school "is to develop the capacity of the faculty to function as a PLC, it must create systems to ensure that each teacher: Receives *frequent and timely feedback* on the performance of his or her students, in meeting an *agreed-upon proficiency standard* established by the collaborative team, on a *valid assessment* created by the team, *in comparison to other students* in the school attempting to meet that same standard" (DuFour et al., 2006:149). This kind of powerful learning, they argue, thrives when schools are transformed into professional learning communities.

A similar line of research and practice are known as Critical Friends Groups (CFGs). According to Daniel Baron (2005), CFGs "are professional-learning communities made up of anywhere from six to twelve teachers, typically" (18). Baron is the coexecutive director of the National School Reform faculty and a booster of the critical friends group approach to school reform.

Both the PLC and the CFG movements seek to improve schools by transforming them into collaborative cultures—communities of practice that redefine the setting for teacher work and for student learning. Ideally, PLCs represent a network of shared practice within which teachers plan together, teach together, and assess results together. CFGs employ meetings and other gatherings to provide intense professional development experiences that teachers then take back to their classroom and use to improve school.

Baron notes that CFGs can be simply

> a small group of teachers at a school who have made a commitment to support each other's learning by meeting once or twice a month, typically for two to two and a half hours, to make their work public to each other. The notion is that teaching has become a very isolated profession and in a sense teachers end up outside the life of a professional community where practitioners make their work public to their peers for the purposes of getting feedback on that work in order to adapt their work to better meet the needs of the learner. So teachers meet regularly and bring their own work to their peers—that being their unit lesson plans, their assessment tools that they have developed—and they bring student work that has been generated by the assignments and assessments. (2005:18)

Examining student work is a powerful way to build community. When teachers together look at student work they come to talk with each other more often and more thoughtfully. This kind of reflection often leads to revising one's practice. As Tina Blythe, David Allen, and Barbara Powell (1999) explain, "there are some purposes for looking at student work that virtually require collaboration and conversation—developing common standards within grade levels or departments, for example. In order to accomplish this aim, a school or a group of teachers must develop not only standards but also a shared understanding of what these standards mean and how to apply them to student work. Examining and discussing student work is virtually the only way to achieve such a goal" (4).

In Chapter 11 standards for authentic learning were discussed. Newmann, Secada, and Wehlage (1995) propose a three-pronged strategy for assessing authentic pedagogy:

1. Assessing the assignments that teachers give students to complete
2. Assessing the dynamics of teaching and learning as classroom instruction is being observed
3. Assessing the work that students actually do

Newmann and his colleagues also provide research-based standards and scoring criteria (see Appendix 11.1, pp. 266–270). They invite readers to refer to "Standards and Scoring Criteria for Assessment of Assignments (Tasks) Teachers Give," and to use the standards and rubrics provided to examine actual assignments that teachers give and actual work that students do. These student work protocols are state-of-the-art and can be adapted in many ways to fit a variety of situations.

COACHING

Few would disagree that teacher learning is a powerful strategy for improving student achievement for all of our students. But we can do better. Too often teacher learning is separated from teaching. Too often learning takes place away from the teacher's classroom. Too often teachers are learning alone. And too often learning is viewed as a private good.

Coaching can change all of this. Good coaching is embedded in the teacher's classroom, takes place at the same time teachers are teaching, is collaborative, and is aimed at the public good. Coaches work side by side with teachers, observing their work, helping them research questions they are interested in, offering critiques, and being models of effective teaching practice. The goal of coaching is to help develop communities of practice within which teachers collaborate to honor a very simple value: when we learn together we learn more, and when we learn more we will more effectively serve our students.

Professional development takes on a different meaning when coaching is involved. Professional development has the following characteristics:

- Is grounded in deep inquiry, reflection, and experimentation
- Is collaborative, focusing on teachers as communities of practice rather than as individuals
- Is sustained and supported by modeling
- Is connected to and driven by teachers' work with their students while teaching is actually going on
- Engages teachers in the work of teaching as they learn
- Is connected to larger purposes (adapted from Darling-Hammond and McLaughlin, 1995; Neufeld and Roper, 2003:3)

Coaching should be driven not only by the needs and interest of teachers, it should be driven as well by the goals and purposes of the school.

COACHES AS ROVING LEADERS

Roving leaders are there when we need them. They are coaches on the move, ready to help at a moment's notice. Max DePree, the famed head of the Herman Miller Furniture Company, describes coaches as "indispensable people in our lives" (Peters and Austin, 1985:328) who sometimes work by appointment, but at other times no appointment is needed. If you need a coach, grab one. Good coaches practice coaching by walking around.

Coaches are not cheerleaders who pump us up by telling us they know we can do it. They are, instead, colleagues who help us to see what we need to do and help us figure out how to do it and do it well. Being a cheerleader puts the leader in the role of bystander. Bystanders work the sidelines but are not involved as colleagues, as partners, as active members of the teacher's shared community of practice. Missing from the cheerleader role is a relationship. At the heart of coaching, say Peters and Austin (1985), is a personal relationship. "Relationships depend on contact. No contact, no relationship" (388). Building relationships is never easy. That is why effective coaching requires an investment of time, attention, and talent.

One important purpose of coaching is to build the capacity of people in such a way that each encounter results in reciprocal learning. Teacher and coach learn together. A second, perhaps more important, purpose is to strengthen the values that are shared in the school, to create a common agenda, and to work together to figure out a better way to achieve our purposes. Why are we here? What are we trying to accomplish? Do our decisions make sense? How does answering these questions help us understand our larger purposes? Coaching is about effectiveness to be sure. But it is also about shaping values and building a normative culture.

Key to coaching are the bonds that develop as trust grows. Coaching is, after all, an intimate strategy for learning. Getting inside another person's practice in a helpful way requires a high level of authenticity. This kind of relationship is threatened when coaches act in the following ways:

- Encourage teachers to become too dependent on them
- Use their coaching role to control what people do rather than to guide and support
- Shield people from bad news
- Tell teachers what they want to hear

AN EVOLVING JOB

Those who practice school-based staff development such as coaching have many job titles. Some are called coaches, but others are called staff development teachers, lead teachers, instructional coordinators, advisors, and mentor teachers. Their duties vary as well. Some are merely clones of assistant principals. Others are responsible for supervising the school's efforts to beat the state accountability testing. Whatever else coaches do they must be academic and pedagogical coaches as well.

SOME REFLECTIONS

1. Prepare a short article for your faculty newsletter that describes good coaching. Use the description of coaching that follows as your framework. Good

coaching is embedded in the teacher's classroom, takes place at the same time teachers are teaching, is collaborative, and is aimed at the public good. Coaches work side by side with teachers, observing their work, helping them research questions they are interested in, offering critiques, and being models of effective teaching practice. The goal of coaching is to help develop communities of practice within which teachers collaborate to honor a very simple value: when we learn together we learn more, and when we learn more we are more effective.

2. In this chapter we noted that there is a shift of emphasis from principals doing things right to principals doing right things. To what extent would this description fit the principals in your school? Provide examples.

$\mathcal{R}$EFERENCES

Baron, Daniel. 2005, Fall. "The National School Reform Faculty: Reforming Schools from the Inside," interview in *Educational Horizons* 84(1), 17–28.

Blythe, Tina, David Allen, and Barbara Schieffelin Powell. 1999. *Looking Together at Student Work: A Companion Guide to Assessing Student Learning.* New York: Teachers College Press.

Cogan, Morris. 1973. *Clinical Supervision.* Boston: Houghton Mifflin.

Darling-Hammond, Linda, and M. W. McLaughlin. 1995. "Policies that Support Professional Development in an Era of Reform," *Phi Delta Kappan* 76(8), 597–604.

DuFour, Richard. 2003. "Building a Professional Learning Community," *The School Administrator* 60(5), 13–18.

DuFour, Richard, Rebecca DuFour, Robert Eaker, and Thomas Many. 2006. *Learning by Doing: A Handbook for Professional Learning Communities.* Bloomington, IN: Solution Tree.

Goldhammer, Robert. 1969. *Clinical Supervision: Special Methods for the Supervision of Teachers.* New York: Holt, Rinehart and Winston.

Neufeld, Barbara, and Dana Roper. 2003. "Coaching: A Strategy for Developing Instructional Capacity," Paper copublished by the Aspen Institute Program on Education and the Annenberg Institute for School Reform.

Newmann, Fred M., W. G. Secada, and G. G. Wehlage. 1995. *A Guide to Authentic Instruction and Assessment: Vision, Standards and Scoring.*
Madison: Wisconsin Center for Education Research.

Newmann, Fred M., BetsAnn Smith, Elaine Allensworth, and Anthony S. Bryk. 2001, Winter. "Instructional Program Coherence: What It Is and Why It Should Guide School Improvement Policy," *Educational Evaluation and Policy Analysis* 23(4), 297–321.

Orihara, Kazuo (Ed.). 1993. *Shogakko: Kenkyu Jugyo no Susume Kata Mikata (Elementary School: Implementing and Observing Research Lessons).* Tokyo: Bunkyo-shoin.

Peters, Tom, and Nancy Austin. 1985. *A Passion for Excellence.* New York: Random House.

Sparks, Dennis. 2000, June 21. "Using Lesson Study to Improve Teaching," *Education Week.*

Stepanek, Jennifer, Gary Appel, Melinda Leong, Michelle Turner Mangan, and Mark Mitchell. 2007. *Leading Lesson Study.* Thousand Oaks, CA: Corwin Press.

Stigler, James W. and James Hiebert. 1999. *The Teaching Gap: Best Ideas from the World's Teachers for Improving Education in the Classroom.* New York: Free Press.

Viadero, Debra. 2004, February 11. "In 'Lesson Study' Sessions, Teachers Polish Their Craft," *Education Week* 23(22), 8.

Wiburg, Karin, and Susan Brown. 2007. *Lesson Study Communities: Increasing Achievement with Diverse Students.* Thousand Oaks, CA: Corwin Press.

Critical Friends Groups in Action: A Day in the Life of Schoolwide CFGs

At Souhegan, once a month there is a two-hour delay to the start of the school day. About 125 faculty and staff use this time for the many meetings of the school's critical friends groups. Here we look at how this time is used, the issues that are examined, and the systems of help that are created to respond to teacher needs.

On a snowy winter morning in Amherst, New Hampshire, faculty and staff members of Souhegan High School gather to help their colleagues with their work. Phil Estabrook wants a new way to look at the assessment criteria for his Vietnam unit; Lisa Kent needs help in setting up a research project for her wellness classes; Melissa Chapman wants to examine a new method of teaching students how to analyze spatial data. A math teacher will ask for help in revising a test; a special education teacher will ask for help in evaluating a site-review plan; an English teacher will request help in fine-tuning a writing assessment. Others want to discuss an article, and some plan to debrief peer observations. While students enjoy a two-hour delay to the start of their school day, more than 125 faculty and staff members participate in this monthly meeting of our Critical Friends Groups (CFGs).

Intrigued by recent research on gender roles in the classroom, wellness teacher Lisa Kent wants to set up gender-specific classes and track her findings. She is also interested in assessing students' fitness before and after their participation in wellness courses. She confessed to her group that although she wants to learn more about both topics, she lacked a sense of how to proceed. Through questions and discussion, Lisa's CFG identified several promising starting points. They suggested that Lisa raise awareness of gender-specific studies by disseminating articles for teachers to read and then discuss. Because her plan to teach gender-specific classes would involve many other people to arrange her schedule, the CFG thought that she needed a more comprehensive research strategy before beginning the work. The group then helped Lisa develop a survey to assemble the data she needed to begin the assessment of her students' fitness. Ten colleagues invested two hours helping Lisa get what she needed to improve her practice.

Lisa appreciates the sense of connection the CFG provides:

> I like knowing that there is a group of people who will help me figure things out in my work. I spend my day in a gym, pretty far removed from classroom life. I love listening to colleagues present lessons from their subject areas. I like visiting my colleagues' classrooms, and I always come away from those visits with some new management idea or a new perspective on some of the kids I teach. Between our monthly meetings, some members of our CFG meet to discuss articles.

As Phil Estabrook's students study the Vietnam War, they focus on the question of what is worth fighting for. Their final exhibition requires them to create a scrapbook with artifacts from a list that includes poetry, letters, movies, art, literature, photography, music, speeches, interviews, and protest writings. The scrapbook must also contain pieces responding to the Vietnam Wall memorial and examining the war's aftermath.

Phil's dilemma is that although he has samples of exemplary work from some students, overall student performance is inconsistent. No matter how he alters the unit or increases points of instruction, some students perform poorly.

"This unit has such potential, and parts of it are absolutely solid," says Phil. "It occurs in May, just before the end of our year. Students have acquired many tools of studying history; now I want them to tell one American story from a particular time period, using primary sources to examine history. I have worked on this unit for years, but I know right now that some kids will not succeed in this assignment. I want to figure out what I can do to increase student success without lowering performance standards. I have done so many things to ensure that kids get traction early in this work, but even at the end of their sophomore year, some of them lack the abstract-thinking skills that this work demands."

Phil's CFG spent time examining his project sheet, assignments, and examples of student work. Using a structured protocol, the group then discussed Phil's quandary while he sat silent, taking notes. Participants commented on Phil's exhaustive preparation. The unit was carefully layered to build on the students' growing knowledge of that era and the central issues behind the Vietnam War. Several noticed the richness of primary sources available to students; someone else commented on the strength of asking students to adopt personas from various perspectives.

The conversation soon turned to the abstract thinking the project requires. Participants wondered what specific lessons Phil teaches to build skills in abstract thinking. Some asked if Phil thought that gender played a role in student success. One individual wondered if Phil had considered a menu of choices for the required exhibition. Another wondered if Phil could use his current events teaching on the war in Iraq to pre-teach some of the skills students would need for this later unit.

Eventually, Phil reentered the conversation. He sighed at the work ahead of him, although he was grateful for questions that pushed his thinking: "The biggest 'Aha!' for me was recognizing that I already could predict the exact students who will not succeed. I can see that I need to create assignments that build abstract-thinking skills."

In debriefing the discussion, Phil noted that every time he requested help with this particular project, colleagues were always complimentary about his work—the project sheet, the activities, all the discrete pieces that culminated in the scrapbook. However, when he asked people to study the student work samples, gaps between teacher work and student performance were evident. "That's what keeps me coming back to my CFG with this work," said Phil. "I always see it differently when I examine it through my colleagues' lenses."

Melissa Chapman, a conservation-biology teacher, frequently brings her work to her CFG:

> Our group has been together for a long time. We know each other's work and each other's style of working. That provides such a shortcut for me. I bring work because I want other perspectives on how to make it more accessible to students. When English teachers and art teachers and math teachers examine work that I do, they see ways to improve it that I could never see.
>
> I was excited to show my CFG the new thinking I was doing about helping students in their preparation for working with very sophisticated geographical information system (GIS) software. I had been concerned that students lacked the analytical skills they needed to draw conclusions from spatial data represented on maps. I tried a low-tech approach to building their skills, requiring them to symbolize their field data using color blocks based on a range of values for their data. I then asked them to display the data in a way that represented our field site. I guided them through a series of questions about their maps, then studied their responses to a written exam. I think that I am on to something by taking them through a very methodical step-by-step process to build their skills in spatial analysis, but I go back and forth between that and simply letting them learn from using the software alone, so I asked my CFG to help me think through three questions: Am I asking the right question? Does it matter whether students have this layer of understanding? How will this activity influence student understanding of technology?
>
> When I took my CFG through the sequence of instruction and activities that I provide for my students, I gained a better awareness of what I was doing. Their questions helped me to answer many of my own questions about the activity. My CFG identified ways of making this work more transparent to students, and affirmed both my intentions and my results. The opportunity to think out loud in front of trusted colleagues is invaluable to my work.

Lisa, Melissa, and Phil are only three of a dozen faculty members who presented their work that morning in January. Each left with some answers, some new questions, and some new ways of approaching their work. Each received help that will improve student learning.

appendix *13.1* **Continued**

We are often asked how we can demonstrate improved student learning. The answers are as complex as the question implies. First, when teachers present their lesson plans, unit ideas, or assessment tools, their colleagues' questions help them to forge tighter links between goals for student learning and the work demonstrating students' increased knowledge and skills. When teachers focus on student work to improve student learning, their questions and their multiple perspectives point out subtleties that might have been missed during the unit design. Finally, when colleagues ask a series of whys—why someone chose a particular text or essay questions, why a teacher expected that all students could demonstrate a particular skill or process, or why this assessment tool will document student learning—we are forced to reflect on our strategies, deepening our understanding of how to help students.

There are also tangible ways of tracking improved student learning. Aimee Gibbons has noted her students' deeper understanding of both the literary text and the historical period from the help she received in revising the students' performance assessments of *The Great Gatsby*. Although Aimee once relied heavily on chapter quizzes and essay questions, she now asks her students to depict some aspect of the text or the times in an art piece and requires them to delve into the text for their artwork. As a result, students have demonstrated a far more thorough understanding of literary symbolism. In addition, more students are completing their final assignments and reporting a greater level of appreciation for the unit and their learning.

Aimee also relied on her CFG colleagues to help her think through a successful children's literature unit. Their suggestion that Aimee invite young children into her classroom to listen to the children's books and offer feedback to her students ramped up the standards significantly. Once her students knew that they would have a "real" audience for their work, they worked diligently to write stories and create illustrations of high interest to the young readers. Looking at the various incarnations of that exhibition of student performance, even a casual observer can see strong evidence of improved student learning. Each time Aimee has requested help from her peers, her expectations for student learning have become more sophisticated—and therefore both more demanding and more rewarding for students than they were before.

Scott Prescott, one of Souhegan's deans of faculty, oversees the CFG initiative:

CFGs are our most significant professional development experience, so we support it with a variety of resources, time, money, training. We monitor this work carefully, and we don't "mess" with this valuable time. CFGs are essential to us, and we show that through our actions as well as our words.

We meet with our CFG coaches three times each year for a full-day, off-site retreat. We engage in new learning through texts and protocols; we discuss dilemmas occurring in our particular CFGs; and we develop and support teacher leadership. These meetings provide an essential link to the work of each individual CFG.

What I am currently working on is making each individual's participation in his CFG more meaningful. How can we connect each other's work to our own practice—how can we ensure personal growth through a focus on another's work? Those are the questions driving our collective focus right now. At our most recent off-site retreat, we developed an essential question to help us deepen the conversation: "How can our collective practice help each adult learner continuously improve student learning?"

To push this thinking, we are asking people to think about what they will take away from each CFG meeting—what the impact of this new learning can teach them about their own work. We want to be more transparent about our desire for them to forge those connections in a more direct way.

We survey our staff every year to determine our progress in CFG work, and we use those data in our meetings with coaches. We put a lot of emphasis on personalized learning at Souhegan, and that concept applies to every learner in our building. In our CFG work, we all make mutual investments in each other's practice with the goals of helping students learn. We hold each other accountable for continuous improvement on behalf of our students. That is the direct impact of the sustained focus our Critical Friends Groups provide.

Each of Souhegan's thirteen CFGs meets nine times each year; that means that there are at least 117 teachers who have the opportunity to present their work for feedback. Each of those teachers represents ninety students who benefit from this professional development. We find it to be our most worthy investment of time and energy.

Source: Peggy Silva (2005, Fall), "A Day in the Life of Schoolwide CFGs," *Educational Horizons* (84)1, 29–35. Used with permission. Peggy Silva is the writing coordinator at Souhegan High School in Amherst, New Hampshire, and a national facilitator for the National School Reform Faculty (NSRF).

14

MOTIVATION, COMMITMENT, AND THE TEACHER'S WORKPLACE

*M*uch is known about how to arrange job dimensions and work conditions within schools so that teachers are more personally satisfied and are inspired to work harder and smarter on behalf of teaching and learning. When teaching is intellectually satisfying, professionally rewarding, and just plain more fun for teachers, they are likely to keep improving their effectiveness as the years go by. Students are more successful learners as a result. That is why few topics are more important. When high motivation and strong commitment are absent, teachers are likely to be connected to their jobs on a "fair day's work for a fair day's pay" basis (Sergiovanni, 1968). Instead of giving their best, teachers emphasize meeting basic work requirements in exchange for extrinsic benefits. If teachers become dissatisfied, their performance is likely to fall below even this fair day's work level (Brayfield and Crockett, 1955; Vroom, 1964). If they experience loss of meaning and significance with what they are doing, they are likely to become detached, even alienated, from their jobs (Argyris, 1957). Commitment erodes and performance decreases.

Despite what is known about how to improve teacher motivation and commitment and the links between such improvement and effective schooling, this knowledge base does not inform policy development and administrative practice very much. State and local policy makers, for example, frequently mandate changes in school organizational patterns, curriculum, and teacher evaluation in ways that contradict the motivation research. Although well intended, these policy initiatives can actually inhibit—even lower—teacher motivation and commitment, with predictable effects on effective schooling.

PROBLEMS AND CONTRADICTIONS IN POLICY AND PRACTICE

Two examples of policies and practice that seem to contradict what motivation research tells us are examined in this section: mandating and implementing highly structured, prescriptive, and standardized curriculum and teaching formats that result in increasing bureaucracy in the classroom; and school organizational patterns that encourage isolation, privatism, and lack of social interaction among teachers.

Bureaucracy in the Classroom

Exhibit 14.1 contains the "Quality of Work Life in Teaching," scale that is adapted from a more general one developed by Marshall Sashkin and Joseph J. Lengermann (Pfeiffer and Goodstein, 1984). The scale is designed to assess perceptions of job conditions in one's work setting. If you are a teacher, please respond to the questions following the directions provided. If you are a principal, respond in the way you think the teachers in your school would respond.

Response patterns indicate the extent to which one perceives her or his job to be growth oriented on a number of dimensions that are considered important by job-enrichment theorists and researchers. Later in this chapter, the instrument will be scored, and response patterns will be examined as the concept of job enrichment is discussed.

The instrument can also be used to assess the extent to which one's job is bureaucratized. Responses to items 1, 3, 4, 6, 8, 11, and 24 hint at the extent to which the teaching job you describe is bureaucratic. Item 6 is scored in reverse. The more prevalent the job characteristics described in the items, the more bureaucratic that job is likely to be.

It is generally assumed that teaching is a profession, although perhaps a fledgling one. Professionals and bureaucrats operate quite differently at work. The work of bureaucrats is programmed for them by their work system. The work of professionals emerges from an interaction between available professional knowledge and individual client needs. Webster, for example, describes a bureaucrat as "a government official following a narrow, rigid, formal routine." In contrast, professionals are assumed to command a body of knowledge enabling them to make informed judgments in response to unique situations and individual client

exhibit
14.1
Quality of Work Life in Teaching

Directions: The following questions ask you to describe the objective characteristics of your job, as well as the activities of your coworkers and supervisor. Try not to use these questions to show how much you like or dislike your job; just be as factually correct as possible—imagine what an outside observer would say in response to these questions. Circle the appropriate letter.

(A)ll of the time, (M)ost of the time, (P)art of the time, (N)ever

1. Teachers in my school are allowed to make some decisions, but most of the decisions about their work have to be referred to their supervisor or are shaped by rules, curriculum requirements, or testing requirements.   A   M   P   N
2. Teachers in my job normally move on to better jobs as a direct result of the opportunities my job offers.   A   M   P   N
3. Teachers in my school are required to produce or cover a specific amount of work each day or each week.   A   M   P   N
4. Teachers in my school perform tasks that are repetitive in nature.   A   M   P   N
5. My work requires me to coordinate regularly with other teachers.   A   M   P   N
6. Teachers in my school have a great deal of control over their work activities.   A   M   P   N
7. Teachers in my job have the opportunity to learn new skills in the course of their work.   A   M   P   N
8. Teachers in my school must work according to a fixed schedule; it is not possible to let the work go for a time and then catch up on it later.   A   M   P   N
9. Teachers in my job are required to follow certain procedures in doing their work that they wouldn't choose if it were up to them.   A   M   P   N
10. Teachers in my position work alone on their teaching, with little or no contact with other teachers.   A   M   P   N
11. When they encounter problems in their teaching, teachers in my school must refer these problems to their supervisor; they cannot take action on their own.   A   M   P   N
12. My work requires me to learn new methods in order to keep up with changes and new developments.   A   M   P   N
13. Teachers in my position must work very rapidly.   A   M   P   N
14. My work involves completing a "whole" task.   A   M   P   N
15. Teachers in my position are able to help out one another as they teach.   A   M   P   N
16. My principal acts on some of the suggestions of teachers in my school.   A   M   P   N

(continued)

exhibit *14.1* **Continued**

17. Teachers in my position are encouraged to try out methods of their own when teaching.	A	M	P	N
18. Teachers in my position have considerable control over the pace or scheduling of work.	A	M	P	N
19. Jobs at my level fail to bring out the best abilities of teachers because they are designed too simply.	A	M	P	N
20. Teachers in my position must interact with other teachers as they teach.	A	M	P	N
21. Teachers at my level can make their own decisions without checking with anyone else or without consulting approved teaching and curriculum requirements.	A	M	P	N
22. Teachers at my level have the opportunity to learn about the teaching that is occurring at other grade levels and in other departments.	A	M	P	N
23. My work must be completed on a set schedule.	A	M	P	N
24. Teachers in my position perform the same series of tasks all day.	A	M	P	N
25. My work requires a great deal of contact with other teachers.	A	M	P	N

Source: Adapted from "Quality of Work Life Conditions" by Marshall Sashkin and Joseph J. Lengermann, 1984, *The 1984 Annual,* pp. 140–141, San Francisco: Pfeiffer/Jossey-Bass. Copyright © 1984 Pfeiffer/Jossey-Bass Inc., Publishers. Reprinted with permission of Pfeiffer, a subsidiary of John Wiley & Sons.

needs. Essential to professionalism is sufficient discretion for professionals to use informed judgment as they practice.

Beginning in the 1970s and continuing to the present, there has been a trend toward greater centralization in deciding what will be taught in schools: when, with what materials, to whom, and for how long. There are many legitimate and desirable reasons for the state to be involved in matters of education, and many alternatives are open to states as they set standards, provide guidelines, promote equity, and ensure accountability. The problem lies in how far the state should go and the consequences of going too far. Providing leadership to local districts is an important responsibility. Legislating learning to the point of installing a system of bureaucratic teaching is quite another matter (Wise, 1979).

Some standards advocates argue that standards-based reforms promote professionalism by giving teachers and schools discretion over means. Schools and their teachers, so the argument goes, are free to make decisions they think are necessary providing state standards are reached. These standards are measured by tests the state provides. But in reality, the ends invariably drive the means. Thus, the tests soon become the curriculum. That curriculum is soon linked (*aligned with* is the jargon) to specific models of teaching, scheduling formats, and other scripts that must be followed. The rhetoric of empowerment and the reality of standardized outcomes and assessments are in many ways like oil and water.

By and large the educational establishment views the problem as follows. When curriculum and teaching decisions are programmed in a way that diminishes the influence of students and teacher in making teaching and learning decisions, then impersonal, standard, and formal learning goals dominate; teaching and learning become "teacher-proof" and "student-proof"; instructional leadership is discouraged as the teacher spends more time managing the learning process by monitoring, inspecting, regulating, and measuring; and commitment to "authentic" teaching and learning by both teacher and students is lessened. For students, the consequences can be more emphasis on learnings and meanings defined by the school, which functions as an agent of the state (Coombs, 1959; MacDonald, 1964) and less emphasis on intrinsic motivation for learning, on responding to students' needs and interests, on students setting standards for themselves, and on other locally defined learnings and meanings. Student learning is enhanced when teaching is characterized by a balanced emphasis on personally and school-defined meanings and learning outcomes and on students being intrinsically motivated to learn. These characteristics are not encouraged by bureaucratic teaching.

In sum, schools are racing toward adopting uniform standards mandated by states as part of a high-stakes, standards-based approach to school improvement (see, e.g., Tucker and Codding, 1998). The approach is high stakes because standards are measured by state-mandated tests. Schools that do well on the tests are rewarded. Most states provide for low-scoring students to receive special assistance but if test scores do not improve, negative sanctions quickly follow. Often, there are exit tests that students must pass as a requirement for graduation or as a requirement to pass on to the next grade.

Many principals believe that setting high standards and assessing progress makes sense when most of the standards are decided at the local level by teachers, parents, students, and others. Uniform standards mandated from afar or imported en masse from afar, by contrast, too often erode local discretion, place a school's organizational character at risk, and compromise the school's ability to be responsive to local aspirations and needs. Over time, this erosion hampers efforts to provide effective teaching and learning.

Testing expert George F. Madaus (1999) points out, "If important decisions are presumed to be related to test results, then teachers will teach to the test" (80). Teachers are inclined to disregard the subjects that are not tested and, with the subjects that are being taught, to neglect the topics that are not tested, resulting in a narrowing, even skewing, of the curriculum. Madaus states further, "In every setting where a high-stakes test operates, a tradition of past exams develops, which eventually de facto defines the curriculum" (83). Making the test the curriculum may seem like a rational and reasonable response that teachers and schools face. But, as Madaus points out, when a teacher's professional worth is determined by test scores, she or he will corrupt the concepts and skills assessed by reducing them to strategies in which students are drilled. Still another principle offered by Madaus is, "Teachers pay particular attention to the form of questions on a high-stakes test (for example, short answer, essay, multiple-choice) and adjust their instruction accordingly" (85). As Meier points out (in Madaus, 1999:86), teaching reading (and other subjects) comes to resemble closely the practice of taking reading tests. Curriculum materials are added or discarded based on what is tested rather than on what is valued. And finally, Madaus asserts, "A high-stakes test transfers control over the curriculum to the agency which sets or controls the exam" (87). These are hardly empowering conditions that encourage teachers to behave as self-managing professionals. Nor, as we discuss next, do these conditions build efficacy in teaching and encourage teachers to behave as "Origins."

The research on motivation to work suggest that Madaus's observations are troublesome (see, e.g., Deci, 1995, and Kohn, 1993). In a recent study of the motivational impact of school-based performance awards, Kelley (1999) observes:

> When incentive systems work as they are intended, employees will shift behaviors toward what is being rewarded and away from everything else. . . . Thus, the design of the incentive system and the assessment instrument is critical because outcomes that are not measured, or not readily measurable, will be de-emphasized in the curriculum. . . . Some teachers indicated that the focus of the assessment on higher-order skills was leading to decreased attention to basic skills. Other teachers indicated that the need to cover a large amount of material was forcing them to maintain a strict schedule. For example, one teacher indicated that when a student asked an interesting but tangential question, in the past she would have pursued it in order to encourage and stimulate students' love of learning. With the high-stakes assessment in place, she felt the need to deflect these questions and maintain a focus on the skills and topics to be assessed. (320)

Teachers as Origins and Pawns

What are the consequences of legislated learning and bureaucratic teaching on motivation and commitment of teachers? Is there a link between teacher motivation and commitment and school effectiveness? In successful schools, teachers are more committed, harder workers, more loyal to the school, and more satisfied with their jobs. The research on motivation to work (Hackman and Oldham, 1980; Herzberg, 1966; Peters and Waterman, 1982) suggests that these highly motivating conditions are present when teachers

- Find their work lives to be *meaningful,* purposeful, sensible, and significant, and when they view the work itself as being worthwhile and important
- Have reasonable *control over their work activities* and affairs and are able to exert reasonable influence over work events and circumstances

■ Experience *personal responsibility* for the work and are personally accountable for outcomes

Meaningfulness, control, and personal responsibility are attributes of teachers functioning as "Origins" rather than as "Pawns." According to De Charms (1968), "An Origin is a person who perceives his behavior as determined by his own choosing: a Pawn is a person who perceives his behavior as determined by external forces beyond his control." He continues:

> An Origin has a strong feeling of personal causation, a feeling that the locus for causation of effects in his environment lies within himself. . . . A Pawn has a feeling that causal forces beyond his control, or personal forces residing within others, or in the physical environment determine his behavior. This constitutes a strong feeling of powerlessness or ineffectiveness. (274)

Personal causation is an important dimension of motivation. People strive to influence the events and situations of their environment, to be Origins of their own behavior.

Legislated learning and bureaucratic teaching threaten personal causation by creating work conditions more associated with Pawn feelings and behavior. In referring to Pawn feelings and behavior among teachers, economist and Nobel laureate Theodore Schultz (1982) states:

> Most of these attitudes of school teachers should have been anticipated in view of the way schools are organized and administered. The curriculum is not for them to decide; nor is the content of the course to be taught and the plans to be followed. . . . In assessing the performance of teachers, it is a dictum of economics that incentives matter. School teachers are responding to the much circumscribed opportunities open to them. They are not robots but human agents who perceive, interpret, and act in accordance with the worthwhile options available. (43)

*B*UT IT IS NOT THAT SIMPLE

There is a paradox at play here. On the one hand, clear mandates, mission statements, lists of standards, goals and purposes, and high achievement expectations for teachers provide them with a needed sense of direction and clear signal of what is important and significant. This realization was an important leadership theme of earlier chapters, which discussed the concepts of purposing and symbolic and cultural aspects of leadership. On the other hand, if such mandates are described and prescribed in such detail that teachers come to feel and behave like Pawns rather than Origins, problems in motivation arise. Still it seems important for teachers to know what the school's purposes are and to be able to convert them into operational goals and objectives.

Expectancy theory (Vroom, 1964), for example, suggests that teachers are motivated when goals are understood, when teachers believe they have the means and resources to achieve the goals, and when achieving the goals will result in outcomes that they personally value. Taken together, these two powerful cousins provide still another tightrope for principals to walk. Goals make sense, but they will backfire if they are so pervasive and so detailed that they script what teachers do.

Principals are responsible for monitoring the delicate balance between goals that work and goals that unduly limit what teachers do. It helps if principals seek to ensure that mandates are sensibly interpreted and articulated into practices that promote Origin feelings and behaviors among teachers. They must ask whether interpretation and implementing decisions will promote professionalism or bureaucracy in teaching. Responsive to unique situations, professionals take their cues from the problems they face and the students they serve. They draw on the wealth of knowledge and technology available to them as they create professional knowledge in use in response to student needs. Bureaucrats, by contrast, are not driven by student problems but by the technology itself. They are appliers of rules, regulators of formats, direction followers, and managerial implementers. They strive for a one-best-way to treat all cases, and, pursuing standard outcomes, they apply formal procedures in standardized ways. It is in this sense that legislated learning and bureaucratic teaching encourage Pawn feelings and behaviors among teachers and students, contributing to less effective teaching and learning.

Public or Private Good?

Should the teaching and learning purposes and outcomes of a teacher's practice and should the professional development agenda of that teacher be viewed as public or private goods (see, e.g., Elmore, 2002)? As private goods the prime beneficiary is the teacher. Here the teacher is given maximum discretion to make decisions that affect the kinds of teaching and learning that takes place, and the teacher makes decisions about what will be her or his professional development agenda. Different teachers will make different decisions because they have different interests and needs and because the contexts for their practice differ. I may decide, for example, to bone up on my computer skills or to learn more about how to teach algebra skills in the elementary grades. You might have a completely different agenda. As a result of my inquiry, I might reach a new level of competence in using the computer, even though I still do not use it very much in my teaching. I benefit nonetheless. Had professional development been viewed as a public good then the standard would be not just how much I learned but to what extent the school's purposes were advanced as well. As a public good the teachers' decisions and the teachers' professional development agenda has to be linked to what the school is interested in, what the school needs, and what the collective context for practice is.

The question of public or private good determines how professionalism is understood (Elmore, 2000). When the private good is dominant teaching is viewed as an individual practice that requires individual judgment and the development of unique solutions to unique problems. The more discretion that is allowed, the more professional is the teacher presumed to be.

To take away discretion by insisting on common goals, shared lesson plans, and the adoption of standard teaching strategies, many feel, will bureaucratize the school. But it is not that simple. The answer is not in adopting one view or the other but in insisting on enough commonness, enough standardization, and enough connections to bring about and to sustain instructional coherence. Instructional coherence is different from instructional rigidity. Rigidity narrows the amount of discretion teachers have while coherence yields enough discretion to bring about a common purpose and common effort but still allows teachers enough wiggle room to be responsive to the situations they find themselves in. Instructional coherence is key, for without it teachers experience a practice that is either isolated or so unpredictable as to be unmanageable. When we have instructional coherence we have a framework in place and a sense of direction in place that makes our practice purposeful. And purposeful practice is something that teachers want and need. A framework for coherence is just that. It is not a script but a set of ideas that helps us steer a sensible course.

Isolation in Teaching

Teaching can be a lonely profession. Typically, teachers work alone. As a result, few others in the school know what they are doing or how well they are doing it (Bidwell, 1975; Lortie, 1975; Waller, 1932). Related to isolation in teaching are tendencies to encourage the value of privatism and the consequences of this value on social interaction. Privatism forces teachers to look inward, discourages sharing, and encourages competition; furthermore, it promotes feelings of inadequacy and insecurity. Lack of social interaction deprives teachers of opportunities to help and seek help from others, to give feedback, and to get feedback from others—both essential ingredients in most motivation to work models. These conditions not only contradict what is known about sound management practices but they also impede professional growth and effective teaching. Despite the debilitating effects of isolation in teaching, schools persist in organizational structures and supervisory and evaluation practices that encourage these conditions. Let's examine further the effects of isolation, privatism, and lack of social interaction in teaching.

Rosenholtz (1984) identifies isolation as one of the major impediments to school improvement. Her review of the research on this topic leads to the following conclusions:

> In isolated settings, teachers come to believe that they alone are responsible for running their classrooms and that to seek advice or assistance from their colleagues constitutes an open admission of incompetence.

Teacher isolation is perhaps the greatest impediment to learning to teach, or to improving one's existing skills, because most learning by necessity occurs through trial and error. One alarming consequence of trial and error learning is that teachers' limits for potential growth depend heavily on their own personal ability to detect problems and to discern possible solutions.

Another consequence is that teachers in isolated settings have few role models of good teaching to emulate. As a matter of fact, it is more typical of teachers in isolated settings to use role models that they recall from their own student days than to seek models of teaching excellence among their contemporaries.

. . . [I]n interpreting and formulating solutions to classroom problems, teachers realize little benefit from the advice, experience, or expertise of colleagues with whom they work. That is, any pre-existing practical knowledge is seldom passed along to new recruits, who must then, of their own accord, sink or swim.

For teachers restricted to trial-and-error learning then, there is a limit to their capacity to grow in the absence of others' professional knowledge. . . . Teachers teach their prime after about four or five years and thereafter, perhaps because of little teaching input, their effectiveness with students actually begins to decline. (4–6)

Lieberman and Miller (1999) point out that being private means not sharing experiences about teaching, classes, students, and learning. By being private, teachers forfeit the opportunity to share their successes with colleagues but gain the security of not having to disclose shortcomings. Having worked in isolation and not having accurate knowledge of the teaching of others, teachers tend to assume that they are not measuring up to colleagues.

Isolation and privatism contribute to fewer social interaction opportunities among teachers. The three conditions combine to force teachers to look inward for sources of feedback and rewards. Indeed, teachers rely almost exclusively on interactions with students as sources of satisfaction in teaching (Lortie, 1975; Waller, 1932). The question, though, is whether the satisfaction derived from student social interaction is enough to provide the kind of motivation and commitment needed for effective schooling. How does social interaction with adults fit into the picture?

Social interaction is a key ingredient in the supervisory process. Contrary to myth, teachers report increases in satisfaction as supervision increases moderately (Dornbush and Scott, 1975). Moderate increases in supervision seem also to be related to increases in teaching effectiveness. From his research, Natriello (1984) concludes: "Teachers who report more frequent evaluation activities also report being markedly more effective in teaching tasks" (592). Social interaction, as a form of feedback about one's teaching, is a contributor to these findings. Social interaction is also the medium by which recognition is given and received. Furthermore, social interaction seems to be a key factor in evoking the power-influence, achievement, and affiliation motives of persons at work and is an integral part of most motivation-to-work and job-enrichment models emerging from the research (Hackman and Oldham, 1980).

Many experts believe that social interaction among teachers, and between teachers and supervisors, is essential for promoting and institutionalizing change in schools and is related as well to successful staff-development efforts. With respect to institutionalizing changes, Clark, Lotto, and Astuto (1984) point out that the focus of staff development must reach beyond the development of new teaching skills to the development of new concepts and behaviors within a supportive school climate. Their review of the research on effective school improvement efforts leads them to conclude that interaction among teachers, and between teachers and administrators, provides the needed opportunities for technical and psychological support that enhances effective implementation. "Teachers report that they learn best from other teachers. Teacher-teacher interactions provide for technical and psychological support as well as personal reinforcement" (Clark et al., 1984:58). Although more than social interaction opportunities may be necessary for school improvement efforts to be successful, success will not be likely without social interaction. Informal professional development efforts are also linked to social interaction among teachers. When provided with opportunity and encouragement, teachers learn a great deal from one another and trust one another as sources of new ideas and as sharers of problems they face (Glatthorn, 1984; Keenan, 1974).

Appendix 14.1, "Studying the Climate of Your School," provides a brief overview of the concept of school climate and how this climate can be assessed. The appendix relies on the work of Rensis Likert, a pioneer in the organizational climate literature.

Legislated learning and bureaucratic teaching, isolation in the workplace, the tradition of privatism, and lack of social interaction are urgent problems that principals and their faculties must address as they work to improve the quality of work life in schools, encourage professional development, increase teacher motivation and commitment, and build professional community in our schools. Community, McLaughlin and Talbert (Bradley, 1993:7) conclude, is not only good for teachers but it is also good for students. Their research reveals that teachers who belong to learning communities have more positive views of students and are more successful in changing their practice for the better.

USING MOTIVATION THEORY AND RESEARCH TO INFORM PRACTICE

In Chapter 7, it was pointed out that leadership practice might usefully be understood through use of the metaphor "developmental stages." Four stages were discussed: leadership by bartering, building, binding, and bonding. Virtually all the available research on motivation addresses the first two stages, leadership by bartering and building. Leadership by bartering makes the assumption that the interests of leaders and those being led are different, and therefore a bargain needs to be struck whereby the leader gives to the led something they want in return for their compliance with the leader's wishes. For the most part, the trading that takes place in leadership by bartering focuses on extrinsic factors. Trade-offs occur in leadership by building as well, although they tend to address higher-order need factors and intrinsic motives of the led.

These ideas are captured by the theorizing of the psychologist Abraham Maslow (1943) and by the research of Frederick Herzberg (1966). These experts make the assumption that people have many needs and that the needs stem from at least two human desires—avoidance of pain, hardship, and difficulty; and the desire for growth and development in an effort to realize one's potential (e.g., Herzberg, 1966:56). Perhaps most well known is the need classification scheme proposed by Maslow (1943). He proposed that human needs could be classified into five broad categories: physiological, security-safety, social-belonging, esteem, and self-actualization. Key to Maslow's theory is that the need categories are arranged in a hierarchy of prepotency, with individual behavior motivated to satisfy the need most important at the time. Furthermore, according to theory, the strength of this need depends on its position in the hierarchy and the extent to which lower-order needs are met or satiated. The press from esteem needs, for example, will not be very great for individuals whose security needs are not met. Maslow's ideas form much of the basis for the material and psychological bartering that takes place between leader and led as each seeks an accommodation of their needs. The leader needs to get work done in a certain way. The led need to get certain needs met. One is traded for the other.

Maslow's ideas are helpful, but have limitations. When applied in the management literature, an assumption is often made that some of the needs in his theory are more valued than others. Esteem, autonomy, and self-actualization, for example, are considered to be better than belonging. Indeed, belonging needs are sometimes considered to be a nuisance that must be met to get a person motivated at a higher level. The higher the level, the more motivated a person will be and the more productive that person will be. This is spurious thinking, especially when applied to young people. To most students, belonging is the most important need.

Another problem is that Maslow's needs are typically viewed as being universally applicable; however, needs are culturally determined. Belonging may be less valued in one culture and more valued in another. The same thing is true of achievement and the other needs in Maslow's formulation.

The work of Frederick Herzberg (1966) and his colleagues (Herzberg, Mausner, and Snyderman, 1959) provides a more sophisticated set of ideas for engaging in this kind of bartering. Herzberg's approach, often referred to as *two-factor theory,* is based on the premise that job characteristics contributing to work motivation are different from those contributing to work dissatisfaction. He called the first set of factors *motivators* and the second *hygienic*. According to the theory, if hygienic factors are not attended to by principals, poor work hygiene will occur, with corresponding feelings of teacher job dissatisfaction and poor performance. However, tending to these factors and eliminating job dissatisfaction will not result in increased teacher commitment or job performance. The motivation factors that contributed to increased teacher performance when present seemed not to result in job dissatisfaction or work performance that was below par when absent. According to the theory, if principals do not attend to the motivation factors, teachers will not be motivated to work, but they will not be dissatisfied either. They will perform up to a certain level considered satisfactory, but will make little or no effort to exceed this level (Sergiovanni, 1966).

The factors identified by Herzberg and his associates as being related to work hygiene included interpersonal relationships with students, teachers, and supervisors; quality of supervision; policy and administration; working conditions; and personal life. The factors related to work motivation were achievement, recognition, the work itself, responsibility, and advancement.

The two-factor theory suggests that job satisfaction and motivation to work are related to two decision possibilities for teachers: participation and performance (Sergiovanni, 1968). The decision to participate in one's job is associated with the fair day's work concept. When participating, one takes a job and does all that is necessary to meet minimum commitments; in return, one receives "fair pay" in the form of salary, benefits, social acceptance, courteous and thoughtful treatment, and reasonable supervision. Because these dimensions are expected as part of fair pay, they tend not to motivate a person to go beyond. The decision to perform, however, results in exceeding the fair day's work for a fair day's pay contract. This decision is voluntary because all that school districts can require from teachers is fair work. Rewards associated with the fair day's work are for the most part extrinsic, focusing on the conditions of work. Rewards associated with the performance investment tend to be more intrinsic (e.g., recognition, achievement, feelings of competence, exciting and challenging work, interesting and meaningful work).

Principals need to be concerned with both extrinsic and intrinsic rewards. Schools cannot function adequately unless the participation investment is made and continued by teachers. However, schools cannot excel unless the majority of teachers make the performance investment as well. The two-factor theory can provide principals with a cognitive map for ensuring that administrative, organizational, curricular, and teaching practices provide for both levels of work investment by teachers. Yet, a map is different than a recipe, not everything will work for everyone. Much trial and error will be necessary as principals practice leadership by bartering.

The Potential of Work Itself as a Motivator

A major problem with leadership by bartering is that it relies heavily on making deals. At the heart of the deals are bureaucratic and psychological authority as the means to obtain compliance. Bureaucratic authority promises sanctions and punishments if compliance is not forthcoming. Psychological authority gives rewards in exchange for compliance. Both forms of authority are limited in two ways. First, they lead to calculated involvement. A person's compliance is contingent on either the avoidance of penalties or the obtaining of rewards. When neither is forthcoming, continued compliance is often risky and sometimes nonexistent.

Both rewards and penalties are based on the economic concept of utility function. Human beings are driven by a desire to maximize their self-interests, thus, they continually calculate the costs and benefits of all their options, choosing the course of action that either makes them a winner or keeps them from losing. In Chapter 4, it was pointed out that the concept of utility function is now being successfully challenged by a new economics that does not dismiss the importance of self-interest but gives equal weight to emotions and values—to expressive and moral authority as motivators (Etzioni, 1988). Leadership by bartering is based on the principle that "what gets rewarded gets done." Leadership by building, by contrast, is based on the principle "what *is* rewarding gets done." Here, the emphasis is on intrinsic returns and expressive reasons for involvement in one's work. To these, Etzioni would add the principle "what is right and good gets done." He has in mind the addition of moral authority as a means to understand why people choose to do something and to do it well.

Job-Enrichment Theory

Another window through which one might view the potential of the work itself to motivate is provided by the research of Hackman and Oldham (1980). These scholars have developed a theory of job enrichment—the Job Characteristics model—that has been successfully applied in practice. Key to the model is the presence of three psychological states found to be critical in determining a person's work motivation and job satisfaction:

1. *Experience meaningfulness,* which is defined as the extent to which an individual perceives her or his work as being worthwhile or important by some system of self-accepted values
2. *Experience responsibility,* which is defined by the extent to which a person believes that she or he is personally accountable for the outcomes of efforts
3. *Knowledge of results,* which is defined as the extent to which a person is able to determine, on a fairly regular basis, whether or not performance is satisfactory and efforts lead to outcomes (Hackman et al., 1975:57)

According to the Job Characteristics model, when these psychological states are experienced, one feels good and performs better—internal work motivation occurs. Internal work motivation means how much an individual experiences positive feelings from effective performance. Hackman and Oldham have found that the content of one's job is an important critical determiner of internal work motivation. Furthermore, when certain characteristics of one's job are improved or enhanced, internal work motivation can be increased. They found, for example, that experiencing meaningfulness is enhanced by jobs characterized by skill variety, task identity, and task significance. Autonomy was the job characteristic related to experiencing responsibility, and feedback was related to knowledge of results.

The Job Characteristics model suggests that in teaching, jobs that require (1) different activities in carrying out the work and the use of a variety of teacher talents and skills (skill variety); (2) teachers to engage in tasks identified as whole and comprising identifiable pieces of work (task identity); (3) teachers to have substantial and significant impact on the lives or work of other people (task significance); (4) substantial freedom, independence, and direction be provided to teachers in scheduling work and in deciding classroom organizational and instructional procedures (autonomy); and (5) teachers be provided with direct, clear information about the effects of their performance (feedback) are likely to evoke the psychological states of meaningfulness, responsibility, and knowledge of results. Hackman and Oldham's research reveals that these conditions result in high work motivation, high-quality performance, high job satisfaction, and low absenteeism among teachers.

Figure 14.1 illustrates the Job Characteristics model. In addition to job dimensions, psychological states, and personal and work outcomes, an "implementing concepts" panel is included. Implementing concepts are suggestions the researchers offer to principals interested in building more of the job dimensions into the work of the school. The principle of combining tasks, for example, suggests that, as much as possible, fractionalized aspects of teaching should be put together into larger, more holistic modules. Comprehensive curriculum strategies, interdisciplinary teaching approaches, and team-group teaching modes all contribute to the combining of teaching and curriculum tasks. Combining teaching tasks increases not only skill variety for teachers, but their identification with the work as well.

Although establishing close relationships with students ("clients") is a natural part of teaching and learning, some patterns of school organization and teaching encourage impersonal relationships between teachers and students. Forming "natural work units" points to the importance of thinking in community terms. The intent of such units would be to increase one's sense of ownership and continuing responsibility for identifiable aspects of the work by more closely connecting people to each other and by connecting them more closely to their work. The self-contained elementary school classroom comes closer to this concept than does the departmentalized and quick-moving secondary school teaching schedule. But even in the elementary setting, the building of teaching teams that plan and work

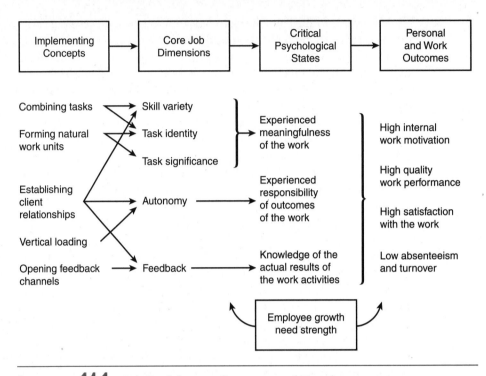

figure **14.1**   **Job Enrichment Concepts and Practices**

Source: From "A New Strategy for Job Enrichment" by J. R. Hackman, G. Oldham, R. Johnson, and K. Purdy. © 1975 by the Regents of the University of California. Reprinted from *California Management Review*, Vol. XVII, no. 4, p. 62, by permission of the Regents.

together and whose members share a common responsibility for students is often lacking. "Vertical loading" suggests strategies that bring together actual teaching and planning to teach. Providing teachers with more control over schedules, work methods, evaluation, and even the training and supervision of less experienced teachers might be examples of vertical loading.

"Opening feedback channels" is another way of saying that the more principals are able to let teachers know how well they are doing, the more highly motivated they will be. Indeed, motivation and satisfaction are neglected benefits of teacher-evaluation supervisory programs designed to provide teachers with helpful feedback. Examples of helpful programs would be those that include clinical supervision, peer supervision, target settings, and similar formats. Principals should strive to create ways in which feedback to teachers occurs naturally from their day-to-day activities and from working closely with colleagues.

The Job Characteristics model suggests that virtually every decision principals make about schooling, classroom organization, curriculum development and implementation, selection of materials, and teaching itself has implications for building motivation and commitment of teachers. Principals need to assess the consequences of a particular decision on promoting job-enrichment opportunities for teachers.

Friendship opportunities and opportunities to work with others are two other dimensions identified in the Job Characteristics model (Sashkin and Morris, 1984). "Friendship opportunities" refers to the extent to which the work setting provides for the development of close contacts among teachers and the development of friendly patterns of interaction. "Working with others" refers to the extent to which the accomplishment of tasks requires that teachers interact with other teachers in order to complete the work successfully. These dimensions seem related to the extent to which workers are involved in their jobs, experience satisfaction, and report improvements in work quality (Sashkin and Morris, 1984).

In summary, the Job Characteristics model provides principals with a conceptual framework allowing them to make informed decisions about the nature and structure of the work of teaching to help teachers feel that their job is meaningful, to enable them to learn the actual outcomes of their efforts, to provide them with feelings of control and responsibility for results, and to help them become part of a social unit. These conditions are related to high intrinsic work motivation, increases in quality performance, high job satisfaction, and lower absence and turnover rates.

Appendix 14.2 contains a key that allows you to score your responses to the Quality of Work Life in Teaching form. Please score by following the directions provided. Note that five subscores are provided, each corresponding to an important dimension of most job-enrichment models. With the exception of work speed and routine, the higher the score, the more enriched is the job, the greater are the possibilities for increased motivation and commitment, and the more likely that connections between and among people will embody community.

*W*OMEN AS A SPECIAL CASE

Much of the available motivation literature is subject to male bias; thus, the accompanying prescriptions for practice may not apply to women. The problem, according to Shakeshaft (1987), is *androcentrism,* defined as "the practice of viewing the world and shaping reality from a male perspective [and] the elevation of the masculine to the level of the universal and the ideal and honoring of men and the male principle above women and female" (94). Maslow's theory, the two-factor theory, and the job enrichment theory, for example, give heavy emphasis to competition, the setting of task goals, individual achievement, the building of self-competence and self-esteem, individual autonomy, and self-actualization. Women, by contrast, give emphasis to such themes as cooperation, intimacy, affiliation, the construction of interpersonal networks, and community building. In using teamwork as an example, Shakeshaft (1987) points out that men tend to view the concept in terms of goals, roles, and responsibilities. A team must first define what needs to be done and then allocate responsibilities to roles making clear not only what is expected, but how one person's niche fits that of others who comprise the team. The metaphor for team, in this context, is sport in the form of baseball, basketball, or football. For women, teamwork is not the parallel play of men, but the meshing of individual identities to create a new configuration and the bonding together of people in a common cause.

Key in applying the concepts from traditional motivation theory is redefining concept indicators. Achievement, for example, can mean the accumulation of a series of individual successes on the one hand or the successful constructing of a learning community on the other. Application of the motivation theory and research should therefore be idiosyncratic. If you want to know what motivates people start by asking them.

$\mathcal{M}$OTIVATION, EFFICACY, AND STUDENT PERFORMANCE

When motivation is down and discretion is low, a teacher's sense of self-esteem becomes blurred, resulting in the erosion of professional confidence. Ultimately, efficacy is affected. As suggested earlier in our discussion of Origin and Pawn feelings and their effects, teacher efficacy is directly related to how teachers behave in the classroom, to students' behavior in the classroom, and to the quality of student achievement they obtain.

"All students can learn" has become a slogan that is repeated by administrators trying to urge teachers to work harder or to change their practice. Most teachers will swear allegiance to this slogan publicly but privately many do not believe it. In their research, Ashton and Webb (1986) found, for example, that teachers with a low sense of efficacy had come to believe that many students cannot learn and will not learn and that there is not much they can do about it. Teachers with a high sense of efficacy, by contrast, believe that all students are capable of learning and that teachers can do a great deal to increase student achievement.*

Ashton and Webb note that there is a second dimension to teachers' sense of efficacy. Not only does it refer to one's belief that students can learn if taught, but also to a particular teacher's belief that she or he has the ability to do the right kind of teaching that will result in student performance. With this two-part definition of efficacy in hand, Ashton and Webb found that teachers with a high sense of efficacy exhibited teacher behaviors that were characterized by warmth. They were more accepting of student responses, more accepting of student initiatives, and more attentive to student needs. Students responded by being more enthusiastic

---

*This discussion follows closely the discussion of efficacy and student achievement in Chapter 7, "Teachers, Keys to School Improvement," in Sergiovanni (2000).

and by initiating more interactions with the teachers. Further, student achievement was higher in both tests of high school mathematics and tests of language basic skills.

Enhancing Efficacy

The good news is that teachers' sense of efficacy can change. Teachers can come to feel more efficacious or less efficacious depending on a variety of factors. Further, higher levels of motivation and commitment and higher levels of efficacy seem to be related to each other. What are the factors that contribute to these higher levels? How do these factors interact with each other? Ashton and Webb (1986) found that school climates that are supportive, teaching and learning environments that are characterized by collegial values and shared decision making, and a school culture that provides a sense of purpose and a shared covenant as a basis for accountability are important. Together, these factors contribute to cooperative relationships and higher levels of interaction; higher levels of personal responsibility for outcomes; and higher standards and expectations as well as a sense that the work of teaching is meaningful and significant. These relationships, summarized from Ashton and Webb's research, are provided here:

1. **a.** A school climate where teachers support each other, and principals support teachers, encourages cooperative relationships and high levels of social interaction among teachers
   b. Collegial values where shared decision making is present and shared inquiry prevails encourages feelings of high personal causation among teachers and high responsibility for work outcomes
   c. A school culture where sense of purpose, shared values and ideas, and a system of accountability based on these ideas is found encourages high standards and expectations, high pride and self-esteem, and the feeling that one's work is meaningful and significant

2. **a.** Cooperative relationships and high levels of social interaction among teachers encourage a high sense of efficacy, motivation, and commitment by teachers
   b. Feelings of high personal causation and high responsibility for work outcomes encourage a high sense of efficacy, motivation, and commitment by teachers
   c. Having high standards and expectations, high levels of pride and self-esteem, and expanding personal meaning and significance at work encourage a high sense of efficacy, motivation, and commitment by teachers

3. A high sense of teacher efficacy, motivation, and commitment
   a. Leads to teacher behaviors that are warm and accepting of student responses, accepting of student initiatives, and attentive to the needs of students

b. Leads to student behaviors characterized by student enthusiasm for learning and student initiation of interaction with teachers
c. Leads to higher student achievement as measured by high school mathematics and language basic skills test scores

In sum, efficacy is important: Individual efficacy is an important part of the professional and cultural world of teachers, and collective efficacy is an important part of the professional and cultural world of schools. Both suffer when bureaucratic policies, management systems, and mandated one-size-fits-all standards and assessments are placed at the center and thus determine the cultural worlds of teachers and other locals.

$\mathcal{T}$HE POWER OF BELIEFS

In this and other chapters, adding moral authority as a basis for leadership to bureaucratic and psychological authority was recommended. Doing so depends on schools being able to develop a set of shared values and beliefs that spells out who they are, what they want to accomplish, and how. These centers of ideas, once accepted, function as covenants that provide the basis for bonding people together as members of a learning community that knows why it exists. Further, covenants detail what the community owes its members and what its members in turn owe the community. This theme was at the heart of earlier discussions of leadership and school culture.

Interpreted properly, the theory and research in the area of teacher motivation and commitment can be helpful in understanding why covenants that lead to building professional communities of practice for teachers are important and how they enable more effective teaching and learning. Often, our policy mandates, administrative directives, and complacency in insisting on "business as usual" present conditions and practices at odds with this knowledge base. School practices, for example, too often encourage bureaucratic teaching, promote isolationism among teachers, encourage privatism, and discourage social interaction. These conditions are typically associated with decreases in teacher motivation and commitment. Effective teaching and learning and other school improvement efforts are enhanced as teachers work harder and smarter and as their commitment to the school and its success is increased. This gap between present practice and what we know represents a test of leadership for principals.

Even more challenging is the attempt to broaden present conceptions of the nature of human potential. Without dismissing the importance of self-interest, principals and faculties must give far more attention to expressive and moral reasons for determining courses of action. As expressive and moral authority gain acceptance as legitimate ways of working with teachers, professional learning communities emerge. Attention will need to be given, as well, to applying these same ideas to students.

SOME REFLECTIONS

1. Use the climate protocols in Appendix 14.1 to study the climate of your school. Review the 72 items and eight categories. Select from 20 to 30 items that will be the focus of your study. These items may reflect one or two of the eight category themes, or they may be a sampling of all the items. Plot your scores on the Profile Scoring Sheet. Using Rensis Likert's theory, how would you describe your school? What changes would you like to make? Where would you begin?

REFERENCES

Argyris, Chris. 1957. *Personality and Organization.* New York: Harper & Row.

Ashton, Patricia T., and Rodman B. Webb. 1986. *Making a Difference: Teachers' Sense of Efficacy and Student Achievement.* New York: Longman.

Bidwell, Charles E. 1975. "The School as a Formal Organization," in James O. March (Ed.), *Handbook of Organizations* (pp. 972–1022). Chicago: Rand McNally.

Bradley, Ann. 1993, March 31. "By Asking Teachers about 'Context' of Work, Center Moves to Cutting Edge of Research," *Education Week,* 7.

Brayfield, A. H., and W. H. Crockett. 1955. "Employee Attitudes and Employee Performance," *Psychological Bulletin* 52(1), 415–422.

Clark, David L., Linda S. Lotto, and Terry A. Astuto. 1984. "Effective Schools and School Improvement: A Comparative Analysis of Two Lines of Inquiry," *Educational Administration Quarterly* 20(3), 41–68.

Coombs, Arthur W. 1959. "Personality Theory and Its Implication for Curriculum Development," in Alexander Frazier (Ed.), *Learning More about Learning.* Washington, DC: Association for Supervision and Curriculum Development.

De Charms, Richard. 1968. *Personal Causation.* New York: Academic Press.

Deci, Edward L. 1995. *Why We Do What We Do.* New York: G. B. Putnam's Sons.

Dornbush, S. M., and W. R. Scott. 1975. *Evaluation and the Exercise of Authority.* San Francisco: Jossey-Bass.

Elmore, Richard F. 2000. *Building a New Structure for School Leadership.* Washington, DC: Albert Shanker Institute.

Elmore, Richard F. 2002. *Bridging the Gap between Standards and Achievement: The Imperative for Professional Development in Education.* Washington, DC: Albert Shanker Institute.

Etzioni, Amitai. 1988. *The Moral Dimension: Toward a New Economics.* New York: Free Press.

Glatthorn, Allan A. 1984. *Differentiated Supervision.* Alexandria, VA: Association for Supervision and Curriculum Development.

Hackman, J. R., and G. R. Oldham. 1980. *Work Redesign.* Reading, MA: Addison-Wesley.

Hackman, J. R., G. Oldham, R. Johnson, and K. Purdy. 1975. "A New Strategy for Job Enrichment," *California Management Review* 17(4).

Herzberg, F. 1966. *Work and the Nature of Man.* New York: World Publishing.

Herzberg, F., B. Mausner, and B. Snyderman. 1959. *The Motivation to Work.* New York: Wiley.

Keenan, Charles. 1974. *Channels for Change: A Survey of Teachers in Chicago Elementary Schools.* Doctoral dissertation. Urbana: Department of Educational Administration, University of Illinois.

Kelley, Carolyn. 1999. "The Motivational Impact of School-Based Performance Awards," *Journal of Personnel Evaluation in Education* 12(4), 309–326.

Kohn, Alfie. 1993, September–October. "Why Incentive Plans Cannot Work," *Harvard Business Review.*

Lieberman, Ann, and Lynne Miller. 1999. *Teachers—Transforming Their World and Their Work.* New York: Teachers College Press.

Lortie, Dan. 1975. *School Teacher.* Chicago: University of Chicago Press.

MacDonald, James. 1964. "An Image of Man: The Learner Himself," in Ronald R. Doll (Ed.), *Individualizing Instruction.* Washington, DC: Association for Supervision and Curriculum Development.

Madaus, George F. 1999. "The Influence of Testing on the Curriculum" in Margaret J. Early and Kenneth J. Rehage (Eds.), *Issues in Curriculum: A Selection of Chapters from NSSE Yearbooks.* Ninety-Eighth Yearbook of the National Society for the Study of Education. Part II. Chicago: University of Chicago Press. (Note: This chapter originally appeared in the 1988 Yearbook.)

Maslow, A. H. 1943. "A Theory of Human Motivation," *Psychological Review* 50(2), 370–396.

Natriello, Gary. 1984. "Teachers' Perceptions of the Frequency of Evaluation and Assessments of Their Effort and Effectiveness," *American Educational Research Journal* 21(3), 579–595.

Peters, Thomas J., and Robert H. Waterman, Jr. 1982. *In Search of Excellence.* New York: Harper & Row.

Pfeiffer, J. William, and Leonard D. Goodstein. 1984. *The 1984 Annual: Developing Human Resources.* San Diego, CA: University Associates.

Rosenholtz, Susan J. 1984. "Political Myths about Educational Reform: Lessons from Research on Teaching." Paper prepared for the Education Commission of the States, Denver, CO.

Sashkin, Marshall, and William C. Morris. 1984. *Organizational Behavior Concepts and Experiences.* Reston, VA: Reston Co.

Schultz, Theodore W. 1982. "Human Capital Approaches in Organizing and Paying for Education," in Walter McMahan and Terry G. Geste (Eds.), *Financing Education: Overcoming Inefficiency and Inequity* (pp. 36–51). Urbana: University of Illinois Press.

Sergiovanni, Thomas J. 1966. "Factors Which Affect Satisfaction and Dissatisfaction of Teachers," *Journal of Educational Administration* 5(1), 66–82.

Sergiovanni, Thomas J. 1968. "New Evidence on Teacher Morale: A Proposal for Staff Differentiation," *The North Central Association Quarterly* 62(3), 259–266.

Sergiovanni, Thomas J. 2000. *The Lifeworld of Leadership: Creating Culture, Community, and Personal Meaning in Our Schools.* San Francisco: Jossey-Bass.

Shakeshaft, Charol. (1987). *Women in Educational Administration.* Beverly Hills, CA: Sage.

Tucker, Marc S., and Judy B. Codding. 1998. *Standards for Our Schools: How to Set Them, Measure Them, and Reach Them.* San Francisco: Jossey-Bass.

Vroom, V. H. 1964. *Work and Motivation.* New York: Wiley.

Waller, Willard. 1932. *Sociology of Teaching.* New York: Wiley.

Wise, Arthur E. 1979. *Legislated Learning: The Bureaucratization of the American Classroom.* Berkeley: University of California Press.

Studying the Climate of Your School

The pioneering work of Rensis Likert and his colleagues at the Institute for Social Research, University of Michigan, from the late 1950s through the 1960s, placed the concept climate in the mainstream of management thought. This research introduced into practice the idea that principals and other school administrators needed to focus not only on "end results"—indicators of effectiveness of their policies, actions, and decisions—but also on the "mediating" indicators as well (Likert, 1961, 1967).

Mediating Variables

According to Likert's theory, school policies, standard operating procedures, and accompanying administrative actions and decisions do not directly influence school effectiveness and other end results variables. Instead, they influence how teachers, students, and others perceive and feel, the attitudes and values they share, the trust and support binding them together, and the degree to which they are motivated to work and are committed to school goals and purposes. It is these mediating indicators that in turn influence school effectiveness.

Initiating → mediating → school effectiveness variables

Likert reached these conclusions by studying the characteristics of more and less effective work groups and organizations. He found that differences in the mediating variables of these group and organization types followed consistent patterns. He was able to identify four distinct patterns of management: Systems 1, 2, 3, and 4. System 1 resembles a rigid bureaucracy and is characterized by little mutual confidence and trust among supervisors and workers, direct supervision, high control, centralized decision making, detailed rules and regulations and work operating procedures, top-down communications, and routine work regulation by inspection. System 4 reflects a commitment to the development and use of human resources and is characterized by trust, supportive relationships, goal clarity and commitment, autonomy with responsibility, group decision making, authority more closely linked with ability, team work, social interaction, and controls linked to agreed-upon goals and purposes. Systems 2 and 3 are at intermediate positions on this continuum. Although they represent a distinct improvement over the rigid bureaucratic management of System 1, they do not recognize human potential as fully as does System 4.

The basic features of Likert's theory are illustrated in Figure 14.2. The principal's assumptions and resulting behavior with regard to leadership, control, organization, goals and purposes, and the motivation of teachers and students provide a specific pattern of management that can be described on a continuum from System 1 to 4. This management system elicits a predictable response from teachers at work that influences their motivation and performance. Teacher attitudes and behavior, it follows, have predictable consequences on school effectiveness. The effects of management systems 2 and 3 on mediating and school effectiveness variables would fall somewhere between the indicators provided in Figure 14.2.

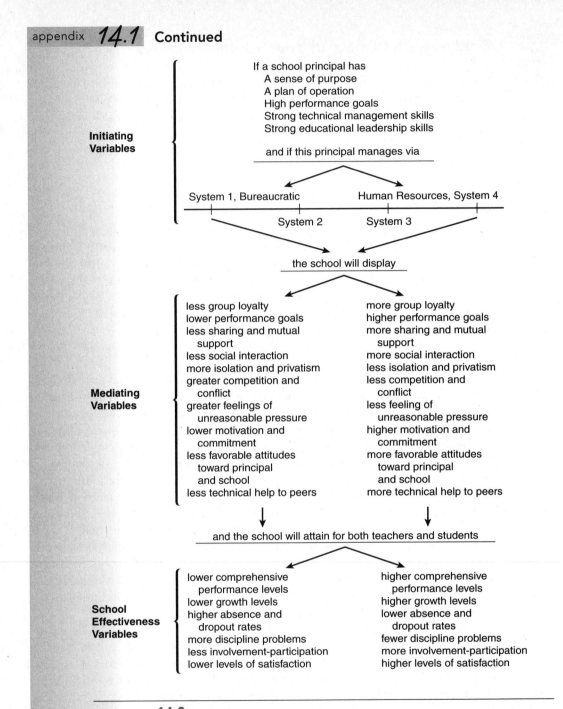

Initiating Variables

If a school principal has
  A sense of purpose
  A plan of operation
  High performance goals
  Strong technical management skills
  Strong educational leadership skills

and if this principal manages via

System 1, Bureaucratic   Human Resources, System 4

System 2   System 3

the school will display

Mediating Variables

less group loyalty	more group loyalty
lower performance goals	higher performance goals
less sharing and mutual support	more sharing and mutual support
less social interaction	more social interaction
more isolation and privatism	less isolation and privatism
greater competition and conflict	less competition and conflict
greater feelings of unreasonable pressure	less feeling of unreasonable pressure
lower motivation and commitment	higher motivation and commitment
less favorable attitudes toward principal and school	more favorable attitudes toward principal and school
less technical help to peers	more technical help to peers

and the school will attain for both teachers and students

School Effectiveness Variables

lower comprehensive performance levels	higher comprehensive performance levels
lower growth levels	higher growth levels
higher absence and dropout rates	lower absence and dropout rates
more discipline problems	fewer discipline problems
less involvement-participation	more involvement-participation
lower levels of satisfaction	higher levels of satisfaction

figure **14.2** **How Management Systems 1 and 4 Influence Mediating and School Effectiveness Variables**

Sources: Summarized from *New Patterns of Management* by Rensis Likert, 1961, New York: McGraw-Hill, and *The Human Organization: Its Management and Value* by Rensis Likert, 1967, New York: McGraw-Hill.

Evaluating the Climate of Your School

Likert (1967) developed the Profile of Organizational Characteristics (POC) as a tool for measuring and charting system characteristics of the organizations he studied. The POC provides an indication not only of which management system characterizes a particular organization, but of that organization's climate as well.

The POC was adopted for school use in the form of the Profile of a School. An abbreviated version of the profile appears in Figure 14.3. Figure 14.4 provides a score sheet for the profile. Use the instrument and the score sheet to evaluate your school or another school you know very well. Try to imagine how most of the teachers who work in this school would respond if they had the chance. Following the directions, plot your scores on the score sheet and draw a profile depicting your perceptions of that school's climate.

There are limitations in evaluating school "secondhand"; nonetheless, comparing your responses with those of others who know this school should reveal some similarities. Chances are your profile line reveals that this school can be characterized as System 2 or 3. Consistencies are likely in your ratings as you move from item to item, although your profile line probably has certain peaks toward System 4 and dips toward System 1. Peaks represent unusually strong qualities of the school's climate. Dips, by contrast, suggest areas where improvements are needed. Analyzing peaks and dips on the profile line allows principals and teachers to diagnose the school climate.

Dips can also be used as benchmarks for evaluating school climate improvement efforts. Imagine a school with relatively low climate scores on dimensions describing the extent to which students trust teachers and feel free to consult with them on academic and nonacademic matters. Principals and teachers might agree on a plan to improve this situation. Perhaps they decide to initiate voluntary open forum sessions for students and teachers on a weekly basis. They might agree as well to conduct weekly "that was the week that was" sessions in homerooms, in which students are free to summarize their academic week, pointing out highs and lows. More informally, teachers might resolve to be more sensitive to this issue as they interact with students. After several months, a second reading of the school climate might be taken; new responses could be compared with benchmark responses to detect improvements.

One implicit benefit of the POS and other climate instruments is that they provide handy structures for encouraging conversation and dialogue about events and conditions that ordinarily are difficult to discuss. It is much easier, for example, for teachers and principals to discuss items and item responses and their meanings than to engage in more unstructured conversations about school conditions and school improvements.

Take a moment to reflect on the climate of the school that you just evaluated. Using the POS, in its entirety, or a shortened version comprised of items that you select, evaluate the climate by first indicating how you would like it to be. What discrepancies

Organizational Variable	System 1	System 2	System 3	System 4

A. Leadership Processes Used:

	RARELY	SOMETIMES	OFTEN	VERY OFTEN
1. How often is your behavior seen by students as friendly and supportive?	① ②	③ ④	⑤ ⑥	⑦ ⑧

How often does the principal seek and use your ideas about:

2. academic matters	① ②	③ ④	⑤ ⑥	⑦ ⑧
3. nonacademic school matters	① ②	③ ④	⑤ ⑥	⑦ ⑧
4. How often do you see the principal's behavior as friendly and supportive?	① ②	③ ④	⑤ ⑥	⑦ ⑧

	VERY LITTLE	SOME	QUITE A BIT	A VERY GREAT DEAL
5. How much confidence and trust does the principal have in you?	① ②	③ ④	⑤ ⑥	⑦ ⑧
6. How much confidence and trust do you have in the principal?	① ②	③ ④ SOMEWHAT	⑤ ⑥	⑦ ⑧

	NOT FREE	FREE	QUITE FREE	VERY FREE
7. How free do you feel to talk to the principal about school matters?	① ②	③ ④	⑤ ⑥	⑦ ⑧

	VERY LITTLE	SOME	QUITE A BIT	A VERY GREAT DEAL
8. How much confidence and trust do you have in students?	① ②	③ ④	⑤ ⑥	⑦ ⑧
9. How much confidence and trust do students have in you?	① ②	③ ④ SOMEWHAT	⑤ ⑥	⑦ ⑧

	NOT FREE	FREE	QUITE FREE	VERY FREE
10. How free do students feel to talk to you about school matters?	① ②	③ ④	⑤ ⑥	⑦ ⑧

How often are students' ideas sought and used by the principal about:

	RARELY	SOMETIMES	OFTEN	VERY OFTEN
11. academic matters	① ②	③ ④	⑤ ⑥	⑦ ⑧
12. nonacademic school matters	① ②	③ ④	⑤ ⑥	⑦ ⑧
13. How often does the principal use small group meetings to solve school problems?				

B. Character of Motivational Forces:

	DISLIKE	SOMETIMES DISLIKE IT, SOMETIMES LIKE IT	USUALLY LIKE IT	LIKE IT VERY MUCH
14. What is the general attitude of students toward your school?	① ②	③ ④	⑤ ⑥	⑦ ⑧

How often do you try to be friendly and supportive to:

	RARELY	SOMETIMES	OFTEN	VERY OFTEN
15. the principal	① ②	③ ④	⑤ ⑥	⑦ ⑧
16. other teachers	① ②	③ ④	⑤ ⑥	⑦ ⑧

	USUALLY A WASTE OF TIME	SOMETIMES A WASTE OF TIME	OFTEN WORTH-WHILE	ALMOST ALWAYS WORTH-WHILE
17. In your job is it worthwhile or a waste of time to do your best?	① ②	③ ④	⑤ ⑥	⑦ ⑧

	NOT SATISFYING	SOMEWHAT SATISFYING	QUITE SATISFYING	VERY SATISFYING
18. How satisfying is your work at your school?	① ②	③ ④	⑤ ⑥	⑦ ⑧

To what extent do the following feel responsible for seeing that educational excellence is achieved in your school:

	VERY LITTLE	SOME	CONSIDER-ABLE	VERY GREAT
19. principal	① ②	③ ④	⑤ ⑥	⑦ ⑧
20. department heads	① ②	③ ④	⑤ ⑥	⑦ ⑧
21. teachers	① ②	③ ④	⑤ ⑥	⑦ ⑧
22. To what extent do students help each other when they want to get something done?	① ②	③ ④	⑤ ⑥	⑦ ⑧
23. To what extent do students look forward to coming to school?	① ②	③ ④	⑤ ⑥	⑦ ⑧
24. To what extent do students feel excited about learning?	① ②	③ ④	⑤ ⑥	⑦ ⑧
25. To what extent do you look forward to your teaching day?	① ②	③ ④	⑤ ⑥	⑦ ⑧
26. To what extent are you encouraged to be innovative in developing more effective and efficient educational practices?	① ②	③ ④	⑤ ⑥	⑦ ⑧

C. Character of Communication Process:

	VERY LITTLE	SOME	QUITE A BIT	A VERY GREAT DEAL
27. How much do students feel that you are trying to help them with their problems?	① ②	③ ④	⑤ ⑥	⑦ ⑧
28. How much accurate information concerning school affairs is given to you by students?	① ②	③ ④	⑤ ⑥	⑦ ⑧

figure **14.3**   Profile of a School: Teacher Form

Organizational Variable	System 1	System 2	System 3	System 4

D. Character of Interaction-Influence:

How much influence do the following *have* on what goes on in your school?

	VERY LITTLE	SOME	QUITE A BIT	A VERY GREAT DEAL
29. principal	① ②	③ ④	⑤ ⑥	⑦ ⑧
30. teachers	① ②	③ ④	⑤ ⑥	⑦ ⑧
31. central staff of your school system	① ②	③ ④	⑤ ⑥	⑦ ⑧
32. students	① ②	③ ④	⑤ ⑥	⑦ ⑧

How much influence do you think the following *should have* on what goes on in your school?

33. principal	① ②	③ ④	⑤ ⑥	⑦ ⑧
34. teachers	① ②	③ ④	⑤ ⑥	⑦ ⑧
35. central staff of your school system	① ②	③ ④	⑤ ⑥	⑦ ⑧
36. students	① ②	③ ④	⑤ ⑥	⑦ ⑧

37. How much influence do you think students *have* on what goes on in your school? ① ② ③ ④ ⑤ ⑥ ⑦ ⑧

38. How much influence do you think students *should have* on what goes on in your school? ① ② ③ ④ ⑤ ⑥ ⑦ ⑧

USUALLY IGNORED	APPEALED BUT NOT RESOLVED	RESOLVED BY PRINCIPAL	RESOLVED BY ALL THOSE AFFECTED

39. In your school, how are conflicts between departments usually resolved? ① ② ③ ④ ⑤ ⑥ ⑦ ⑧

VERY LITTLE	SOME	QUITE A BIT	A VERY GREAT DEAL

40. How much do teachers in your school encourage each other to do their best? ① ② ③ ④ ⑤ ⑥ ⑦ ⑧

EVERYONE FOR SELF	LITTLE COOPERATIVE TEAMWORK	A MODERATE AMOUNT OF COOPERATIVE TEAMWORK	A VERY GREAT AMOUNT OF COOPERATIVE TEAMWORK

41. In your school, is it "everyone for self" or do principals, teachers, and students work as a team? ① ② ③ ④ ⑤ ⑥ ⑦ ⑧

VERY LITTLE	SOME	QUITE A BIT	A VERY GREAT DEAL

42. How much do different departments plan together and coordinate their efforts? ① ② ③ ④ ⑤ ⑥ ⑦ ⑧

E. Character of Decision-Making Processes:

RARELY	SOMETIMES	OFTEN	VERY OFTEN

43. How often do you seek and use students' ideas about academic matters, such as their work, course content, teaching plans and methods? ① ② ③ ④ ⑤ ⑥ ⑦ ⑧

44. How often do you seek and use students' ideas about nonacademic matters, such as student activities, rules of conduct, and discipline? ① ② ③ ④ ⑤ ⑥ ⑦ ⑧

VIEWED WITH GREAT SUSPICION	SOME VIEWED WITH SUSPICION, SOME WITH TRUST	USUALLY VIEWED WITH TRUST	ALMOST ALWAYS VIEWED WITH TRUST

How do students view communication from:

45. you	① ②	③ ④	⑤ ⑥	⑦ ⑧
46. the principal	① ②	③ ④	⑤ ⑥	⑦ ⑧

NOT WELL	SOMEWHAT WELL	QUITE WELL	VERY WELL

47. How well do you know the problems faced by students in their school work? ① ② ③ ④ ⑤ ⑥ ⑦ ⑧

VERY LITTLE	SOME	CONSIDERABLE	VERY GREAT

48. To what extent is the communication between you and your students open and candid? ① ② ③ ④ ⑤ ⑥ ⑦ ⑧

49. To what extent does the principal give you useful information and ideas? ① ② ③ ④ ⑤ ⑥ ⑦ ⑧

FROM THE TOP DOWN	MOSTLY DOWN	DOWN AND UP	DOWN, UP, AND LATERALLY

50. What is the direction of the flow of information about academic and nonacademic school matters? ① ② ③ ④ ⑤ ⑥ ⑦ ⑧

VIEWED WITH GREAT SUSPICION	SOME VIEWED WITH SUSPICION, SOME WITH TRUST	USUALLY VIEWED WITH TRUST	ALMOST ALWAYS VIEWED WITH TRUST

51. How do you view communications from the principal? ① ② ③ ④ ⑤ ⑥ ⑦ ⑧

USUALLY INACCURATE	OFTEN INACCURATE	FAIRLY ACCURATE	ALMOST ALWAYS ACCURATE

52. How accurate is upward communication to the principal? ① ② ③ ④ ⑤ ⑥ ⑦ ⑧

(continued)

figure **14.3** Continued

Organizational Variable	System 1	System 2	System 3	System 4
	NOT WELL	SOMEWHAT WELL	QUITE WELL	VERY WELL
53. How well does the principal know the problems faced by the teachers?	① ②	③ ④	⑤ ⑥	⑦ ⑧
To what extent is communication open and candid:	VERY LITTLE	SOME	CONSIDERABLE	A VERY GREAT DEAL
54. between principal and teachers	① ②	③ ④	⑤ ⑥	⑦ ⑧
55. among teachers	① ②	③ ④	⑤ ⑥	⑦ ⑧
	VERY LITTLE	SOME	QUITE A BIT	A VERY GREAT DEAL
56. How much help do you get from the central staff of your school system?	① ②	③ ④	⑤ ⑥	⑦ ⑧
	VERY LITTLE	SOME	QUITE A BIT	A VERY GREAT DEAL
57. How much are students involved in major decisions affecting them?	① ②	③ ④	⑤ ⑥	⑦ ⑧
	AT MUCH TOO HIGH LEVELS	AT SOMEWHAT TOO HIGH LEVELS	AT QUITE SATISFACTORY LEVELS	AT THE BEST LEVELS
58. Are decisions made at the best levels for effective performance?	① ②	③ ④	⑤ ⑥	⑦ ⑧
	VERY LITTLE	SOME	CONSIDERABLE	VERY GREAT
59. To what extent are you involved in major decisions related to your work?	① ②	③ ④	⑤ ⑥	⑦ ⑧
60. To what extent are decision makers aware of problems, particularly at lower levels?	① ②	③ ④	⑤ ⑥	⑦ ⑧
F. Character of Goal Setting:				
61. To what extent does the principal make sure that planning and setting priorities are done well?	① ②	③ ④	⑤ ⑥	⑦ ⑧
G. Character of Control Processes:	HIGHLY AUTHORI-TARIAN	SOMEWHAT AUTHORI-TARIAN	CONSUL-TATIVE	PARTICI-PATIVE GROUP
What is the administrative style of:				
62. the principal	① ②	③ ④	⑤ ⑥	⑦ ⑧
63. the superintendent of schools	① ②	③ ④	⑤ ⑥	⑦ ⑧
How competent is the principal:	NOT COMPETENT	SOMEWHAT COMPETENT	QUITE COMPETENT	VERY COMPETENT
64. as an administrator	① ②	③ ④	⑤ ⑥	⑦ ⑧
65. as an educator	① ②	③ ④	⑤ ⑥	⑦ ⑧
H. Performance Goals:	VERY LITTLE	SOME	CONSIDERABLE	VERY GREAT
66. To what extent does the principal try to provide you with the materials, equipment, and space you need to do your job well?	① ②	③ ④	⑤ ⑥	⑦ ⑧
	VERY LITTLE	SOME	QUITE A BIT	A VERY GREAT DEAL
67. How much do you feel that the principal is interested in your success as a teacher?	① ②	③ ④	⑤ ⑥	⑦ ⑧
68. How much interest do students feel you have in their success as students?	① ②	③ ④	⑤ ⑥	⑦ ⑧
69. How much does the principal try to help you with your problems?	① ②	③ ④	⑤ ⑥	⑦ ⑧
70. To what extent do students accept high performance goals in your school?	① ②	③ ④	⑤ ⑥	⑦ ⑧
	INADEQUATE	SOMEWHAT INADEQUATE	QUITE ADEQUATE	VERY ADEQUATE
71. How adequate are the supplies and equipment the school has?	① ②	③ ④	⑤ ⑥	⑦ ⑧
	LOW	ABOUT AVERAGE	QUITE HIGH	VERY HIGH
72. How high are the principal's goals for educational performance?	① ②	③ ④	⑤ ⑥	⑦ ⑧

f i g u r e **14.3** Continued

Source: Items and scoring formats are from the Profile of a School, Form 3, Teacher Form. Items have been regrouped and renumbered, and system designations have been added. The original questionnaire contains additional items that enable evaluation of high school departments, grade levels, or teaching teams. Used by permission of Rensis Likert Associates, Inc., Ann Arbor, Michigan, 48104. Copyright © 1977 by Jane Gibson Likert and Rensis Likert. Distributed by Rensis Likert Associates, Inc. All rights reserved. No further reproduction in any form authorized without written permission of Rensis Likert Associates, Inc., Ann Arbor, Michigan, 48104.

Item	System 1		System 2		System 3		System 4	
1	1	2	3	4	5	6	7	8
2	1	2	3	4	5	6	7	8
3	1	2	3	4	5	6	7	8
4	1	2	3	4	5	6	7	8
5	1	2	3	4	5	6	7	8
6	1	2	3	4	5	6	7	8
7	1	2	3	4	5	6	7	8
8	1	2	3	4	5	6	7	8
9	1	2	3	4	5	6	7	8
10	1	2	3	4	5	6	7	8
11	1	2	3	4	5	6	7	8
12	1	2	3	4	5	6	7	8
13	1	2	3	4	5	6	7	8
14	1	2	3	4	5	6	7	8
15	1	2	3	4	5	6	7	8
16	1	2	3	4	5	6	7	8
17	1	2	3	4	5	6	7	8
18	1	2	3	4	5	6	7	8
19	1	2	3	4	5	6	7	8
20	1	2	3	4	5	6	7	8
21	1	2	3	4	5	6	7	8
22	1	2	3	4	5	6	7	8
23	1	2	3	4	5	6	7	8
24	1	2	3	4	5	6	7	8
25	1	2	3	4	5	6	7	8
26	1	2	3	4	5	6	7	8
27	1	2	3	4	5	6	7	8
28	1	2	3	4	5	6	7	8
29	1	2	3	4	5	6	7	8
30	1	2	3	4	5	6	7	8
31	1	2	3	4	5	6	7	8
32	1	2	3	4	5	6	7	8
33	1	2	3	4	5	6	7	8
34	1	2	3	4	5	6	7	8
35	1	2	3	4	5	6	7	8
36	1	2	3	4	5	6	7	8
37	1	2	3	4	5	6	7	8
38	1	2	3	4	5	6	7	8
39	1	2	3	4	5	6	7	8
40	1	2	3	4	5	6	7	8
41	1	2	3	4	5	6	7	8
42	1	2	3	4	5	6	7	8
43	1	2	3	4	5	6	7	8
44	1	2	3	4	5	6	7	8
45	1	2	3	4	5	6	7	8
46	1	2	3	4	5	6	7	8
47	1	2	3	4	5	6	7	8
48	1	2	3	4	5	6	7	8
49	1	2	3	4	5	6	7	8

(continued)

figure **14.4** **Profile of a School Scoring Sheet**

Item	System 1		System 2		System 3		System 4	
50	1	2	3	4	5	6	7	8
51	1	2	3	4	5	6	7	8
52	1	2	3	4	5	6	7	8
53	1	2	3	4	5	6	7	8
54	1	2	3	4	5	6	7	8
55	1	2	3	4	5	6	7	8
56	1	2	3	4	5	6	7	8
57	1	2	3	4	5	6	7	8
58	1	2	3	4	5	6	7	8
59	1	2	3	4	5	6	7	8
60	1	2	3	4	5	6	7	8
61	1	2	3	4	5	6	7	8
62	1	2	3	4	5	6	7	8
63	1	2	3	4	5	6	7	8
64	1	2	3	4	5	6	7	8
65	1	2	3	4	5	6	7	8
66	1	2	3	4	5	6	7	8
67	1	2	3	4	5	6	7	8
68	1	2	3	4	5	6	7	8
69	1	2	3	4	5	6	7	8
70	1	2	3	4	5	6	7	8
71	1	2	3	4	5	6	7	8
72	1	2	3	4	5	6	7	8

figure **14.4** Continued

do you note between your ideal and real responses? Assume that your responses represent average responses for the entire faculty. Based on the scoring profile that you prepare, what improvements need to be made in the climate of this school?

An important strength of the POS is that climate is not conceived as the product of only the principal's behavior or of any other single source. As one reads the items, it becomes clear that climates are based on a mix of attitudes, beliefs, and behaviors of everyone who lives and works in the school. They are manifestations of the school's culture. This being the case, school improvement efforts require that teachers and principals work together. Striving toward a System 4 climate, for example, requires a shared commitment. As you review the climate profile of the school you evaluated, what ideas come to mind as to how you as principal (and the faculty whose responses are represented by your responses) can plan to work together to improve the school?

References

Likert, Rensis. 1961. *New Patterns of Management.* New York: McGraw-Hill.
Likert, Rensis. 1967. *The Human Organization: Its Management and Value.* New York: McGraw-Hill.

Quality of Work Life in Teaching Scoring Form

Instructions: Transfer your answers to the questions on the QWLinT instrument (Exhibit 14.1) to the scoring grid below, circling the number below the letter of the answer you selected. When you have transferred all answers and circled the appropriate numbers, add up all the numbers circled in each of the columns and enter the total in the empty box at the bottom of the column. Each of these totals refers to one of the scales in the QWLinT. Note that high scores for autonomy, personal growth, work complexity, and task-related interaction indicate a strong presence of thse characteristics and suggest high job-enrichment opportunities in one's job. High scores for work speed and routine indicate a weak presence of this characteristic and low job enrichment.

Q.1				Q.2				Q.3				Q.4				Q.5			
A	M	P	N	A	M	P	N	A	M	P	N	A	M	P	N	A	M	P	N
1	2	3	4	4	3	2	1	1	2	3	4	1	2	3	4	4	3	2	1
Q.6				**Q.7**				**Q.8**				**Q.9**				**Q.10**			
A	M	P	N	A	M	P	N	A	M	P	N	A	M	P	N	A	M	P	N
4	3	2	1	4	3	2	1	1	2	3	4	1	2	3	4	1	2	3	4
Q.11				**Q.12**				**Q.13**				**Q.14**				**Q.15**			
A	M	P	N	A	M	P	N	A	M	P	N	A	M	P	N	A	M	P	N
1	2	3	4	4	3	2	1	1	2	3	4	4	3	2	1	4	3	2	1
Q.16				**Q.17**				**Q.18**				**Q.19**				**Q.20**			
A	M	P	N	A	M	P	N	A	M	P	N	A	M	P	N	A	M	P	N
4	3	2	1	4	3	2	1	4	3	2	1	1	2	3	4	4	3	2	1
Q.21				**Q.22**				**Q.23**				**Q.24**				**Q.25**			
A	M	P	N	A	M	P	N	A	M	P	N	A	M	P	N	A	M	P	N
4	3	2	1	4	3	2	1	1	2	3	4	1	2	3	4	4	3	2	1

Autonomy	Personal Growth Opportunity	Work Speed and Routine*	Work Complexity	Task-Related Interaction

Scale Score Interpretation:

Low job enrichment: 5–9   Moderate job enrichment: 10–15   High job enrichment: 16 to 20

---

*High scores for work speed and routine indicate low job enrichment.

15

THE CHANGE PROCESS

Schools in the United States and Canada are busy changing: New standards have been mandated, curriculum is being developed that is aligned with these standards, assessments follow to complete the instructional delivery package, and everywhere teachers are being trained in how to teach to the test, to align things to get students ready, to adapt mandates to local situations, to beef up their subject-matter knowledge so they can competently teach to higher standards, and to learn new pedagogies. Despite this frenzy of change activity, one wonders what is really going on. Are teachers changing their practice for the better? Are students better off? Will the changes of the 1990s sustain themselves over time? Do the things that have changed the most really matter the most?

Some schools, provinces, and states, for example, can point to sharp increases in student test scores as a result of changes introduced to help students meet "world-class standards." But are the gains achieved indicators that students are learning to use their minds well? Are they able to problem solve, particularly when confronted with new information? Are they more self-sufficient learners able to tackle new tasks? We don't know the answers to these questions. Though many changes have been introduced, though schools appear to be doing things differently, and though higher test scores indicate some improvements in learning—at least in what is being tested—real changes come hard. Adopting changes is not the same as implementing changes and implementing changes may not produce the intended results.

$\mathcal{M}$ORE THAN ADOPTION, MORE THAN IMPLEMENTATION

Much of the literature on change in schools assumes that adoption is the same as implementation. The two, however, are different (Gaynor, 1975). Schools frequently adopt innovations that are not implemented or, if implemented, innovations are shaped to the way things were to the point that the "change is hardly noticeable." The open-space concept, popular during the late 1960s and early 1970s, is a classic example. "Implementation" of open space was characterized by carving schools into traditional classrooms through the use of bookcases, room dividers, lockers, and other partitions. Goodlad and Klein (1970) make a similar observation with respect to the adoption of team teaching and the ungraded classroom concept. Frequently, implementation was characterized by "turn" teaching and the creation of grades within grades. From your own experiences you probably know of a junior high school that has adopted, but not really implemented, the middle school concept. In a similar vein, today's standards movement is intended to ensure a broad yet deep education for students. Yet, the standards, curriculum, and assessment changes seem to be narrowing the curriculum and limiting what is learned.

Sometimes changes have unanticipated consequences that, when forced on the system, make things worse than they were. Site-based management, for example, has been widely adopted, but instead of becoming a means to help us get somewhere, it often is an end in itself. Not only can site-based management become a nonevent in the teaching and learning life of the school but it can also create problems. Lichtenstein, McLaughlin, and Knudsen (1992) explain:

> We observed and read about instances in which site-based authority resulted in little of consequence in the classroom. Rather than feeling empowered to exercise greater authority in their teaching, many teachers found their time bound up with committees wrestling with decisions about what color to make the curtain on the auditorium stage, or whether to spend $500.00 on a slide projector or bookcases. In some cases, we discovered that "restructuring" mandates provided weak school administrators an excuse to delegate significant responsibilities to teachers who then floundered because of insufficient orientation, resources, support, and expertise. Further, we saw instances where efforts to expand teacher's authority without also attending to their capacity resulted in the ironic outcome of *diminished* performance of school, classroom, or system. (39)

Too often, changes are introduced that contradict each other. As a result, they raise havoc and cause confusion. Espousing Deming's (1993) philosophy and touting "Total Quality Management" (TQM) or using TQM to create the "Quality School" are good examples. Deming rarely uses the word *quality* in his writing and lectures, and does not recommend its use. Furthermore, the notion of totally managing something is alien to him. To Deming, the secret is not to manage for control (the word *management*, for example, is derived from the Latin word *manus* and its Italian cousin *maneggio*, which means the training or handling of a horse), but to honor variation. He takes exception to the use of the word *customer* in educational settings. Unlike most appliers of TQM to practice, Deming believes that one cannot view his 14 principles as a buffet of ideas from which one picks and chooses only the ideas that are liked. Deming's ideas comprise a whole and must be applied as a whole. That means the slogan *TQM* has to be dropped because slogans are out. It means that grading and testing students as well as evaluating teachers, honor rolls, and other student rankings cannot be used because they violate two of his principles (eliminating work standards on the one hand and extrinsic rewards on the other).

At times, Deming's ideas are packaged together with other movements, such as Outcomes-Based Education (OBE) or today's standards movement. But like oil and water, Deming's philosophy and theses approaches cannot be readily mixed. In OBE, process is not important; one must focus on outcomes and let process take care of itself. People are free to do whatever they want as long as the job gets done. The only requirement is to "design down" what you do from the outcomes. To Deming, outcomes are part of the problem; his answer is to focus on process. It is the activity of teaching and learning, the curriculum, the classroom climate, and the numerous social contracts that are struck between teachers and students, among teachers, and among students that count the most. Tend to these and the outcomes will take care of themselves. No wonder change comes so hard—new ideas are accompanied by mixed signals. Too often, new ideas come in prepackaged forms and are marketed as if they were a new breakfast food.

Even successful implementation of a change in schooling is not enough. School improvement requires that such implementation be sustained over time; this, in turn, requires that the change be institutionalized. Institutionalization means that the change is "built in" to the life of the school (Miles, 1983). As Huberman and Crandall (1982) point out: "New practices that get built into the training, regulatory, staffing, and budgetary cycles survive, others don't. Innovations are highly perishable goods" (cited in Miles, 1983:14). Institutionalization is a process of making a change routine; it becomes part of the ordinary life of the school. Changes requiring new dollars, for example, become institutionalized when these new dollars become regularly budgeted dollars. Changes requiring new structural arrangements become institutionalized when regular school policies are revised to reflect these arrangements. Changes requiring new patterns of behavior become institutionalized when the regular reward system (salary, promotions, psychological rewards) is adjusted to reflect these patterns. Institutionalization cannot be taken for granted. Thus, school improvement requires that adoption, implementation, *and* institutionalization become the principal's goals.

A SYSTEMS VIEW OF CHANGE

For every successful school improvement effort, one hears horror stories about unsuccessful efforts. One reason for failure, beyond lack of management and leadership effort by the principal, is a limited view of what the process of change involves. Unsuccessful school improvement efforts tend to put "all their eggs in one basket" by using a one-best-way to approach the problem.

Some experts advocate engineering the social and political context within which the school exists in an effort to provide the necessary support and momentum for change. Other experts emphasize the development of favorable school climates that provide the necessary interpersonal support for change. In recent years, scholars from this group have focused on the concept of school culture and have emphasized the importance of developing values and norms that include the proposed changes. Still other experts concentrate almost exclusively on the individual and her or his needs, dispositions, stages of concern for the proposed change, and the driving and restraining forces that pull and tug, causing resistance to the change. Finally, some experts give primary attention to engineering the work context as a means to program and structure teacher behavior to ensure that the school improvement effort is implemented properly. All these concerns are important, but none alone is an adequate model for school improvement. More recently the focus is on change as a moral imperative (Fullan, 2003a; Sergiovanni, 1992) and on viewing the problems of change as problems of sustainability (Hargreaves and Fink, 2004). Do we have our purposes right? How do we support the changes that we have made so that they last?

When one brings together each of these concerns, a systems view begins to emerge—one that provides a dynamic, integrative, and powerful view of change. Within this view, the unit of change is not limited to the individual teacher, the school, the work flow of teaching and schooling, or the broader political and administrative context. Instead, the four are viewed as interacting units of change, all requiring attention. When attended to properly, these units of change are the roads to successful school improvement.

The systems view is depicted in Figure 15.1. Note that the direct road to changes relating to teaching and learning is through structuring the work flow of schooling. However, teaching is human-intensive, which means that regardless of how hard one might try to introduce change, teachers cannot be ignored. They count, whether one wants them to or not. They make the day-to-day and minute-to-minute decisions influencing what happens to students. For changes in the work flow of teaching to count, they must be directly linked to changes in teaching behavior, and this inevitably means changes in the attitudes and beliefs of individual teachers and the faculty as a whole. Teaching and learning change as teachers change.

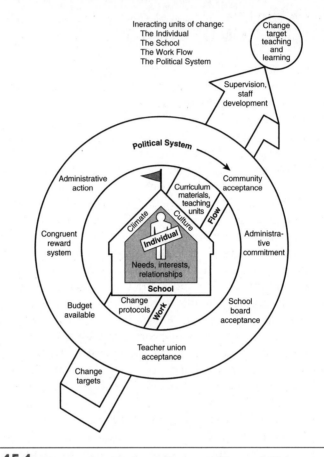

figure **15.1** **Interacting Units: A Systems View of Change**

Teachers typically work alone. This isolation has telling negative consequences on teaching effectiveness and school improvement (Lieberman and Miller, 1984; Rosenholtz, 1989). Still, teachers are members of social groups that make up the larger school faculty. Social groups create norms, customs, and traditions that define ways of living. *School culture* is the term often used to refer to the sense of order and being that emerges. School culture defines what is of worth for teachers, specifies acceptable limits of behavior and beliefs, and is a powerful factor in promoting or resisting school improvement efforts (Sarason, 1971).

Schools do not exist in isolation; thus, another dimension of importance in the school improvement process is the broader administrative, social, and political environment. School climates, for example, are influenced by actions and attitudes of the teachers' union, the school board, and central office school district administrators (Kirst, 1984). Influences from this political system trickle down from the school level to the individual teacher and finally to the work flow. All four levels—

individual, school, work flow, and political context—are interacting units of change needing attention as principals promote school improvement. Deep, continuous, meaningful, and effective change cannot be just top down or just bottom up.

*O*VERCOMING RESISTANCE TO CHANGE

Resistance to change occurs when one's basic work needs are threatened. Although individual differences among teachers exist in the relative importance of specific work needs, four fairly universal needs can be identified (Mealiea, 1978):

1. *The Need for Clear Expectations.* Most of us require fairly specific information about our jobs to function effectively. We need to know what is expected of us, how we fit into the total scheme of things, what our responsibilities are, how we will be evaluated, and what our relationships with others will be. Without such information, our performance is likely to decline and our job satisfaction will be lessened (Katz and Kahn, 1978). Change upsets this "equilibrium" of role definition and expectations.
2. *The Need for Future Certainty.* Closely related to knowing how we fit into the job system is being able to predict the future. We need to have some reliability and certainty built into our work lives to provide us with security and allow us to plan ahead (Coffer and Appley, 1964). Change introduces ambiguity and uncertainty, which threaten our need for a relatively stable, balanced, and pre-dictable work environment.
3. *The Need for Social Interaction.* Most of us value and need opportunities to interact with others. This interaction helps us to define and build our own self-concepts and to reduce anxiety and fear we experience in the work en-vironment. We seek support and acceptance from others at work. Change is often perceived as threatening to these important social interaction patterns, and the prospects of establishing new patterns can present us with security problems. Collaborative cultures and communities of practice have been persistent themes in this book, and both are powerful means to promote the support and direction teachers need for learning. Learning, in return, is a pre-requisite for changing.
4. *The Need for Control over Our Work Environment and Work Events.* Most of us want and seek a reasonable degree of control over our work environment (Ar-gyris, 1957). We do not wish to be at the mercy of this system. As suggested in the last chapter, we want to be Origins and not Pawns (De Charms, 1968) when it comes to making decisions that affect our work lives.

When control is threatened or reduced, the net effect for teachers is not only less job satisfaction but also a loss of meaning in work that can result in job in-difference and even alienation. Change efforts that do not involve teachers and changes that threaten to lessen their control over teaching, learning, and other aspects of schooling can have serious consequences for school effectiveness.

Teachers vary in the intensity with which the four universal needs are held. The greater the intensity, the more likely change threats will be felt. Still, for all teachers, change will likely create some disturbance in their present situation. Principals can help get teachers back onto a more comfortable and stable course by providing as much relevant information as possible about the change and how it affects the work of teaching. Teachers need to know what will be expected of them as the change is put into operation. Allowing—indeed, welcoming—teacher participation in planning the proposed change will help provide for these needs and will very likely result in ideas about how to improve the proposal. Keeping the proposed change simple and implementing aspects of the change gradually will increase teachers' confidence in themselves as successful implementers.

Mealiea (1978) suggests that changes be accompanied by a nonevaluation period during which the teacher's performance cannot have a negative effect on income, career, or other school benefits. During this period, the emphasis would be solely on providing feedback to teachers to help them learn more about the change and to increase proficiency in implementing the change. Directing change efforts first to teachers who might be considered as role models and who optimally would become early adopters of the change can be helpful to successful school improvement. If teachers who are widely respected by others are moving ahead with the change, a certain confidence and calm are likely to occur and resistance is likely to be lessened.

Keep in mind that though teachers may not initially support a change, if they are provided with help, the learning, and the information they need to succeed, they will come to like it. The more successful is a teacher in implementing a change, the greater is his or her support for the change. Principals often spend too much time trying to get support beforehand when in fact it may be more important to help people be successful so that they come to support something in a more sustained way. The lesson here seems to be that the principal should move forward when enough start-up commitment is cultivated. But this "tipping point" may not require a majority of people actively supporting the change. Once the change implementation process begins, teachers will come to support the change if they are successful in implementing it. This is one reason why learning is an important part of the change process, and this is one reason why support networks are so important.

Expectancy theory of motivation can be helpful here. According to expectancy theory, before motivation to change occurs, teachers need answers to the following four questions:

1. Do I know what it is that needs to be accomplished?
2. Are the benefits of accomplishment important to me and desired by me?

3. Do I have a clear idea of exactly what it is that I need to do to accomplish this?

4. Should I attempt accomplishment; will I be successful?

A no answer to any of these questions means that teachers will not be motivated to participate in the school improvement effort. Yes answers that result in motivation depend on the attention principals give to learning. Particularly key is the supervisory support available to teachers to ensure successful implementation. Capacity building is the key to success.

A THEORY OF SCHOOL IMPROVEMENT

Susan Fuhrman (2003) argues that reform may be the wrong metaphor for gauging changes that matter in schools—changes that actually affect teaching and learning in a deep and sustained way. Her view is that we have tried reform. We have reorganized schools in various and seemingly endless configurations as if we were preoccupied with structure—with changing the way things look in schools but not improving the results that schools are getting. In her words:

> So, if "reform" is not the answer, what is? Perhaps we need to shift the metaphor from "reform" to "improvement." Reform is a matter of policies swooping down from on high. Improvement is a matter of continued attention to the basics of teaching and learning—the heart of schooling. Improvement is slow, unending, not particularly glamorous, hard work. It involves deep investment in teacher quality and knowledge, through recruiting, compensating, and developing teachers. It involves thoughtful, well-funded professional development that is intensive, extensive (over a period of time), focused on the curriculum that teachers are teaching, and followed up by coaching and other on-site support. (10)

Richard Elmore believes that the best solution to problems of student achievement in both the short and long term is for local districts, state officials, teachers, and others to together focus their resources and efforts on developing strong theories and practices of school improvement (Elmore, 2003). These theories and practices, Elmore says, would encompass a number of parameters including the following five assumptions:*

1. *Internal accountability precedes external accountability.* Before schools can respond effectively to external accountability policies, they must first develop strong

---

*The five assumptions in italics are direct quotes found in Elmore (2003), pp. 9–10. The discussion that follows each assumption is drawn from the same source with direct quotes noted.

professional norms about what constitutes high-quality teaching practice. Without a consensus on norms of instructional practice the students will not be able to pull together the monitoring and feedback systems that are needed for schools to gauge their progress as they work to improve. Elmore reminds us that "internal coherence around instructional practice is a prerequisite for strong performance . . ." (9).

2. *Improvement is a developmental process that proceeds in stages; it is not a linear process.* When improvement is viewed as a linear process "schools are required to make progress against a continually increasing gradient of performance" (9). Elmore's experience is that "schools increase their internal coherence and capacity around instruction in several discernible stages" (9). Significant gains in measured performance is followed by times when improvement in quality and capacity continue to rise but improvement in student performance goes flat. Gains followed by flat periods that are in turn followed by gains is a common pattern that makes sense when teachers and students are treated as learners. "Performance often lags behind practice. Schools are 'improving' just as much when they are changing practices as they are when they are changing performance . . ." (10).

3. *Leadership is a cultural practice.* Effective leaders have an explicit set of ideas, an explicit theory of what good instruction looks like. They lead with ideas. Key among these ideas is that success requires changing a weak instructional core and a weak encompassing culture into a strong and explicit body of knowledge about effective teaching and learning. They are convinced that cultures can be changed, new norms can be created, and new patterns of practice can be achieved.

4. *Powerful leadership is distributed because the work of instructional improvement is distributed.* Relying on Spillane, Halverson, and Diamond's (2001) idea of distributed leadership, Elmore (2003) concludes that "instructional improvement requires that people with multiple sources of expertise work in concert around a common problem; this distributed expertise leads to distributed leadership" (10).

5. *Knowledge is not necessarily where you think it is.* It is typically assumed that low-performing schools don't know what they are doing and that high-performing schools have something to teach others. But the success of high-performing schools may have more to do with the social capital base of their students and families than with superior knowledge about teaching, curriculum, and other matters of instruction. Elmore points out that he is in routinely low-performing schools that are competent in the process of instructional improvement.

This is not an all-inclusive list of assumptions needed to develop strong theories and practices of school improvement. Take a moment to visit with a colleague, for example, and see if together you can come up with two other assumptions. A good candidate for adding to the Elmore list is "given the proper investment of time, talent, and other resources, when schools are low-performing because teachers fail to teach effectively, the problem is usually not dumb teachers but more likely to be a lack of focus on the teaching techniques and other instructional practices that teachers need to master in order to succeed." In Elmore's words, "The work of turning a school around entails improving 'capacity' (the knowledge and skills of teachers)—changing their command of content and how to teach it—and helping them to understand where their students are in their academic development. Low-performing schools, and the people who work in them, *don't know what to do.* If they did, they would be doing it already. You can't improve a school's performance, or that of any teacher or student in it, without increasing the investment in teachers' knowledge, pedagogical skills, and understanding of students" (2002b:37).

SUSTAINING IMPROVEMENT

Change is not enough. Change must lead to improvement. We now know how to change the way things look but we have been less successful in bringing about the sustained improvement that leads to achievement of our purposes. Elmore puts it more pointedly: "the pathology of American schools is that they know how to change. They know how to change promiscuously and at the drop of a hat. What schools do not know how to do is improve, to engage in sustained and continuous progress toward a performance goal over time" (2002a:not numbered).

We have sustainability when not only do we have improvements but these improvements last over time. Hargreaves and Fink (2003) suggest that sustainability in educational change comprises five interrelated characteristics as follows:

1. Improvement that sustains learning, not merely change that alters schooling
2. Improvement that endures over time
3. Improvement that can be supported by available or achievable resources
4. Improvement that does not impact negatively on the surrounding environment of other schools and systems
5. Improvement that promotes ecological diversity and capacity throughout the educational and community environment. (438)

LEADING IMPROVEMENT AND SUSTAINING LEARNING

Leading improvement is at the center of the principal's leadership role as is sustaining learning. The two are inseparable. Schools succeed when they are able to show continuous improvement in achieving their learning purposes over time. And these purposes cannot be achieved without sustained learning by students and by everyone else who shares responsibility for student learning. Hargreaves and Fink (2003) sum up these relationships as follows: "In our view, leaders develop sustainability by how they approach, commit to and protect deep learning in their schools; by how they sustain others around them to promote and support that learning; by how they sustain themselves in doing so, so that they can persist with their vision and avoid burning out; and by how they try to ensure the improvements they bring about last over time, especially after they themselves have gone" (440). Their research reveals seven principles that are commonly held by successful leaders of improvement. The principles are summarized in Exhibit 15.1.

Change Facilitator Styles

Some leadership styles are more likely to lead to sustainable improvement than others. Other leadership styles describe leaders who are focused on change but not improvement. Let's begin our inquiry into this topic by describing the behavior of a principal whose school is, or has recently been, involved in a change effort. It is hard to separate all the aspects of a principal's change facilitator style from her or his general style or orientation; thus, you will want to focus on both the general style and the change style as we begin our analysis. What kind of leadership does the principal bring to the school? What does the leader stand for, and how effective is she or he in communicating these standards to teachers? What kind of interpersonal leader is the principal? How does the principal work to facilitate change that will result in school improvement? Before continuing further, turn to the Change Facilitator Styles Inventory (CFSI), which appears as Appendix 15.1; following the directions, describe the principal you have been thinking about.

The CFSI is based on an extensive research program investigating links between principal behaviors and successful school improvements (Hall et al., 1983). This research was conducted at the Research and Development Center for Teacher Education at the University of Texas at Austin. The investigators were able to group principal leadership behaviors into three general change facilitator styles: Responder, Manager, and Initiator. These three styles correspond to the *R, M,* and *I* response categories on the CFSI and are described in the following extract (Hall and Rutherford, 1983):

> *Responders* place heavy emphasis on allowing teachers and others the opportunity to take the lead. They believe their primary role is to maintain a smooth-running school by focusing on traditional administrative tasks, keeping teachers content, and treating students well. Teachers are viewed as strong professionals who are able to carry out their instructional role with little guidance. Responders emphasize the personal side of their relationships with teachers and others. Before they make decisions they often give everyone an opportunity to have input so as to weigh their feelings or to allow others to make the decision. A related characteristic is the tendency toward making decisions in terms of immediate circumstances rather than in terms of longer-range instructional or school goals. This seems to be due in part to their desire to please others and in part to their limited vision of how their school and staff should change in the future.

exhibit
15.1

Seven Principles of Sustainable Leadership

1. *Sustainable Leadership Matters.* Sustainable leadership goes beyond temporary gains in achievement scores to create lasting, meaningful improvements in learning.

2. *Sustainable Leadership Lasts.* Sustainable leadership demands that leaders pay serious attention to leadership succession. We can achieve this goal by grooming successors to continue important reforms, by keeping successful leaders in schools longer when they are making great strides in promoting learning, by resisting the temptation to search for irreplaceable charismatic heroes to be the saviors of our schools, by requiring all district and school improvement plans to include succession plans, and by slowing down the rate of repeated successions so teachers do not cynically decide to "wait out" all their leaders.

3. *Sustainable Leadership Spreads.* Leadership succession . . . means distributing leadership throughout the school's professional community so others can carry the torch after the principal has gone. Sustainable leadership must be a shared responsibility.

4. *Sustainable Leadership Is Socially Just.* Sustainable leadership benefits all students and schools—not just a few at the expense of the rest.

5. *Sustainable Leadership Is Resourceful.* Such systems provide time and opportunity for leaders to network, learn from and support one another, and coach and mentor their successors. Sustainable leadership is thrifty without being cheap. It carefully husbands its resources in developing the talents of all its educators rather than lavishing rewards on a few proven stars.

6. *Sustainable Leadership Promotes Diversity.* Standardization is the enemy of sustainability. Sustainable leadership recognizes and cultivates many kinds of excellence in learning, teaching, and leading, and it provides the networks for sharing these different kinds of excellence in cross-fertilizing processes of improvement. Sustainable leadership does not impose standardized templates on everyone.

7. *Sustainable Leadership Is Activist.* In the past few years, Durant's (one of the schools in Hargreaves and Fink's research) courageous new principal has activated his personal and professional networks and forged strategic alliances with the community in a tireless campaign to preserve the school's mission. He has written articles for local and state newspapers, appeared on radio and television programs, and supported students and parents who, in a symbolic gesture, protested in straitjackets outside the district offices. He organized conferences on the adverse effects of high-stakes testing and worked assiduously with his allies throughout the state to push for a request for group variance from the state tests, receiving for his efforts a temporary exclusion from state policy. Durant's story shows that, especially in an unhelpful environment, sustainable leadership must have an activist dimension.

Source: Summarized from "Seven Principles of Sustainable Leadership," by Andy Hargreaves and Dean Fink, 2004, *Educational Leadership* 61(7), 9–13. For further development of the principles, see Andy Hargreaves and Dean Fink, 2005, *Sustainable Leadership,* San Francisco: Jossey-Bass.

Managers represent a broader range of behaviors. They demonstrate both responsive behaviors in answer to situations or people and they also initiate actions in support of the change effort. The variations in their behavior seem to be linked to their rapport with teachers and central office staff as well as how well they understand and buy into a particular change effort. Managers work without fanfare to provide basic support to facilitate teachers' use of the innovation. They keep teachers informed about decisions and are sensitive to teacher needs. They will defend their teachers from what are perceived as excessive demands. When they learn that the central office wants something to happen in their school, they then become very involved with their teachers in making it happen. Yet, they do not typically initiate attempts to move beyond the basics of what is imposed.

Initiators have clear, decisive long-range policies and goals that transcend but include implementation of the current innovation. They tend to have very strong beliefs about what good schools and teaching should be like and work intensely to attain this vision. Decisions are made in relation to their goals for the school and in terms of what they believe to be best for students, which is based on current knowledge of classroom practice. Initiators have strong expectations for students, teachers, and themselves. They convey and monitor these expectations through frequent contacts with teachers and clear explication of how the school is to operate and how teachers are to teach. When they feel it is in the best interest of their school, particularly the students, Initiators will seek changes in district programs or policies or they will reinterpret them to suit the needs of the school. Initiators will be adamant but not unkind, they solicit input from staff and then decisions are made in terms of the goal of the school even if some are ruffled by their directness and high expectations. (84)

Which of these general change facilitator styles best corresponds with your response patterns on the CFSI? Can you estimate which of these styles were most and least associated with successful school improvement efforts? Hall and Rutherford (1983) found that Initiator principals were more likely to be successful than were Manager and Responder principals. Responders were least likely to be successful. As you review the principal behavior descriptions on the CFSI associated with each of these styles, note that Initiators have a clear sense of what needs to be accomplished and take more active roles in planning, prodding, encouraging, advising, participating, checking, stimulating, monitoring, and evaluating change efforts. Furthermore, they assume more direct roles in obtaining and providing the necessary material and psychological support for successful change efforts. Initiators are able to empower the change process by both enabling and empowering teachers to be active in their change roles. To this end, they are neither laissez-faire supporters nor micromanagers of the change process.

Levels of Leadership Behavior

As a result of their research on principals at work, Leithwood and Montgomery (1986) identified four levels of leadership behavior, each with a different focus and style and each with different consequences for principal effectiveness. They found that the "higher" the level of principal behavior, the more effective the school. Effectiveness was defined as gains in student achievement in the "basics" and increases in student self-direction and problem solving.

Each of the levels represents increasingly complex and effective principalship behaviors. Principals functioning at level one, *Administrators*, believe that it is the teacher's job to teach and the principal's job to run the school. Principals functioning at level two, *Humanitarians*, believe that the basis of a sound education is a good interpersonal climate. Principals functioning at level three, *Program Managers*, believe that their job is to provide the best possible programs for students. Principals functioning at level four, *Systematic Problem Solvers*, are committed to doing whatever is necessary by way of invention and delivery in order to give students the best possible chance to learn. Program Managers and Systematic Problem Solvers both bring to their practice a focus on students, but Program Managers are largely committed to proper implementation of officially sanctioned goals and programs. They are more dependent on established guidelines, resources, and procedures than are Systematic Problem Solvers.

> Systematic Problem Solvers are "bottom liners" virtually all of the time; the bottom line is the goals held for students by their school. Their focus is largely unconstrained by established practice and their client orientation leads them to the invention and delivery of whatever legitimate services are likely to realize the goals held by their school for students. (Leithwood and Montgomery, 1986:83)

Important to Leithwood and Montgomery's formulation is the concept of level. What Administrators do at level one is not necessarily ineffective, only less effective than the other three levels if this behavior pattern is dominant. Humanitarians at level two carry with them some of the Administrator style but focus primarily on more complex behaviors that emphasize human relationships. Although more effective than Administrators, Humanitarians are not as effective as Program Managers. Program Managers bring aspects of the Administrator and Humanitarian style to their practice but focus primarily on more complex matters of educational program development and implementation. Finally, the Problem Solvers focus primarily on students' success. This entrepreneurial stance is supported, nonetheless, by competent administrative, human relations, and program management skills.

Leithwood and Montgomery's research suggests that as principals come to view their jobs in more complex ways they become more effective operating at higher levels of practice. They recognize, of course, the important management demands in their job and the need to provide an environment that supports and enhances human relationships. Yet, neither management nor human relations processes are viewed as ends in themselves. They believe that process always serves substance. The substance of the school is defined by its educational programs and levels of commitment to teaching and learning. Yet, neither process nor substance can be viewed as something static, they are, instead, pursued in a context characterized by an array of demands, constraints, and choices. Realizing that expanding choices results in better schooling, principals at level four work for this expansion by taking a problem-solving, even entrepreneurial, approach to their leadership practice.

$\mathcal{S}$OME ETHICAL QUESTIONS

Principals often feel uncomfortable when they are asked to assume fairly direct roles in bringing about change. Change, be it ordinary or the kind that leads to improvement, is a form of "social engineering"; and, as one becomes more skilled at bringing about change, ethical issues are naturally raised. Are we talking about leadership or are we really talking about manipulation? No easy answer exists to this question, but one thing is certain—principals have an obligation to provide leadership to the school, and this involves following a course of action leading to school improvement. The change agent role is therefore unavoidable.

Benne (1949) proposes a set of guidelines for principals to ensure that their change behavior is ethical. He believes that the engineering of change and the providing of pressure on groups and organizations to change must be collaborative. Collaboration suggests that principals and teachers form a change partnership, with each being aware of the intentions of others. Change intents are honest and straightforward. Teachers, for example, do not have to endure being "buttered up" today for the announced change of tomorrow.

First, the engineering of change should be educational to those involved in the process. *Educational* suggests that principals will try to help teachers become more familiar with the process of problem solving and changing so that they are less dependent on her or him. Giving a teacher a solution is not as educational as helping the teacher muddle through a problem. Second, the engineering of change should be experimental. *Experimental* implies that changes will not be implemented for keeps but will be adopted tentatively until they have proven their worth or until a better solution comes along.

Finally, engineering of change should be task oriented; that is, controlled by the requirements of the problem and its effective solution rather than oriented to the maintenance or extension of prestige or power of the principal and others who are encouraging changes. Task orientation refers to one's primary motive for change. The principal should have job-related objectives in mind first—objectives that are concerned with improving teaching and learning for students. If such school improvement efforts are successful, the principal and others responsible for the change enjoy personal success and a certain amount of fame as well. These are the rewards for hard work, but they are not the reasons for bringing about the change in the first place. Principals who emphasize change to get attention from their supervisors or to improve their standing or influence in the school district may well be violating this ethical principle.

THE CHANGE FACILITATING TEAM

This is a book for principals; therefore, it is natural to emphasize the principal's role and its significance in school improvement efforts. Yet, as discussions of distributive leadership have revealed, the principal cannot do it alone. In highlighting this issue, Hord, Hall, and Stiegelbauer (1983) point out: "This rhetoric, abundant in literature, quite obviously hangs like a heavy mantle on the principal. However, what is becoming equally certain and abundantly clear is that the principal does not bear the weight of leadership responsibility alone" (1). Their research reveals that often one or two other key people in the school emerge as key change facilitators. As a result of their research on school improvement and analysis of the change literature, Loucks-Horsley and Hergert (1985) conclude, "The principal is not *the* key to school improvement. Although the principal is important so are many other people" (ix). Teachers and supervisors have important roles to play, as do superintendents and specialists at the central office.

The research suggests that it may be more useful to view the principal as the leader of the change facilitating team (Hall, 1988), with as many as four change facilitators serving on the team. The principal, for example, might be viewed as the primary change facilitator. Very often, a second change facilitator (assistant principal, department chairperson, resource teacher, or teacher on a special assignment) was identified by the researcher. Frequently, a third level of change facilitator existed. Typically, facilitators at this level were teachers whose roles were less formalized but whose help was substantial and sought by their peers (Hord et al., 1987). This group of facilitators served the process of change primarily by modeling the use of the new practices, disseminating information to other teachers, cheerleading, and providing support. The principals who were most effective in implementing change were team oriented, working closely with these other levels of change facilitators. Often, structures were built that allowed them to work together as a change facilitator team.

> In some schools, they may meet each week to review data about the school improvement process, generate ideas, and plan who will do what during the ensuing week. When they meet again, they debrief to ascertain what went well and what needs more attention. In other schools we observe a more hierarchical organization of facilitators: the first CF (the principal) appeared to interact only with the second CF, who in turn related to the third CF. All communications flowed through this "chain of command." Whether the team of CFs has a "flat" or horizontal collegial structure or a more hierarchical one, however, the important aspects to remember are what they need to do as group. (Hord et al., 1987:85)

These researchers identified even a fourth category, the *external facilitator*. Frequently, this role was filled by someone from the central office who served as a facilitative link between the office resources and the school.

*T*HE MEANING OF EDUCATIONAL CHANGE

One theme emerges from this discussion of the process of change. Although principals are important, and their visions key in focusing attention on change and in successfully implementing the process of change, what counts in the end is bringing together the ideas and commitments of a variety of people who have a stake in the success of the school. As this distributed leadership process unfolds, principals can often find themselves on thin ice. They need to be clear about what it is that they want but cannot be so clear that they are providing people with road maps. They need to allow people to have an important say in shaping the direction of the school and deciding on the changes needed to get there, but they cannot be so detached that these individual aspirations remain more rhetorical than real. Michael Fullan (1991), after reviewing Lighthall's (1973) work, points out that there is strong support for the assertion that

> leadership commitment to a particular version of a change is negatively related to ability to implement it. . . . Educational change is a process of coming to grips with the *multiple* realities of people who are the main participants in implementing change. The leader who presupposes what the change should be and acts in ways which preclude others' realities is bound to fail. (95)

Key, of course, are the visions of teachers. If change is not responsive to the world of teaching as teachers experience it, it is likely to be viewed as irrelevant if not frivolous (Lortie, 1975). Fullan (1991) believes that the assumptions that principals and others make about change are key because they represent powerful, although frequently unconscious, sources of one's actions.

School improvement may not be easy, but it is well within reach of most schools. Successful efforts depend on the principals taking a comprehensive view of the problem. This view acknowledges the importance of leadership density and emphasizes implementation and institutionalization of change as well as adoption. Most changes don't count for very much. Some changes actually make things worse. This is why the school change and school improvement distinction is so important. School improvement is anchored in gains the school makes over time in achieving its purposes. Some of the purposes have to do with student learning. Other purposes have to do with teacher learning. And still other purposes deal with other themes. School change often happens in a random pattern. School improvement requires a much more targeted approach than is usually the case.

*M*ORAL PURPOSE IS KEY

Michael Fullan, a leading expert on change theory and change practice, argues that at the heart of sustainable change and sustainable leadership is moral purpose. Chapter 1 of this book focused on moral themes that are at the very heart-beat of school leadership. It is fitting, therefore, for us to return to this theme as this book closes. In Fullan's words,

> In addition to the direct goal of making a difference in the lives of students, moral purpose plays a larger role in transforming and sustaining system change. Within the organization, how leaders treat all others is also a component of moral purpose. At a larger level, moral purpose means acting with the intention of making a positive difference in the (social) environment. The goal here is system improvement (all schools in the district). This means that school principals have to be almost as concerned with the success of other schools in the district as they are about their own school. This is so because sustained improvement of schools is not possible unless the whole system is moving forward. This commitment to the social environment is precisely what the best principals must have. (2003b:452–453)

Fullan continues, "Moral purpose means closing the gap between high performing schools and lower performing schools—and between high performing and lower performing students—by raising the level of achievement of all, while closing the gap. This is the only way for a large-scale, sustainable reform to occur—and it is moral purpose of the highest order" (2003b:453).

$\mathcal{S}$OME REFLECTIONS

1. Review Richard Elmore's five assumptions for planning and developing change strategies. To what extent do you agree with Elmore? What other assumptions would you propose?
2. Use the Change Facilitators Styles Inventory (CFSI) depicted in Appendix 15.1 to assess the leadership behaviors your principal uses. With which principal style—responder, manager, or initiator—are you most comfortable?

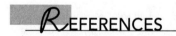$\mathcal{R}$EFERENCES

Argyris, Chris. 1957. *Personality and Organizations.* New York: Harper & Row.

Benne, Kenneth D. 1949. "Democratic Ethics and Social Engineering," *Progressive Education* 27(4).

Coffer, C. N., and M. H. Appley. 1964. *Motivation: Theory and Research.* New York: Wiley.

De Charms, Richard. 1968. *Personal Causation: The Internal Affective Determinants of Behavior.* New York: Academic Press.

Deming, W. Edwards. 1993. *The New Economics for Industry, Government, and Education.* Cambridge, MA: MIT Press.

Elmore, Richard F. 2002a, January/February. "The Limits of 'Change,'" Harvard Education Letter Research Online, http://edletter.org/past/issues/2002-jf/limitsofchange.shtml, accessed November 3, 2003.

Elmore, Richard F. 2002b. "Testing Trap," *Harvard Magazine* 105(1), 35–37, 97.

Elmore, Richard F. 2003. "A Plea for Strong Practice," *Educational Leadership* 61(3), 6–10.

Fuhrman, Susan H. 2003. "Is 'Reform' the Answer for Urban Education?" in *Penn GSE: A Review of Research.* Philadelphia: University of Pennsylvania.

Fullan, Michael. 1991. *The New Meaning of Change* (2nd ed.). New York: Teachers College Press.

Fullan, Michael. 2003a. *The Moral Imperative of School Leadership.* Thousand Oaks, CA: Corwin Press.

Fullan, Michael. 2003b. "Principals in a Culture of Change" in Brent Davies and John West-Burnham (Eds.), *Handbook of Educational Leadership and Management.* London: Pearson Longman.

Gaynor, Alan K. 1975, March 27–30. "The Study of Change in Educational Organizations: A Review of the Literature." Paper presented at the University Council for Educational Administration, Ohio State University Career Development Seminar, Columbus.

Goodlad, John I., and Frances M. Klein. 1970. *Behind the Classroom Door.* Worthington, OH: Charles A. Jones.

Hall, Gene E. 1988. "The Principal as Leader of the Change Facilitating Team," *Journal of Research and Development in Education* 22(1).

Hall, Gene E., Shirley M. Hord, Leslie L. Huling, William L. Rutherford, and Suzanne M. Stiegelbauer. 1983, April. "Leadership Variables Associated with Successful School Improvement." Papers presented at the Annual Meeting of the American Educational Research Association, Montreal, Canada.

Hall, Gene E., and William L. Rutherford. 1983, April. "Three Change Facilitator Styles: How Principals Affect Improvement Efforts." Paper presented at the Annual Meeting of the American Educational Research Association, Montreal, Canada.

Hargreaves, Andy, and Dean Fink. 2003. "Sustaining Leadership," in Brent Davies and John West-Burnham (Eds.), *Handbook of Educational Leadership and Management.* London: Pearson Longman.

Hargreaves, Andy, and Dean Fink. 2004. "The Seven Principles of Sustainable Leadership," *Educational Leadership* 61(7), 9–13.

Hord, Shirley M., Gene E. Hall, and Suzanne Stiegelbauer. 1983, April. "Principals Don't Do It Alone: The Role of the Consigliere." Paper presented at the Annual Meeting of the American Educational Research Association, Montreal, Canada.

Hord, Shirley M., William L. Rutherford, Leslie Huling-Austin, and Gene E. Hall. 1987. *Taking Charge of Change.* Alexandria, VA: Association for Supervision and Curriculum Development.

Huberman, A. M., and D. P. Crandall. 1982. *People, Policies and Practices: Examining the Chain of School Improvement. Vol. IX: Implications for Action.* Andover, MA: The Network.

Katz, Daniel, and Robert L. Kahn. 1978. *The Social Psychology of Organization* (2nd ed.). New York: Wiley.

Kirst, Michael W. 1984. *Who Controls Our Schools?* New York: Freeman.

Leithwood, Kenneth A., and Deborah J. Montgomery. 1986. *Improving Principal Effectiveness: The Principal Profile.* Toronto: Ontario Institute for Studies in Education Press.

Lichtenstein, Gary, Milbrey W. McLaughlin, and Jennifer Knudsen. 1992. "Teacher Empowerment and Professional Knowledge" in Ann Lieberman (Ed.), *The Changing Context of Teaching,* Ninety-First Yearbook of the National Society for the Study of Education, Part I. Chicago: University of Chicago Press.

Lieberman, Ann, and Lynne Miller. 1984. *Teachers, Their World and Their Work: Implications for School Improvement.* Alexandria, VA: Association for Supervision and Curriculum Development.

Lighthall, F. 1973, February. "Multiple Realities and Organizational Nonsolutions: An Essay on Anatomy of Educational Innovation," *School Review.*

Lortie, Dan. 1975. *Schoolteacher: A Sociological Study.* Chicago: University of Chicago Press.

Loucks-Horsley, Susan, and Leslie F. Hergert. 1985. *An Action Guide to School Improvement.* Arlington, VA: Association for Supervision and Curriculum Development and the Network.

Mealiea, Laird W. 1978. "Learned Behavior: The Key to Understanding and Preventing Employee Resistance to Change," *Group and Organizational Studies* 3(2), 211–223.

Miles, Matthew B. 1983. "Unraveling the Mystery of Institutionalization," *Educational Leadership* 41(3), 14–19.

Rosenholtz, Susan J. 1989. *Teachers Workplace: A Social-Organizational Analysis.* New York: Longman.

Sarason, Seymour B. 1971. *The Culture of the School and the Problem of Change.* Boston: Allyn and Bacon.

Sergiovanni, Thomas J. 1992. *Moral Leadership.* San Francisco: Jossey-Bass.

Spillane, James P., Richard Halverson, and John B. Diamond. 2001. "Investigating School Leadership Practice: A Distributed Perspective," *Educational Researcher* 30(3), 23–28.

Change Facilitator Styles Inventory

This inventory contains descriptions of principal behavior grouped by style. The items are drawn from actual research comparing more and less effective principals involved in school improvement. The inventory provides an opportunity for you to describe a principal you know (or perhaps yourself) and to compare your responses with the change facilitator styles of these principals.

Each item comprises three different descriptors of principal behavior. Using a total of 10 points, distribute points among the three to indicate the extent to which each describes your principal's behavior. Record your responses on the score sheet provided.

Score Sheet

Principal Behaviors		R	M	I	Totals
A. Vision	1.	____	____	____	10
	2.	____	____	____	10
	3.	____	____	____	10
B. Structuring the school as a workplace	4.	____	____	____	10
	5.	____	____	____	10
	6.	____	____	____	10
	7.	____	____	____	10
	8.	____	____	____	10
C. Structuring involvement with change	9.	____	____	____	10
	10.	____	____	____	10
	11.	____	____	____	10
	12.	____	____	____	10
	13.	____	____	____	10
	14.	____	____	____	10
D. Sharing of responsibility	15.	____	____	____	10
	16.	____	____	____	10
	17.	____	____	____	10
E. Decision making	18.	____	____	____	10
	19.	____	____	____	10
	20.	____	____	____	10
F. Guiding and supporting	21.	____	____	____	10
	22.	____	____	____	10
	23.	____	____	____	10
	24.	____	____	____	10
	25.	____	____	____	10
	26.	____	____	____	10

Principal Behaviors		R	M	I	Totals
G. Structuring his/her professional role	27.	——	——	——	10
	28.	——	——	——	10
	29.	——	——	——	10
	30.	——	——	——	10
	31.	——	——	——	10
	32.	——	——	——	10
	33.	——	——	——	10
	34.	——	——	——	10
	35.	——	——	——	10
	36.	——	——	——	10
	37.	——	——	——	10
Totals					370

Score	Style Emphasis
0–39	Very Low
40–136	Low
137–233	Medium
234–330	High
331–370	Very High

Change Facilitator Styles Inventory (CFSI)

Principal Behaviors	R	M	I
A. Vision	1. Accepts district goals as school goals	Accepts district goals but makes adjustments at school level to accommodate particular needs of the school	Respects district goals but insists on goals for school that give priority to this school's student need
	2. Future goals/direction of school are determined in response to district level goals/priorities	Anticipates the instructional and management needs of school and plans for them	Takes initiative in identifying future goals and priorities for school and in preparing to meet them
	3. Responds to teachers', students', and parents' interest in the goals of the school and the district	Collaborates with others in reviewing and identifying school goals	Establishes framework of expectations for the school and involves others in setting goals within that framework

(continued)

Principal Behaviors	R	M	I
B. Structuring the school as a work place	4. Maintains low profile relative to day-by-day operation of school	Very actively involved in day-by-day management	Directs the ongoing operation of the school with emphasis on instruction through personal actions and clear designation of responsibility
	5. Grants teachers autonomy and independence, provides guidelines for students	Provides guidelines and expectations for teachers and students	Sets standards and expects high performance levels for teachers, students, and self
	6. Ensures that district and school policies are followed and strives to see that disruptions in the school day are minimal	Works with teachers, students, and parents to maintain effective operation of the school	First priority is the instructional program; personnel and collaborative efforts are directed at supporting that priority
	7. Responds to requests and needs as they arise in an effort to keep all persons involved with the school comfortable and satisfied	Expects all involved with the school to contribute to effective instruction and management in the school	Insists that all persons involved with the school give priority to teaching and learning
	8. Allows school norms to evolve over time	Helps establish and clarify norms for the school	Establishes, clarifies, and models norms for the school
C. Structuring involvement with change	9. Relies on information provided by other change facilitators, usually from outside the school, for knowledge of the innovation	Uses information from a variety of sources to gain knowledge of the innovation	Seeks out information from teachers, district personnel, and others to gain an understanding of the innovation and the changes required
	10. Supports district expectations for change	Meets district expectations for change	Accommodates district expectations for change and pushes adjustments and additions that will benefit his/her school

Principal Behaviors	R	M	I
C. Structuring involvement with change *(continued)*	11. Sanctions the change process and strives to resolve conflicts when they arise	Involved regularly in the change process, sometimes with a focus on management and at other times with a focus on the impact of the change	Directs the change process in ways that lead to effective use by all teachers
	12. Expectations for teachers, relative to change, are given in general terms	Tells teachers that they are expected to use the innovation	Gives teachers specific expectations and steps regarding application of the change
	13. Monitors the change effort principally through brief, spontaneous conversations and unsolicited reports	Monitors the change effort through planned conversations with individuals and groups from informal observations of instruction	Monitors the change effort through classroom observation, review of lesson plans, reports that reveal specific teacher instruction involvement, and specific attention to the work of individual teachers
	14. May discuss with the teacher information gained through monitoring	Discusses information gained through monitoring with teacher in relation to teacher's expected behavior	Gives direct feedback to teacher concerning information gained through monitoring, which includes a comparison with expected behaviors and a plan for next steps, possibly including improvements
D. Sharing of Responsibility	15. Allows others to assume the responsibility for the change effort	Tends to do most of the intervening on the change effort but will share some responsibility	Will delegate to carefully chosen others some of the responsibility for the change effort

(continued)

Principal Behaviors		R	M	I
D. Sharing of Responsibility *(continued)*	16.	Others who assume responsibility are more likely to be outside the school, e.g., district facilitators	Others who assume responsibility may come from within or from outside the school	Others who assume responsibility are likely to be from within the school
	17.	Others who assume responsibility have considerable autonomy and independence in which responsibilities they assume and how they carry them out	Coordinates responsibilities and stays informed about how others are handling these responsibilities	First establishes which responsibilities will be delegated and how they are to be accomplished, then works with others and closely monitors the carrying out of tasks
E. Decision making	18.	Makes decisions required for ongoing operation of the school as deadlines for those decisions approach	Actively involved in routine decision making relative to instructional and administrative affairs	Handles routine decisions through established procedures and assigned responsibilities, thereby requiring minimal time
	19.	Makes decisions influenced by the immediate circumstances of the situation and formal policies	Makes decisions based on the norms and expectations that guide the school and the management needs of the school	Makes decisions based on the standard of high expectations and what is best for the school as a whole, particularly learning outcomes and the longer-term goals
	20.	Willingly allows others to participate in decision making or to make decisions independently	Allows others to participate in decision making but maintains control of the process through personal involvement	Allows others to participate in decision making and delegates decision making to others within carefully established parameters of established goals and expectations

Principal Behaviors	R	M	I
F. Guiding and supporting	21. Believes teachers are professionals and leaves them alone to do their work unless they request assistance or support	Believes teachers are a part of the total faculty and establishes guidelines for all teachers to be involved with the change effort	Believes teachers are responsible for developing the best possible instruction, so expectation for their involvement with innovation is clearly established
	22. Responds quickly to requests for assistance and support in a way that is satisfying to the requester	Monitors the progress of the change effort and attempts to anticipate needed assistance and resources	Anticipates the need for assistance and resources and provides support as needed as well as sometimes in advance of potential blockages
	23. Checks with teachers to see how things are going and to maintain awareness of any major problems	Maintains close contact with teachers involved in the change effort in an attempt to identify things that might be done to assist teachers with the change	Collects and uses information from a variety of sources to be aware of how the change effort is progressing and to plan interventions that will increase the probability of a successful, quality implementation
	24. Relies on whatever training is available with the innovation in order to aid in the development of teacher's knowledge and skill relative to the innovation	In addition to the regularly provided assistance, seeks out and uses sources within and outside the school to develop teacher knowledge and skills	Provides increased knowledge or skill needed by the teachers through possible utilization of personnel and resources within the building
	25. Provides general support for teachers as persons and as professionals	Provides support to individuals and to subgroups for specific purposes related to the change as well as to provide for their personal welfare	Provides direct programmatic support through interventions targeted to individuals and to the staff as a whole

(continued)

appendix *15.1*   **Continued**

Principal Behaviors	R	M	I
F. Guiding and supporting *(continued)*	26. Tries to minimize the demands of the change effort on teachers	Moderates demands of the change effort to protect teachers' perceived overload	Keeps ever-present demands on teachers for effective implementation
G. Structuring her/his professional role	27. Sees role as administrator	Sees role as avoiding or minimizing problems so instruction may occur	Sees role as one of ensuring the school has a strong instructional program with teachers teaching students so they are able to learn
	28. Believes others will generate the initiative for any school improvement that is needed	Engages others in regular review of school situation to avoid any reduction in school effectiveness	Identifies areas in need of improvement and initiates action for change
	29. Relies primarily on others for introduction of new ideas into the school	Is alert to new ideas and introduces them to faculty or allows others in school to do so	Sorts through new ideas presented from within and from outside the school and implements those deemed to have high promise for school improvement
	30. Is concerned with how others view him	Is concerned with how others view the school	Is concerned with how others view the impact of the school on students
	31. Accepts the rules of the district	Lives by the rules of the district but goes beyond minimum expectations	Respects the rules of the district but determines behavior by what is required for maximum school effectiveness
	32. Opinions and concerns of others determine what will be accomplished and how	Is consistent in setting and accomplishing tasks and does much of it herself/himself	Tasks determined and accomplished are consistent with school priorities but responsibility can be delegated to others

appendix *15.1* **Continued**

Principal Behaviors	R	M	I
G. Structuring her/his professional role *(continued)*	33. Maintains a general sense of "where the school is" and of how teachers are feeling about things	Is well informed about what is happening in the school and who is doing what	Maintains specific knowledge of all that is going on in the school through direct contact with the classroom, with individual teachers, and with students
	34. Responds to others in a manner intended to please them	Responds to others in a way that will be supportive of the operation of the school	Responds to others with concern but places student priorities above all else
	35. Develops minimal knowledge of what use of the innovation entails	Becomes knowledgeable about general use of the innovation and what is needed to support its use	Develops sufficient knowledge about use to be able to make specific teaching suggestions and to troubleshoot any problems that may emerge
	36. Indefinitely delays having staff do tasks if perceiving that staff are overloaded	Contends that staff are already very busy and paces requests and task loads accordingly	Will knowingly sacrifice short-term feelings of staff if doing a task now is necessary for the longer-term goals of the school
	37. Ideas are offered by each staff member, but one or two have dominant influence	Some ideas are offered by staff and some by the principal; then consensus is gradually developed	Seeks teachers' ideas as well as their reactions to her/his ideas; then priorities are set

Note: The items on this inventory were identified as a result of an extensive research program investigating the relationship between principal behavior and successful school improvement. This program was conducted at the Research and Development Center for Teacher Education, University of Texas, Austin. The items are from Gene E. Hall and William L. Rutherford (1983), "Three Change Facilitator Styles: How Principals Affect Improvement Efforts," paper presented at the Annual Meeting of the American Educational Research Association, Montreal, April. Available from the RDCTE, Austin, TX, document number 3155. See also "Leadership Variables Associated with Successful School Improvement" (Austin, TX: RDCTE, 1983).

Index